Cities and the Grand To[u]

How did eighteenth-century travellers experience, describe and represent the urban environments they encountered as they made the Grand
Tour? This fascinating book focuses on the changing responses of the
British to the cities of Florence, Rome, Naples and Venice, during a
period of unprecedented urbanisation at home. Drawing on a wide
range of unpublished material, including travel accounts written by
women, Rosemary Sweet explores how travel literature helped to create
and perpetuate the image of a city; what the different meanings and
imaginative associations attached to these cities were; and how the
contrasting descriptions of each of these cities reflected the travellers'
own attitudes to urbanism. More broadly, the book explores the construction and performance of personal, gender and national identities,
and the shift in cultural values away from neo-classicism towards medievalism and the gothic, which is central to our understanding of eighteenth-century culture and the transition to modernity.

ROSEMARY SWEET is Professor of Urban History at the Centre for
Urban History, University of Leicester. Her previous publications
include *The English Town, Government, Society and Culture* (1999) and
Antiquaries: The Discovery of the Past in Eighteenth-Century Britain
(2004).

Cambridge Social and Cultural Histories

Series editors:

Margot C. Finn
University College London

Colin Jones
Queen Mary, University of London

Robert G. Moeller
University of California, Irvine

Cambridge Social and Cultural Histories publishes works of original scholarship that lie at the interface between cultural and social history. Titles in the series both articulate a clear methodological and theoretical orientation and demonstrate clearly the significance of that orientation for interpreting relevant historical sources. The series seeks to address historical questions, issues or phenomena which – although they may be located in a specific nation, state or polity – are framed so as to be relevant and methodologically innovative to specialists of other fields of historical analysis.

A list of titles in the series can be found at:
www.cambridge.org/socialculturalhistories

Cities and the Grand Tour

The British in Italy, c. 1690–1820

Rosemary Sweet

CAMBRIDGE
UNIVERSITY PRESS

CAMBRIDGE
UNIVERSITY PRESS

University Printing House, Cambridge CB2 8BS, United Kingdom

Cambridge University Press is part of the University of Cambridge.

It furthers the University's mission by disseminating knowledge in the pursuit of education, learning and research at the highest international levels of excellence.

www.cambridge.org
Information on this title: www.cambridge.org/9781107529205

First published 2012
First paperback edition 2015

A catalogue record for this publication is available from the British Library

Library of Congress Cataloguing in Publication data

Sweet, Rosemary.
Cities and the grand tour : the British in Italy, c.1690–1820 / Rosemary Sweet.
pages   cm. – (Cambridge social and cultural histories)
Includes bibliographical references and index.
ISBN 978-1-107-02050-4 (Hardback)
1. Italy–Description and travel.   2. British–Travel–Italy–History–18th century.
3. Travelers–Great Britain–History–18th century.   4. Travelers' writings, British–
18th century.   5. British–Travel–Europe–History–18th century.   I. Title.
DG425.S94 2012
914.504′7–dc23

2012014614

ISBN 978-1-107-02050-4 Hardback
ISBN 978-1-107-52920-5 Paperback

In memory of John Philip McMurdo Sweet
10 June 1927–2 July 2009

Contents

List of figures   *page* viii
Acknowledgements   x
List of abbreviations   xii

Introduction   1

1   Experiencing the Grand Tour   23

2   Florence: a home from home   65

3   Rome ancient and modern   99

4   Naples: leisure, pleasure and a frisson of danger   164

5   Venice: a place of singularity and spectacle   199

6   Medievalism on the Grand Tour   236

    Conclusion   267

Bibliography   291
Index   322

Figures

1 'Vue Générale de l'Etat actuel des fouilles ordonées par le
  Roi de Naples dans le lieu que l'on pense avoir été le camp ou
  Quartier des soldats à Pompeii' (View of the excavations ordered
  by the King of Naples in the place thought to be the soldiers'
  barracks at Pompeii) from Jean Claude Richard de Saint-Non,
  *Voyage pittoresque ou description des royaumes de Naples et de
  Sicilie*, 5 vols. (Paris, 1782–5). Reproduced by kind permission
  of the Syndics of Cambridge University Library.   *page* 48
2 'The Palazzo Pubblico, in Bologna', from John Smith, *Select
  Views in Italy with Topographical Descriptions in England and
  France*, 2 vols. (1792–6). Reproduced by kind permission
  of the Syndics of Cambridge University Library.   60
3 'Florence from Fiesole', from James Hakewill, *A Picturesque
  Tour of Italy from Drawings Made in 1816, 1817* (1820).
  Reproduced by kind permission of the Syndics of Cambridge
  University Library.   69
4 'Florence from the Ponte alla Carraia', from James Hakewill,
  *A Picturesque Tour of Italy from Drawings Made in 1816,
  1817* (1820). Reproduced by kind permission of the Syndics
  of Cambridge University Library.   74
5 'Veduta della Piazza del Popolo', from Giovanni Battista
  Piranesi, *Vedute di Roma*, 2 vols. (Rome, n.d.). Reproduced
  by kind permission of the Society of Antiquaries.   100
6 'Temple of Jupiter Stator, Rome, showing the excavation',
  from Edward L. Cresy and G. L. Taylor, *The Architectural
  Antiquities of Rome*, 2 vols. (1821). Reproduced by kind
  permission of Special Collections, David Wilson Library,
  University of Leicester.   118
7 'Interior view of the Coliseum', from Edward L. Cresy and
  G. L Taylor, *The Architectural Antiquities of Rome*, 2 vols. (1821).
  Reproduced by kind permission of Special Collections,
  David Wilson Library, University of Leicester.   119

8 'Veduta della Piazza della Rotonda', from Giovanni Battista
Piranesi, *Vedute di Roma*, 2 vols. (Rome, n.d.). Reproduced by
kind permission of the Society of Antiquaries.   144
9 'Veduta dell'insigne Basilica Vaticana coll'ampio Portio e
Piazza adjacente', from Giovanni Battista Piranesi, *Vedute di
Roma*, 2 vols. (Rome, n.d.). Reproduced by kind permission
of the Society of Antiquaries.   152
10 'Vue de la Ville de Naples prise du Faubourg de Chiaja'
(View of Naples from the Chiaja), from Jean Claude
Richard de Saint-Non, *Voyage pittoresque ou description des
royaumes de Naples et de Sicilie*, 5 vols. (Paris, 1782–5).
Reproduced by kind permission of the Syndics of
Cambridge University Library.   166
11 'Vue de l'intérieur de l'Eglise Cathédrale de St Janvier à
Naples' (View of the interior of the cathedral of San Gennaro),
Jean Claude Richard de Saint-Non, *Voyage pittoresque ou
description des royaumes de Naples et de Sicilie*, 5 vols.
(Paris, 1782–5). Reproduced by kind permission of the
Syndics of Cambridge University Library.   182
12 'Mazanielle haranguant le Peuple de Naples dans la Place du
Marché des Carmea pendant la fameuse sedition de 1647'
(Masaniello haranguing the people of Naples in the Piazza del
Mercato during the famous rebellion of 1647), Jean Claude
Richard de Saint-Non, *Voyage pittoresque ou description des
royaumes de Naples et de Sicilie*, 5 vols. (Paris, 1782–5).
Reproduced by kind permission of the Syndics of
Cambridge University Library.   184
13 Michele Marieschi, 'Prospectus Plateae Divi Marci Venetiarum,
et eiusdem Basilicae cum redibus D Marci Procuratorum
(The Piazza San Marco and Basilica) (private collection).   206
14 Antonio Canaletto, 'Pons Rivoalti, utrinque Ripae, et Aedes
ad Orientem (The Rialto Bridge from the east), engraved by
Giovanni Battista Brustoloni (private collection).   216
15 'Specimen of the Architecture of the Baptistery at Pisa', from
Robert Smirke, 'An account of some remains of gothic
architecture in Italy and Sicily', *Archaeologia*, 15 (1806).
Reproduced by kind permission of Special Collections,
David Wilson Library, University of Leicester.   249
16 View of Assisi, from John Smith, *Select Views in Italy
with Topographical Descriptions in England and France*, 2 vols.
(1792–6). Reproduced by kind permission of the Syndics of
Cambridge University Library.   258

Acknowledgements

At the end of an overdue project there is considerable satisfaction in finally acknowledging the debts that have steadily accrued. My thanks are due first to the University of Leicester for providing me with two periods of study leave during which essential research and writing took place. Over the course of two summers, I was able to spend time in the company of British Studies at Oxford, where the combination of enthusiastic students, congenial faculty and the proximity of the Bodleian created a productive environment for research; I owe a particular debt of gratitude to Michael Leslie for facilitating this. The project received valuable impetus in 2005 with a grant from the Paul Mellon Foundation which enabled me to spend a period at the British School at Rome. I am deeply grateful to the Mellon Foundation and to the staff of the BSR who did so much to make it an enjoyable as well as a productive visit. In particular I would like to thank the librarian, Valerie Scott, and the Assistant Director, Susan Russell. Much of the writing was completed during a period of leave in 2009 when I was awarded a visiting fellowship at the Institute for Advanced Studies in the Humanities at the University of Edinburgh. I would like to thank the Director, Susan Manning, for welcoming me to such a congenial academic environment. My parents and siblings generously provided accommodation and distraction during various periods of research in London, Cambridge and Edinburgh, and even feigned interest on occasion. I am particularly grateful to my cousin Lainie McAdam for extended use of her sofabed during the winter of 2009.

Research has been carried out at a number of other libraries and archives and I would like to thank the staff in the following repositories for their assistance: the Bodleian Library, the Brinsley Ford Archive at the Paul Mellon Centre for the Study of British Art, the British Library, the British School at Rome, Cambridge University Library, Durham University Archives and Special Collections, Edinburgh University Library, Gloucestershire Archives, Magdalen College Oxford, the National Archives, the National Archives of Scotland, the National

Library of Scotland, the National Library of Wales, Norfolk Record Office, Record Office of Leicester, Leicestershire and Rutland, the Society of Antiquaries, St Andrews University Library, Surrey History Centre, Trinity College Cambridge, Wadham College Oxford, and the University of Leicester Special Collections.

Versions of every chapter have been presented at a number of conferences, workshops and seminars at the British School at Rome, Lamport Hall, the Society of Antiquaries and the universities of Birkbeck Cambridge, Edinburgh, Leeds, Leicester, Northumbria, Oxford, Tokyo, Warwick and York and I am grateful for comments and feedback from all those who listened. Earlier versions of Chapters 2 and 3 were published by the *Historical Journal* and the *Journal for Eighteenth-Century Studies* and I am grateful to the publishers for permission to reproduce material here.

Many colleagues at Leicester and elsewhere have provided me with valuable advice and information or have commented on draft chapters. In particular, I would like to thank Hannah Barker, Elaine Chalus, Robert Colls, Simon Gunn, Clare Haynes, Joanna Innes, Katy Layton-Jones, Prashant Kidambi, Phillip Lindley, Helen Meller, Julian Pooley, Carol Richardson, Richard Rodger and Jo Story. I would also like to thank Professor Douglas Tallack, the Head of the College of Arts, Humanities and Law, for making it possible for me to take leave of some administrative responsibilities during the final stages of writing over the summer of 2011, and to express my gratitude to my colleagues for their willing cooperation.

I would also like to thank Elizabeth Friend-Smith at Cambridge University Press and the series editors for their constructive criticism and encouragement. The book is infinitely better for their comments; its remaining deficiencies and errors are all my own. Finally, I must express my gratitude to Linda Randall who was all that one could wish for in a copy-editor, and more.

Abbreviations

Archives

BL	British Library
Bodl	Bodleian Library
CUL	Cambridge University Library
DUASC	Durham University Archives and Special Collections
GA	Gloucestershire Archives
MCO	Magdalen College Oxford
NAS	National Archives of Scotland
NLS	National Library of Scotland
NLW	National Library of Wales
NRO	Norfolk Record Office
ROLLR	Record Office for Leicester, Leicestershire and Rutland
SAL	Society of Antiquaries of London
TCC	Trinity College Cambridge
TNA	The National Archives
WCO	Wadham College Oxford

Periodicals

AHR	*American Historical Review*
HJ	*Historical Journal*
JWCI	*Journal of the Warburg and Courtauld Institutes*
ODNB	*Oxford Dictionary of National Biography*
P&P	*Past and Present*
TRHS	*Transactions of the Royal Historical Society*

Introduction

Long before the eighteenth century, Italian cities such as Rome and Venice occupied a very particular place in the British imagination. But as travel on the continent became increasingly commonplace amongst the British elite from the late seventeenth century onwards, with the rise of what has become known as the 'Grand Tour', this familiarity increased and the influence of Italian history and culture upon Britain grew steadily stronger. Books and prints describing Italy, its cities and its art and antiquities proliferated, consumed by armchair travellers and grand tourists alike. Returning travellers brought with them Italian fashions in art, music and architecture and the wealthiest redesigned their houses and their gardens to evoke an Italianate classical ideal and to display the art and antiquities they had collected. Italian poetry captured the imagination of an increasingly broad swath of the literate classes and learning Italian became a fashionable accomplishment, particularly for young women. As a consequence of these changes, the physical image, history and reputation of the principal cities of the Italian tour – Florence, Rome, Venice and Naples – were readily recognised by a wide range of travellers and readers, being invoked in novels and poetry, commemorated in prints and engravings and emulated in architecture and civic design. The foundations of the recognition which these cities still command today were securely established in the eighteenth century. This book, therefore, is not conceived as a survey of the Grand Tour as a cultural institution or a study of the broader influence of Italy on British culture; it is not even specifically concerned with what travellers saw and did. There are numerous books which cover this ground already.[1]

[1] Ilaria Bignamini and Andrew Wilton (eds.), *Grand Tour: The Lure of Italy in the Eighteenth Century* (1997); Jeremy Black, *The British Abroad: The Grand Tour in the Eighteenth Century* (Stroud, 1985); Jeremy Black, *Italy and the Grand Tour* (New Haven and London, 2003); Edward Chaney, *The Evolution of the Grand Tour: Anglo-Italian Cultural Relations since the Renaissance* (1998); Chloe Chard, *Pleasure and Guilt on the Grand Tour: Travel Writing and Imaginative Geography, 1600–1830* (Manchester, 1999); Christopher Hibbert, *The Grand Tour* (1969); Clare Hornsby (ed.), *The Impact of Italy: The Grand*

Rather, its focus is upon recovering and understanding how these urban centres were experienced, described and represented as places; how the image of a city was created and perpetuated through the medium of travel literature; what the different meanings and imaginative associations attached to these cities were; and how the contrasting descriptions of each of these cities reflected the travellers' own attitudes to urbanism. More broadly, this book explores other themes central to our understanding of eighteenth-century culture and the transition to modernity such as the construction and performance of personal, gender and national identities, and the shift in cultural values away from neo-classicism towards medievalism and the gothic.

The European Grand Tour was essentially a prolonged journey based around the principal cities of Europe rather than an exploration of the countryside and rural pleasures. It generally started in France or the Low Countries from where travellers made their way south, either passing over the Alps into northern Italy or making their way down to the Mediterranean and crossing over to the Ligurian coast via the Gulf of Spezzia. Having made the tour of Italy, they would either travel back via the major cities of Austria-Hungary, Germany and the Low Countries, or through France again. The length of time spent in 'making the tour' fell over the course of the century, but even in the early nineteenth century many tours lasted six months at the very least, and the costs could be prohibitive.[2] The conventional understanding of the Grand Tour is that it was intended to provide the final education and polish for elite young men, before they embarked upon fully fledged adulthood.[3] As we shall see, however, in practice the range of travellers undertaking these continental tours was more diverse than the traditional

Tour and Beyond (Rome, 2000). Recent literature on the Grand Tour is surveyed in two review articles: Barbara Ann Naddeo, 'Cultural capitals and cosmopolitanism in eighteenth-century Italy: the historiography of Italy and the Grand Tour', *Journal of Modern Italian Studies*, 10 (2005), 81–99; John Wilton Ely, ' "Classic ground": Britain, Italy, and the Grand Tour', *Eighteenth-Century Life*, 28 (2004), 136–65.

[2] Costs varied enormously, depending on the length of the tour, the style of travel and the quantity of purchases made. The kinds of expenses incurred are discussed in Black, *Italy and the Grand Tour*, 94–101.

[3] Bruce Redford, *Venice and the Grand Tour* (New Haven and London, 1996), 14, argues that 'The Grand Tour is not the Grand Tour unless it includes the following: first, a young British male patrician (that is, a member of the aristocracy or gentry); second, a tutor who accompanies his charge throughout the journey; third, a fixed itinerary that makes Rome its principal destination; fourth, a lengthy period of absence, averaging two or three years.' It is also the definition used by many other historians of the Grand Tour, such as Christopher Hibbert, for all that he frequently cites a much more eclectic range of sources, including female travellers such as Mariana Starke, Catherine Wilmot or Beaujolais Campbell, older men travelling for professional purposes, such as the musician Charles Burney, and French travellers such as Charles de Brosses.

image implies. Nevertheless, most of those undertaking a tour had at least some ambition to acquire cultivation and refinement; to improve their taste by studying the finest specimens of art and architecture; and to participate in the leisure pursuits and sociability of polite company in the different countries through which they passed. All these goals were pursued in the environment of towns and cities. This is not to say that the countryside was without interest: indeed, remarks relating to the fertility of the soil, the state of agriculture, the condition of the labouring population or the existence of manufactures all comprised an important element of travellers' observations and represented a crucial means of evaluating the prosperity and governance of the state.[4] Moreover, travel in pursuit of picturesque scenery or sublime landscape was becoming increasingly popular in the latter part of the eighteenth century, as was evident, for example, in the growing popularity of exploring the Swiss Alps from the 1780s. But for most purposes, the itinerary of the Grand Tour continued to be based around urban centres with people travelling *through* the countryside and staying *in* towns and cities.

It is only to be expected, then, that the observations recorded in travel journals and letters home, as well as the information provided in travel literature, tended to be structured around the description of particular cities. From this information, it is possible to draw some general conclusions about the kind of criteria by which eighteenth-century travellers judged the cities through which they passed; the kinds of questions that most interested them about the history, governance or social life of a city; and how these changed over the course of the century. We can also build up a sense of *how* visitors viewed a new town or city, both physically and imaginatively. In certain cities, visitors made much more extended stays of weeks, or even months, and here it is possible to arrive at a rather fuller understanding of how these cities were perceived and represented by the British, the meanings with which they were associated and the narratives that were told around them. Because so many British travellers went to Italy and recorded their impressions, either for private circulation or for publication, the published and unpublished material describing these cities is uniquely rich and varied, and allows one to trace the continuities and discontinuities and to identify the hackneyed clichés or the sudden aperçus with particular clarity. In describing the towns and cities through which they passed, travellers were able to rehearse various narratives by means of which the British understood their own history and identity as well as their relationship to other European

---

[4] See, for example, Josiah Tucker, *Instructions to Travellers* (1758), or Leopold Berchtold, *An Essay to Direct and Extend the Inquiries of Patriotic Travellers*, 2 vols. (1798).

societies. Thus, accounts of the cities which were encountered on the Grand Tour can be read on one level simply as records of where travellers stayed and what was seen. But we can also see how particular narratives or tropes were constructed around specific cities, which in turn predetermined the expectations and reactions of subsequent travellers. However, the ways in which these descriptions were framed and the choices that were made regarding what observations to include were also reflective of shifting attitudes towards urban society in general and of an evolving sense of what it meant to be British. For this was a period when Britain itself was undergoing rapid urban growth, not just in London but in provincial towns and cities throughout the country.[5] It was a society that was becoming increasingly aware of itself as 'polite and commercial' and by extension urban: towns and cities were an object of interest and inquiry, both for their historical importance in the past but also as the centres of economic growth, political power and cultural achievement in the present. Urban centres were scrutinised, discussed and described, and local and urban histories were a rapidly proliferating genre.[6] Travellers' comments on Italian cities are therefore revealing for what they imply about attitudes to urbanism back in Britain as well as for their observations relating directly to Italy.

In analysing the sources used in this study – travel literature, guidebooks, diaries, journals, correspondence – it is important to bear in mind the practical and cultural constraints that influenced the scope of much of what could be written. At the most basic level, the physical limitations on travel, enforced by the nature of the transport infrastructure and the availability of inns, roads, coaches and guides, ensured considerable standardisation and continuity to the itinerary and the experience of travel in Italy over the course of the eighteenth century.[7] Visitors' comments, not unexpectedly therefore, frequently display a significant degree of homogeneity: the travellers visited the same sites, went on the same excursions, read the same books and made the same observations in their own journals and correspondence. Moreover, what travellers observed and recorded was always heavily determined by conventions within the genre of travel writing and by the anticipated readership: their observations, therefore, cannot be taken as statements

---

[5] For an overview of urban population growth in this period see John Langton, 'Urban growth and economic change: from the late seventeenth century to 1841', in Peter Clark (ed.), *The Cambridge Urban History of Britain*, vol. II (Cambridge, 2000), 453–90.

[6] Rosemary Sweet, *The Writing of Urban Histories in Eighteenth-Century England* (Oxford, 1997).

[7] Judith Adler, 'Travel as performed art', *American Journal of Sociology*, 94:6 (1989), 1371–2.

of the simple immediacy of experience.[8] The literary formats of the day shaped the range of responses it was possible to express and did much to determine what was visited and described.[9] Thus, travellers were not free agents either in what they chose to see or how they described it. Although this is a drawback in terms of recovering the specificity of a given individual's experience, it can also be seen as a strength when we are seeking to understand the broader cultural meaning of particular places for eighteenth-century society and in explaining how these meanings changed – or failed to change – over the course of the century.

This book covers what may loosely be called the 'long eighteenth century', a period extending from roughly 1690 to around 1820. In the earlier part of this period, the dominant mode of writing about Italy, which characterised many of the published accounts as well as more personal, unpublished diaries and correspondence, was the trope of 'classical nostalgia', epitomised by publications such as Joseph Addison's *Remarks on Several Parts of Italy* (1705). It reflected the civic humanist education and the dominance of the classical ideal amongst the social elite who comprised the majority of travellers.[10] Addison's *Remarks on Several Parts of Italy*, and other works contemporary to it, were primarily textual in orientation: his travels were effectively undertaken and described as illustrations to classical quotations. Addison's was the most literary of tours, but the fascination with antiquity which *Remarks on Several Parts of Italy* represented helped to shape almost every tour, published and unpublished, that was made in the first half of the eighteenth century. But even when the literary and historical references were more sparsely provided, the classical frame of reference still determined the agenda of sightseeing throughout Italy, so that even at Genoa, a city with no ostensible remains of antiquity to boast of, one of the established fixtures on the tourist

[8] Charles Batten, *Pleasurable Instruction: Form and Convention in Eighteenth-Century Travel Literature* (Berkeley, 1978), 4.
[9] On the development and diversification of travel writing in this period see ibid.; Judith Adler, 'Origins of sightseeing', *Annals of Tourism Research*, 16:1 (1989), 7–29; Chard, *Pleasure and Guilt*; Barbara Korte, *English Travel Writing from Pilgrimages to Postcolonial Explorations*, trans. Catherine Matthias (Basingstoke, 2000), 40–65; Mary Louise Pratt, *Imperial Eyes: Travel Writing and Transculturation* (2nd edn, 2008); Katherine Turner, *British Travel Writers in Europe 1750–1800. Authorship, Gender and National Identity* (Aldershot, 2001); J. Viviès, *English Travel Narratives in the Eighteenth Century: Exploring Genres* (Aldershot, 2002); and on developments in the early nineteenth century, see James Buzard, *The Beaten Track: European Tourism, Literature, and the Ways to Culture, 1800–1918* (Oxford, 1993).
[10] Philip Ayres, *Classical Culture and the Idea of Rome in Eighteenth-Century England* (Cambridge, 1997).

itinerary was the rostrum from the Roman galley that had been placed over the entrance of the old Arsenale.[11]

Many of these accounts seem today dry, descriptive catalogues of objects or perfunctory lists of buildings. The conventions of topographical and antiquarian writing of the time, however, which shaped both published and unpublished accounts, demanded that writers should eschew the personal response or the individual opinion in order to guarantee the objectivity of descriptions: readers expected to find a disinterested approach and a highly factual content, typically presented in the format of enumerated lists and catalogues of building, works of art and antiquities.[12] This mode of writing was characteristic not just of descriptions of Italy, but of topographical literature much more generally: place and locality were defined by antiquities whether in the cities of Italy or the remoter corners of Great Britain.[13] Yet, for all that they shared a common 'classical nostalgia', the published tours of the first half of the century still offered a considerable variety in approach, coverage and emphasis, which, as we shall see, allowed for some variation in how particular cities were described. George Lewis Langton, travelling in 1737, weighed up the relative merits of the texts that he consulted in preparation for his trip to Italy: Edward Wright's *Some Observations Made in Travelling through France, Italy* (1730) offered 'great Exactness' but a 'very high degree of coarseness in his reflections and baseness in his style'. Nevertheless, his 'quaint conceits' and 'impertinent stories' were, apparently, to be preferred to the account of Maximilien Misson, first translated into English in 1695 as *A New Voyage to Italy*. Richard Lassels' *Voyage of Italy* (1670) was 'dull', and in the eyes of a Protestant such as Langton, full of Catholic 'superstition'. The Bishop of Salisbury, Gilbert Burnet, offered a more satisfactorily Protestant perspective, but Langton found him 'affected', and unreliable as an authority. John Breval, author of the two-volume *Remarks on Several Parts of Europe* (1726) was, by implication, more reliable but overly long, requiring 'an uncommon Share of Patience and Leisure' on the part of the traveller. Addison's *Remarks on Several Parts of Italy* – mercifully shorter – were 'made & expressed with a Delicacy that makes you lament his being so superficial & incorrect'.[14]

---

[11] Edward Wright, *Some Observations Made in Travelling through France, Italy, &c in the Years 1720–21 and 1722*, 2 vols. (1730), I, 26.

[12] Batten, *Pleasurable Instruction*, 13.

[13] Rosemary Sweet, *Antiquaries: The Discovery of the Past in Eighteenth-Century Britain* (2004), 314–16.

[14] R. J. Colyer, 'A Breconshire gentleman in Europe, 1737–8', *National Library of Wales Journal*, 21 (1979–80), 285.

The heyday of the aristocratic Grand Tour, however, is said to have passed by 1760, and in the last third of the eighteenth century this model of classical nostalgia and objective observation began to fragment as the social constituency of travellers to Italy broadened and the genres of travel writing multiplied.[15] Yet, even at mid-century, not all travel was being funded by the agricultural rentals of the great estate. Thomas Nugent's volume of travels, which was first published in 1744, offered tips on how to save money and to travel economically. Although Nugent (or his publisher) entitled his book, *The Grand Tour, or, a Journey through the Netherlands, Germany, Italy and France*, his target readership was self-evidently not exclusively the nobility and gentry. Amongst those whom he predicted would find his volume useful, he included 'all such as who travel for business'.[16] Nugent was attempting to catch some of the reflected lustre associated with aristocratic travel, perhaps, when he selected his title, but the choice of words is also indicative of how commonplace it had become to describe any kind of extended continental journey as a 'Grand Tour'. By 1760, young men from the landed elite were still being sent to Italy for the final polish to their education, although more and more writers were questioning the value of such a practice.[17] Increasingly, however, they were being joined by older men, professional writers, wealthier members of the middle classes, wives and family groups.[18] Merchants might send their sons abroad to mix business with education and pleasure; a bookseller could combine a business trip to purchase a library with a continental tour.[19] Artists and architects

---

[15] Redford, *Venice and the Grand Tour*, 15. It is important to recognise that this dimension to travel in Italy did not disappear: 'classical nostalgia' continued to shape travel accounts into the nineteenth century, see, for example, Richard Colt Hoare, *A Classical Tour through Italy and Sicily* (1819) and John Chetwode Eustace, *A Tour through Italy*, 2 vols. (1813), republished as *A Classical Tour through Italy*, 2 vols. (1814; revised edn, 4 vols., 1817).

[16] Thomas Nugent, *The Grand Tour, or, a Journey through the Netherlands, Germany, Italy and France*, 4 vols. (2nd edn, 1756), I, v.

[17] See, for example, Richard Hurd, *Dialogues on the Use of Foreign Travel Considered as Part of an English Gentleman's Education* (1764); Vicesimus Knox, *Liberal Education: or, a Practical Treatise on the Methods of Acquiring Useful and Polite Learning*, 2 vols. (9th edn, 1788), II, 296–309; Michèle Cohen, *Fashioning Masculinity: National Identity and Language in the Eighteenth Century* (1996), 54–63.

[18] John Towner, 'The Grand Tour: a key phase in the history of tourism', *Annals of Tourism Research*, 12 (1985), 308–12, provides a preliminary quantitative analysis of the social background of travellers to Italy; Katherine Turner, *British Travel Writers* emphasises the role of the middle classes, and women, in the composition of travel narratives in the later eighteenth century; Brian Dolan, *Ladies of the Grand Tour* (2001), also focuses on female travellers.

[19] See the diaries of the Norfolk textile merchants John Patteson and Robert Harvey: D. Cubitt, A. L. Mackley and R. G. Wilson (eds.), *The Great Tour of John Patteson, 1778–1779*, Norfolk Record Society, 67 (2003), and Harvey journal NRO MS 20677; or the

travelled to Italy in increasing numbers and whilst these travellers were clearly of a different social status to the 'tourists' proper, they often mixed with them socially, and frequently supplemented their earnings by acting as drawing masters and guides to their fellow Britons: social boundaries could prove less impermeable and more flexible within the artificial environment of a British community abroad.[20] The changing profile of travellers had become even more marked by the turn of the century. By this time, travel guides were routinely being published which deliberately promoted Italy as somewhere cheap to live – a place where one could follow the way to be 'rich and respectable' at minimal outlay.[21] Thus Henry Coxe's *Picture of Italy* (1815) was prefaced with over fifty pages of advice, most of which consisted of instructions on how to live economically but genteely without giving the appearance of scrimping. Coxe made his recommendations on the assumption that readers would be travelling without servants and he offered tips on a wide range of matters from the best way of dealing with bedbugs to the appropriate etiquette for dining at the table d'hôte at inns.[22]

These later travellers had different agendas; they did not necessarily subscribe to the nostalgia for classical antiquity and were prepared to challenge some of the assumptions on which the traditional itinerary of the 'Grand Tour' had been based. Travellers from commercial and professional backgrounds, for example, might ask rather different questions and note different features in the urban landscape.[23] At the same time, a buoyant domestic market for travel literature encouraged the diversification of style, content and approach. The popularity of conjectural history, which emphasised the value of the study of 'manners and customs' as reflections of the legal, moral and economic state of a society, lent new value to such observations. The description of 'manners and

---

journal of London bookseller, James Robson, BL Add. MS 38837. For an earlier example of a merchant making the tour of Italy, see Richard Chiswell's journal of 1696, Bodl. MS Don. c. 181.

[20] Some of the most vivid observations on Italian cities come from artists or their relatives. See for example, Paul Oppé (ed.), *Memoirs of Thomas Jones of Penkerrig, Radnorshire, 1803*, Walpole Society, 32 (1946–8); Susan Pearce and Frank Salmon (eds.), *Charles Heathcote Tatham in Italy*, Walpole Society, 65 (2005); John Ingamells (ed.), *John Ramsay's Italian Diary 1782–4*, Walpole Society, 65 (2003) (John Ramsay was the son of the artist and antiquary, Allan Ramsay); diary of Ann Flaxman, Flaxman journal BL Add. MS 39787 and BL Add. MS 39780 correspondence of both Ann and John Flaxman from Italy.

[21] Thomas Martyn, *A Gentleman's Guide in his Tour through Italy* (1787), xx–xiii.

[22] Henry Coxe, *Picture of Italy; Being a Guide to the Antiquities and Curiosities of that Classical and Interesting Country* (1815), i–l.

[23] Margaret Hunt, 'Imperialism and the traveler's gaze in eighteenth-century England', *Journal of British Studies*, 32:4 (1993), 346–53.

customs' offered fresh topics for discussion and opportunities for using the medium of travel writing in a more reflective way to debate issues of morality and national difference as well as to explore individual subjectivities. 'I never trouble you with descriptions of churches and palaces', wrote the surgeon Samuel Sharp, 'but, rather, with the customs and manners of the people I visit.'[24] True to his promise, his description of cities such as Florence and Venice barely even mentioned the usual highlights of the tourist itinerary, concentrating instead on discussions of the problem of beggars, the conventions of the *conversazione* and the perennially fascinating subject (for Englishmen at least) of the morality of Italian women and the married ladies' custom of taking a supposedly platonic lover, the *cicisbeo*. Laurence Sterne's *Sentimental Journey* (1768) inspired an emulative stream of sentimental narratives, in which the traveller's emotional responses and personal reflections took precedence over the collation of factual information, changed the tenor and content of topographical literature. Moods and feelings, personal encounters and anecdotal stories took the place of the comprehensive catalogues of sites to be seen and objects to be admired. John Owen, whose travels were published in 1796, went to great lengths to explain what he was *not* going to write about: he was not a connoisseur, not a naturalist, not an expert in painting, physics, mountains or wildlife. Rather, his interest was in human nature 'in all her varieties'.[25] The emergence of the picturesque equally had a decisive impact on the way that travel 'got done and written about' both in Britain and in Europe.[26] Female travellers, whose published works began to appear in increasing numbers from the 1770s, confirmed this trend away from the more rigidly classical and antiquarian mode of observation, which their gender disqualified them from adopting.[27] More broadly, however, travel writing of the early nineteenth century is distinguished by the impact of romanticism, with its heightened sensitivities and exquisite emotions, which influenced male and female travellers alike. Travellers were taught to feel and articulate an emotional response to Italy through reading *Childe Harold* or *Corinne* that displaced the didactic intent of earlier narratives. A divergence

[24] Samuel Sharp, *Letters from Italy, Describing the Customs and Manners of that Country in the Years 1765 and 1766* (1766), 243.
[25] John Owen, *Travels into Different Parts of Europe, in the Years 1791 and 1792: With Familiar Remarks on Places, Men and Manners*, 2 vols. (1796), I, 2.
[26] James Buzard, 'The Grand Tour and after (1660–1840)', in Peter Hulme and Tim Youngs (eds.), *The Cambridge Companion to Travel Writing* (Cambridge, 2002), 38.
[27] Turner, *British Travel Writers*, ch. 4, discusses some of the dominant features of women's travel writing in this period. The contrasts between the accounts of male and female travellers are considered in more detail in Chapter 1.

emerged between the informative, objective and edifying literature of travel writing and the more literary narratives of personal observation and reflection, based upon 'first impressions' and subjective responses.[28] This book, however, does not purport to be a study of the travel writing per se, but developments in the genre are important in so far as they changed the way in which cities were described and represented, and how this in turn determined the experiences of subsequent travellers and the reproduction of a particular image or narrative of a city.

The foundations of the Grand Tour were laid long before the *milordi inglesi* began to descend on Rome in their hundreds.[29] Nevertheless, it is generally seen as a quintessentially eighteenth-century experience. Accordingly, this study starts in the late seventeenth century, the period when numbers travelling to Italy began to rise appreciably, and ends in the 1820s when the numbers travelling and the diversification of itinerary saw continental travel evolve into a different kind of leisure phenomenon, albeit one which was still very clearly rooted in the traditions of eighteenth-century travel.

Many studies of the Grand Tour conclude in 1793 when the outbreak of the French Revolutionary Wars made continental travel problematic, if not impossible. But for all that fewer Britons were travelling in Italy between 1790 and 1815, this period and the years immediately following are crucial in arriving at an understanding of how the 'classical' vision of Italy in the eighteenth century evolved into *Italia romantica* of the early nineteenth century. Although war was an impediment to travel, the interruption was far from absolute for the entire duration. The British were present in large numbers for much of the 1790s and were quick to resume their pattern of continental travels in 1802 following the Peace of Amiens.[30] This window of opportunity was swiftly closed, however, with the resumption of hostilities a year later in 1803. Travellers such as Joseph Forsyth, who was seized by the French army in Turin as he made his way back from Italy in May 1803, were held for the duration of the hostilities in prisoner of war camps.[31]

[28] Maura O'Connor, *The Romance of Italy and the English Imagination* (1998), 1–54; Nigel Leask, *Curiosity and the Aesthetics of Travel Writing, 1770–1840* (Oxford, 2002); and Buzard, *The Beaten Track.*

[29] See notably Chaney, *The Evolution of the Grand Tour; John Stoye, English Travellers Abroad, 1607–1667: Their Influence in English Society and Politics* (London, 1952); and Cesare de Seta, *L'Italia del Grand Tour da Montaigne a Goethe* (3rd edn, Naples, 2001), 61–72.

[30] See, for example, Hudson Gurney's manuscript journal (SAL MS 677) and the published travels of John Chetwode Eustace, Lewis Engelbach, Joseph Forsyth and J. G. Lemaistre.

[31] Joseph Forsyth composed the greater part of his *Remarks on Antiquities* whilst held in a prisoner of war camp by the French in the hope that it might assist in securing his release if brought to the attention of Napoleon. *Remarks on Antiquities, Arts and Letters, during an Excursion in Italy, in the Years 1802 and 1803* (2nd edn, 1816), 4–8.

Thereafter, overland travel became increasingly dangerous and by 1807 the sea routes had become impossible also. Between 1807 and 1814, there was almost a complete hiatus in continental travel. But the steady stream of publications on continental travel throughout this period, however, indicates that interest remained very much alive.[32] This was a fact of which writers and publishers were not unaware: in 1814, when peace seemed likely, Mariana Starke wrote to her publisher, John Murray, suggesting that he would do well to expedite the next edition of her *Letters from Italy* for 'it seems reasonable to suppose the emigration from this Country will be immediate & immense, in case of peace'.[33] She was proved right. Even before the peace was signed, the British travelling public raced across the Channel to visit the continent once more, both to see those sites that had been so long closed to them, but also to observe the changes wrought by Napoleon and his armies. The clergyman and antiquary Robert Finch decided to travel to Italy in 1814, before Napoleon's escape from Elba. He was not alone: in April 1815, he sat down to dinner at a hotel in Florence with twelve other travellers, seven of whom were English. By 1818, it was estimated that 2,000 British tourists visited Rome.[34] Recent events added a new dimension to the itinerary within Italy: the passage over the Alps evoked Napoleon and Marengo, as well as Hannibal; a visit to Genoa included a day trip to Elba.[35] Travellers were quick to notice changes. Some were positive: a perceived improvement in manners; better roads; cleaner streets and excavations of the forum in Rome and at Pompeii. Other changes were received less favourably – chiefly the absence of some of the most highly esteemed works of art

[32] Guides and tours of Italy published in this period include: J. G. Lemaistre, *Travels after the Peace of Amiens, through Parts of France, Switzerland and Italy*, 3 vols. (1806); Robert Semple, *Observations on a Journey through Spain and Italy to Naples and thence to Smyrna and Constantinople*, 2 vols. (1807); Eustace, *Tour through Italy*; Forsyth, *Remarks on Antiquities*.
[33] Mariana Starke to John Murray, 13 Mar. 1814, NLS Acc 12604.
[34] Lynne Withey, *Grand Tours and Cook's Tours: A History of Leisure Travel, 1750 to 1915* (New York, 1997), 59. By the 1830s, the estimated figure had risen to 5,000.
[35] Eustace, *Classical Tour*, II, 296; Coxe, *Picture of Italy*, 38; Lemaistre, *Travels after the Peace of Amiens*, I, 192. John Milford reported that he met Napoleon frequently on the island during a fortnight's stay. The prisoner apparently ate abundantly and with great celerity, whilst drinking vast quantities of coffee. *Observations, Moral, Literary and Antiquarian Made during a Tour through the Pyrenees, South of France, Switzerland, the Whole of Italy and the Netherlands, in the Years 1814 and 1815*, 2 vols. (1818), I, 233–5; Richard Colt Hoare, who had been one of the few travellers to visit Elba before the revolution, saw his opportunity, and brought out an illustrated description of Elba, *A Tour through the Island of Elba* (1814). 'The extended and varied scenes of Napoleon's *triumphs*', announced the preface, 'are in general well known; but those of his destined *retirement* have been hitherto unfrequented and imperfectly noticed. To illustrate the latter by Views and Descriptions, is the object of my present Publication.'

which had been removed to Paris and a breakdown of law and order (brigandage) in the Neapolitan kingdoms. Some visitors, predictably, regretted the loss of political autonomy suffered by states such as the Venetian Republic, but others welcomed the French invasion as a necessary preliminary step towards modernity, progress and ultimately Italian unification. British travellers did not, on the whole, concern themselves with the vicissitudes suffered by the Italian people during this period of instability and their remarks were mostly confined to such changes as affected themselves directly.

But was the Napoleonic era in itself such a caesura in the experience of travel? Despite the very obvious changes wrought by war, in many senses these were superficial and did little to change the itinerary of the tour or the experience of travel except to make it rather smoother and more comfortable in certain places, such as the Alpine passes. In the short term at least, the political situation reverted to the status quo ante in much of Italy after the Treaty of Vienna, with the restoration of Habsburg power in Tuscany and northern Italy, papal authority in the Roman states and the Bourbon monarchy in Naples.[36] The biggest change was the subjugation of the Venetian Republic to Austria-Hungary. The real and apparent continuities with the earlier period were sustained not least by the ongoing availability of eighteenth-century books of travels which spanned the period of war. Addison's *Remarks on Several Parts of Italy*, for example, was still being republished even in the nineteenth century, although it was rarely used as a practical guide. The most widely consulted books of travel in the period after 1815, however, were those by Eustace, Forsyth and Starke, all of whom had been travelling on the continent in the 1790s or during the respite afforded by the Peace of Amiens in 1802. These works established a bedrock of continuity with the eighteenth century which it is important to explore. One of the objectives of this book, therefore, is to consider more closely the changes that were taking place and transforming the experience of travel in this interim period between the eighteenth-century 'Grand Tour' and the period of 'romantic travel' in the 1820s and 1830s. By this time, the itinerary of the continental tour itself was beginning to show clearer signs of modification: longer periods

---

[36] Stuart Woolf, *A History of Italy 1700–1860: The Social Constraints of Political Change* (1979), 231; John A. Davis, *Naples and Napoleon: Southern Italy and the European Revolutions, 1780–1860* (Oxford, 2006), 276–9. Formerly independent duchies such as Parma and Modena fell under the sway of the Habsburgs, as did the Venetian Republic, while Lucca went to the Bourbons. Many of the changes – sale of land, closure of monasteries and financial reform – introduced by the French were not reversed, but these were not matters that most travellers took it upon themselves to study.

were being spent in Switzerland in the Alps; journeys into the south of Italy and Sicily became more commonplace; the Rhine, made popular by *Childe Harold's Pilgrimage*, began to rival Italy as a favourite destination.[37] With the arrival of railways, travel became quicker, cheaper and easier, opening the way to the development of a new form of leisure travel by mid-century.[38] But the hegemony of classicism and the values which it sustained was beginning to fall apart, even before the introduction of rail and steam. As the numbers of British abroad increased, some travellers made a virtue of disregarding the traditions of the Grand Tour which had become hackneyed and commonplace. They began deliberately to seek to escape their compatriots and to demonstrate their superiority over those who travelled with insufficient taste or knowledge to appreciate the hidden secrets of Italy: this was the period when going 'off the beaten track' began to acquire a cultural value in its own right.[39]

This book is based upon a combination of both published works of topography and antiquarianism and unpublished narratives, journals and correspondence written over the course of the long eighteenth century. The various authors come from a broad range of social backgrounds: in addition to the aristocratic young men and their bearleaders, there are young women and older matrons, merchants and booksellers, artists and architects and even gentlemen's gentlemen. The various authors, diarists and correspondents come from a mixed range of English, Scottish, Welsh and some Irish travellers. The English were the most numerous amongst British travellers, but there was always a substantial minority from Scotland and Ireland (many were Catholics attracted to the Pretender's court in the earlier part of the century) and a scattering of Welsh gentry, but in the face of foreign society they tended to refer to themselves as 'English' too.[40] From the perspective of the Italians, however, they were all *milordi inglesi*, and whilst there are certain distinctions that emerge in the comments of English, Scottish, Irish or Welsh travellers respectively,

---

[37] The continued popularity of the continental tour as evidenced in publications in the period following the end of the Napoleonic Wars has been analysed by Benjamin Colbert. Italy retained its market share up to 1818, outnumbered only by tours to France. In the 1820s, Italy and France still dominated publications, but the tours of the Rhine and Switzerland were rapidly rising in popularity and would eventually surpass the tours to Italy in number. Benjamin Colbert, 'Bibliography of British travel writing, 1780–1840: the European Tour, 1814–18 (excluding Britain and Ireland)', *Cardiff Corvey Articles*, XIII.1, www.cardiff.ac.uk/encap/journals/corvey/articles/cc13_n01.html, accessed 31 July 2009.

[38] Withey, *Grand Tours and Cook's Tours*, ch. 3.   [39] Buzard, *The Beaten Track*, 6.

[40] Roger Robertson included himself amongst the 'English' when telling his mother how he and other compatriots had met together at the Princess Borghese's box at the theatre in Rome. Robertson to his mother, 26 Jan. 1752, NLS Acc 12244.

these are relatively minor and are heavily outweighed by the overwhelming influence of the common cultural background of the eighteenth-century social elite. This book, therefore, treats them collectively as British travellers in recognition of their geographical origins, but this should not necessarily be taken to assume a common British identity.

Taken individually, the published tours offer insights into the development of the genre of travel writing and its use in the construction of subjectivities; they offer material for the articulation of theories of taste and aesthetics and allow for the elaboration of concepts of national identity, race and ethnicity.[41] My approach has not been to focus on any particular genre or any single author but rather to use a broad variety of different kinds of source in order to establish the full range of what could be said – or left unsaid – about the cities that were visited. Taken together en masse over a century or more, the combination of published and unpublished material allows one to explore how attitudes and expectations evolved; to trace the common themes that travellers rehearsed and which sustained their English or British identity; to identify recurrent preoccupations or to pinpoint the unusual observation and how these altered over time. For all that the eighteenth-century tour is dominated by the image of aristocratic young men on a gap year, none of the published accounts was written by them, although the correspondence between them and their parents often survives. The image of Italy that we derive from the print culture of the day was rather the product of the middling sorts: the travelling tutors, clergymen, aspiring men (and women) of letters, architects, antiquaries and artists, lawyers, botanists and physicians. Writing a volume of travels served to demonstrate their literary credentials and to display their learning and taste; it might also earn some additional income. The sources that have been used also include those lengthier works which were generally consulted in a library before or after the journey, but which framed the expectations and informed the understanding of the places that were visited, and the shorter guides which were designed to be carried in the pocket of the traveller. In addition, locally published guides and histories have been used in order to acquire a sense of the range of information that

---

[41] Batten, *Pleasurable Instruction*; Elizabeth Bohls, *Women Travel Writers and the Language of Aesthetics, 1716–1815* (Cambridge, 1995); Buzard, *The Beaten Track*; J. B. Bullen, *Continental Crosscurrents: British Criticism and European Art 1810–1910* (Oxford, 2005); Chard, *Pleasure and Guilt*; Leask, *Curiosity and the Aesthetics of Travel Writing*; Dennis Porter, 'Uses of the Grand Tour: Boswell and his contemporaries', in Dennis Porter (ed.), *Haunted Journeys: Desire and Transgression in European Travel Writing* (Princeton, 1991), 25–68; Patricia Meyer Spacks, 'Splendid falsehoods: English accounts of Rome, 1760–1798', *Prose Studies*, 3:3 (1980), 203–16; Turner, *British Travel Writers*.

was available to travellers on the spot. Alongside these printed sources, a wide selection of unpublished journals, diaries and correspondence has also been consulted. These have the advantage of being less constrained by the literary conventions of the time or the dictates of the market place and frequently offer a more immediate and personal insight into the experience of travel. Such unpublished sources, studied alongside the published tours, also highlight the extent to which so many narratives were self-conscious rhetorical performances. The fragmentary, partial and often inconsequential content of correspondence and diaries offers an alternative perspective on the expectations and experiences of travel.

Each different type of source, however, raises problems of inter-pretation.[42] The published tours and volumes along the lines of 'Letters from Italy' would routinely stress their claims to originality, veracity and accuracy. To do otherwise would have been to flout all the expectations of travel writing as truthfulness, and truth depended on personal witness and precise observation.[43] But such claims deserve to be met with an element of caution. Tours were rarely published immediately upon the traveller's return: in most cases, there was a considerable time lag between the journey and publication during which revisions might be made, additional material added from other sources and other obser-vations excised.[44] Given the number of publications that appeared on continental travel during the eighteenth century, some claim to original-ity had to be made to differentiate one book of travels from another. Many such claims were spurious: a straightforward comparison of dif-ferent texts shows multiple borrowings and repetitions, sometimes acknowledged, at other times involving outright plagiarism. In some cases, such as Thomas Nugent's *The Grand Tour*, there is no evidence that the author ever went to Italy at all.[45] He and John Northall, the author of *Travels through Italy* both cut and paste from other authorities, such as Addison, Misson and Keysler. Henry Coxe (the pseudonym used by John Millard) performed a similar exercise in his popular *Picture of Italy* (1815). Even where the author can be shown to have travelled to Italy, there is no guarantee that he or she actually saw the places that

[42] See also the discussion of sources in Black, *Italy and the Grand Tour*, 17–22.
[43] Adler, 'Origins of sightseeing', 18.
[44] Turner, *British Travel Writers*, 175–8, discusses the relationship between Piozzi's 'Thraliana' and her journals.
[45] There is no reference to Thomas Nugent in John Ingamells (ed.), *A Dictionary of British and Irish Travellers in Italy, 1701–1800* (New Haven and London, 1997), nor does the entry in *ODNB* suggest that he ever visited Italy in person. Elizabeth Baigent, 'Nugent, Thomas (c. 1700–1772)', ODNB, Oxford University Press, 2004 (www.oxforddnb.com/view/article/20402, accessed 31 July 2011).

they described. Robert Harvey, a merchant from Norwich, recorded his conversation with an innkeeper at Turin who told him that Tobias Smollett had never stirred from his room for the entire period of his stay 'but took all his information from his valet de place'. Readers of Smollett's *Travels in France and Italy*, however, generally assumed he had been there: as Harvey observed to himself in his own journal, 'this man's travels are read & esteem'd'.[46] Travellers might use their guides critically, often commenting when their authority appeared to have been mistaken or to have misled them. But for the most part, there was a basic level of trust amongst travellers, and an acceptance that the books that they were reading were reasonably accurate, authentic and reliable. The historian's trust has to be rather more qualified.

Topographical literature and the information of the local guides or *ciceroni* were essential in giving meaning to what visitors encountered: the information imparted in these sources was repeated in journals and letters, and subsequently filtered into another generation of published tours. Individual texts had a much longer shelf life than those that are published today – Gilbert Burnet's comments on the depopulated Roman *campagna*, for example, were still being repeated at mid-century more than fifty years after he had first made the observations.[47] Similarly, James Boswell took great pleasure in seeing Italy through the *Spectator*'s eyes after a similar lapse of time.[48] Writing in 1813, the Roman Catholic bearleader John Chetwode Eustace still thought it worth warning his readers against the 'strong prejudices' of Addison.[49] The literature of eighteenth-century travel is thus characterised by important continuities and a high level of interdependence and intertextuality. Sometimes, this occasioned reflective commentary on the part of the traveller, in other cases, as already noted, its appearance simply constituted straightforward plagiarism.

Diaries, journals and correspondence allow one to access a far wider range of responses to Italy. They also offer what is apparently a more immediate view of Italy in that they generally appear to have been less premeditated, less self-conscious in their composition. Robert Finch, who kept a detailed record of his travels, began to plan an account of Italy based upon his journals in the 1820s but died with little progress having been made. His wife undertook some preparatory work on the

---

[46] Harvey journal NRO MS 20677, 47.

[47] Francis Blackburne (ed.), *Memoirs of Thomas Hollis Esq FR and ASS*, 2 vols. (1780), I, 33.

[48] Boswell to Johnston, 28 Nov. 1764, in Ralph Walker (ed.), *Correspondence of James Boswell and John Johnston of Grange* (1966), 146–7. Joseph Addison, author of *Remarks on Several Parts of Italy etc in the Years 1701, 1702, 1703* (1705) was best known for his contributions to the *Spectator* periodical.

[49] Eustace, *Classical Tour*, i, xxxiv–v.

manuscripts after his death and references to 'private parts' and pubic hair in his description of Titian's *Venus de Medici* are now scored through: a visible demarcation of the divergence between what was deemed suitable for private and public consumption.[50] Many 'journals' however, were kept originally as rough notes and the volumes that survive in record offices are the fair copies that were written up subsequently, often with additional material interpolated at a subsequent date. Some of these were clearly prepared with a view to publication, or at least private circulation, such as Francis Drake's lengthy and unpublished account of his tour 1750–2, and do not show such a clear distinction between works intended for a private as opposed to a public readership as might be expected. William Forbes' hefty multivolume manuscript of his family's travels in Italy in 1792–4, with its ponderous record of everything from the dimensions of their apartments to the names of those whom they met on their travels, was never intended for circulation beyond his private circle. Despite the disclaimer that he had written it only for the eyes of his wife and daughter, he almost certainly did not conceive of the project for their satisfaction alone.[51] Given that he had himself benefited from perusal of the journal kept by his friend Sir James Hall of his own travels in Europe a decade earlier, it is likely that Forbes would have expected to share his journals within his circle of friends.[52] As such, the journal was a demonstration of the wide reading and erudition that would confirm his reputation as a gentleman of taste and judgement. The completion of his 'tour' in the fair copy that now survives in the National Library of Scotland seems to have been an exercise that occupied him for several winters after his return to Edinburgh. When Forbes' notes were inadequate, or when he deemed it appropriate to refer to the expertise of a higher authority, he copied out long passages from the relevant text, be it Gibbon, Robertson or Roscoe, in the manner of a commonplace book.

Most travellers were more succinct than Forbes or Finch in keeping their journals and frequently simply referred themselves to the relevant volume that they had been reading or to a particular print or engraving when it came to describing a building or recording specific information. In the case of Sarah Bentham, for example, she merely noted the relevant passage in her son's journal on subject matter which she felt he had covered more competently than she.[53] Omission of detail,

---

[50] Finch journal Bodl. MS Finch e. 15, fol. 13v; on Finch's career see Elizabeth Nitchie, *The Reverend Colonel Finch* (New York, 1940), 10.

[51] Forbes journal NLS MS 1539, fol. 3.   [52] Hall journal NLS MSS 6324–7.

[53] Bentham journal TNA PRO 30/9/43, 107, 168.

therefore, did not necessarily correlate with a lack of interest. For many, the purpose of keeping a diary was largely factual: it was an aide-mémoire, a record of what had been seen and when, rather than an opportunity to explore personal impressions, reactions or opinions. It is for this reason that comments on Rome, where there was the most to be seen (and a ready supply of printed guides and engraved images to refer to), are frequently disappointingly laconic. As Whaley Armitage, recently graduated from Cambridge, explained in his journal: 'I propose leaving off giving any particulars in this Journal of the different articles which I see in any Churches &c as it takes up some time & I find I but imperfectly sketch what may be found at large in the description of Antient and Modern Rome which I have.' His notes focussed instead upon his social engagements and his programme of reading.[54]

Whereas journals might deteriorate into cryptic notes, letters back home to relatives, who were often paying for the tour, had to be rather fuller and, depending upon the addressee, covered different ground. Some travellers kept a journal as well as writing letters; the journals therefore tended to record the factual detail of what was seen and the letters 'are intended rather to tell you what I feel, to give you the ideas which employ my mind at the time I write' as Boswell put it.[55] But the intended readership has always to be borne in mind. As subsequent chapters will show, travellers carefully tailored their comments to their audience. There was no point in regaling one's mother, whose knowledge of ancient history was limited, with a summary of what one had been told by the *cicerone* at the Coliseum. Equally, it was probably best not to inform one's father of the full scale of sociability which had been indulged in. Some collections of correspondence, like that of Roger Robertson of Ladykirk, whose letters to his mother, father and sisters survive together, offer particularly revealing contrasts in what was deemed suitable for whom. It was his mother to whom he tried to justify his expenses (having first softened her up with the promise of a fan), priming her with the excuses for his extravagance with which she was to win over his more formidable father. He had to buy another suit, he wrote, as he had only the one which he had bought in Paris; but when mixing with so many great people, fine clothes were necessary; and he begged her to assure his Papa that he had chosen the plainest and genteelest clothes that he could get.[56] Lord Winchilsea, another dutiful

[54] Armitage journal TCC Add. MS a 226 37 (1), unfoliated MS, 22 Oct. 1790.
[55] Boswell to Johnston, 30 Dec. 1765, Walker (ed.), *Correspondence of James Boswell*, 205.
[56] Robertson to his parents, 6 Nov. 1751, NLS Acc 12244.

son, constantly reassured his mother on his excellent state of health, which he attributed to his habit of always putting on a greatcoat when going out into the cold, after having become heated from dancing at balls.[57] Mothers were always anxious for reassurance on the state of their offspring's physical and moral health.[58] Indeed, it is often in the letters home to female family members that one is able to gain an insight into the more personal dimension of travel, the emotions and anxieties experienced, and a sense of the family dynamics: young men were more likely to admit to anxiety or to homesickness and to tell them more about the mundane practicalities of life.[59] Amusing anecdotes were saved for entertaining younger sisters. Letters were always a rhetorical performance, however. Even if there was no intention of publication, there was always the expectation that they would be circulated around family members at the very least and content would be manipulated accordingly.

The term 'Grand Tour' has considerable heuristic value in that it signals the remarkable homogeneity of both the itinerary of the tour and the experiences of those travelling over the long eighteenth century. However, it also disguises important differences: both change over time, which will be explored more fully in subsequent chapters, and the variety of experiences reflecting the individual traveller's respective religion, social status or gender. The majority of the texts that survive, and on which this study is based, were written by Protestants and from the social elite, comprising the aristocracy, gentry and wealthy merchants and members of the professions.[60] Within that social elite there was, of course, considerable variation, and the eye of the merchant might see a town differently from that of the landed gentleman; similarly, the moral values of a clergyman might colour his perceptions in a rather different shade from that of the aristocrat. These are themes that will run through subsequent chapters. A large body of materials, however, also survive which were written by women, and these allow one to

---

[57] Winchilsea to his mother, 19 Jan. 1773, ROLLR Finch MSS DG 7/4/12 box 4953 bundle 32.

[58] See Martha Patteson's letters to her son in Cubitt, Mackley and Wilson (eds.), *Great Tour of John Patteson.*

[59] See for example, Lord Kildare's letters to his mother in Elizabeth Fitzgerald (ed.), *Lord Kildare's Grand Tour, 1766–1769* (Cork, 2000), or Brian Fitzgerald (ed.), *The Correspondence of Emily Duchess of Leinster*, 3 vols. (Dublin, 1957).

[60] The occasional journal written by a servant survives, offering a rather different perspective on the experience of travel, largely unmediated by knowledge of classical history, antiquarianism or art: see, for example, the journal of Edmund Dewes (1773), Bodl. MS Eng. misc. d. 213; or Geoffrey Trease (ed.), *Matthew Todd's Journal: A Gentleman's Gentleman in Europe 1814–20* (1968).

explore in greater depth the differences – and the similarities – between the masculine and feminine experience of travel in Italy. However, because the Grand Tour was so deeply implicated in the construction of elite masculinity, the tendency in most contemporary and subsequent discussions has been for the experiences of women travellers to be elided with those of men.[61] The first chapter is therefore devoted to exploring in greater detail what the Italian tour involved for both men and women and the extent to which the practice of travel was constrained by the norms of gender relations. The tour's importance as a stage for the performance of elite masculinity has long been accepted, but the participation of women on the tour has never been adequately scrutinised: what difference did their gender make in the itinerary of sightseeing and in their experiences of the cities through which they passed? Considering the feminine as well as the masculine experience of travel, and paying closer attention to how gender determined what was seen, what was done and how it was described, complicates and enriches our understanding of the experience and representation of the Grand Tour.

Chapters 2–5 concentrate on the principal cities of the Italian tour: Florence, Rome, Naples and Venice. By emphasising breadth and consulting a wide range of both published and unpublished materials, rather than focussing upon one or two particular texts or travellers, the objective has been to arrive at an appreciation of the range of observations that were made, how individual cities were seen and experienced over the long term and also more broadly what this can tell us about attitudes to cities and urban society in the eighteenth century. This approach allows us to understand how a particular city was viewed and experienced; to develop an understanding of how the image and reputation of these cities evolved over time; and to explore how these changing perceptions in turn were inflected by the gender and social background of the visitor. By the nineteenth century, the major cities of Italy were being described in far greater variety, depth and detail than had been the case a century earlier; one consequence of this was a much sharper sense of how the cities' historical development could be traced through their physical fabric. Travellers of the nineteenth century were more adept in reading the city as a product of complex historical change than their early

---

[61] Turner's study *British Travel Writers* offers an exception; neither Dolan, *Ladies of the Grand Tour* nor Kathryn Walchester, *Our Own Fair Italy: Nineteenth-Century Women's Travel Writing and Italy 1800–1844* (Bern, 2007), engages with the question of how and why the feminine experience differed from the masculine. Nor is this a question that engages standard authorities which also draw on the testimony of female travellers; see, for example, Hibbert, *Grand Tour*, or Black, *Italy and the Grand Tour*.

eighteenth-century predecessors and rather more interested in viewing it as a community of people rather than simply as the physical centre of power and authority. Thus we also see how descriptions of cities evolved away from a mode of comprehensive listing, focussing on the public and the monumental, towards a more discursive format that sought to evoke atmosphere and a sense of place, that looked for the essence of the city in its streets and its people and which saw more emphasis on the experience of walking through the streets as a means of encountering and understanding the city.[62] By focussing on the specific place, rather than more general themes, the distinctive identity and interpretative function of each city within the itinerary of the tour can be analysed and interpreted, whilst at the same time commonalities in the experience of viewing and describing these urban centres are established. Each city had a particular narrative to be told around it which heavily determined what was seen and what was ignored. However, these narratives also changed over the course of our period, both in relation to the fortunes of the city itself and in relation to developments within British culture and society of the time.

The way in which a city was experienced was always influenced by the information with which a traveller was equipped. Guidebooks were powerfully constitutive of the experience of sightseeing; they determined what was seen and in what order, and shaped what judgements were made. One of the principal themes of chapters that follow will be the extent to which a visitor's perception of the town was shaped by what he or she had already read: travellers in this period for the most part discovered the city that they had been taught to expect. But other influences could have a bearing on what attracted visitors' attention, and the content of travel literature and guidebooks changed, often in response to the shifting values or interests of their intended market. This becomes particularly apparent in the final chapter where the argument again moves away from a focus upon specific cities to concentrate on one of the key ways in which the classical hegemony of the Grand Tour began to break down. This chapter examines the gradual process by which British travellers became aware of the medieval past in Italian cities and the gothic architecture in which it assumed its most visible form. The enthusiasm for gothic antiquities, which became an increasingly dominant feature of domestic tourism and topographical literature in later eighteenth-century Britain, could not undermine the rationale for the pursuit of classical antiquities on the Italian tour altogether. It did,

---

[62] The contrast drawn here corresponds roughly to that identified by Michel de Certeau in *The Practice of Everyday Life*, trans. Steven Randall (Berkeley, 1984), 92–4.

however, cast familiar cities in a different light and endowed other less-well-regarded centres such as Pisa, Orvieto or Assisi with new meaning and importance. It also laid the foundations on which later travellers, such as John Ruskin, could discover an entirely different vision of Italy for British readers.

1 Experiencing the Grand Tour

Introduction

From the inception of the 'Grand Tour' as a cultural institution in the seventeenth century, it was ascribed particular value in the construction of elite, masculine identity. Richard Lassels, whose *Voyage of Italy* (1670) helped to establish the phenomenon of the Grand Tour and who is often credited with having coined the term, explained how the independence and self-reliance wrought by travel would equip the young man with the necessary qualities of masculinity. It would preserve the young nobleman from 'surfeiting of his parents', and wean him 'from the dangerous fondness of his mother'. The endurance required for early rising, hunger and long hours in the saddle, ensured that the youth was separated from the comfort and ease of home, where female influence prevailed, and developed the fortitude to withstand personal discomfort and danger with courage and without complaint.[1] The education that it offered in politics, statecraft, antiquity and connoisseurship were all crucial attributes for the construction of elite manhood.[2] Travel facilitated social polish through conversation in aristocratic salons, through mixing with the polite society of other nations and through the acquisition of accomplishments such as dancing and swordsmanship, which gave the young man poise and social grace. For older men, who might be presumed to have acquired such attributes, a visit to Italy offered the opportunity to display those

---

[1] Richard Lassels, *The Voyage of Italy* (1670), preface.
[2] Redford, *Venice and the Grand Tour*, 5–25; Henry French and Mark Rothery, ' "Upon your entry into the world": masculine values and the threshold of adulthood among landed elites in England, 1680–1800', *Social History*, 33:4 (2008), 402–22; Cohen, *Fashioning Masculinity*, 54–63; Michèle Cohen, 'Manliness, effeminacy and the French: gender and the construction of national character in eighteenth-century England', in Tim Hitchcock and Michèle Cohen (eds.), *English Masculinities, 1660–1800* (1999), 44–62; Clare Haynes, *Pictures and Popery: Art and Religion in England, 1660–1760* (Aldershot, 2006), 14–45.

qualities of taste and connoisseurship that defined their membership of a cosmopolitan (and largely masculine) social elite.[3]

The language in which the Grand Tour was discussed was accordingly highly gendered, reinforcing the normative values of elite masculinity. In 1729, Conyers Middleton compared the voyage to Italy to the journey of life, that is the masculine life. France, he suggested, represented the pleasures of youth – gay and fluttering – and was, by implication, feminine. It was only as one advanced towards Rome that the 'solid, manly, and rational' attributes were acquired, and in Rome itself they reached their perfection.[4] At the other end of the century, Archibald Alison similarly defined the delight in viewing antiquities and visiting Rome in exclusively masculine terms: 'And what is it that constitutes that emotion of sublime delight, which every man of common sensibility feels upon the first prospect of ROME?', he asked. 'It is ancient Rome which fills his imagination. It is the country of Caesar, and Cicero, and Virgil, which is before him.'[5] The imagination that was being thus stimulated was one which had been nurtured on the manly texts of ancient history and classical literature and inculcated with the virtues of honour, duty, courage and loyalty. Even the way in which the city was supposed to be viewed developed masculine attributes: generations of Englishmen made their way around Rome measuring monuments with tape measures and quadrants, comparing their results against those of other authorities. Thus, they acquired the skills of mensuration, surveying and draughtsmanship which demonstrated their command of mathematics and scientific instruments, as well as enhancing their familiarity with the monuments themselves.[6]

---

[3] On the importance of Roman antiquity for elite cultural values see Ayres, *Classical Culture*. On the centrality of the classics in male education, see M. V. Wallbank, 'Eighteenth-century public schools and the education of the governing elite', *History of Education*, 8 (1979), 1–19.

[4] Conyers Middleton, *A Letter from Rome: Shewing an Exact Conformity between Popery and Paganism, or the Religion of the Present Romans to be Derived Entirely from that of their Heathen Ancestors* (1729), 8.

[5] Archibald Alison, *Essays on the Nature and Principles of Taste* (Dublin, 1790), 25.

[6] Richard Pococke's letters to his mother (BL Add. MS 22978) record how he and his pupil measured almost every monument they encountered. See also Misson's recommendation that travellers should carry with them a measuring cane and waxed packthread for measuring monuments, Maximilien Misson, *A New Voyage to Italy*, 4 vols. (1739), II, 357. On the importance of architectural drawing and surveying as a part of elite masculine education see Michael McCarthy, 'The education in architecture of the man of taste', *Studies in Eighteenth-Century Culture*, 5 (1985), 337–53, and Ann Bermingham, *Learning to Draw: Studies in the Cultural History of a Polite and Useful Art* (New Haven and London, 2000), 33–73.

Not unsurprisingly, therefore, discussions of the Grand Tour tend to treat it in undifferentiated terms as part of the *rite de passage* of elite manhood and to assume that this ideal remained a constant. But constructions of masculinity were not immutable over the course of the eighteenth century and the model of elite manhood that had arisen in the European courts of the later seventeenth century was both challenged and modified by new ideals of masculine behaviour that were better adapted to a society that was taking on an increasingly bourgeois tone. Courtly civility and its descendant 'politeness' declined in importance by mid-century; the manly qualities of independence, sincerity, and even taciturnity, displaced the earlier skills of social display such as dancing, swordsmanship and conversational facility. Increasingly, English or British manhood was defined against the effeminate, foreign other.[7] Those who were critical of the practice of foreign travel construed their arguments in terms of the negative consequences for masculinity, arguing that it promoted habits of effeminacy and compromised the masculinity of British youth, exposing them to dangerous influences at an impressionable age.[8] Similarly, the didactic value of classical antiquity, which the Grand Tour exemplified, did not go unquestioned: outside the world of public schools, educational curricula expanded to take in new subjects of greater relevance to a modern, commercial age. Travel was still valued as a means of educating young men, but for writers such as Josiah Tucker, its benefit lay in the acquisition of knowledge (commercial, agricultural, political) rather than in the acquisition of taste and social polish. But whilst Tucker saw travel as a responsibility and commitment, there was a parallel development that saw the promotion of travel for leisure and pleasure.[9] Recreational and valetudinarian travel, at home and abroad, became increasingly commonplace towards the end of the century.

As the raison d'être for travel broadened not only did the social background of travellers become more diverse, but the travellers increasingly included women amongst their number. Yet, the image of the masculine grand tourist is so dominant that it is easy to overlook how many women also accompanied husbands, fathers and brothers on a continental tour.

---

[7] Cohen, *Fashioning Masculinity*; Cohen, 'Manliness, effeminacy and the French'; Gerald Newman, *The Rise of English Nationalism: A Cultural History, 1740–1830* (New York, 1997), 81–2.

[8] See, for example, the discussion in Hurd, *Dialogues on the Uses of Foreign Travel*, or Tobias Smollett, *Travels through France and Italy*, 2 vols. (1766), discussed in Redford, *Venice and the Grand Tour*, 40–6; John Brown's jeremiad against foreign influence, *An Estimate of the Manners and Principles of the Times* (1757); Knox, *Liberal Education*, II, 296–309.

[9] Tucker, *Instructions to Travellers*.

As early as 1733, Joseph Spence commented to his mother on the numbers of Englishwomen he had encountered in Florentine society, observing with a touch of irony that 'it is now all the fashion for ladies to travel'.[10] The fashion became ever more marked as the century progressed. With rising disposable incomes and improving travel conditions, more and more women were joining their male relatives travelling on the continent. Young men returned in middle age with their wives and partners, or took a newly married wife to the continent for an extended honeymoon. Brothers travelled with their sisters.[11] Wives and daughters would be taken to recover their strength in the warmer climate of Italy.[12] Daughters accompanied by their parents learnt Italian, French, refined their knowledge of art and acquired social polish: it was no longer just young men whose education was finished in Italy; rather, it had become 'the fashion for the whole house to transport themselves together', as Patrick Home noted in 1775.[13] Widowed matriarchs such as Lady Templetown and Lady Berwick travelled to Italy with daughters in tow, in the hope of snaring a husband en route.[14] The widowed Lady Charlotte Campbell took her five children to Italy in 1817 in pursuit of a more economical lifestyle.[15] The occasional woman, such as the otherwise unidentified Mrs Motte encountered by Sarah Bentham in 1794, even travelled on her own, accompanied only by her female servant.[16] By the time that Jane Waldie published her *Sketches Descriptive of Italy*, based upon a tour she had made with her sister and brother in 1816, she was able to claim that there were many

[10] Slava Klima (ed.), *Joseph Spence: Letters from the Grand Tour* (Montreal and London, 1975), 138.

[11] John Carr of Dunston Hill, Durham, travelled to Italy 1791–4 with his sister Harriet for the sake of her health: Ingamells (ed.), *Dictionary of British and Irish Travellers*, 185–6; A. W. Purdue, 'John and Harriet Carr: a brother and sister from the north-east on the Grand Tour', *Northern History*, 30 (1994), 122–38; Lady Charlotte Lindsey travelled with her brother Frederick in 1815 (Bodl. MS Eng. c. 7052–3).

[12] Sir William Forbes took his wife to Italy with their daughter, in order to try to recover her health (NLS MSS 1539–45); Sarah Bentham travelled with her consumptive daughter-in-law in an unsuccessful attempt to recover her health (TNA PRO 30/9/43–4).

[13] Home journal NAS GD 267/33/2, fol. 37; Sarah Bentham reported that the Advocate General of Jamaica, James Pinnock, whom she met in Naples, had travelled there with his wife and three daughters for their education: TNA PRO 30/9/43, 151. The Duchess of Beaufort originally brought her granddaughter and daughter to Italy for their health; in Rome, she engaged James Byres to 'read architecture' with them, Ingamells (ed.), *Dictionary of British and Irish Travellers*, 66.

[14] The latter was gratified to see her eldest daughter married to the impulsive Charles Lord Bruce in Florence in 1793, although the other two daughters remained unmarried. Ingamells (ed.), *Dictionary of British and Irish Travellers*, 86–7, 144.

[15] The family's journey was recorded by the third daughter, Harriet Charlotte Beaujolais Campbell, *A Journey to Florence in 1817*, ed. G. R. de Beer (1951).

[16] Bentham journal TNA PRO 30/9/43, 259.

parties of English ladies travelling all over Italy without any male friends at all.[17] Thus, women travelled to Italy as companions, for their health, to escape domestic embarrassment at home, but also because they too, like men, were fascinated by Italy and subscribed to the same canons of taste and the same understanding of history that made it so important a destination for male travellers. By the later eighteenth century, the presence of women was commonplace, and had indeed become an essential element of the Grand Tour: they facilitated the reproduction of patterns of sociability from London to the continent in the expatriate communities of British in the various cities around which the Grand Tour was based.

In the chapters that follow, women's observations will feature with considerable regularity, not least because they often had different kinds of observations to make, or offered different emphases. Gender was a key determinant in how travellers experienced, perceived and represented the places through which they passed. The purpose of this chapter, therefore, is to consider in greater depth what difference gender (as opposed to other factors such as social status, religious background or nationality) made and to interrogate more closely how the experience and performance of travel was shaped by the coercive power of normative gender roles.

Taste, virtue and erudition

Although the exercise of taste and virtue was almost invariably discussed as a masculine attribute, in practice it was not an exclusively masculine preserve; most elite women wanted to, and indeed were expected to, appreciate the antiquities of ancient Rome (even if their enthusiasm for antiquities waned elsewhere) and they laid claim to the language of taste and virtue accordingly.[18] Women had to tread a line between the display of too much antiquarian learning, which would have been deemed unfeminine, and sufficient knowledge of ancient history and literature to allow them legitimately to lay claim to the legacy of taste and the promised land of Rome itself. Thus, when the artist Thomas Jones

---

[17] Jane Waldie, *Sketches Descriptive of Italy in the Years 1816 and 1817*, 4 vols. (1820), I, 282.

[18] On the gendering of the language of taste, see John Barrell, 'The dangerous goddess: masculinity, prestige and the aesthetic in early eighteenth-century England', in John Barrell, *The Birth of Pandora and the Division of Knowledge* (1992), 63–87. It should be acknowledged, however, that the evidence presented here is weighted towards those women whose interest inspired them to record what they had seen, make notes on what they had read and inform their correspondents back in Britain. The bored and disengaged traveller (of both sexes) is inevitably underrepresented in the sources.

described Saunders Welch's daughter, who had bullied her father into making the tour of Italy, as 'a Lady who piqued herself much on her classic learning and *Virtu*' his irony was directed at her unfeminine pretensions.[19] But equally, the inability to show at least a measure of interest in Rome demonstrated a culpable and feminine want of seriousness: in 1815, Robert Finch was outraged by Lady Westmorland's failure fully to appreciate the glories of Rome. 'When she was here', he complained, 'she got up at twelve or one o' clock, spent five minutes in the Capitol, five minutes in one gallery, and five minutes in another'. In a protest against this invasion of the masculine domain of taste and virtue by the inanity of feminine superficiality, he demanded that 'such triflers should be forbid entrance into a city like Rome. They almost pollute it's [sic] sacred air.'[20] The laughable (and possibly apocryphal) ignorance of Mrs Coutts, who thought that the Coliseum would be 'a *very* pretty building' once it was finished and whitewashed, lent itself to ridicule, but also confirmed expectations that women could have no proper understanding of antiquity.[21]

But attaining the appropriate ideal of cultivated virtue was not straightforward for either sex. Viewing Rome was an opportunity for displaying one's taste and scholarship, but this depended upon a knowledge of literature and history, not the uncritical compilation of trivial detail that was associated with the worst excesses of antiquarianism. Whilst antiquaries were preoccupied with technical detail and matters of proof, the gentleman aspired to the lofty overview unencumbered by an excess of specialist knowledge or undigested information.[22] Gentlemen had therefore to guard against the dangers of antiquarian pedantry, which would discredit their masculine taste and judgement.[23] Meanwhile, the *abbati* and *ciceroni* who showed the British around Rome were ridiculed for their obsession with fragments and trifling objects (in itself a feminine characteristic). When Edward Wright was guided round Rome with his pupil George Parker by the antiquary and *cicerone* Francesco de' Ficoroni, the latter carefully showed him the hydraulic mechanisms behind the Roman fountain, the *meta sudante*, which he had personally excavated. But Wright never mentioned these details of

---

[19] Oppé (ed.), *Memoirs of Thomas Jones of Penkerrig*, 64.
[20] Finch journal Bodl. MS Finch e. 16, fol. 159r.
[21] Ingamells (ed.), *Dictionary of British and Irish Travellers*, 245.
[22] For a discussion of the gendering of antiquarianism and its broader cultural reputation in the eighteenth century see Sweet, *Antiquaries*, 69–79.
[23] See, for example, the guidance issued by the Earl of Chesterfield to his illegitimate son travelling in Europe, *Letters Written by the Late Right Honourable Philip Dormer Stanhope, Earl of Chesterfield, to his Son, Philip Stanhope*, 4 vols. (1774), II, 69–70.

Roman engineering in his *Observations Made in Travelling through France and Italy*, despite the fact that, according to Ficoroni's account of Rome's antiquities, it was the 'Inglese Wright' who had accompanied him when making the excavation.[24] The elaboration of such mechanical details in a published work would have constituted a breach of gentlemanly good taste.

At the other end of our period, Charlotte Eaton also defined herself against the traditions of antiquarian scholarship as a rational woman (although she drew freely on the insights of antiquarianism), dismissing the credulity of antiquaries and *ciceroni* who would pin any attribution upon the most unlikely object and quibble over the most trivial points. Such 'antiquarian lore' she claimed was fit only for 'laqueys'. 'Lore', like folktales and legends, was more commonly associated with the irrationality and gullibility of women: indeed, elsewhere she referred to the old women loitering around the monuments, eager to impart their 'antiquarian lore' to the unwilling visitor.[25] Her target was, of course, the degenerate and effeminate Italian *cicerone*.[26] For Eaton, neither reason and taste, nor their antitheses credulity and pedantry, were the exclusive property of either gender: indeed, effeminate irrationality defined the national difference between the British and the Italians rather than that between the sexes.

Connoisseurship, the ability to appreciate the aesthetic qualities of works of art, was prized as a gentlemanly attribute, but could also be dangerous to masculinity if carried to excess: thus, John Moore, the author of a widely read volume of travels in the late eighteenth century, expressed the hope that his readers would not 'think him a connoisseur' for admiring busts and statues.[27] Connoisseurship could edge perilously close to pedantry but was also frequently associated – in negative terms – with indulgence in sensuality and, by extension, luxury and effeminacy.[28] At the other extreme, travellers were quick to condemn the ignorant philistinism of those who failed to appreciate the surroundings in which

---

[24] Francesco de' Ficoroni, *Le vestigie e rarità di Roma antica ricercate, e spiegate da Francesco de' Ficoroni* (Rome, 1744), 37.

[25] D. R. Woolf, 'A feminine past? Gender, genre, and historical knowledge in England, 1500–1800', *AHR*, 102 (1997), 645–79.

[26] Charlotte Eaton, *Rome in the Nineteenth Century*, 3 vols. (Edinburgh, 1820), I, 130, 228.

[27] John Moore, *A View of Society and Manners in Italy; With Anecdotes Relating to Some Eminent Characters*, 2 vols. (1781), I, 1.

[28] Barrell, 'The dangerous goddess'; Harry Mount, 'The monkey with the magnifying glass: constructions of the connoisseur in eighteenth-century Britain', *Oxford Art Journal*, 29:2 (2006), 167–84. Early eighteenth-century attitudes to connoisseurship are surveyed by Brian Cowan, 'An open elite: the peculiarities of connoisseurship in early modern England', *Modern Intellectual History*, 1:2 (2004), 151–83.

they found themselves, such as the bored youths encountered by James Boswell in the ducal gallery in Florence, who 'tried for a bet who should hop first to the end of it'.[29] Such behaviour was as much an indictment of gentlemanly masculinity as was a show of precious pedantry. Whilst young male travellers generally found no problem in conforming to many aspects of normative masculine behaviour – the drinking, the gambling and the sexual exploits – the ideal of polite masculinity was rather harder consistently to maintain.[30] Failure to experience pleasure in Rome, for example, constituted a demonstrable shortcoming in those qualities of taste that defined one's membership of the gentlemanly, educated elite. For many, viewing Rome involved a highly self-conscious act of performance to which few of them were prepared openly to admit even in letters and journals.[31] It was the textile merchant John Patteson, combining a business trip with a 'tour' and mixing uneasily between the worlds of commerce and fashionable society, who broke rank in this performance of polite taste. He confessed to his mother how boring he found the endless round of antiquities, paintings and virtù in Rome, but was relieved to find that in reality most of his compatriots were of a similar opinion. 'Otherwise', he continued, 'I should be induced to believe my conception and understanding infinitely below the common run.'[32]

Less was expected of women, therefore, in the performance of taste and appreciation of virtù. Nevertheless, unlike Mrs Coutts, most women who were in a position to travel to Italy would have had sufficient knowledge of the literature and history of ancient Rome to make some sense of what they saw. Knowledge of ancient and modern history was regularly recommended in educational treatises for girls.[33] Women from the classes of the travelling elite generally knew their classical history and many put themselves through a reading programme in preparation, in which Charlotte Eaton for one claimed to show a diligence that 'few of my countrymen possessed'.[34] Some aristocratic women, like the fourth

---

[29] Cited in Elizabeth Manwaring, *Italian Landscape in Eighteenth-Century England* (1965), 31.

[30] See, for example, Philip Carter's discussion of James Boswell's problems in negotiating the tensions between his sexuality and the norms of polite masculinity: 'James Boswell's manliness', in Tim Hitchcock and Michèle Cohen (eds.), *English Masculinities 1660–1800* (1999), 111–30.

[31] Boswell has proved a particularly rich case study to explore in this respect: see Richard de Ritter, ' "This changeableness in character": exploring masculinity and nationhood on James Boswell's Grand Tour', *Scottish Literary Review*, 2:1 (2010), 23–40.

[32] Cubitt, Mackley and Wilson (eds.), *Great Tour of John Patteson*, 248.

[33] See, for example, Hester Chapone, *Letters on the Improvement of the Mind Addressed to a Young Lady*, 2 vols. (1773), II, 227–56.

[34] In the preface to *Rome in the Nineteenth Century*, Eaton described her two-year preparation for her continental tour: 'I availed myself to the utmost of every means of

Duchess of Beaufort, had been educated alongside their brothers. As a girl, the duchess had learnt Latin, Italian, French and history, but when her brother had gone on the Grand Tour with their tutor, George Barclay, she was left behind. Her decision to travel, once the death of her husband gave her the freedom to do so, appears to have fulfilled a longstanding ambition.[35] And there were plenty of other female travellers who shared in the kind of imaginative rapture outlined by Alison: Ann Flaxman travelled with her husband to Rome in 1787 and recorded her excitement as they finally approached the city: 'To describe our Joy when we beheld from far the Gates of Rome would be almost as difficult as to do Justice to the City itself.'[36] Like their male counterparts, women relished the experience of standing in the place where famous events had taken place or which were associated with familiar scenes from literature. Even the frequently lukewarm Lady Holland acknowledged that there was 'some pleasure in the consideration of being in this same spot [Rome] one has read of so much'.[37] Nor was an education in Latin necessary for familiarity with the literature and history of ancient Rome: histories of Rome were widely read by women as well as men, and the verse of the major Latin poets – notably Virgil – was readily available in English and French translations. Thus, when Anne Miller purportedly wrote to her mother describing the statue of Laocoon or the contents of the tribuna in Florence she referred her to the relevant passages in Dryden's translations of Virgil and Juvenal.[38] Translations, as Jane Waldie noted, made the 'classic ground' of Italy accessible to every schoolgirl, as well as every schoolboy.[39]

---

intelligence, of access to rare books, of the opinions of the best informed, and above all, of the diligent study of history, pursued solely with this view' (I, x).

[35] Her classical and antiquarian tastes were evident in her reading programme of Cicero, Horace and Virgil and her completion of a six-week course of antiquities with James Byres in Rome. Ingamells (ed.), *Dictionary of British and Irish Travellers*, 66–7. See also Maura Aileen Henry, 'The fourth Duchess of Beaufort's Grand Tour (1769–1774) and the making of the aristocracy', Harvard University Ph.D. thesis (1996).

[36] Flaxman journal BL Add. MS 39787, fol. 37v.

[37] Lady Holland to the Duchess of Leinster, 9 Nov. 1766, in Fitzgerald (ed.), *Correspondence*, I, 483.

[38] Anne Miller, *Letters from Italy, Describing the Manners, Customs, Antiquities, Paintings etc of that Country*, 3 vols. (1776), II, 109, 149. See also Amanda Vickery, *The Gentleman's Daughter: Women's Lives in Georgian England* (New Haven and London, 1998), 259, on the widespread availability for literate female readers of translations of classical texts. On the place of Latin and Greek in girls' education see Michèle Cohen, ' "To think, to compare, to combine, to methodise": girls' education in Enlightenment Britain', in Sarah Knott and Barbara Taylor (eds.), *Women, Gender and Enlightenment* (Basingstoke, 2005), 224–42.

[39] Waldie, *Sketches Descriptive of Italy*, I, xvi.

Women did not, however, on the whole, undermine the prevailing models of female knowledge and taste by directly challenging male authority in areas of connoisseurship or antiquarian and historical expertise. After a visit to San Paolo, the Countess of Pomfret came up with the (erroneous) 'conceit' that the main body of the basilica had not originally been intended for a church, but she did so in the comparative privacy of a letter to her friend the Countess of Hartford.[40] In general, women were reluctant to venture their opinion on antiquities: they deferred, instead, to the greater learning of husbands, brothers and *ciceroni*. For those, like Anne Miller or Hester Piozzi, who published their tours, the abdication of any pretence to antiquarian expertise was an important part of constructing a suitably acceptable authorial identity, which in Miller's case she elaborated with some care. Miller's self-fashioning of herself as a submissive wife is particularly clear when covering topics of traditional masculine expertise, such as antiquities or politics: at Genoa, she claimed that she was copying out her husband's notes on antiquities. And at Perugia, it was her husband who, in true antiquarian spirit, had wanted to visit the site of the battle of Trebia where Hannibal's army had been defeated, despite the fact that, as Miller acerbically noted, no 'vestiges of antiquity' survived to indicate where it might have been.[41] Whilst in Naples, she adopted the role of antiquarian helpmate and expressed the hope that 'by [my] industry' she would soon be able to assist her husband in his researches after antiquity without being an interruption to him.[42] In private letters home to family members (as opposed to letters written with a view to publication), women were similarly reluctant to venture an opinion on antiquarian topics, either omitting all mention of them or by promising that their husband or brother would describe such matters. So at Portici, for example, Ann Flaxman declined to describe the antiquities they had seen at the museum for her father, promising that her husband, 'Flaxman' would do so, and so she would not trouble herself.[43]

But because there was less expectation that women should display erudition or that they should be able to engage in antiquarian debate, the

[40] R. Phillips (ed.), *Correspondence between Frances, Countess of Hartford (afterwards Duchess of Somerset), and Henrietta Louisa, Countess of Pomfret, between the Years 1738–42*, 3 vols. (1805), III, 93, commented on the body of San Paolo *fuori le mure* which was 'very large' and 'I believe is not originally designed for a church; but this is a conceit of my own, from the difference between that building and the upper part of the cross upon it; and because, round an old Mosaic, at the upper end, there is, in letters of the same, an inscription, that Theodorus began and Honorius finished this hall.'
[41] Miller, *Letters from Italy*, I, 380.   [42] Ibid., II, 228.
[43] Flaxman journal BL Add. MS 39787, fol. 67v.

public performance of taste (whether in visiting art and antiquities or in writing about what had been seen) was less important for women than for men. Men would generally demur from the persona of the gentleman of taste only in the comparative privacy of personal correspondence or when wishing to adopt a deliberately provocative tone.[44] This did not, of course, apply to women. It follows from this that it was more acceptable for a woman to admit to boredom at the endless round of antiquities in Rome or Florence than it was for a man. Thus Betsey Wynne, whose family was resident in Italy for much of her youth in the 1790s, found the antiquities in the museum at Verona dull and disappointing, but was frankly delighted to see the tomb of Romeo and Juliet.[45] Indeed, it was almost expected that a woman should affect a measure of *ennui* and detachment in the face of relentless antiquarianism in order to demonstrate her femininity: as James Russel put it in a letter to his sister from Rome in 1740, 'the ruins which time and age have made in what was once very beautiful, can be no ways agreeable to one of your sex'.[46] Lady Mary Fortescue was the patiently passive companion to her husband's ill-informed but over-enthusiastic interest in antiquities. 'Poor Lady Mary', as her friend Lady Lyttelton observed, 'who seems not to have known that the old Romans ever existed, is obliged to go with him to every fragment of an old wall and to every broken shaft of a crumbling column, where he keeps her an hour to examine what it might have been, without a *cicerone*, so that he makes nothing out'.[47] A woman like Lady Holland could afford to be disarmingly frank in her letters to her sister Emily, Duchess of Leinster, about the 'few very fine things and the vast deal of tiresome stuff' in the ducal galleries at Florence. The tribuna, with its showpieces such as the *Venus de Medici*, was all very well, she allowed, but there were endless busts of emperors and cabinets of coins and medals to be walked through first. These she had found tedious and boring.[48]

Whether Anne Miller really did defer to the learning of her husband in the way that she described is impossible to know, but this kind of rhetorical strategy certainly reinforced the prevailing expectation that women could have nothing of value to say on matters of antiquarianism.

---

[44] See, for example, Smollett, *Travels through France and Italy*.

[45] Anne Fremantle (ed.), *The Wynne Diaries*, 3 vols. (Oxford, 1937), II, 78.

[46] James Russel, *Letters from a Young Painter Abroad to his Friends in England*, 2 vols. (2nd edn, 1750), I, 37.

[47] Mrs Hugh Wyndham (ed.), *Correspondence of Sarah Spencer, Lady Lyttelton 1787–1870* (1912), 217.

[48] Lady Holland to Duchess of Leinster, 18 Nov. 1766, in Fitzgerald (ed.), *Correspondence*, I, 480.

Similarly, Hester Piozzi generally depicted herself as deferring to the *cicerone*, Mr Byres, or her travelling companion Bertie Greethead on matters of Roman antiquity. The latter was on one occasion 'angry with me for admiring spiral columns, as he said pillars were always meant to support something, and spiral lines betrayed weakness'.[49] Piozzi had apparently fallen into the classic feminine trap of being seduced by the superficial artifice of the ornaments rather than understanding the principles and true manly worth of correct classical architecture.[50] Even when describing antiquities, Piozzi's comments were characteristically more pragmatic and less concerned with finding the appropriate literary allusion than those of many male travellers. Her interest in the manners and mores of Italian society, and the place of women in particular, was projected back to antiquity as well. At the Coliseum, for example, she marvelled at its size and was intrigued by the evidence which she was shown for supper rooms, taverns and shops within the complex.[51] It would appear from her comments, and those of other women, that James Byres, who was one of the leading antiquarian guides for the British in the later eighteenth century, made an effort to make the Coliseum more interesting to his female clients by pointing out such features as would particularly appeal to them, that is features that could be specifically identified with women and their activities in antiquity. Bononi, who guided the Misses Berry round Rome, apparently followed a similar strategy, for they recorded having been shown the remains of 'closed boxes' for 'noble ladies' where they could have sat 'without being much seen'.[52] In a similar way, women consistently singled out representations of women in their observations when viewing antiquities: either as a statement of common sisterhood or because they consciously or subconsciously wished to conform to the normative expectation that they should be more interested in women. At the Duke's Galleries in Florence, female visitors such as Ann Flaxman or Catherine Wilmot chose to focus on the busts of the imperial wives and daughters in the chronological display of Roman emperors – busts which were generally invisible in the accounts of male visitors, who had eyes for the emperors

[49] Hester Piozzi, *Observations and Reflections Made in the Course of a Journey through France, Italy and Germany*, ed. Herbert Barrows (Ann Arbor, 1967), 300.
[50] See also Ann Bermingham's discussion of the feminine aesthetic of ornamental detail, 'The picturesque and ready-to-wear femininity', in Stephen Copley and Peter Garside (eds.), *The Politics of the Picturesque: Literature, Landscape and Aesthetics since 1770* (Cambridge, 1994), 81–119; Jane Stabler, 'Taking liberties: the Italian picturesque in women's travel writing', *European Romantic Review*, 13:1 (2002), 15–16.
[51] Piozzi, *Observations and Reflections*, 197.
[52] Lady Theresa Lewis (ed.), *Extracts of the Journals and Correspondence of Miss Berry from the Year 1783–1852*, 3 vols. (1865), I, 105.

only: 'What would have pleas'd you most of anything', enthused Wilmot to her sister, 'was an arrangement of Roman Emperors from Julius Caesar to Gallienus, with their frightful Empresses smirking opposite to them like tête à têtes in a magazine'.[53]

Given that one of the primary sources of pleasure for men of the Italian tour was to view those places made familiar through the schoolboy's education, the more limited education which most women had undergone struck some as a barrier to the full enjoyment of what they saw. Piozzi, in self-consciously bluestocking mode, complained that every day she lost enjoyment for want of learning, having to rely on her travelling companions for information on Greek literature and antiquity.[54] Others, however, had fewer pretensions and were content to accept what they saw at face value; they did not apparently regret their want of a detailed historical and literary framework against which to interpret what they saw and were able to find their pleasure elsewhere. Antiquities meant little to Sarah Bentham, for example, and her comments on particular monuments are revealingly vague: the church of Sta Costanza, she noted, was supposed to have been the Temple of Bacchus because the sarcophagus had 'carvings of children playing with bunches of grapes'.[55] Many of those whose education had not prepared them for an interest in architecture or antiquities simply preferred not to participate in the gruelling antiquarian courses offered by the *ciceroni*. They would pick and choose, only attending sociable outings as part of a party to the more famous sites such as St Peter's, the Coliseum or the more notable museums and palazzi. There were, moreover, practicalities to be borne in mind: the sights in Rome were dispersed over an extensive area and a full antiquarian programme involved a considerable amount of walking outside, much of it in the rough terrain of the *disabatio*, where, as Anne Miller noted, a lady's complexion was in constant danger of becoming tanned.[56] Few ladies had the stamina of male tourists, who

[53] Flaxman journal BL Add. MS 39787, fol. 33; Thomas U. Sadleir (ed.), *An Irish Peer on the Continent (1801–1803). Being a Narrative of the Tour of Stephen, 2nd Earl Mount Cashell, through France, Italy, etc as Related by Catherine Wilmot* (1920), 127.
[54] Piozzi, *Observations and Reflections*, 285. Piozzi had learnt Latin as a teenager with Dr Arthur Collier: Michael J. Franklin, 'Piozzi, Hester Lynch (1741–1821)', *ODNB* (www.oxforddnb.com/view/article/22309, accessed 31 July 2011).
[55] Bentham journal TNA PRO 30/9/43, 204. The sarcophagus, now in the Vatican Museum, actually displays Christian motifs of vine branches and children bearing grapes, peacocks and a ram.
[56] 'I believe I shall find it [an improvised pasteboard hat] extremely convenient in the mornings when we are walking amongst the Ruins; for constantly going out in the Roman fashion, with nothing to shade my face but a black lace hood hanging down over my eyes, has tanned me to such a degree, that I know not whether all the strawberry water in Rome will be able to whiten me again.' Miller, *Letters from Italy*, III, 37–8.

might walk the circuit of the city walls, purely to establish to their own satisfaction the walls' extent. Miller was indefatigable in her determination to view all that was to be seen in Rome (declining offers of hospitality in order to accomplish this) but even she decided against accompanying her husband to view a bridge built by Augustus because access was said to be difficult.[57] But for many female travellers, antiquities were a less dominant aspect of their experience of Rome, or indeed any other city: they were in Italy first as companions, rather than out of a particular personal desire to see Italy. It is only to be expected, therefore, that they experienced a measure of detachment from the routines of antiquarianism and connoisseurship prescribed for male visitors.

Italy was 'classic ground', most often understood through the prism of classical literature. But by the end of the eighteenth century, it had begun to take on a different kind of 'classic' status for British travellers. Modern literature became increasingly important as a medium through which to experience and interpret Italy, and it was one with which women were frequently equally if not more familiar than men. Unlike Latin, a knowledge of Shakespeare, poetry and modern languages was considered suitable for female reading by even the most conservative writers on education. Thus, as we have seen, for Betsey Wynne, Verona was the city of the doomed lovers, Romeo and Juliet, but she was far from being the only one to see Verona in Shakespearean rather than classical terms.[58] 'My Head ran more on Romeo than on Virgil at Mantua and Verona' confessed Hester Piozzi in a letter to her daughter,[59] and Venice was 'classic ground' for Lady Webster, because of its associations with Otway and Shakespeare.[60] But such associations were not just the resort of those who lacked familiarity with classical antiquity: for James Boswell, who had insisted on conversing in Latin with his guide in Rome, Verona was above all the city of Romeo and Juliet and Venice the setting for Pierre and Jaffeir's conspiracy in *Venice Preserved*.[61] Similarly, the widespread popularity of Italian literature amongst educated men and women of the eighteenth century offered another set of literary associations for travellers. Tasso and Ariosto were held in particularly high esteem.

[57] Ibid., III, 174.
[58] 'I have been a pilgrimage to Juliet's tomb, who was of this city', Mary Carter to Lady Nelthorpe, 17 Oct. 1793, in Frances Nelthorpe (ed.), *Mrs Mary Carter's Letters* (1860), 9.
[59] Piozzi to Hester Maria Thrale, 22 Apr. 1785, in Edward A. Bloom and Lilian D. Bloom (eds.), *The Piozzi Letters: Correspondence of Hester Lynch Piozzi, 1784–1821*, 6 vols. (London and Toronto, 1989), I, 14.
[60] Lady Webster to Lady Sheffield, 10 Oct. 1792, in Jane H. Adeane (ed.), *The Girlhood of Maria Josepha Holroyd* (2nd edn, 1897), 189.
[61] Boswell to Johnston,13 July 1765 and 23 July 1765, in Walker (ed.), *Correspondence of James Boswell*, 170–1, 176.

John Harington's translation of *Orlando Furioso* had first appeared in 1591; a new translation was published by William Huggins in 1755, while Temple Henry Croker and John Hoole brought out a different translation again in 1767. Similarly, *Gerusalemme Liberata*, which had been a success ever since its first translation in 1600, was issued in a new translation again by Hoole in 1763. Its popularity was such that it had gone through ten editions by 1815.[62] Translations of *Orlando Furioso* or *Gerusalemme Liberata* were also undertaken by many young women as an educational exercise; some of these were published.[63] Tasso and Ariosto, and to a lesser extent Dante and Petrarch, accordingly became the focus of a modern literary pilgrimage for both men and women, which took travellers not just to Florence and Venice, but to Ferrara, where Tasso died and Ariosto was imprisoned, and Arezzo where Petrarch was born. Indeed, the principal attraction of the otherwise desolate city of Ferrara was the opportunity to pay homage at Ariosto's tomb.[64] The gondoliers of Venice, who were supposed to serenade each other with Tasso's verse, were regularly sought out by the British visitors to Venice. In the early nineteenth century, with the hugely popular success of both *Corinne* and Byron's poetry, the tour of Italy was rapidly imbued with new layers of literary association for both sexes. In the 1820s, women such as Jane Waldie, Marianne Colston or Anna Jameson described a literary landscape that illustrated the texts of Byron and de Staël, rather than those of Virgil and Horace.[65] Waldie acknowledged in the introduction to her *Sketches Descriptive of Italy* that she could not pretend to antiquarian learning or to pronounce on matters of antiquity. She offered instead a description of Italy based upon her personal

[62] Roderick Cavaliero, *Italia Romantica: English Romantics and Italian Freedom* (2005), 68–71; C. Brand, *Italy and the English Romantics: The Italianate Fashion in Early Nineteenth-Century England* (Cambridge, 1957), 49; Roderick Marshall, *Italy in English Literature 1755–1818: Origins of the Romantic Interest in Italy* (1934), 59–60.

[63] Susanna Watts translated *Gerusalemme Liberata* and completed a life of Tasso, which she circulated privately, but personal circumstances meant that she was unable to publish it (Susanna Watts to John Nichols, 31 [sic] Sept. 1796, Bodl. MS Eng. Lett. c. 368, fol. 116). Isobel Grundy, 'Watts, Susanna (*bap.* 1768, *d.* 1842)', rev. *ODNB* (www.oxforddnb.com/view/article/38113, accessed 31 July 2011); the Countess of Pomfret referred to her own efforts to translate the letters of Tasso ROLLR Finch MSS DG 7/4/12a, fol. 3. Marshall notes that the number of Italian masters publishing grammars, readers and dictionaries at least doubled after 1770, indicating that many more people wanted to read Italian poetry or literature in the original (*Italy in English Literature*, 159).

[64] Adam Walker, *Ideas Suggested on the Spot in a Late Excursion through Flanders, Germany, France and Italy* (1790), 184.

[65] This is a principal theme in Kathryn Walchester's discussion of female-authored nineteenth-century texts, *Our Own Fair Italy*. Walchester emphasises the generic instability of women's travel writing and their borrowings from novelistic and poetic genres (see especially 39–70).

experience, filtered by her reading of Mrs Radcliffe, de Staël and Byron.[66] In this, she was typical of numbers of other travellers (male and female) of the early nineteenth century, both published and unpublished.[67] 'The immortal Corinna and the 4th Canto of Childe Harold' according to Colston were 'the best guides to Rome that have been written'.[68] But although the sensitivity enjoined by a reading of *Corinne* was often used to reject the dead antiquarian empiricism of guidebooks such as that by John Chetwode Eustace, whose learned and literary descriptions left little scope for the expression of sensibility,[69] for his part, Eustace warmly recommended *Corinne* as the best guide or rather 'companion' to inspire the reader with the 'lofty temper of mind' with which fully to appreciate 'the great and the beautiful in art or in nature'.[70] Thus Italy, seen through the novels of de Staël and the poetry of Byron, was equally the imaginative property of men and women.

Sociability and social life

For men and women, an important aspect of travel was the opportunities it afforded for sociability. Social intercourse filled otherwise unoccupied hours and could also be a means of acquiring social connections which might be of use on one's return home. The rituals of sociability defined the traveller's position within English-speaking society in Italy and amongst that part of Italian society that mixed with the British. As in Britain, the responsibilities of sociability weighed more heavily on women than on men: the Countess of Pomfret, for example, noted in her letters on a number of occasions that she had stayed at home in the morning rather than going out sightseeing in order to leave herself sufficient time to dress for an invitation to dinner.[71] Women's time was heavily taken up with the social responsibilities of calling on the other British visitors, and those Italians who were willing to receive British company, and receiving calls in turn. They entertained their compatriots, inviting them to dinner and to drink tea, or they adopted as Lady

---

[66] Waldie, *Sketches Descriptive of Italy*, I, xvi–xvii.

[67] With expectations shaped by his reading of Radcliffe's novels, Henry Matthews sought out the church of San Nicolo where key scenes in *The Italian* had been set; only to complain that the service of vespers he witnessed failed to live up to Mrs Radcliffe's romantic descriptions. Henry Matthews, *The Diary of an Invalid Being the Journal of a Tour in Pursuit of Health in Portugal, Italy, Switzerland and France in the Years 1817, 1818 and 1819* (2nd edn, 1820), 163.

[68] Marianne Colston, *Journal of a Tour in France, Switzerland, and Italy, during the Years 1819, 20, 21*, 2 vols. (Paris, 1822), I, 199.

[69] Eaton, *Rome in the Nineteenth Century*, I, vii.   [70] Eustace, *Classical Tour*, I, xxxv.

[71] Phillips (ed.), *Correspondence*, II, 308.

Holland did, the Italian practice of holding *conversazioni*. Their role in facilitating this kind of social intercourse was crucial to the enjoyment of other travellers.[72] British travellers, particularly young men, frequently professed to find Italian company dull, not least because the participation of women was strictly limited. It was confined to the *conversazioni* held in the evening and the sociability of theatre-going. Where there were few other 'English' present, and particularly where the amount of mixed company was limited, travellers frequently complained of 'dullness' and boredom and longed for the enlivening presence of more feminine company.[73]

Because the rituals of society generally assumed a greater importance in their daily lives than it did for men, women devoted more attention to recording such details of sociability and the spaces in which it took place in their diaries and correspondence and in this respect their records offer a valuable supplement to the more prolific documentation produced by men. The most detailed accounts of what it was like to attend a *conversazione*, for example, come from women. Rather than descriptions of antiquities or churches, the entries to Sarah Bentham's journal concentrated on the social life amongst the British community in Rome and her reactions to the Italian society which she encountered, chiefly through *conversazioni* held at the palazzi of those members of the Roman nobility who were willing to receive the English. As she left Rome, after a sojourn of six weeks, she noted in her journal with some satisfaction that there had been only one evening on which she had not been engaged. Each engagement merited an entry; social space was described, whilst art and antiquities were absent. She even itemised the different kinds of ice-cream (lemon, currant and milk) served as the *rinfresco* at the *conversazioni* in Rome and noted, with some satisfaction, that the tea and coffee were served from pots that looked remarkably like Staffordshire or Wedgwood-ware.[74] Similarly, Bentham and Miss Derbishire give us a much better sense of the interior arrangement and decoration of the Italian palazzi where they were entertained and the lodgings in which they stayed than one finds in the accounts of most male travellers, providing notes on the upholstery, wall-hangings, curtains, carpets (or lack of), the lighting and the provision for heating. At the theatre in Venice, Bentham took note of the furniture, the blinds and the commode

---

[72] Smollett noted that English ladies of fashion generally kept an assembly 'to which the British subjects resort', *Travels through France and Italy*, II, 93.
[73] Lord Kildare to Duchess of Leinster, 19 Jan. 1767, in Fitzgerald (ed.), *Correspondence*, III, 452. Thomas Brand to his sister, 27 Dec. 1790, CUL Add. MS 8670 (c) /36.
[74] Bentham journal TNA PRO 30/9/43, 181–2.

in the corner in each of the boxes, but said nothing about the play. She always paid particular attention to the sequence of rooms through which the company passed in order to reach the main reception room, acutely aware of how this contributed to the Italians' sense of status and how it signified the importance of the occasion. At the Villa Lantri in Rome she admired the bedsteads for servants, which slid on castors under the table; and with her own recent experience of nursing an invalid clearly still very much in mind, she noted that they might be of great use in sickness, as they could be pushed 'under a toilet table' when not in use.[75] Derbishire, who travelled as companion to Dr Philip Lloyd and his wife, was particularly taken by the elaborate decorations for the Marquis de Bayanne's new year's ball in Rome in 1788, recording the festoons of artificial flowers, the lutestring drapes as well as the occupational hazard of catching her heels in the cracks of the brick floor when dancing.[76] By contrast, when Patrick Home viewed the apartments of Cardinal Corsini in Rome he noted the Cardinal's reading habits: *Lives of the Saints*, a Latin Bible and Muratori's *Annals of Italy*, but recorded nothing regarding the furnishings or domestic arrangements.[77]

All female travellers were careful to record whom they met and where, the appearance and dress of the company, and that of ladies in particular, and any peculiarities of social convention. The restrictions placed against Italian women appearing in company were always worthy of comment, highlighting as they did the greater liberty enjoyed by women in Great Britain (which in itself was an indication of Britain's more advanced state of civility and freedom) and reinforcing stereotypes about the Italians' propensity to jealousy.[78] Given the constraints upon women's appearance in public, the relative freedom extended to women in Venice to appear in the coffee houses, albeit masked, was always remarked upon. Men as well as women noted this, but female observers, such as Hester Piozzi and Anne Miller, made a particular point of examining the custom as it affected their own sex. Miller recorded that the Senate had been forced to allow women to enter the coffee houses in response to violent public remonstrations when the partitions that had

---

[75] Ibid., 111, 253.

[76] Derbishire journal NRO DCN 118/6, 1. Lloyd was Dean of Norwich cathedral; it has not been possible to identify Derbishire more precisely.

[77] Home journal NAS GD 267/33/2, fol. 13v. On women's identification with domestic interiors in this period see Amanda Vickery, *Behind Closed Doors: At Home in Georgian England* (New Haven and London, 2009).

[78] For a recent analysis of the relationship between women, civility and society in eighteenth-century thought see Karen O'Brien, *Women and Enlightenment in Eighteenth-Century Britain* (Cambridge, 2009), esp. 36–67.

formerly divided up the coffee houses were taken down rendering them open and public.[79] Elizabeth Craven, travelling on the continent in order to escape the aftermath of the breakdown of her marriage, was particularly struck by the ease with which Venetian women were apparently able to procure a divorce.[80] The phenomenon of the *cicisbeo* or *cavaliere servente* and the ceremony of a nun taking the veil upon entering a convent were recurring subjects of fascination and comment. As Chloe Chard has argued, the practice of cicisbeism, along with that of monasticism, exemplified to British travellers how the Italians' immoderate restraint (in the form of the Catholic church and the restrictions placed upon daughters' freedom of behaviour) led to improper licence.[81] It was a subject that interested male and female travellers equally and the profession of a nun was similarly a set piece of Grand Tour writing for both sexes. Descriptions of the ceremony and the nuns' way of life were frequently taken as an opportunity to highlight the hypocrisy of the Catholic church as an institution: travellers emphasised the extent to which the nuns were able to integrate with the outside world and the laxity of the regulations which governed their dress and their behaviour such that they were allowed to receive mixed company.[82]

As far as the actual ceremony was concerned, male observers tended to emphasise both the element of titillation and the theme of ritual sacrifice, often drawing comparisons with Iphigenia.[83] In a letter to his aunt, Mrs Atkinson, John Baker Holroyd wrote of how he had seen two nuns taking the veil in Lucca – 'the most melancholy spectacle that ever was seen' – but also an occasion on which 'the Association of Religion and Vice was drolly conspicuous'. He described the ceremony in both its social and religious dimensions in suggestive detail, including the disrobing of the two girls 'till they appeared all white in their stays and

[79] Miller, *Letters from Italy*, III, 287–8.

[80] Elizabeth Craven, *A Journey through the Crimea to Constantinople* (1789), 95; Katherine Turner, 'Elizabeth, margravine of Brandenburg-Ansbach-Bayreuth [*other married name* Elizabeth Craven, Lady Craven] (1750–1828)', *ODNB* (www.oxforddnb.com/view/article/576, accessed 31 July 2011).

[81] Chard, *Pleasure and Guilt*, 91–2. See, for example, Alexander Drummond, *Travels through Different Cities of Germany, Italy, Greece, and Several Parts of Asia* (1754), 41.

[82] Drummond, *Travels through Different Cities*, 74–5.

[83] Drake journal MCO MS MC F16 vol. 2, 99. The extent to which such descriptions had become a rhetorical trope is apparent in Sir William Forbes' account some forty years later. Forbes was somewhat literal-minded and frequently expressed his impatience at discrepancies between what he experienced and the heightened language of much contemporary travel literature. Having attended one such ceremony in Naples he professed himself 'a great deal disappointed' that it was not a more melancholy event and that 'it had nothing of horror' in it. Rather, the young ladies and their families appeared to treat it with cheerful equanimity. Forbes journal NLS MS 1541, fol. 164.

under-petticoats'. For Holroyd, the ceremony was charged with sexual frisson: 'the nearer they approached to their birth suit, the more I was affected', he wrote. But it was also profoundly unsettling: 'I went away more uncomfortable than if I had seen a dozen rascals hanged.'[84] Holroyd was clearly hoping to entertain, even to shock, his female relatives. James Russel's account of a similar ceremony written for his sister, however, was constructed with a view to reminding her of her good fortune in enjoying the superior liberties of an Englishwoman and as a warning not to 'tease' any future lovers, lest a similar fate befall her.[85] Catherine Wilmot described the ceremony she witnessed in Naples in the conventional language of sacrifice and wasted lives: she recorded how the men as well as the women of the English party were moved to indignant tears and one hot-blooded young man 'instinctively lay'd his hand upon his sword, swearing that such heart-rending superstitious cruelties ought to be extirpated from off the face of the earth'.[86] But Miss Derbishire took a slightly different perspective from that of most male visitors: attending the entrance of one of the daughters of the Princess Sta Croce into a Franciscan convent at Rome, she saw the ceremony not just as an occasion of pathos (she hoped the 'poor thing' would be happy, but noted eyes 'swimming' with tears) but also as a female-dominated family drama. Her description emphasised the participation of the different family members and the family dynamics and affection on display, as she recorded how the mother lifted up the little five-year-old brother to touch his sister's crown of thorns.[87]

Derbishire's comments, and those of other female travellers, demonstrate their identification with other women, be they Italian or English, and their interest in Italian society and family; this was an interest which was also reflected in the letters which male travellers wrote home to their families. Whilst fathers expected to receive an enumeration of sights seen and money spent, the letters of sons to their mothers show that the latter were particularly interested to know with whom their offspring had been mixing and what the nature of Italian society was like. Elite women were, of course, brought up to be hostesses and social facilitators; such information was therefore of particular interest to them whether as travellers or as recipients of news. The Duchess of Leinster, for example, explicitly requested that

---

[84] J. B. Holroyd, to his aunt, Mrs Atkinson, 2 Oct. 1764, BL Add. MS 3488, fol. 159r–v.
[85] Russel, *Letters from a Young Painter Abroad*, I, 66–7.
[86] Sadleir (ed.), *An Irish Peer on the Continent*, 153–4.
[87] Derbishire journal NRO DCN 118/6, 15–16.

her son, Lord Kildare, should send her a list of the English with whom he had been mixing.[88] Male travellers were making notes on the customs of society, the dress of women and the practice of cicisbeism long before describing the 'manners and customs' of a country became a major preoccupation of travel writers. They did so not least because this was the kind of information that they thought appropriate for the understanding of their female correspondents, and which the women in turn wished to hear. It was less usual to comment on the dress of men, and such remarks as were made generally referred simply to the fact that in Genoa, for example, it was the custom for all men to wear black or that in Venice the nobility wore 'prodigious' wigs. It was the women's dress and finery that bore witness to the Italians' love of empty ornament and display; as such it was a far more important signifier of the local manners and customs than that of men, as well as offering an index of the taste of society and the spread of fashion. John Holroyd's letters home to his uncle, Dr Baker, and to his mother and his aunts illustrate the divergent interests of both the vicarious and the real travellers. In letters to his uncle he fantasised about seeing the ghost of Scipio walking in the forum and described the objects of virtù he had seen in Rome. To his mother and aunts he described the court at Turin, the horse races in Rome during carnival, the appearance of the Pretender and the pope ('who is so over whelmed with Vestments that he much resembles a Tortoise with a little Head standing out'), provided lists of the English present and gave an account of a theatrical performance of a 'long comic dance' called Vauxhall in England.[89] The picture of Italy that he offered them was more sociable and more humorous than that which he represented to his uncle.

Other leisure practices such as shopping were also transposed to the Italian urban environment as the British made their residence in the various cities of the tour. Men rarely made references either to shops or what they purchased, unless to itemise prints and books or paintings and antiquities which they were having shipped back to Britain. Nor did they refer to 'going shopping' as an activity. In this respect, their behaviour matches the pattern that historians have identified amongst consumers in Britain: shopping, that is the purchase of goods, was carried out

---

[88] Lord Kildare referred to the fact that his mother had requested a list of the English with whom he had been mixing. Fitzgerald (ed.), *Correspondence*, III, 524. See also Thomas Pelham's correspondence with his parents, BL Add. MS 33127, or the Earl of Winchilsea's letters to his mother, ROLLR Finch MSS DG 7/4/12 box 4953 bundle 32.

[89] Holroyd to Dr Baker, 5 Nov. 1764 and to Mrs Holroyd, 6 Jan. 1765, BL Add. MS 3488, fols. 160r and 164v.

equally by both sexes but as a pastime it was particularly associated with women.[90] It is no surprise, then, to find that female travellers were more likely to take note of the shops, what was sold and what they themselves purchased (whether fabric or souvenirs or more humdrum items such as gloves and paper), and to refer to 'going shopping' as an activity worthy of record in their journals or letters. The shops in Milan were found to be particularly well stocked, larger and 'more showy' than in any other town in Italy, boasting Manchester goods and Birmingham cutlery.[91] Naples was a city for buying souvenirs: objects made from lava, fans, combs and other knick knacks decorated with designs inspired by local antiquities, such as Anne Miller's purchase of a comb decorated with an Etruscan design taken from an antique vase.[92] Venice, which always enjoyed a reputation for the sale of expensive goods and baubles, stood out both for the luxuries on show and the skill and artifice with which they were displayed – even the greengrocers made an architectural arrangement of their fruit and vegetables, as Anne Miller noted with delight.[93] Bologna offered a fine selection of fabrics – but no stiletto knives, much to the disappointment of the Misses Berry, who had hoped to purchase one as a souvenir.[94] Whilst some days were certainly taken up with excursions or visits to palazzi and churches, few women were as remorseless in their sightseeing as Anne Miller. Many days were also spent in a more mundane fashion: walking in the Borghese Gardens in Rome or the Boboli Gardens in Florence, reading, and shopping for everyday items of consumption. Far more so than did men, women replicated the routines of polite urban society in the cities in which they were temporarily resident.

After a day's sightseeing in Rome, Sarah Bentham was unimpressed: 'I was much disappointed in Seeing Rome', she complained. Her disenchantment arose not so much because the city failed to live up to heightened expectations cultivated since infancy or images of Rome inspired by Piranesi's engravings, but because she found it 'narrow, dirty and filthy'.[95]

---

[90] Helen Berry, 'Polite consumption: shopping in eighteenth-century England', *TRHS*, 6th ser., 12 (2002), 375–94; Margot Finn, 'Men's things: masculine possession in the consumer revolution', *Social History*, 25:2 (2000), 133–55; Amanda Vickery, 'His and hers: gender, consumption and household accounting in eighteenth-century England', *P&P*, supplement 1 (2006).

[91] Derbishire journal NRO DCN 118/6, 17; Bentham journal TNA PRO 30/9/44, 359.

[92] Miller, *Letters from Italy*, II, 243.

[93] Ibid., III, 258–9. Hester Piozzi also admired the 'beautiful' poulterers' and fruiterers' shops and the window displays of the gunsmiths that turned 'instruments of terror into objects of delight'. *Observations and Reflections*, 81.

[94] Piozzi, *Observations and Reflections*, 130; Lewis (ed.), *Extracts of the Journals and Correspondence*, I, 52.

[95] See also Chapter 3 on Rome.

In short, 'Rome has nothing within, nor without its walls to make it desirable for an English person to be an inhabitant.'[96] This is a crucial distinction: Mrs Bentham was evaluating Rome as a place to live, rather than as a connoisseur viewing a collection of sights, wonders and curiosities, full of imaginative associations. When travelling round the city and recording what she saw, she did not employ any of the 'framing' devices commonly used to describe antiquities, detaching them from their surroundings, and thereby enabling the writer to pass over the dirt and clutter with which antiquities in the eighteenth-century city were surrounded.[97] At the Arch of Vespasian, she observed nothing about its appearance, but noted the 'narrow dirty path' used by the Jews to avoid walking through it, as they made their way to and from the ghetto. Her eye for practicalities took in the manner of drying washing in Italian cities: in many streets, she observed 'there was Linnen hanging to dry upon cords festooned from house to house on the opposite sides of the street and our coachman was frequently obliged to stoop as he drove under the went linen'. Her remarks on Naples were necessarily constrained by the fact that she was nursing, and subsequently mourning, her terminally consumptive daughter-in-law. Nevertheless, she embarked upon a certain amount of sightseeing; her comments, however, never succumbed to the conventional patterns of hyperbole and delight that most travellers employed. Instead, we find a much more pragmatic view of Naples, one which was not overlaid with the conventions of literary tourism. The Chiaja, she allowed, was magnificent, but she was dismayed by the levels of poverty and degradation that she saw around her: ladies, she noted, could not walk on the streets because of the number of half naked men wandering around, filthy and disfigured by sores. She was similarly repelled by the custom of women openly checking their families' heads for vermin in the streets. And she alone of all the visitors to Naples commented upon the lines of washing strung out to dry for half a mile or more along the length of the Chiaja, the promenade of the Neapolitan social elite.[98]

Domesticity

Throughout her travels, Bentham was an acute assessor of the cleanliness or otherwise of the places in which she stayed. Observations of this kind were a standard part of any traveller's evaluation of a town or city

---

[96] Bentham journal TNA PRO 30/9/43, 133; contrast this with William Drake, who in a letter dated 5 June 1769, piously informed his father that 'Out of England, I believe Rome is the place I should choose to fix my residence in', Centre for Buckinghamshire Studies D – DR/8/2.

[97] Chard, *Pleasure and Guilt*, 226.

[98] Bentham journal TNA PRO 30/9/43, 132, 164, 198.

and operated at both a literal and metaphorical level. Men also made comments on the conditions at inns or the state of the streets and even on the personal hygiene of the Italians,[99] but women seem to have used cleanliness more consistently as a yardstick by which to judge the cities through which they passed. This was not just because feminine sensibilities could not be expected to put up with dirt and discomfort with the same insouciance as those of men. Rather, comments on the cleanliness or otherwise of any city represented the kind of quotidian detail that fell 'naturally' to a woman's sphere of observation, as opposed to the generalities and abstractions to which the gaze of the gentleman laid claim.[100] As Hannah More explained, women 'excel in details; but they do not so much generalize their ideas as men'.[101] Similarly, women's responsibility for household management may have made them particularly alert to deficiencies in this area when travelling. Moreover, the subject of domesticity was also one upon which women could write with authority without compromising their femininity. Finding fault with Italian (or French or German) standards of cleanliness was also a means of asserting the superiority of British domesticity, as well as the better regulation of public order and police in their own country. As subsequent chapters will show, comments on the dirt or cleanliness of the various cities that they visited became an increasingly prominent element of tourists' descriptive armoury, not least because it was becoming an increasingly important index of civility and improvement at home. As the streets of London and provincial England were paved, swept, watched and illuminated with the passage of local improvement acts, expectations of the urban environment steadily increased and became associated with England's claims to civility.[102]

This attention to dirt or domestic arrangements is also representative of the kind of 'disruptive detail' that has often been associated with female travel writing, a mode of description that was defined against the masculine traditions of antiquarian connoisseurship.[103] However,

---

[99] See, for example, John Mitford's delighted description of Cristoforo Spinola's private machine 'for administering a clyster' in the Palazzo Spinola, Genoa, and his reflections on the lack of cleanliness amongst French and Italians. Mitford journal GA D 2002/3/4/1, vol. 2, 74–5.

[100] John Barrell, 'The public prospect and the private view: the politics of taste in eighteenth-century Britain', in John Barrell, *The Birth of Pandora and the Division of Knowledge* (1992), 41–61.

[101] Hannah More, *Strictures on the Modern System of Female Education* (1799), 127, quoted in Ann Bermingham, 'The accomplished woman in the culture of connoisseurship', *Oxford Art Journal*, 16:2 (1993), 14.

[102] Rosemary Sweet, 'Topographies of politeness', *TRHS*, 6th ser., 12 (2002), 355–75.

[103] A phrase used by Stabler, 'Taking liberties', 17.

such comments became more frequent in the early nineteenth century as succeeding chapters will show in more detail. This trend, as James Buzard has argued, may be understood as part of a rhetoric of disappointment and unfulfilled expectations. As such, it was a general characteristic of travel literature in this period and cannot be associated exclusively with women.[104] Sensitivity to the relative cleanliness of one's surroundings, however, irrespective of any metaphorical functions that such comments might bear, was a more significant factor in shaping women's responses to the urban environment. Women tended to evaluate urban space from a feminine perspective of household management, noting the washing, the markets selling household provisions, the dirt or, indeed, cleanliness, and in the case of Charlotte Eaton, asserting a feminine responsibility for maintaining the cleanliness of the environment. Having decried the filth and noisome rubbish surrounding the Pantheon, she pronounced her ambition to come in with a mop and clean the Piazza Rotonda at her own expense.[105]

The feminine interest in domesticity is also apparent in the responses of female travellers to Herculaneum and Pompeii where the everyday life of the ancient Romans was, for the first time, made visible to all: Roman antiquities were no longer the monopoly of the dry researches of numismatists and epigraphists. Both men and women were intrigued by the insights into the private life of antiquity offered by the buried cities. There was a series of standard observations which almost all tourists made, which reflected the dependence of visitors on Italian guides and a limited range of guidebooks, but these comments are also indicative of which features struck British travellers particularly strongly. The width of the streets and pavements, for example, and the furrows left by wheels, demonstrated that Roman cities had suffered from traffic congestion as much as any eighteenth-century town. The series of shops seemed uncannily familiar, so much so that many referred to the marble counters in one, which was evidently some kind of tavern, that bore the stains of coffee cups. The fact that coffee could not possibly have been served in first-century Pompeii does not appear to have troubled them. The houses were a source of surprise, however, for they were small, apparently only one storey high, and with few windows. Visitors assumed that the inhabitants of Pompeii had

[104] Buzard, *The Beaten Track*, 173–4; in illustration of his point he cites William Hazlitt's disappointment at the sight of the 'mass of tawdry, fulsome *common places*' in Rome: *Notes of a Journey through France and Italy* (1826), 279.
[105] Eaton, *Rome in the Nineteenth Century*, I, 340. Kathryn Walchester makes the rhetoric of domesticity and British superiority a central theme in her analysis of Charlotte Eaton's writing: *Our Own Fair Italy*, 105–36.

Figure 1 View of the excavations at the soldiers' barracks at Pompeii, from Jean Claude Richard de Saint-Non, *Voyage pittoresque ou description des royaumes de Naples et de Sicile*, 5 vols. (Paris, 1782–5).

taken advantage of the balmy climate to spend little time indoors. However, women responded particularly eagerly to a version of Rome with which they could identify much more readily than that of the military heroes and political orators. Lady Charlotte Lindsey described her visit to Pompeii as the 'most curious and interesting thing that I have seen in my travels'. Like so many other visitors, Lindsey's excitement stemmed from the fact that, as she put it, 'Nothing can convey a more exact idea of the domestic life, manners occupations & amusements of the Ancient Romans than you receive from examining the ruins of Pompeii.'[106] But whilst male visitors might walk through the Roman forum and conjure up the ghost of Cicero, Lindsey's fancies in Pompeii took a more empathetic, personal turn as she and her companions tried to imagine what kind of character had inhabited each of the empty houses and what their lifestyle had been: 'we amused ourselves with finding out the House of a good Economist that made the most of every thing, of a Man of good taste, of another of fanciful taste, and of a rich vulgar <u>parvenu</u>'.[107] Anne Miller was particularly interested in the practical arrangements for plumbing and sanitation, noting that the theatre had conveniences similar to English water closets, with leaden pipes for the conveyance of water.[108] Lady Holland, whose views on Florence and Rome had been jaded to say the least, found in Pompeii antiquities to which she could relate on a personal level, greatly preferring them to the monuments of public life in Rome. She was clearly intrigued at the sights such as the interior of the soldiers' barracks and the street of private houses, but, as she complained to her sister, 'the simpletons throw the earth back again, and don't go on when they come to what they imagine was a private house, which is provoking, as one should have infinite more curiosity to see that than any public building' (see Figure 1).[109]

At the museum in Portici, where the objects excavated from both Pompeii and Herculaneum were on display, visitors were shown culinary implements laid out as if in a kitchen, doctors' instruments, writing equipment, jewellery and hair pins. Again, there is a discernible contrast between what caught the eye of the female visitors and what the men

---

[106] Lindsey journal Bodl. MS Eng. c. 7052, fol. 27.

[107] Ibid. This was in keeping with women's supposed preference for the biographical and 'private' side of history, as opposed to the narration of public matters and events that comprised traditional narrative history. Mark Salber Phillips, *Society and Sentiment: Genres of Historical Writing in Britain, 1740–1820* (Princeton, 2000), 110–14.

[108] Miller, *Letters from Italy*, II, 299.

[109] Lady Holland to Duchess of Leinster, 20 Feb. 1767, in Fitzgerald (ed.), *Correspondence*, I, 498.

highlighted: male visitors tended to see these collections as auxiliary to the written word. Their value as antiquities derived from the illumination that they offered to the literary text. Roger Robertson enumerated the various utensils he had seen at the museum in a letter to his father: there was 'in short everything that you need for the home'. But rather than dwelling upon the insight that such objects offered into the domestic life of the Romans, he saw their value in terms of the light they might shed upon Latin literature. They would, he suggested, be 'tres utile pour eclairer pleusieurs endroits dans les Anciens Auteurs, combien de disputes ont etées arrivé parmi les plus grands Esprits et Connoisseurs de l'Antiquité'.[110] Miller could summon up little enthusiasm for the collection of coins and the numerous styli displayed in one cabinet, but noted her husband's interest and also the fact that he was prompted to recollect a passage in Horace which described similar styli. Charles Abbot likewise was particularly taken with the writing apparatus.[111] For herself, Miller was far more intrigued by the cooking utensils and associated paraphernalia such as the jars for storing dormice, the moulds for ices and the cutters for ornamenting pastry. The ancients, she concluded in amazement, appeared to have employed more refinements in their entertainments than the moderns and served up a greater variety of dishes. Evidence for luxury that surpassed even that of modern urban society may not have been morally edifying, but as a hostess she could also appreciate what the moderns could learn from antiquity in more practical terms: 'Another article for culinary use, which would be very convenient and agreeable in England is, a kind of portable kitchen, which does not exceed the size of a commodious plate-warmer; This would be a most convenient machine for the use of those who like to eat in parks or garden.'[112] Men and women were captivated by the alternative vision of antiquity that they encountered at Pompeii and the sense of immediacy that the intimate objects of everyday life conveyed. But for women, whose self-identity was so closely bound up with household management and domesticity – rather than the public affairs of politics, wars and religion to which the ruins of Rome gave witness – Pompeii and Herculaneum were a welcome revelation.

---

[110] Robertson to his father, 27 Nov. 1751, NLS Acc 12244. Robertson regularly wrote to his father in French.

[111] Abbot journal TNA PRO 30/9/41, 303.

[112] Miller, *Letters from Italy*, II, 261, see also Miss Derbishire's comment on the various receptacles for holding hot and cold water: 'one pleased me extreamly, it was a flat square, with 4 little castles at the corners with a lid, & a cock in front, so that you might have hot water constantly without any trouble in a moment'. Derbishire journal NRO DCN 118/6, 24.

Art and its appreciation

In general, women were more likely to take an interest in art and paintings than in antiquities or architecture. Some female travellers, it is true, declined to engage in the appreciation of art as well as antiquities: Miss Derbishire, for example, was unimpressed by Guido's ceiling fresco of Aurora at the Palazzo Ruspigliosi, conventionally deemed as one of the artistic highlights of Rome, dismissing it as 'uninteresting'.[113] But there were also, it should be remembered, plenty of male travellers who professed to be unmoved by the canonical works of art.[114] For female travellers, however, the study of paintings was a more accessible pastime, both physically and intellectually, than the study of antiquities and they therefore tended to be enthusiastic viewers of art; some were also discriminating. Paintings were hung in palazzi, museums, churches, which were social spaces where women could venture without any fear of impropriety or discomfort. Just as in London, where exhibitions and artists' studios had become places of mixed, polite sociability as well as spaces in which to inspect and discuss art,[115] so too in Rome and Florence visitors congregated in these rooms, and particularly those studios belonging to female artists such as Angelica Kauffman or Elizabeth Vigée le Brun.[116] Art criticism, as defined by practitioners and theorists such as Lord Shaftesbury, Jonathan Richardson or Joshua Reynolds, was expressed in masculine terms and in such a way as to exclude women by definition. Having evolved from the language of civic humanism, it retained an emphasis on the inculcation of virtue and the promotion of the public good. The ability to abstract the general from the particular and to grasp universal truths lay at the basis of Reynolds' theory of art, and it was a skill that resided with men.[117] But the growth of the art market and exhibitions and the proliferation of print discussing art had created a viewing

---

[113] Derbishire journal NRO DCN 118/6, 10.

[114] See John Patteson's comments above; note also Nigel Llewellyn's scepticism regarding the active pursuit of art connoisseurship amongst male travellers: ' "Those loose and immodest pieces": Italian art and the British point of view', in Shearer West (ed.), *Italian Culture in Northern Europe in the Eighteenth Century* (Cambridge, 1999), 77.

[115] John Brewer, *The Pleasures of the Imagination. English Culture in the Eighteenth Century* (1997), 218–51; David Solkin, *Painting for Money: The Visual Arts and the Public Sphere in Eighteenth-Century England* (New Haven, 1992); Mark Hallett, ' "The business of criticism": the press and the Royal Academy exhibition in eighteenth-century London', in David Solkin (ed.), *Art on the Line: Royal Academy Exhibitions at Somerset House, 1780–1836* (New Haven and London, 2002), 65–75.

[116] Bentham journal TNA PRO 30/9/43,173; Lewis (ed.), *Extracts of the Journals and Correspondence*, I, 56–7, 61, 70–1; Piozzi, *Observations and Reflections*, 293.

[117] Barrell, 'The dangerous goddess'; and John Barrell, *The Political Theory of Painting from Reynolds to Hazlitt* (New Haven and London, 1995), 69–162.

public that was very different to Reynolds' ideal, of which women were equally a part.[118] They may well have been attracted by 'trivial' details and 'inconsequential' narratives, but this did not prevent them from consulting the treatises on art, which provided advice on how to view a painting and form a judgement, or, indeed, from reading Reynolds' *Discourses* themselves.[119] John Chetwode Eustace, the author of *A Classical Tour*, advised his readers that a knowledge of Du Fresnoy's *Art of Painting* and Reynolds' *Discourses* was sufficient to equip the traveller: this was a reading list that was equally at the command of women as men.[120] Whereas fully to appreciate the monuments of ancient Rome demanded knowledge of Roman history, literature and antiquities on the part of the sightseer, the appreciation of art lent itself much more readily to female practitioners who were less likely to have enjoyed such an education. It depended upon the authority of eye witness rather than that of classical learning, as the advertisement to Anne Miller's *Letters from Italy* made clear.[121]

Thus, the viewing of art and paintings tended to assume a more dominant place in the experiences of female tourists. Elizabeth Gibbes, for example, was part of a family group travelling through Italy in 1789–90. Her journal was kept as an aide-mémoire – erratically at times – and included humdrum notes on paying the shoemaker as well as more extended commentary on what she and her family had seen on a daily basis. She had no great interest in antiquities – which, unless particularly well known, she often dismissed with comments such as 'nothing in particular' or 'nothing of interest' – but she was a dedicated viewer of paintings, filling her notebook with observations on all that she saw. Her observations were frequently far more extensive than those of most male travellers. Whilst she was clearly reliant on information she had read in guidebooks or supplied to her by *ciceroni*, she nevertheless expressed her own distinctive view, which might not have conformed to the criteria of taste, as set out by the theorists, but which reflected her own careful observation. She looked at works of art for the story that they conveyed and the emotional relationships that they depicted rather

[118] Solkin, *Painting for Money*, 3–4; David Solkin (ed.), *Art on the Line: Royal Academy Exhibitions at Somerset House, 1780–1836* (New Haven and London, 2002), esp. C. S. Matheson, ' "A shilling well laid out": the Royal Academy's early public', 39–54, and K. Dian Kriz, ' "Stare cases": engendering the public's two bodies at the Royal Academy', 55–63.

[119] See, for example, the comments of Mary Berry on the Raphael Stanze, which contain clear echoes of Reynolds' *Discourses* on Raphael. Lewis (ed.), *Extracts from the Journals and Correspondence*, I, 62–3.

[120] Eustace, *Classical Tour*, I, xxvii.

[121] Miller, *Letters from Italy*, I, advertisement; see also Chard, *Pleasure and Guilt*, 35–6. On feminine claims to superior taste, see Vickery, *Behind Closed Doors*, esp. chs. 5 and 6.

than for their qualities of form and style. Composition was discussed in terms of its effectiveness in conveying the personal poignancy of the moment: commenting on Tintoretto's *Last Supper* in the Scuola San Rocco, she approved of the fact that the artist had avoided the usual 'hackneyed' representation, and had chosen instead to show Christ 'conversing naturally' with one of his disciples. At the Palazzo Zampieri in Bologna, she was taken with a 'fine picture' of the sacrifice of Abraham, Agar and Ishmael, concentrating again on the pathos of the scene and the emotional relationship between the figures. It was, she wrote, 'a striking mixture of surprise, indignation & in the muscles of the mouth grief, in the face of Agar: Little Ishmael is hiding his head with his hands, & Abraham is a fine majestic patriarch in a Turban'.[122]

Anne Miller's *Letters from Italy* (1776) had made similarly detailed and personal observations upon the paintings that she viewed, although there is no evidence that Gibbes read this volume (or that of Piozzi who was equally eloquent on the subject of painting) as a guide. Miller's *Letters from Italy* was prefaced with an advertisement from her publisher, that expressed the hope that her comments might prove useful to those in Britain who wished to commission the purchase of art in Italy. It is fair to assume, however, that her decision to concentrate heavily on discussing art did not stem solely from a disinterested wish to assist the aspiring art collector. It gave her a chance to establish a distinctive voice in topographical literature.[123] Many of Miller's comments were highly derivative of other authorities such as Charles Nicholas Cochin's *Voyage d'Italie* (1758) or Abbé de Lalande's *Voyage en Italie* (1769), but she added numerous instances of personal observation, and in particular her own emotional response to the paintings which particularly impressed her. Whilst she and Piozzi never challenged the established orthodoxy as to what constituted a fine painting or sought to undermine the accepted canon, they took delight at times in correcting or disagreeing with the male authorities whom they cited, and in asserting an independent judgement which they would not have ventured on the subject of antiquities. Miller, for example, took a particular dislike to Correggio's acclaimed *Virgin and Child with St Jerome* at Bologna, a painting widely admired by all the connoisseurs. The Virgin's face was like that of a peasant woman, she complained; the Magdalen looked like an idiot,

---

[122] Gibbes journal TNA PRO 30/9/7/10, unfoliated MS, entries for 24 Oct. and 2 Nov. 1789.

[123] On Miller's use of the epistolary genre to establish her own cultural capital, see Susan E. Whyman, *The Pen and the People: English Letter Writers, 1660–1800* (Oxford, 2009), 193–200.

St Jerome like an old beggarman, whilst the singing angel opened his mouth like a John Dory. Whilst at Bologna, Miller made a detour from the standard route to visit Cento, the birthplace of Guercino. Her great pleasure in finding a painting (the *Appearance of the Risen Christ to Mary*) which she held to be superior to the celebrated canvases in the Palazzo Zampieri in Bologna, was consistent with the whole tenor of her tour, which was to create a rhetorical space in which she could assert an opinion without having constantly to defer to male authority and inter-pretations.[124] Horace Walpole took a dislike to Miller and ridiculed her literary pretensions,[125] but her detailed comments were seriously received by others as a reliable source of information: the architect John Soane took Miller's letters with him on his voyage to Italy, and planned an extra-illustrated edition.[126] Sir William Forbes made frequent refer-ence to Miller's volumes when he came to write up his travels to Italy, and at one point took a pedantic pleasure in establishing that she, rather than his *cicerone* in Rome, Patrick Moir, was correct with regard to the number of columns in the courtyard of the Palazzo Borghese.[127] Some travellers, such as the botanist James Edward Smith, made a point of trying to fault her accuracy and described her comments as 'whimsical', 'ludicrous' and 'extravagant', treating male authorities with greater leniency. But he also frequently referred to her *Letters from Italy* for their factual content and often agreed with her judgements: he was as much displeased with Correggio's *Virgin and Child with St Jerome*, he admitted, as was Lady Miller herself.[128]

Physical and cultural boundaries

But being a woman did, of course, impose some limitations upon what one could see and do in Italy. At the most basic level, it determined the itinerary of the tour. Few went any further south than Paestum, and even this was an excursion which a number of women declined to make on the grounds of the discomfort of the journey.[129] Even the journey from

---

[124] Miller, *Letters from Italy*, I, viii.

[125] Ruth Hesselgrave, *Lady Miller and the Batheaston Literary Circle* (New Haven, 1927), 4.

[126] Gillian Darley, *John Soane: An Accidental Romantic* (New Haven, 1999), 26. Pierre de la Raffinière Du Prey, *John Soane: The Making of an Architect* (Chicago, 1982), describes Miller as Soane's 'constant companion' in his tour of Italy. Soane's reading and use of Miller's *Letters from Italy* is discussed in greater detail, ibid., 132–44.

[127] Forbes journal NLS MS 1544, fol. 302.

[128] James Edward Smith, *Sketch of a Tour on the Continent in the Years 1786 and 1787*, 3 vols. (1793), III, 33.

[129] Hester Piozzi declined to join a party to Paestum: 'my cowardice kept me at home, so bad was the account of the roads and accommodation': Piozzi, *Observations and*

Rome to Naples, as Lady Holland informed her sister, was a 'most tedious and most uncomfortable journey for a woman to take'.[130] The roads south of Naples deteriorated; inns were few and far between and of a poor quality, and as a consequence the usual custom was to stay at monasteries. For obvious reasons, this was not an option available to women, and southern Naples, Sicily and Malta remained an almost entirely masculine preserve for travellers.[131] Physical exertion was not entirely ruled out, however, and was most obviously required in the ascent of Vesuvius. Men, let alone women, found this a physically demanding endurance test due to the steepness of the gradient and the difficult terrain.[132] Whether they reached the crater or not, the ascent was frequently tackled by female British travellers – much to the amazement of the local Italians – and thereby presented an opportunity for British women (encouraged by their male compatriots) to demonstrate the superior qualities of British womanhood. Italian women by contrast refused to walk anywhere, let alone climb Vesuvius, insisted on travelling by chair or by coach, and were regarded by the British as commensurately weaker and less healthy.[133] (The ladies of Florence, complained Francis Drake, preferred to 'loll in their chariots' at the gates of the Boboli Gardens rather than 'walk amongst their enchanting delights'.)[134] In 1788, Ann Flaxman accompanied her husband in the ascent of the volcano. Halfway up they stopped for refreshments and she was assailed by doubts: 'but womanlike when they [her companions] offer'd to return and send the mules away I began to be asham'd of my weakness and resolutely resolv'd at all Events to go forward. I took an additional draught of strong Beer was placed on my mule and brought up the rear most gallantly singing.' Once the soil became sandy and too steep for the

Reflections, 246. The indefatigable Ann Flaxman accompanied her husband on a trip to Paestum in February 1788, but found the roads so bad that she was forced to get out and walk for fear of being thrown out of the carriage. The party was reduced to staying overnight in a 'peasant hovel' given the absence of any other form of accommodation. Flaxman journal BL Add. MS 39787, fols. 69v–70r.

[130] Lady Holland to Duchess of Leinster, 8 Nov. 1766, in Fitzgerald (ed.) Correspondence, I, 479.

[131] There were exceptions: Sir William Hamilton took his first wife on a trip to south of Italy.

[132] Francis Drake argued that it was 'no great feat to boast of in our sex, when several English ladys [sic] had the courage to goe [sic] to the very top, tho' they durst not descend into the crater'. Drake journal MCO MS MC F16, vol. 3, 55.

[133] Mrs Patrick Home, Hester Piozzi, Catherine Wilmot, Miss Derbishire, Elizabeth Gibbes all made the ascent. William Forbes noted that it was conventional for most women (including his invalid wife) to go no further than a view point above the 'hermitage' near the bottom of the mountain. Forbes journal NLS MS 1541, fol. 88.

[134] Drake journal MCO MS MC F16 vol. 2, 86; see also Sharp, Letters from Italy, 208 who complained that Italian women 'hardly know what it is to walk'.

mules they dismounted and followed the guide up on foot. Flaxman,
however, found that she was rapidly sinking in up to her calves and was in
danger of losing her shoes through the weight of the sand: 'in some
places', she told her family, 'I mounted Heroically alone with the help
of a Club but in others I was forc'd to submit to lay hold of the Guides
Girdle and let him lug me up.' But she reached the top in triumph, and
on the descent she and her male companions linked hands, running
and sliding down the mountainside on their backsides.[135] Vesuvius was
a unique natural phenomenon and its exceptional quality appears to have
allowed a relaxation of the norms of appropriate behaviour to take place,
enabling women to undertake a distinctly unfeminine level of physical
activity without incurring disapproval. But Naples itself, as we shall see,
was a place where greater licence in all sorts of behaviour seems to have
been tolerated or even expected.

   Women also encountered restrictions on what they might see. In
Rome, Mary Berry noted that she and her sister were not allowed into
the Anfiteatro Castrense, located in the gardens of a Cistercian convent,
simply because they were women.[136] Veronese's *Marriage at Cana*, hanging in the refectory of the monastery of San Giorgio in Venice, was
similarly out of bounds to all women, including Hester Piozzi, much to
her annoyance. As she wrote to her daughter: 'Mr Piozzi and Mr Parsons
went *in* this Morning to look at it, & left me on the *out*side of the Wall'
(her italics).[137] Monastic institutions in general were problematic, but
Elizabeth Gibbes appears to have found a number of monks and friars
who were willing to turn a blind eye to the presence of female visitors
in the more public areas of the monastery.[138] (Equally, of course, we
should note that men were unable to enter convents beyond the public
parlour, and had to wait whilst the female members of their party viewed
the interior rooms and spaces).[139] However, it was more commonly the
subject matter rather than specific spaces from which women were
excluded. Thus, the more overtly phallic objects, such as the items in
Signor Bianchi's cabinet and the lion's priapus in the ducal galleries at

[135] Flaxman journal BL Add. MS 39787, fols. 70v–72r.
[136] Lewis (ed.), *Extracts of the Journals and Correspondence*, I, 95.
[137] Piozzi to Hester Maria Thrale, 22 Aug. 1785, in Bloom and Bloom (eds.), *The Piozzi
Letters*, I, 135.
[138] Gibbes journal TNA PRO 30/9/7/10 and 11.
[139] Bentham journal TNA PRO 30/9/43, 254–5; Sarah Bentham's record of a visit to the
convent of 'La Madonna de Sept Dolores' in Rome noted how the male members of
the party had to wait in the public parlour for the women, who were being shown
around the interior of the convent. Similarly, Elizabeth Gibbes in Venice was permitted
to be shown the interior of the Ospedale della Pietà after attending a concert, because
she was a woman: Gibbes journal TNA PRO 30/9/7/10, 25 Oct. 1789.

Florence, were kept covered or in closed cabinets in deference to the presence of female visitors.[140] Some paintings were also deemed unsuitable for feminine eyes: Sir William Forbes' daughter was prevented by their guide from seeing the painting of *Leda and the Swan* in the Palazzo Bovi at Bologna, depicted in what Forbes described as an 'equivocal' attitude. The guide insisted on taking Miss Forbes out of the room before drawing back the curtain that covered the painting and protected young ladies' modesty (Lady Forbes, as her husband noted drily, was allowed to remain).[141] Certain items, however, such as the statue of the goat and the satyr at Portici, seem to have acquired notoriety amongst male travellers and an established place in elite homosocial libertine culture.[142] 'Mind to have an order to see the satyr f – g the Goat', the Earl of Pembroke instructed his son, 'We did not see it.'[143] Other objects and works of art, such as the painting of *Leda and the Swan*, noted above, were rarely commented upon, except in the more private context of family correspondence or personal journals. The only other specific reference to this particular depiction comes from the Norwich merchant, Robert Harvey, who was no less taken aback than Forbes but rather more excited by the explicit content of the painting: 'The Leda by Giulio Romani [sic] is in the most louching [sic] & voluptuous attitude the swan has his tongue in Leda's mouth who his [sic] quite naked & his body is betwixt her thighs. Ye Gods what ideas it awakens.'[144]

In general, a stronger sense of prudery, which had a discernible influence upon the tenor of visitors' comments as we shall see in subsequent chapters, began to make itself felt towards the end of the eighteenth century, although it was considerably less fully articulated than it would be under the Victorians. This trend reflected both the increasing number of women and family parties making the tour of Italy, a development that undermined the strain of libertinism that certain aspects of the Grand Tour had engendered, and a climate of morality in Britain that had become more censorious about such matters.[145] Nevertheless, even in the early

[140] Mitchell journal BL Add. MS 58315, fol. 18v; Georges A. Bonnard (ed.), *Gibbon's Journey from Geneva to Rome* (1961), 45; John Northall, *Travels through Italy* (1766), 64.
[141] Forbes journal NLS MS 1540, fols. 237–8.
[142] On aristocratic libertinism see Jason Kelly, *The Society of Dilettanti* (New Haven and London, 2009), esp. chs. 2 and 7.
[143] Lord Herbert (ed.), *Henry, Elizabeth and George (1734–1780): Letters and Diaries of Henry 10th Earl of Pembroke and his Circle* (1939), 197.
[144] Harvey journal NRO MS 20677, 96.
[145] See, for example, Robert Gray, *Letters during the Course of a Tour through Germany, Switzerland and Italy, in the Years MDCCXCI and MDCCXCII* (1794), 314–15. See also discussion on pp. 196–7 below. The issue of women's exposure to 'indecent' classical sculpture was also being raised in the British press at the time, see Kriz, ' "Stare cases" ', 58.

nineteenth century the British were apparently more blasé about such matters than the Italians, or at least they affected to be surprised by the heightened sensitivities they encountered in Italy. Italian squeamishness on sexual matters was always represented as another instance of Roman Catholic hypocrisy: Italian society, and the church in particular, were prepared to sanction excessive freedom and immodesty with regard to sexual mores, but displayed unwarranted modesty over inanimate works of art.[146] The British – men and women – were amused by attempts to cover up genitalia on statues with fig leafs and by the petticoats that had been added to cover the indecency of Michelangelo's nudes in the *Last Judgement*.[147] In Venice, where the courtesans were by repute more brazen than anywhere else, Charles Abbot noted, with a touch of irony, that Titian's *Toilet of Venus* in the Palazzo Barberigo had been daubed over 'for decency's sake'.[148] But travellers were also irritated by the impairment that such modifications presented to their appreciation of these works of art – not least the King of Sardinia's decision to cut in half those canvases which he considered to be too revealing – and the limitations such censorship placed upon their experience.[149] Lady Charlotte Campbell was, according to her daughter Harriet, highly entertained by the efforts of their *laquais de place* in Milan to prevent them from viewing the statues at the Palazzo Brera: they were, he informed them, not suitable for their female eyes to see. Fourteen-year-old Harriet, on the other hand, was deeply aggrieved.[150]

---

[146] Richard Rawlinson recorded that, at the instigation of his confessors, the Grand Duke of Tuscany had ordered Bandinelli's nudes of Adam and Eve to be removed from the duomo and all the statues in his collections on public display to be castrated 'or the nudities ill covered'. Rawlinson journal Bodl. MS Rawl. d. 1181, 715, 21 Dec. 1722. Likewise, on his second visit to Italy, John Breval noticed the disappearance of Adam and Eve, but was told that they had been removed on the Archbishop's orders 'out of an over-scrupulousness upon the Account of the *Nudities*'. John Breval, *Remarks on Several Parts of Europe Relating Chiefly to their History and Antiquities ... since 1723*, 2 vols. (2nd edn, 1738), I, 169.

[147] Robert Finch noted that 'Some of the figures have been covered with drawers and petticoats, to the shame of those who could feel offended at the sight of the unveil'd form of nature.' Finch journal Bodl. MS Finch e. 16, fol. 255r. Female visitors were similarly surprised by papal prudery: Eaton, *Rome in the Nineteenth Century*, II, 374, 'It seems that one of the Popes (I forget which) in an unfortunate fit of prudery, was seized with a resolution of dressing all the naked figures in this great painting' (the *Last Judgement*).

[148] Abbot journal TNA PRO 30/9/41, 431. Abbot also complained that the figure of Venus was 'too robust' for his taste.

[149] Miller, *Letters from Italy*, I, 125. Miller was not impressed by the King of Sardinia's 'ridiculous prudery' (ibid., 119). Sir Richard Colt Hoare in his notes on painting in Italy complained that 'the present Prince Colonna has spoilt the effect of many of his finest pictures by painting over the nudities; fortunately only with water colour'. CUL Add. MS 4155, fol. 3v (n.d.).

[150] Campbell, *Journey to Florence*, 70.

Some expressions of concern were made, generally by men, who were more likely to express anxiety about the possible dangers to female modesty represented by male nudes. If women were offended they kept quiet; even to acknowledge impropriety might suggest immodesty. In Bologna, at the fountain of Piazza Nettuno, John Moore was taken aback by how little Giambologna's magnificent nude *Neptune* left to the imagination (see Figure 2). Female travellers, he suggested primly, would be better advised to admire the sculptor's skill in the drapery of the robes on the nearby statue of the pope 'than the anatomical accuracy in forming the majestic proportions of the Sea Divinity'.[151] But these were rare observations and, judging from other accounts, by both men and women, Giambologna's statue was apparently viewed without provoking embarrassment or adverse comment. John Moore, in fact, seems to have been unusually sensitive to the potential impropriety of classical and renaissance statuary, objecting not only to Giambologna, but also to the statues of hermaphrodites in the Duke's Galleries in Florence and at the Borghese Palace in Rome.[152] The silent rather than explicit condemnation of travellers is harder to interpret. It is only through the stray comments of travellers such as Robert Harvey (noted above) or Richard Rawlinson, who was intrigued by the 'lewd' paintings in the duomo at Florence, where he noted a devil 'inserting fire' into the 'privy parts' of a woman,[153] that it becomes apparent how much was being tacitly ignored. Such silence arose either because the subject matter was unsuitable for communication in the public or semi-public domain of correspondence, or because the paintings were effectively invisible given both the poor lighting of so many churches and galleries and the dependence of visitors upon the discretion of local guides and guidebooks in directing them as to what to see.

Female nudes, however, did not in the eighteenth century provoke concern, amongst either male or female travellers. Even John Moore raised no objections against the *Venus de Medici*, although he did argue its inferiority to the *Apollo Belvedere*.[154] Both John Barrell and John Hale have analysed the responses of male viewers to the *Venus de Medici* over the course of the eighteenth century, and drawn attention to the sensuality of many of the descriptions. It certainly elicited some highly sexualised responses from male travellers, particularly in the latter part of the eighteenth century when, as Barrell argues, the stoic abnegation of

---

[151] Moore, *View of Society and Manners*, I, 300.   [152] Ibid., II, 367.
[153] Rawlinson journal Bodl. MS Rawl. d. 1181, 714. Rawlinson is the only traveller who commented on these frescos in the sources consulted for this study.
[154] Moore, *View of Society and Manners*, II, 365.

Palazzo Pubblico in Bologna

Figure 2 The Palazzo Pubblico in the Piazza Netuno, Bologna, from John Smith, *Select Views in Italy with Topographical Descriptions in England and France*, 2 vols. (1792–6).

sexuality that characterised Shaftesbury's civic humanist aesthetics gave way to an aesthetics in which the expression of sexuality and desire were legitimate and acknowledged as constituent of elite masculinity.[155] Yet, in general, the nudity of classical and renaissance statues caused little disquiet in this period. Thus, women generally shared their male counterparts' admiration for the *Venus de Medici*, although expressed it in more muted fashion, avoiding the overtly sensual response of some of their male compatriots. Elizabeth Gibbes, for one, admired her head, but found her legs to be 'hideous'.[156] As Chloe Chard has noted, it was the excess and licentious behaviour of modern Italians represented in the flamboyant paintings and statues of the seventeenth century that created more concern.[157] Statuary, by contrast, was associated with decorum and restraint. Indeed, when disapproval was pronounced, the likelihood was that it would be levied against the baroque sensuality of Bernini's *St Theresa* rather than antiquity.[158] When travellers returned to the continent after 1815, they were more shocked by Canova's statue of Pauline Borghese than any antique nude that they encountered.[159] The 'cold, chaste nakedness' of classical statuary represented an ideal of beauty that was deracinated from the narratives which had given rise to it and could consequently be viewed simply as an aesthetic object.[160] It thereby lost much of its potential to shock. Instead, it was admired for the qualities of smooth, flowing lines and the almost tactile properties of the flesh. The fact that Italians might be embarrassed simply displayed their want of true taste.

[155] John Hale, 'Art and audience: the Medici Venus, c. 1750–1850', *Italian Studies*, 31 (1976), 37–58; Barrell, 'Dangerous goddess'. Victorian attitudes, as Hale shows, became much more prudish and censorious.

[156] Gibbes journal TNA PRO 30/9/7/11, 13 May 1790.

[157] Chloe Chard, 'Nakedness and tourism: classical sculpture and the imaginative geography of the Grand Tour', *Oxford Art Journal*, 18:1 (1995), 14–28. There were exceptions, of course: John Moore, as noted above, was one, but see also Gray, *Letters during the Course of a Tour*, 314–16.

[158] Charles Abbot complained of Bernini's 'depraved' taste, which he contrasted with the much 'chaster' and 'nobler' design and execution of John of Bologna (Giambologna). Abbot journal TNA PRO 30/9/40, 245–6. See also Smith's objections to the saint's 'lascivious expression', *Sketch of a Tour*, II, 157.

[159] Campbell, *Journey to Florence*, 124–5.

[160] Matthews, *Diary of an Invalid*, 133. Matthews objected to the 'squeamishness' which led the authorities in Florence and Rome to 'deface' works of antiquity with tin fig leaves: 'One would imagine the Society for the Suppression of Vice had an affiliated establishment in Italy. Nothing can be more ridiculously prudish. That imagination must be depraved past all hope, that can find any prurient gratification in the cold chaste nakedness of an ancient marble. It is the fig leaf alone that suggests any idea of indecency, and the effect of it is to spoil the statue.' See also Kenneth Clark, *The Nude* (1956; repr., 1980), 1–25.

Conclusion

The Grand Tour had an important role to play in the construction of British elite masculinity, providing the opportunity to display the key qualities of taste, virtue and judgement both through the activity of sightseeing and through the reflective performance of writing, whether in letters home, diaries or published accounts. But in practice the Grand Tour, even when narrowly defined, was neither exclusively masculine nor confined to the aristocratic elite. For all that the beliefs and values that provided the rationale for travel to Italy were, in the abstract, discussed in masculine terms, the practice was rather different from the prescriptive norm. Taste was not gender neutral, but it was more flexible than theorists such as Shaftesbury might argue. Women were active participants, not passive bystanders. Whilst most of them had internalised the expectation that their taste and judgement in matters of art and antiquity was inferior to that of men, they were fully capable of appropriating the language of taste and criticism to form their own judgements which they recorded in journals to their own satisfaction. They experienced the same pleasure of recognition at sites of antiquity from their familiarity with the literature and history of ancient Rome, even if it was through translations, and they expressed similar admiration for the canonical works of art. Few women sought to challenge the assumption that they would be more interested in the particular, the personal or the inconsequential, and they sought it out and found it, whether in the kitchen utensils of Pompeii or the portrait busts of Roman empresses at the ducal galleries of Florence. Indeed, they frequently exploited the greater latitude allowed them by virtue of their sex, to disregard the conventions of the 'Grand Tour' and to engage only in those activities in which they were most readily interested.

Women's accounts of their travels, in particular those that were published, have been closely examined by other scholars with regard to the development of travel literature as a genre, or in terms of the creation of authorial subjectivities.[161] This chapter has taken a different approach: on one level it has served to introduce some of the main themes and preoccupations of British travellers in Italy. It has established some of the expectations with which people travelled and the patterns of behaviour to which they subscribed once in Italy. But it has also demonstrated the extent to which women's experience of the Grand Tour, and of Italian cities in particular, differed from that of men. A focus on women helps to

---

[161] Turner, *British Travel Writers in Europe*; Bohls, *Women Travel Writers*; Leask, *Curiosity and the Aesthetics of Travel Writing*; Walchester, *Our Own Fair Italy*.

break down the perception that the eighteenth-century tour was populated solely by the kind of aristocratic young man who had his portrait
painted by Pompeo Batoni. (Although Batoni, it should be remembered,
painted a number of female travellers, and their children, too.)[162]
A significant number of the women who 'made the tour', moreover,
were the authors of widely read texts that mediated representations of
Italy and its cities to a far wider readership of armchair travellers at
home; their influence in the broader cultural reception of Italy during
this period needs to be acknowledged. Further, the detailed practicalities
of travel often received more careful attention from female travellers:
it was the reliable factual content and empiricism of Mariana Starke's
Instructions for Travellers (the revised edition of *Letters from Italy*, first
published in 1800) that provided the model for John Murray's hand-
books to Italy, and the rest of Europe.

Recognising the contribution of women travellers not only highlights
the extent to which the experience of travel was gendered, but also helps
us to understand how the Grand Tour evolved in tone and content
through the eighteenth and into the nineteenth centuries. As the
following chapters will show, by the early nineteenth century British
travellers' representations of Italy had become less rigorously classical,
were more influenced by poetry and novels, showed a greater interest in
manners and customs and expressed a new awareness of Italy's medieval
past. This reinvention of Italy cannot be understood purely in terms of
women's influence or their reluctance to engage with classical antiquity
but their experience was representative of a shift away from the interpretation of Italy and its cities derived from the traditions of civic
humanism that characterised the earlier part of the century. Gender
was not, of course, always the decisive factor in shaping experiences.
Men from a trading background, who had not necessarily been drilled in
the classics since infancy, such as the Norwich merchants John Patteson
or Robert Harvey, could be as underwhelmed by Rome's antiquities as
any female traveller. And while women were excluded from some sights
on account of their sex, so too were men on account of their social status:
at St Elmo in Naples, Harvey encountered a monk who refused to open
up the church for him – a member of the aristocracy would have been
unlikely to have met with such unobliging resistance. John Patteson
similarly straddled the worlds of mercantile and polite society uneasily,

---

[162] For example Sarah, Lady Fetherstonhaugh, Georgiana, Countess Spencer or the three-
year-old Lady Louisa Grenville: see Edgar Peters Bowron and Peter Björn Kerber,
Pompeo Batoni: Prince of Painters in Eighteenth-Century Rome (New Haven and London,
2008), 46, 70, 72.

well aware that his trading connections excluded him from elite company in Naples.[163] Moreover, male and female travellers shared much in common: both subscribed to the cosmopolitan values of taste and virtue that sustained the Grand Tour, and equally they both identified themselves as English or as Britons, in contrast to the effeminacy, corruption, superstition and backwardness that they claimed to encounter in Italy. By the end of our period, a sense of British superiority was being articulated with greater frequency by both sexes. These questions of national difference and national identity will be explored in greater detail in the chapters that follow as well as analysis of the creation of a sense of place and of the evolution in the understanding of the cities themselves.

[163] Harvey journal NRO MS 20677, 153; Cubitt, Mackley and Wilson (eds.), *Great Tour of John Patteson*, 301.

2   Florence: a home from home

Introduction

In the summer of 1785, Hester Piozzi left Florence with considerable regret: 'But I must bid adieu to beautiful Florence', she wrote, 'where the streets are kept so clean one is afraid to dirty them, and not one's self, by walking in them: where the public walks are all nicely weeded, as in England, and the gardens have a homeish and Bath-like look, that is excessively cheering to an English eye.'[1] Piozzi's strong attachment to Florence was far from being unique amongst English-speaking visitors, and, as the quotation above suggests, was not simply based upon admiration of the ducal collections. Rather, it grew out of a sense that Florence was mercifully free of those qualities which rendered Italian cities, for all the magnificence of their art and antiquities, an alien and unfamiliar environment. Florence appeared to offer an oasis of home-like comfort in the midst of lengthy peregrinations in foreign lands. In identifying reassuring familiarity in Florence, the British were also defining those values that they associated most closely with their sense of self and of national identity.

Piozzi's comments are of interest because they indicate which qualities of urban life were regarded as characteristically 'English' and remind us of the alienation and homesickness that could afflict the tourist even in the promised land of Italy. They also highlight how different the eighteenth-century response to Florence was from that of the nineteenth or twentieth centuries. The idealisation of the republican Florentine past that became so widespread in the Victorian era did not even begin to make itself felt until the very end of the eighteenth century. Accordingly, the attractions of Florence as a city of outstanding beauty rested not so much on the combination of towers, loggias and medieval churches, that featured so heavily in nineteenth-century representations, as on its pleasing location in the vale of the Arno, on the quality of the Grand

---

[1] Piozzi, *Observations and Reflections*, 166.

Duke's collection of art and antiquities, and the congenial physical and social environment to which Hester Piozzi referred.

This is not to say that the perception and representation of Florence did not change over the course of the century; on the contrary, there is a clear evolution in the manner in which Florence was described that reflects not only the changing conventions of travel writing, but also the different values that were associated with Florence by the nineteenth century and its meaning in terms of how the British understood both the city's history and its relationship to contemporary British culture. There is a rough pattern we can establish: at the start of the eighteenth century, the standard account of Florence by British visitors would present it simply in terms of the Medici dukedom. Florence's identity and fame rested upon its place as the showpiece of the Grand Dukes' patronage, taste and power. The art and architecture that drew the admiration of the tourist was overwhelmingly that of the sixteenth and the seventeenth centuries: it was the wealth and power of the Medici that had enabled them to 'ransack' Europe and Asia for treasures.[2] The city's republican past, along with the commercial wealth and artistic culture of the fourteenth and fifteenth centuries, were of minor interest. But by the end of the eighteenth century, we find a richer and more diverse range of responses to the city. The term 'renaissance' had not yet been coined, but British travellers were now beginning to attach much more importance to Florence's role in fostering the early revival of the arts. There was also increasing recognition of how its commercial and manufacturing wealth had permitted patronage on a scale which even the wealthiest of the landed elite were bound to admire.[3] Florence acquired a new set of associations for the British visitor, which in turn influenced the way in which it was viewed, experienced and described as a city.

Florence came to be seen not simply as the expression of Medici taste and power, but as a city with a past that had the capacity to inspire the imagination and which endowed the open spaces and built fabric of the city with meaning. Much of the information upon which travellers drew in developing this perception of Florence had always been available: the change in content was not the result of the discovery of new material, but rather a consequence of making better use of sources that had always existed, either in English or Italian. There were changes in the culture of

[2] Breval, *Remarks on Several Parts of Europe* (1738 edn), I, 144.
[3] The best account of Anglophone interest in, and writing on, the renaissance for this period remains J. R. Hale, *England and the Italian Renaissance: the Growth of Interest in its History and Art* (1954; repr. 1996). See also J. B. Bullen, *The Myth of the Renaissance in Nineteenth-Century Writing* (Oxford, 1994).

the British travelling public towards the end of the eighteenth century that made them more receptive to such information. But it should also be recognised that this 're-evaluation' of Florence coincided with a stronger sense of civic patriotism and a revival of interest in the Florentine Republic that was developing within Florence itself at the same time. It is important to bear in mind, therefore, the extent to which British visitors' perceptions of the city drew upon information derived from the printed guides and histories which they would have encountered in Italy, and the degree to which the changing sensibilities of the British were determined by the Florentine view of the city and its past.

One of the striking features of British responses to Florence is that they are remarkable for the consistency of their approbation. Rome, Venice and Naples, the other major centres of the Italian tour, evoked rather more equivocal reactions. Rome was the ultimate goal of the grand tourist, but heightened expectations were often disappointed when confronted with the prosaic reality of ruins which lacked the pristine clarity of Desgodetz's engravings. Further, the British were frequently unimpressed, or at least claimed to be unimpressed, by aspects of the modern city, not least because most observers were locked into a system of thought whereby papal absolutism could not be admitted to be capable of good government or benign rule. More prosaically, the social life and the entertainments on offer were often found wanting. Naples offered a livelier social scene, a benign climate and a wealth of curiosities, geological and antiquarian, in the surrounding *campagna*. But Naples as a city posed dangers as well as attractions. The architecture was too florid; the Catholicism too overt; the *lazzaroni* too idle. Venice was extraordinary, but also claustrophobic, alien and discomfiting. Visitors frequently left it without regret after only a matter of days. Yet Florence, however, was frequently recommended as a most desirable place for prolonged residence in Italy.

The attractions of Florence

One reason for Florence's capacity to charm may be that it suffered less from the burden of unfulfilled expectations and disappointment. Visitors approached Rome and Venice with preconceived ideas, and compared the city to the images that they had previously formed in their imagination, shaped by texts, engravings and paintings. But Florence was not a city whose buildings were familiar through the visual record, as were Rome or Venice. There was no established tradition of *vedute* of Florentine streetscapes to match those of Venice's canals. Engraved views of the buildings of Florence did not feature in the collections of the eighteenth-century British collector. Giuseppe Zocchi, the main print-maker of Florentine *vedute*, never commanded the kind of recognition of Piranesi or Canaletto.[4] Visitors to Florence purchased Etruscan vases or alabaster fire places as souvenirs; if they acquired prints, they were reproductions of the famous paintings and statues, not of the buildings that housed them.[5] Florence, like Naples, was most frequently depicted in a prospect view – seen from a distance, set in a landscape of agricultural fertility, farms and villas – but unlike Naples it lacked the defining landmark features of Vesuvius or the Bay of Naples to render it distinctive. The approach to Florence was attractive but did not generate a buzz of anticipation or provoke exclamations of recognition (see Figure 3). Its reputation, and the justification for its place on the itinerary of the tour, rested overwhelmingly upon the collections of art and antiquity rather than its buildings or its history. Florence earned its sobriquet 'the Fair' as much from the beauty of the star attractions in the collections – the *Venus de Medici* and Titian's *Medici Venus* – as from its innate properties. It is significant that the defining image of Florence and the Grand Tour in the British tradition is Zoffany's group portrait within the tribuna, where the focus was upon the collection and the male tourists, rather than the physical fabric or location of the city itself.

The tradition of writing favourably about Florence was established early in the institutional development of the Grand Tour. Travellers in the late seventeenth century always remarked upon the extent to which Grand Duke Cosimo III was particularly well disposed towards the British and how he welcomed them more warmly to Florence than any other nation, dispensing gifts of wine and fruit to all new arrivals.[6]

[4] E. E. Dee, *Views of Florence and Tuscany by Giuseppe Zocchi 1711–1767. Seventy-Seven Drawings from the Collection of the Pierpont Morgan Library New York* (New York, 1968). Zocchi produced two volumes of engravings of Florentine *vedute* and views of villas in the surrounding *campagna* in 1744. These were reissued in 1754. *Scelta di XXIV vedute delle principali contrade, piazze, chiese, e palazzi della città di Firenze* and the *Vedute delle ville e d'altri luoghi della Toscana*. Charles Abbot noted that it was possible to buy prints of individual buildings at Bouchard, for four and a half pauls each, Abbot journal TNA PRO 30/9/40, 165.

[5] The accounts of Sir Watkin Williams Wynne in Florence in 1768 included purchases for vases, scaoli tables, a 'chequer table of all sorts of marble', '12 pieces of marble made like books', a 'small Florentine work in marble, 2 figures, a woman and a Turk', copies of Virgil and Tasso, ten volumes of prints of the Florentine gallery, two further books of prints and 'views of Florence and sundry country palaces bound in two volumes' which must have been the two Zocchi volumes. NLW Wynnstay MSS Box 115/1, 53.

[6] Anon., 'Remarks on several parts of Flanders, Brabant, France and Italy in the year 1717', Bodl. MS Douce 67, 182–3; Twisden journal Bodl. MS Eng. misc. c. 206, fol. 41r; Le Strange journal NRO LEST/NF 2, 83. Richard Rawlinson noted in 1721 that the 'Grand Duke shows Englishmen a great regard in memory of the great civilities he received when as Grand Prince he travelled to England', Bodl. MS Rawl. d. 1181, 720.

Figure 3 'Florence from Fiesole', from James Hakewill, *A Picturesque Tour of Italy from Drawings Made in 1816, 1817* (1820).

It was clearly in Cosimo's favour to maintain a friendly relationship with Britain, if only with regard to the trading interests of the port of Livorno whose prosperity was heavily dependent upon the continued presence of the English factory, but the English at least chose to believe the friendly reception was in recognition of the hospitality which Cosimo had received when he visited England as a young man in 1668–9.[7] The warmth of his reception did much to temper the criticism which travellers were wont to level against an absolute ruler such as the Grand Duke, who kept cannons trained upon the city in the event of any unrest and oppressed his subjects with high levels of taxation.[8] More trenchant criticism was directed against his successors, who did not enjoy the buffer of being

[7] W. E. Knowles Middleton (ed.), *Lorenzo Magalotti at the Court of Charles II: His relazione d'Inghilterra of 1688* (Waterloo, Ont., 1980).

[8] Wright, *Observations*, II, 429. In 1696, Richard Chiswell had blamed the 'intollerable arbitrary Government' of Florence for its declining population: Bodl. MS Don. c. 181, fol. 15r. He attributed the happy and populous prosperity he saw in Lucca, by contrast, to its traditions of liberty (fol. 17v).

thought a particular friend of Britain, but the sense of affinity with Florence was not eradicated.

The end of the Medici dynasty in 1737 ushered in the absentee rule of Francis Stephen, later Holy Roman Emperor, and the British could no longer expect such preferential treatment from either the ruler or his representatives. They still contrived to find common ground, however: British visitors were ready to believe that the Archduke and his nobility encouraged trade (they noted the custom amongst the nobility of selling wine from their own palazzi) and this, they argued, tempered both the absolutism and the poverty of the country.[9] But Count Richecourt, Francis Stephen's plenipotentiary, definitely did not favour the British (despite the fact that Lady Walpole was his mistress):[10] he was responsible, amongst other policies, for revoking the immunities of the British merchants at Livorno.[11] This hostility from the ducal court was, however, less significant than it might have been in influencing the perceptions of the British because from 1740 they could find a home from home at the house of Sir Horace Mann, who had assumed the role of British Resident in Florence. Mann's boundless hospitality and courtesy to British visitors of all descriptions is well documented, both in his own correspondence and that of the tourists themselves, and does not require reiteration. According to the Earl of Cork, he was the only person he had ever known, whom 'all Englishmen agreed in praising'.[12] Mann died in 1786, but the unusual longevity of his tenure provided a remarkable element of continuity in the experience of British travellers. Young men who enjoyed his hospitality in the 1740s were followed by their offspring a generation later, leading to some touching scenes, such as the occasion when Mann introduced the young Thomas Pelham, heir to the future Earl of Chichester, to the Countess Acciaioli, to whom his father had acted as *cavaliere servente* twenty-five years before.[13]

By the time that Thomas Pelham was making small talk with his father's former mistress in 1777, there had been a change of ruler. Francis Stephen was succeeded by Peter Leopold in 1765, who embarked upon a project of implementing the precepts of enlightened absolutism within

---

[9] Charles Thompson, *The Travels of the Late Charles Thompson Esq. Containing his Observations on France, Italy, Turkey in Europe, the Holy Land, Arabia and Egypt*, 3 vols. (1744), I, 105.
[10] Brian Moloney, *Florence and England: Essays on Cultural Relations in the Second Half of the Eighteenth Century* (Florence, 1969), 41.
[11] Eric Cochrane, *Florence in the Forgotten Centuries, 1527–1800* (1973), 346.
[12] John Duncombe (ed.), *Letters from Italy in the Years 1754 and 1755 by the Late Right Honourable John Earl of Corke and Orrery* (1773), 108.
[13] Thomas Pelham to his father, 13 Sept. 1777, BL Add. MS. 33127, fol. 311.

the dukedom of Tuscany.[14] British tourists generally warmed to Duke Leopold, as he was generally known: with his agricultural reforms, suppression of monasteries, codification of the law and abolition of excessive ceremonial and ritual, he was credited with bringing prosperity and progress to Tuscany.[15] In a country where the British repeatedly decried the enervating and corruptive force of luxury, Duke Leopold earned their approval for his efforts to lessen luxury by discrediting it.[16] He appeared to be introducing the kind of enlightened tolerance and economic progress which the British associated with their own country. Unlike the Roman or Neapolitan *campagna*, which invariably gave rise to reflections on alternatively the pernicious effects of corrupt and absolutist government or the dead hand of feudalism on the affluence of a country, the prosperity which travellers claimed to detect throughout Tuscany, and the flourishing commerce at the free port of Livorno, vindicated their own belief in the benign effects of free trade, toleration and enlightened principles.[17] Of more practical concern to the tourists, perhaps, was the fact that he opened up the Laurentian library to visitors and abolished the expensive and irksome custom of giving perquisites to the guides and servants.[18]

One of the improvements that was particularly singled out was Leopold's reform of the criminal code and the institution of a more effective system of law and order. In the early eighteenth century, visitors had complained about the levels of crime and violence, as they did throughout Italy: the Florentines were prone to homicide wrote one, being 'splenetick and revengeful' and far too quick to resort to

[14] For an overview of Leopold's reforms in Tuscany see Carlo Capra, 'Habsburg Italy in the age of reform', *Journal of Modern Italian Studies*, 10 (2005), 218–33. The intellectual and social contexts to the Tuscan reform programme, and in particular the influence of French physiocratic thought, is explored by Thomas Wahnbaeck, *Luxury and Public Happiness: Political Economy in the Italian Enlightenment* (Oxford, 2004).

[15] See, for example, Moore, *View of Society and Manners*, II, 356.

[16] Paul Mellon Centre, Brinsley Ford Archive, transcript of Thomas Orde's journal at Florence and Siena (1772), 25.

[17] The British would have been influenced by Leopold's own propaganda machine, which produced statistics demonstrating the improvements he had wrought and outlining his plans for improvement. (Cochrane, *Florence in the Forgotten Centuries*, 484–5). Leopold also convinced Arthur Young of the efficacy of his measures. Young became a member of Georgofili society and offered a very favourable assessment of Leopold's improvements in *Travels during the Years 1787, 1788 and 1789* (Bury St Edmunds, 1792), 494. See also Semple, *Observations on a Journey*, II, 36; Forsyth, *Remarks on Antiquities*, 72–4, was equally full of praise for Leopold as a 'philosopher king' who carried out practical reforms.

[18] Abbot journal TNA PRO 30/9/40, 172; Fitzwilliam Museum Cambridge, inv. no. 832.5, 'John Flaxman, Italian journal', fols. 11–13, printed in H. Brigstocke, E. Marchand and A. E. Wright (eds.), *John Flaxman and William Young Ottley in Italy*, Walpole Society, 72 (2010), 95.

the stiletto.[19] Leopold, however, instituted a programme of reform following Beccarian principles, and the botanist James Edward Smith, for example, was curious to discover the effect of the new criminal code upon the police of the Tuscan capital. He claimed to have been told that although the safety of the streets was formerly 'execrable', it was now 'perfect'. Robberies and outrages were apparently unknown and any amount of money could be carried about as safely at midnight as at midday.[20] The effects of the introduction of good police, like agricultural improvements or tariff reform, were often discussed in the context of the duchy of Tuscany, rather than Florence itself, but it is nevertheless noticeable that travellers were far less likely to comment on the dangers posed by crime or by beggars in Florence once Leopold had assumed the dukedom. In Bologna and Padua, stories of secret stabbings with the notorious stiletto abounded; in Naples, the *lazzaroni* in the city and the *banditti* in the countryside represented a constant threat; in Rome, beggars proliferated, the Trasteverini were notorious for violence, and a description of the summary punishment of the *strapado* was commonplace. In Venice, the danger was not so much posed by criminal elements as by the workings of the Council of Ten and the State Inquisition: even the gondoliers were believed to be part of a network of spies and informers. Yet, Florence seemed free of such dangers: at least they seldom, if ever, represented a theme in travellers' observations, reinforcing the sense that one of the city's attractions was that it offered an unthreatening environment.

The dangers presented by other cities, particularly Venice and Naples, were not constituted solely by criminality, but also by sexuality. References to prostitutes or 'public women' in Florence were extremely rare: they formed no part of the discourse around the city, unlike Naples or Venice, or even Rome, where the tacit encouragement of prostitution by the papacy as a means of raising revenue was frequently cited.[21] Rather, Florence's reputation was increasingly one of urbane civility; like any city it was a little staid and boring out of season. But it did not pose any particular threat or discomfort to visitors and offered instead – in addition to the collections of virtù – familiar routines of leisure and sociability and practical domestic comforts, reminiscent of home, that were hard to come by in other centres of the Italian

---

[19] Anon., 'Remarks', Bodl. MS Douce 67, 174.

[20] Smith, *Sketch of a Tour*, I, 319; see also Gray, *Letters during the Course of a Tour*, 308–9.

[21] Francis Drake was a rare exception to this rule: he commented upon the 'actresses' at the theatre, comparing them to those of Covent Garden. Drake journal MCO MS MC F16 vol. 2, 101.

tour.[22] The handsome Florentines, observed Elizabeth Craven with some complacency, are very like the English.[23]

Due to the presence of the English factory at Livorno, supplies of English food and other goods were more readily available in Florence than elsewhere – a matter of no small importance for travellers who often found normal Italian fare hard to stomach. John Swinton, a naval chaplain, who visited Florence during a sojourn in Livorno in 1731, was pleased to discover that the Florentine nobility had acquired a taste for English beer: 'The Italian nobility and Cavaliers', he noted, 'make nothing of drinking 3 or 4 Bottles of the strongest English Beer in a Morning, but ys [this] is no Prejudice to them, their heads being in capable of suffering thereby.'[24] In addition to beer, as numbers of tourists found, the shops were better stocked than elsewhere in Italy with imported luxuries such as Reading sauce and Woodstock gloves, whilst Mariana Starke, whose special concern was the care of travelling invalids, was pleased to reassure her readers that 'Dr. James Fever Powders' were readily available in Florence.[25] By the second half of the eighteenth century, there were several well-established hostelries which were famous amongst the British for being run by their own countrymen. One such was run by Charles Hadfield, who had determined upon establishing a hotel in Florence after his own negative experiences of travel in Italy.[26] He ran his business, which eventually amounted to three different establishments in and around Florence, for thirty years. After his death, one of the hotels was acquired in 1779 by another Englishman, Meggit, who had been servant to Lord Maynard.[27] Meggit continued to cater to the needs of the English for nearly twenty years. Vanini's was run by Widow Vanini, an Englishwoman who had married an Italian and made a profitable living out of catering to the needs of visitors, such as Lady Miller, who relished the 'true English elegance, civility and cleanliness'.[28] Hester Piozzi revelled in the soft clean pillows, currant tarts, beans and bacon,[29] and Ann Flaxman

---

[22] Physical comfort, that is the 'self-conscious satisfaction with the relationship between one's body and its immediate physical environment' has been identified as a distinctive aspect of Anglo-American culture during the eighteenth century and a term that was used with increasing frequency to express 'satisfaction and enjoyment with immediate physical circumstances'. John Crowley, 'The sensibility of comfort', *AHR*, 104 (1999), 749–82.

[23] Craven, *Journey through the Crimea*, 84.

[24] Swinton journal WCO Wadham MS A11.6, 27 Apr. 1731.

[25] Matthews, *Diary of an Invalid*, 40; Mariana Starke, *Letters from Italy between the Years 1792 and 1798*, 2 vols. (1800), II, 300.

[26] Ingamells (ed.), *Dictionary of British and Irish Travellers*, 439–40.   [27] Ibid., 652–3.

[28] Miller, *Letters from Italy*, II, 74.   [29] Piozzi, *Observations and Reflections*, 137.

Figure 4 'Florence from the Ponte alla Carraia', from James Hakewill, *A Picturesque Tour of Italy from Drawings Made in 1816, 1817* (1820).

was delighted to be served good English fare of roast beef and plum pudding.[30] Male travellers tended to be less specific about the creature comforts that they found at these places, but the clean beds and familiar food were as welcome to them as to women. There is a palpable sense of relief evident in their letters and journals as they found themselves amidst more familiar surroundings after the strains of travel.[31] As the artist Thomas Jones remarked with feeling on his arrival at Hadfield's: 'I could hardly help fancying myself in England and that increasing phantom – *distance from home* which continually haunted my Mind at every Other Stage, vanished an Instant.'[32] Comments such as these bring home the sense of estrangement and alienation which was as much a part of the Grand Tour as the emotional transports enjoyed on seeing the *Venus de Medici*.[33]

Florence, then, offered perhaps a higher degree of physical comfort and safety than other Italian cities. But Piozzi's remark, quoted at the outset of this chapter, reminds us that it was as much the physical appearance of the town that she found so 'cheering' as the quality of the accommodation. What impressed the British visitor in Florence was the 'good figure' made by the houses and buildings,[34] the breadth of the main streets (beyond which few tourists penetrated) and the quality of the pavements and the cleanliness. For many tourists, the last place in which they would have made any extended stay in Italy – particularly those who had come by sea from the south of France – would have been Genoa. Here, the streets were notoriously narrow; so much so that they were impassable to carriages, and the elaborately decorated façades could barely be seen from the street. The centre of Florence, however, had the kind of broad streets and spacious squares that were widely appreciated, both for their aesthetic qualities and the freer circulation of air and traffic which they allowed, and the city itself was surrounded by gardens and orchards. The low elliptical arches of the Ponte Sta Trinità invariably elicited approval for the elegance of their design (see Figure 4).[35] The more judgemental tourist might complain that the squares were not regular and that the streets away from the main

---

[30] Flaxman journal BL Add. MS 39787, fol. 30.
[31] Trease (ed.), *Matthew Todd's Journal*, 118: 'Rose to breakfast at 9 o'clock, having enjoyed a most capital bed, with a carpeted room, just like England.'
[32] Oppé (ed.), *Memoirs of Thomas Jones of Penkerrig*, 51.
[33] Lord Kildare wrote to his mother, Emily, Duchess of Leinster: 'I must own I long to be once more comfortable at Carton, but as travelling is a pleasant thing to have over, I am, thank God, very happy and enjoy being abroad much better than I expected.' Fitzgerald (ed.), *Correspondence*, III, 466.
[34] Twisden journal Bodl. MS Eng. misc. c. 206, fol. 40v.
[35] Hall journal NLS MS 6326, fol. 193.

thoroughfare were narrow and confined, but in the principal spaces which the British frequented, Florence appeared open and clean. 'Other towns seem to have grown from small beginnings; this, like the creation, appears to have arisen at once: each part corresponding with the others; and all gay, noble, and convenient.'[36] Moreover, these thoroughfares were paved and cleansed, mitigating the perennial complaint of British visitors to Italy about the filthy state of the streets. 'Poor people', noted Andrew Mitchell, 'go about in the mornings gathering the dung & nastiness in boxes upon asses or horses backs.'[37] Such an arrangement was hardly unusual – indeed, it could be paralleled in many English towns – but the fact that Mitchell singled it out for notice in Florence rather than for any other town is indicative of how significant the cleanliness of the streets was in shaping visitors' impression of the city. 'It is so perfectly clean', the Countess of Pomfret told the Countess of Hertford in 1740, 'that there is not the least ill smell in the streets all the year round.'[38] Even after a shower, noted Ann Flaxman over forty years later, the streets were clean and dry enough for walking.[39]

In emphasising these qualities, British travellers were following in a well-established tradition. As early as 1400, Leonardo Bruni, originally a native of Arezzo, had singled out the cleanliness of Florence for special praise in the *Laudatio Florentinae urbis*, where he associated it with the qualities of republican freedom and celebrated the willingness of all citizens to play their role in keeping the streets clean. The observation was repeated by other observers, such as the Venetian Marco Foscari, in the sixteenth century.[40] Thus, Florence had clearly been recognised for its cleanliness long before the British started to pass judgement and it is reasonable to assume that the city's well-established reputation had some bearing on visitors' accounts, even if it is unlikely that many of them had read the *Laudatio Florentinae urbis*. But, equally, they could have chosen to deny the claims and to ridicule the city's pretensions; that they did not do so, and that they placed so much emphasis upon the absence of dirt or noisome smells, should not be underestimated and is a telling indicator of the positive reputation that Florence had acquired amongst the British.

---

[36] Phillips (ed.), *Correspondence*, I, 211.   [37] Mitchell journal BL Add. MS 58317, fol. 2.
[38] Phillips (ed.), *Correspondence*, I, 211. This was a view that her grandson, the Earl of Winchelsea, reiterated over forty years later in a letter to his mother, 3 Apr. 1773, ROLLR Finch MSS DG 7/4/12 box 4953 bundle 32.
[39] Flaxman journal BL Add. MS 39787, fol. 30.
[40] D. Biow, 'The politics of cleanliness in northern renaissance Italy', *Symposium*, 50:2 (1996), 1–13.

With respect to architecture, British visitors, who often found the baroque curves and columns of Rome and Naples in poor taste, were more in sympathy with the simpler Florentine aesthetic, praising its 'beauty and neatness'.[41] The approbation extended to Florentine architecture by early eighteenth-century travel writers such as Joseph Addison and Edward Wright proved influential: their comments were echoed and repeated by subsequent travellers well into the eighteenth century.[42] The façades of the palazzi and other buildings built in the 'Tuscan' or 'rustic' order were in general widely admired, not least for their perceived similarity to the Palladian style made fashionable in Britain by the Earl of Burlington.[43] There was more magnificence in the 'projecting façade of the rustic order', wrote Francis Drake, 'than in the smooth and uniform front in English architecture'.[44] In the 1770s and 1780s, the simplicity and grandeur of the Florentine façades continued to meet with approval: Sir James Hall, a gentleman with amateur architectural pretensions, described them as striking structures in a 'noble Roman manner'.[45] French visitors, by contrast, were less impressed: Charles de Brosses found the buildings' façades excessively flat, lacking the relief and movement of columns which he admired in the architecture of Borromini and Bernini.[46] By the early nineteenth century, however, there was a trend to find fault with the stark façades and heavy proportions of the palazzi: they were described as gloomy, cumbersome, oppressive and prisonlike.[47] But such comments tended to come from travellers who were developing a more analytical and critical mode of

---

[41] Mitchell journal BL Add. MS 58312, fol. 2.

[42] Nugent, *Grand Tour*, III, 335, and Northall, *Travels through Italy*, 38.

[43] Thompson, *Travels of the Late Charles Thompson Esq*, I, 99, observed of the Tuscan order exemplified in the Palazzo Pitti that 'this Manner of Building is where great rough Stones are set jutting out beyond the plain Superficies; which has been imitated by several *English* Noblemen, particularly the Earl of *Burlington*, in the Pillars before his House in *Piccadilly*'. See also Wright, *Observations*, II, 393, or Colyer, 'A Breconshire gentleman in Europe', 285. See also Sir James Hall's praise for buildings 'in the noble Roman manner without time', Hall journal NLS MS 6326, fol. 175.

[44] Drake journal MCO MS MC F16 vol. 2, 85.

[45] Hall journal NLS MS 6326, fol. 175.

[46] R. S. Gower (ed.), *Selections from the Letters of de Brosses* (1897), 71. French visitors were not uniformly admiring of Italian baroque architecture, however, particularly in its more extreme forms in Naples. As the eighteenth century progressed, their attitude became progressively more critical of the 'mauvais gout' of Neapolitan ecclesiastical architecture: A. Blunt, 'Naples as seen by French travellers 1630–1780', in F. Haskell, A. Levi and R. Shackleton (eds.), *The Artist and the Writer in France. Essays in Honour of Jean Seznec* (Oxford, 1974), 1–14.

[47] John Mayne Colles (ed.), *The Journal of John Mayne during a Tour on the Continent upon its Reopening after the Fall of Napoleon, 1814* (1909), 151; Eustace, *Classical Tour*, II, 195; Forsyth, *Remarks on Antiquities*, 67.

architectural description in general and whose taste was determined by the purism of the Greek revival. Although this trend is significant in terms of the development of a particular discourse within the genre of travel writing, these comments do not appear to have affected the overall favourable impression that the appearance of Florence made on visitors to any great degree. Most visitors continued to enthuse about the city's beauty, despite these reservations. Although there were no architectural glories to match St Peter's or monumental antiquities to compete with the Coliseum, the prevailing impression of Florence was of a city that was uniquely pleasant and agreeable.

It is noticeable that some of the most positive commendations of Florence emanated from female travellers such as Pomfret, Miller, Flaxman and Piozzi, who have already been quoted. Their enthusiasm, and that of other women, seems to suggest that Florence was a city that was particularly attractive to the female traveller.[48] This was not simply because they appreciated the comparative cleanliness of the streets, although this undoubtedly did weigh heavily in their positive evaluation. But in other ways, too, Florence offered a more congenial atmosphere in which women could spend time than did Rome, for example, where the principal objective was supposed to be the study of antiquities – a subject which, as we have seen, was regarded as a particularly masculine pursuit. In Florence, however, the object was not so much the pursuit of antiquity, but the appreciation of art and the cultivation of polite sociability in the *conversazione*, the theatres and the opera houses. Florence lent itself particularly well, therefore, to the female visitor who, armed with a copy of Jonathan Richardson's *An Account of Some of the Statues, Bas-Reliefs, Drawings and Pictures in Italy, with Remarks* (1722) or Charles Nicholas Cochin's *Voyage d'Italie* (1758), could pronounce judgements on works of art as readily as any man – and frequently did.[49] The ducal galleries and the Palazzo Pitti were as attractive to women as to men. Zoffany's conversation piece of grand tourists leering over the *Venus de Medici*, the *Venus d'Urbino* and other choice specimens has helped to create a perception of the Grand Tour as a

[48] Lady Mary Coke wrote that 'I am much better pleased with the town [Florence] and country about it then [sic] I am with any other part of Italy I have seen', quoted in A. Moore, *Norfolk and the Grand Tour* (Fakenham, 1985), 68.

[49] Much of Richardson's success as a theorist lay in the fact that he argued that the 'science of the connoisseur' was dependent upon the exercise of rational faculties rather than an innate quality of mind. Whilst he did not explicitly endorse female connoisseurship, those who followed Locke's arguments for the essential equality of mind between the two sexes could find in Richardson ample justification for women venturing to pronounce upon art. Richardson's theories of connoisseurship are discussed in Carol Gibson Wood, *Jonathan Richardson* (New Haven and London, 2000).

largely masculine experience.[50] Zoffany, however, deployed considerable artistic licence in inserting many objects of virtù which did not
normally reside in the tribuna; his representation of the space as the
preserve of male connoisseurs was hardly any more accurate. Lady
Miller, for one, provided a blow by blow account of how she and her
husband measured every part of the *Venus de Medici's* anatomy: 'round
her shoulders, passing the string under her arms across her breast,
three feet'.[51]

Florence also boasted a well-established social life in which women,
and men, could participate. In Venice, Rome and Naples, the British
found that the majority of the resident nobility were reluctant to entertain at home, preferring to exchange visits in the boxes of the theatre
and the opera house. The Florentine nobility, however, were said to be
particularly civil to foreigners, 'very sociable in a sober way', according
to Edward Wright, and friendlier with strangers than was customary in
other parts of Italy.[52] The air of 'cheerfulness and gaiety' was still being
offered as a defining characteristic of the city in the guides of the early
nineteenth century.[53] Sir Horace Mann was attentive and assiduous in
entertaining British travellers, even to the extent of rigging up lamps on
green poles wrapped with vine branches in order to recreate the effect of
Vauxhall Gardens for their benefit.[54] He also included the Italian
nobility in his invitations, thereby facilitating a greater degree of social
intercourse with the resident Italian society than occurred in the other
major centres. 'I believe there is no place in Europe, where the nobility
and gentry pass their time more agreeably than they do here', wrote
one satisfied visitor in 1756.[55] Mann's efforts were supplemented by
the presence of other long-term English residents, such as the third
Earl Cowper, Lord Tylney, and the Countess of Orford, who similarly
extended hospitality, although on a less inclusive basis.[56] Favourable

[50] Llewellyn, ' "Those loose and immodest pieces" '. Llewellyn's focus on paintings of male
tourists viewing works of art gives undue emphasis to the male gaze and underestimates
the extent to which women travelled in the company of men, particularly in the period
after 1740.
[51] Miller, *Letters from Italy*, II, 111.
[52] Wright, *Observations*, II, 428; Northall, *Travels through Italy*, 103; Moore, *View of Society
and Manners*, II, 390.
[53] See, for example, Milford, *Observations, Moral, Literary and Antiquarian*, II, 122.
[54] Drummond, *Travels through Different Cities*, 41; Mann to Walpole, 4 July 1744, in
Dr Doran, *'Mann' and Manners at the Court of Florence, 1740–86*, 2 vols. (1876), I, 186.
[55] Sacheverell Stevens, *Miscellaneous Remarks Made on the Spot, in a Late Seven Years Tour
through France, Italy, Germany and Holland* (1756), 128.
[56] For biographical details, see Ingamells (ed.), *Dictionary of British and Irish Travellers*,
246–7, 959–60, 725–7. Hester Piozzi commented that Lord and Lady Cowper
'contribute much to English society', *Observations and Reflections*, 140.

perceptions were, perhaps, also influenced by the anglophile tone of Florentine culture: by the 1770s, Italian histories of England, translations of Hume, Robertson and Smollett were available, along with English grammars for those who wished to learn the language themselves.[57] 'I must own', confessed the Earl of Winchelsea to his mother, 'it gives me great pleasure to see the French a little humbled as it is very evident how much the preference is given to the English.'[58] Others noted that the Florentines were 'much like' the English in dress and figure.[59] Adam Walker, like so many others, praised the cleanliness of Florence – in striking contrast with his criticism of the dirt and stench of Rome and Venice: 'something like English cleanliness pervades the place'. But he also praised the rational conversation and communicativeness of the Florentines; again, in telling contradistinction to the scathing criticism he launched against the manners and morals of the modern Romans.[60]

The city of art and culture

Voltaire's description of Florence as a second Athens quickly became a clichéd observation amongst travellers and its importance as a centre of the fine arts and literature under the Medici was widely acknowledged.[61] The overarching narrative that was associated with Florence was not ancient grandeur, or even commercial greatness, but the revival of the arts and literature, exemplified in the patronage of the Medici. It was the Medici collections of art, antiquities and manuscripts – not the city's buildings – that were the principal attraction drawing visitors to Florence and likewise the justification for spending an extended period of time there. Indeed, the physical settings in which the collections were housed – the palazzi, the churches and libraries – were largely incidental for visitors such as Francis Drake, who commented that if the collections were ever to be removed from Florence, it would be visited by strangers 'with as much indifference' as Pisa or Siena (cities which merited a day's visit at most at that time). ''Tis this prodigious collection that induces foreigners to continue here', he concluded.[62] Florence was both described and experienced chiefly as a gallery of paintings and sculptures, rather than as an urban space of streets, piazzas and buildings: a tendency that

---

[57] Moloney, *Florence and England*, 131–6.
[58] Winchilsea to his mother, 20 Dec. 1772, ROLLR Finch MSS DG 7/4/12 box 4953 bundle 32.
[59] Northall, *Travels through Italy*, 105.
[60] Walker, *Ideas Suggested on the Spot*, 145, 310, 320, 359.
[61] Voltaire, *The General History and State of Europe*, 3 vols. (Edinburgh, 1758), II, 5.
[62] Drake journal MCO MS MC F16 vol. 2, 84.

was accentuated by the Florentine tradition of erecting statues throughout the city's streets and squares and thereby enhancing the sense of the city as an open-air space of display.

The city's reputation as a centre of learning had declined since its apogée under Lorenzo de' Medici, but even in the eighteenth century, British visitors were more willing to credit Florence with the cultivation of learning than Venice, Rome or Naples. There were more learned men in Florence, reported Francis Drake, than any other city in Italy.[63] The basis upon which Drake formed his opinion may be open to question, but the point to note is that he had formed (or taken with him) the impression of a city where learning and the arts were still cultivated; an impression assisted in part by the qualities of the collections which he saw – the coins, medals and cameos for the study of antiquity; the collections of manuscripts in the Laurentian library – but also influenced by the fact that those who showed the British round, like Antonio Cocchi, the custodian of the ducal galleries, were noted anglophiles.[64]

Florence was, as Piozzi said, above all the 'residence of the fine arts', and the places where these were to be appreciated were chiefly the Duke's galleries and the Palazzo Pitti. Travellers' diaries show that visitors went straight to the gallery before any other sight upon arrival in Florence, and once at the gallery, it was the treasures of the tribuna, and above all the *Venus de Medici*, which elicited the most extravagant praise. Two weeks were not enough, it was said, to appreciate the glories of that collection alone: Edward Gibbon found that he needed fourteen separate visits fully to appreciate its riches.[65] Philip Yorke, anxious to impress his uncle (who was financing his tour) with his seriousness of purpose, opined that there was sufficient in the gallery to occupy one for a couple of months. In the event, however, he tired of paintings after only two weeks.[66]

Most visitors did, of course, visit more than the gallery and the Palazzo Pitti and took in a number of churches and other palazzi during their visit, but the tourist itinerary was a highly partial and selective one, which sought out monuments and buildings associated with a few key figures and the works of those artists only who were admired according to conventional eighteenth-century canons of taste. Amongst

[63] Ibid.
[64] Swinton journal WCO Wadham MS A11.5, 2 Mar. 1730/1; Duncombe (ed.), *Letters from Italy*, 108, and Klima (ed.), *Letters from the Grand Tour*, 6; see also Joseph Barretti, *An Account of the Manners and Customs of Italy; with Observations on the Mistakes of Some Travellers, with Regard to that Country*, 2 vols. (1768), II, 173.
[65] Bonnard (ed.), *Gibbon's Journey*.
[66] Yorke to his uncle, 12 Oct. 1778, BL Add. MS 35378, fol. 245.

the Florentine artists, Raphael, Michelangelo, Andrea del Sarto and Fra Bartolommeo were held in particular esteem, whilst Giotto and Cimabue deserved acknowledgement, if not admiration, as the first revivers of the art of painting. The duomo, along with the campanile and the baptistery, occupied almost as important a position on the tourist itinerary as did the Medici collections. It was Brunelleschi's octagonal dome, renowned for being the forerunner to Michelangelo's greater effort at St Peter's, which was chiefly admired. The marble clad exterior, by contrast, evinced very mixed responses and only qualified admiration.[67] Inside, the tomb of Giovanni Acuto, the English *condottieri* Sir John Hawkwood was one of the few objects of notice in an interior which was generally deemed disappointingly drear. The campanile was much admired – not least, perhaps, because unlike the famous towers of Pisa and Bologna, it had remained perpendicular. Few visitors missed San Lorenzo where they would marvel at the unfinished riches of the Medici chapel and Michelangelo's Medici tomb in the sacristy. In Sta Croce, Giotto's frescos were invisible in the eighteenth century and its soaring gothic proportions failed to impress; but the tombs of Galileo and Aretino, as well as Dante, Petrarch and Boccaccio, made the church a site of pilgrimage, even before Byron gave Sta Croce and the 'all Etruscan three' literary immortality in *Childe Harold's Pilgrimage*. The conscientious traveller would go also to Santo Spirito to admire Brunelleschi's architecture; Sta Trinità, famous for having been Michelangelo's favourite church; and to Santissima Annunziata, where Andrea del Sarto's frescos adorned the cloisters. With the exception of the baptistery (which was persistently, but erroneously, said to have been originally a Roman temple to Mars) and Giotto's campanile, few buildings erected before the era of Brunelleschi attracted any notice at all.

To a certain extent, this narrowness of vision was determined early on by the nature of the guidebooks which became principal reference works for years to come. Richardson's *Account of Some of the Statues, Bas-Reliefs, Drawings and Pictures in Italy* was one of the most influential works on art appreciation and art theory amongst the English reading public, but it covered only the duomo and San Lorenzo amongst all the Florentine churches in any detail. Subsequent visitors, therefore, found themselves bereft of guidance when viewing other fabrics, and their comments were correspondingly limited. Richardson's preferences were

---

[67] See, for example, Thomas Watkins, *Travels through Switzerland, Italy, Sicily, the Greek Islands to Constantinople, Greece, Ragusa, and the Dalmatian Isles*, 2 vols. (2nd edn, 1794), I, 295, who compared its appearance to a harlequin's jacket, but could find no fault with Brunelleschi's dome.

perpetuated by other widely used guides: Edward Wright and Thomas Martyn, for example, whose published observations were separated by nearly sixty years, both confined their comments on Florence to little more than a description of the duomo, the ducal gallery and San Lorenzo.[68]

In all these comments on the art and architecture of Florence, it is easy to detect the influence of Vasari. Much of what Richardson conveyed to his readers was in fact a condensed summary of the *Lives of the Artists*. It is for this reason, one may assume, that the campanile was so widely admired, given that its pink and white marble design was very far from what was regarded as correct architectural taste in Britain. Vasari's opinions were filtered through into travellers' observations in varying degrees of attenuation, but in the process of translation and transmission, the expression of Florentine pride in the artistic achievements of his native city was diluted and lost, along with the anecdotes that enlivened his biographies. Similarly, had the British consulted Italian guidebooks they could have discovered considerably more about the works of art to be found in the city's churches and monastic foundations.[69] It was not that the Florentine guides were celebrating the merits of early renaissance artists in any great detail – the Florentines shared the same standards of taste and expectations as the British – but these guides provided considerably more information about the subject matter and design of such paintings. Whilst acknowledging the deficiencies in perspective, drawing and composition of the early renaissance artists, they also lauded them for having transcended the barbarity of *i tempi bassi*.[70] Although visitors were willing to accept Vasari's overall argument that the recovery of art began in Florence and was largely the work of Florentine artists, they showed little interest in the stages by which that recovery took place or in the world in which these artists lived and the patrons for whom they worked. The importance of Giotto and Cimabue in the narrative of the restoration of civilisation was always acknowledged, but this rarely extended to admiration for their works of art themselves.[71] Their paintings, if described at all, were deemed dry, hard and unpleasant. Indeed, Francis Drake, who wrote a particularly discursive account of his tour in Italy, incorporating large amounts

[68] Wright, *Observations*, II, 393–433; Martyn, *Gentleman's Guide*, 320–9.
[69] See, for example, Francesco Bocchi and Giovanni Cinelli, *Le bellezze della città di Firenze dove a pieno di pittura di scultura di sacri templi, di palazzi, i più notabili artifizj, e più preziosi si contengono* (Florence, 1677).
[70] Anon., *L'Antiquario fiorentino o sia guida per osservar con metodo le cose notabili della città di Firenze* (Florence, 1765), 13, 93.
[71] Breval, *Remarks on Several Parts of Europe* (1738 edn), I, 170.

of history and commentary on the state of the arts and literature, pointedly refused to take his historical account back further than the late fourteenth century, explaining that it was only at this date that: 'Italy first began to shine out of monkish ignorance, and to point out the path which other nations have since pursued'.[72] In keeping with this rejection of the early renaissance, British visitors would typically decline even to identify artists before the late *quattrocento* and Lorenzo de' Medici's patronage of the great masters Leonardo, Raphael and Michelangelo.

Thus, many tourists never recorded anything in Florence beyond their visit to the gallery and the tribuna.[73] There were, of course, lengthy guides published to take them through the collection and to structure their subsequent observations.[74] But there were also plenty of guides to the city of Florence as a whole available for the visitor to purchase.[75] Based upon the same text and published by Florence's single printing house, the guide was repackaged and expanded in various editions through the eighteenth century. Those who read it would have been alerted to a city which comprised more than the collections of art and virtù of the Medici family. Even the versions produced in the earlier part of the century, at a time when Medici absolutism had effectively dampened Florentines' interest in their own past, offered the visitor something more than a city which was simply a showcase for Medici patronage and collecting. The visitor was taken through a comprehensive tour of the churches, palazzi and charitable institutions of the city. The guides divided the city up into quarters, and documented every church and building of significance within each area. Not only did British tourists ignore the majority of these buildings, but they showed a complete disregard for the topography and the history of the city.

The city republic and the renaissance

Marco Lastri, the author of *L'Osservatore fiorentino* (1776), wrote of how the stones and buildings of which the city was built could only come to

[72] Drake journal MCO MS MC F15 vol. 2, 104.
[73] The responses of British visitors to the collections in the Uffizi are summarised by Jane Whitehead, 'British visitors to the Uffizi, 1650–1789', in Paola Barocchi and Giovanna Ragionieri (eds.), *Gli Uffizi: quattro secoli di una galleria* (Florence, 1983), 287–307.
[74] See, for example, Giuseppe Bianchi, *Ragguaglio delle antichità e rarità che si conservano nella Galleria Mediceo-Imperiale di Firenze* (Florence, 1759).
[75] Many British visitors, particularly those in Italy for educational purposes, took Italian lessons during their stay, but most seem to have been able to read Italian without any difficulty. Anne Miller, for example, directed those of her readers who wished for further information on the collections at the Duke's Galleries to the 'trumpery books' sold at all the booksellers in Florence (Miller, *Letters from Italy*, II, 102).

life if connected to the historical events which gave rise to them and which took place within their walls.[76] The short tourist guides were hardly espousing full-blown Florentine civic republicanism in defiance of Medici absolutism, but the sense of Florentine superiority, civic identity and pride which looked back to the fifteenth-century traditions of civic republicanism was never eliminated.[77] There was a strong tradition of chronicling and history writing, ranging from the fourteenth-century chronicles of Villani to the sixteenth-century histories of Guiccardini and Machiavelli. Eighteenth-century Florentines were deeply conscious of this tradition which also provided the historical basis for the guidebooks. Florentines, like the citizens of any other city, attached considerable importance to the antiquity of their city's foundation, its fortunes under the Romans and decline of the Empire, and the city's resurgence under Charlemagne during 'i tempi bassi'.[78] But Florentine pride in their city's historic antiquity did not impress the British. Most British visitors to Florence were content simply to accept Machiavelli's view that Florence had been founded by a colony of Romans under the triumvirate. The efforts of Florentine antiquaries such as Giovanni Lami or the Academy of Cortona to establish claims for an Etruscan civilization in Florence which preceded that of the Romans were of little concern to most British travellers.[79] Edward Gibbon's interest in the Etruscan antiquities in the ducal collections and his keen admiration for the Florentine antiquaries, Lami and Antonio Francesco Gori, was highly unusual.[80] Other travellers were less than impressed and failed to appreciate the archaeological

[76] Marco Lastri, *L'Osservatore fiorentino sugli edifizi della sua patria per servire alla storia della medesima*, 3 vols. (Florence, 1776), I, 3.

[77] It is noteworthy that most of the Florentine guidebooks were addressed to 'viaggiatori e concittadini' whereas none of the eighteenth-century guidebooks to Rome used such an address or gave any indication that the authors or editors expected the inhabitants of the city to read them.

[78] On the study of history and antiquities in Florence and Tuscany during the eighteenth century see Eric Cochrane, *Tradition and Enlightenment in the Tuscan Academies* (Rome, 1961), 156–205.

[79] Giovanni Lami, *Lezioni di antichità Toscane e spezialmente della città di Firenze recitate nell'accademia della crusca* (Florence, 1766).

[80] Bonnard (ed.), *Gibbon's Journey*, 133, 146, 175–6. The interest of the antiquary and art dealer, James Byres, in Etruscan antiquities should also be noted here; he compiled notes towards a history of the Etruscans: NLS MS Dept 184/4. Thomas Coke's purchase of Thomas Dempster's manuscript history of the Etruscans, later published as *De Etruria regali libri septem* (Florence, 1723–4) had not stimulated any further interest in the Etruscan period amongst British visitors, although it did precipitate further research into Etruscan antiquities amongst a small circle of Florentine antiquaries (M. Cristefani, 'Sugli inizi dell' "Etruscheria": la pubblicazione del *De Etruria regali* di Thomas Dempster', *Mélanges de L'École Française de Rome: Antiquité*, 90 (1978), 577–625).

significance of Etruscan antiquities having no interest in the agenda of Florentine patriotism. Etruscan antiquities were interesting only in so far as they were aesthetic objects: Charles Abbot for one considered that Wedgwood had 'far surpassed all the Urns in this Collection for Elegance of Form'.[81] The British were similarly unmoved by the legend of Charlemagne's role in refounding the city: the story never featured in their accounts.

British visitors also preferred to remain oblivious to the history of the Florentine Republic which was often dismissed simply as a series of revolutions. Important republican structures such as the Piazza della Signoria (the Piazza del Gran Duca as it was then known), the Palazzo Vecchio and its cycle of frescos celebrating the major events of Florentine history (always described in detail by the Florentines) seldom received anything more than a passing comment. When the frescos were mentioned, it was by virtue of having been painted by Vasari, rather than in recognition of the interest of their subject matter. The Palazzo Vecchio itself was almost universally condemned as an ugly gothic building, and its tower, extolled by various Florentine writers as a structure of outstanding beauty, was condemned as the clumsy ineptitude of a rude, uncultivated age.[82] Even John Breval, one of the most sympathetic of English writers on Florence, found it 'bold' but 'somewhat shocking to the Eye, from a Projection, in which the Builder made a Shew of his art at the Expence of his Judgment'.[83] Francis Drake complained that the Ponte Vecchio suffered from a similar 'deformity' as the bridge in Paris and suggested that the houses should be taken down to open up the prospect along the Arno.[84] Forty years later William Forbes compared it to Old London Bridge – which at the time was hardly a commendation.[85] Florence's quaintly picturesque features awaited discovery until the nineteenth century.[86]

The muted interest in Florence's history as a republic is, at first sight, surprising, given the British interest in other republican city states, particularly Venice.[87] But whereas Venice had offered to seventeenth-century commonwealthmen a model of political stability and commercial

[81] Abbot journal TNA PRO 30/9/41, 175.   [82] Anon., *L'Antiquario fiorentino*, 169.
[83] Breval, *Remarks on Several Parts of Europe* (1738 edn), I, 162.
[84] Drake journal MCO MS MC F16 vol. 2, 80.
[85] Forbes journal NLS MS 1540, fol. 274.
[86] See, for example, J. R. Hale (ed.), *The Italian Journal of Samuel Rogers Edited with an Account of Rogers's Life and of Travel in Italy in 1814–1821* (1956), 187.
[87] This attitude contrasts with the widespread interest shown in the history of the Venetian Republic. Gibbon and the Earl of Cork had both planned to write histories of the Florentine Republic. Cork never completed his; Gibbon was distracted by the rather larger task of writing the history of the decline and fall of Rome.

strength, the Florentine Republic could boast no such continuity. Instead, it was a period of factionalism, instability and intrigue that eventually led to subordination under the Medici and the absolute rule of the Grand Dukes of Tuscany. The gradual emasculation of republican freedom through the insidious influence of Medici wealth offered little in the way of politically edifying role models for the eighteenth-century gentleman. Moreover, the Medici propaganda machine, originally set in motion by Lorenzo the Magnificent and perpetuated by authors such as Vasari, ensured that the family's role in art patronage overshadowed that of the republic which they purported to serve. In short, the British were unimpressed by the traditions of republican freedom: the Florentines took great pride in this era of their history, it was said, but the general verdict was that they had allowed themselves to be enslaved by the Medici. Visitors tended to be sternly dismissive of specious arguments that had failed to prevent the Florentine people from sinking into servile submission.[88] Whilst guidebooks claimed that the Florentines were the descendants of the best sorts of Romans, had the noblest spirits and that in the fifteenth century the 'ottimi cittadini' exceeded the senators of Rome in public virtue, British observers found that the modern Florentines had not a 'trace of Roman spirit left in them'.[89]

The mercantile past and the prosperity of the Florentine Republic similarly commanded little notice, particularly when compared with interest in, and awareness of, the rise of the Venetian or the Genoese Republics.[90] Standard works on the history of trade, such as Anderson's *Historical and Chronological Deduction of the Origin of Commerce* (1764), devoted far more attention to the rise of Venice and its commercial might, than to the mercantile prosperity of the Florentine Republic.[91] Given the emphasis on overseas trade in eighteenth-century perceptions of national identity, the fact that Florence was not a maritime city state may have retarded appreciation of the city as a centre of trade and commerce: there was not that automatic sense of common identity that the British felt with Venice or Genoa as sea-going, commercial

---

[88] Duncombe (ed.), *Letters from Italy*, 110.

[89] Raffaello del Bruno, *Ristretto delle cose più notablili della città di Firenze* (5th edn, Florence, 1745), 2–5. Breval pronounced them the most effeminate of Italians, not only because the men played at cards, whilst their wives flirted with other men, but because they had tamely submitted to the Medici's dismantling of republican freedom (*Remarks on Several Parts of Europe* (1738 edn), I, 174).

[90] On perceptions of Venice see Chapter 4. Visitors to Genoa were also generally favourably impressed by the evidence of commercial wealth.

[91] Adam Anderson, *An Historical and Chronological Deduction of the Origin of Commerce, from the Earliest Accounts to the Present Time*, 2 vols. (1764). Florence's role in laying the foundations for the revival of commerce was mentioned briefly, ibid., I, 20.

centres.[92] None of the Florentine guides, of course, offered anything approaching an analysis of the economic history of the city, but they did draw attention to the wealth that 'must have' existed in the city in order to fund the massive building projects of the late thirteenth and fourteenth century. They also highlighted the role of the guilds as patrons of art and sources of funding for the architectural embellishment of the city. None of this had any perceptible influence on British perceptions of Florence. The rise of the Republic and the late thirteenth-century flowering of wealth, when many of the major churches were constructed and when the city clearly assumed its modern form, did not begin to be recognized by British tourists until late in the eighteenth century.

In the last two decades of the century, British perceptions of Florence became less narrowly concerned with the art and antiquities of the Medici. Instead, they began to encompass rather more of the city's history and its specifically urban qualities as a centre of trade and commerce. Interest grew in the city *before* the period of the Medici dukedom, a period when trade and the fine arts had flourished. Part of this is attributable to changes in the social background of those travelling to Italy. Over the course of the century, the profile of visitors, whilst still wealthy, was becoming steadily less aristocratic: by the 1780s, it included many from a commercial or professional background. Indeed, in the last two decades, visitors from gentry, professional and other 'middle-class' backgrounds appear to have outnumbered their aristocratic counterparts.[93] One such was the agricultural writer, Arthur Young, who travelled to Italy in 1789. Young was not a typical tourist, of course. He was in search of economic information rather than *virtù* (although that did not mean that he was immune to the charms of the *Venus de Medici*, which he described in glowing terms at some length). It did mean, however, that he took a notably more informed interest in the state of the economy, and in particular that of Tuscany, which had seen significant improvements under the rule of Leopold. He noted that income from land was now far more important than that derived from trade, and that the major source of employment was domestic service, rather than manufactures. But he was also acutely aware of the former importance of trade for Florence as the basis of her splendour and magnificence. Young drew an explicit connection

---

[92] Charles Philpot, *An Introduction to the Literary History of the Fourteenth and Fifteenth Centuries* (1798), did not mention Florence in the context of his analysis of the relationship between the rise of commerce and the arts, although he did refer to the role played by Venice and Genoa.

[93] Towner, 'Grand Tour', 310.

between the grandeur of the palazzi and the churches and the flourishing state of the Florentine economy from the fourteenth and fifteenth centuries. Rather than simply alluding to the Palazzo Pitti, for example, as yet another sign of Medici splendour or as the palace of a nobleman, which was the conventional description, he pointed out that the Pitti, and all the other palaces, had been built by private merchants, and marvelled at the wealth that must have sustained such conspicuous display. Merchants in London, he observed, might make a yearly profit of £20,000–30,000, but they just lived in brick cottages with a few daubed portraits and earthenware figures on their chimney pieces: they were, he admitted, contemptible in comparison.[94] James Edward Smith, the son of a Unitarian wool merchant, was similarly impressed by the scale of the private mercantile wealth which lay behind the construction of the palazzi.[95] The comments of other tourists offered comparable shifts in emphasis, so that buildings such as the Palazzo Strozzi or Palazzo Riccardo Medici were being described as a merchant's, rather than a nobleman's, house in the 1790s.[96] Similarly, increasing emphasis was being placed upon the Medici's origins in trade and physic, before the family had enriched itself by banking and assumed the role of princes.[97] Such observations were no doubt influenced by contemporary discussion of the relationship between wealth and virtue which had been encouraged under the auspices of Leopold, but as visitors contemplated the civilisation of republican Florence and the contribution of private individuals in sustaining that culture, the conclusions to be drawn were obvious.[98] Taste, genius, literature and the arts fled Rome, to reappear in the Florentine and other Italian Republics, and thence they passed to Holland. Their present sole abode, as Charlotte Eaton was to claim a few years later, was England.[99]

The burgeoning interest in the history of Florence before the *cinquecento* was to some extent part of a much more general interest in the middle ages as a period of historical inquiry which was characteristic

---

[94] Young, *Travels during the Years*, 244–6, 274.
[95] Smith, *Sketch of a Tour*, I, 310.   [96] Young, *Travels during the Years*, 242.
[97] Charles Abbot observed that 'To Understand Florence it is Necessary to recollect that Sylvester de Medicis an Opulent Trader of Florence and who Rose to be Gonfaloniera of the Republick was the Father of Como the Great, some times called Como the Elder.' Abbot journal TNA PRO 30/9/41, 163. See also Francis Garden Lord Gardenstone, *Travelling Memorandums, Made in a Tour upon the Continent of Europe in the Years 1786, 87 and 88*, 3 vols. (Edinburgh, 1791), III, 14: 'The family of the Medicis were originally great interprising [sic] merchants in the Republic of Florence.'
[98] Wahnbaeck, *Luxury and Public Happiness*, 73–135.
[99] Eaton, *Rome in the Nineteenth Century*, I, 27. See also Sydney Morgan, *Italy*, 2 vols. (1821), I, 9–14.

of the later eighteenth century.[100] In his introductory essay to his *History of the Reign of the Emperor Charles V* (1769) William Robertson showed how, in the centuries following end of the Crusades, feudalism was eroded, a spirit of industry revived and commerce began to flourish; towns, and particularly the Italian cities, grew in population, wealth and prosperity.[101] Robertson described Florence as a 'commercial democracy' with institutions particularly favourable to commerce; its magnificence, sponsored by the Medici, had come about through trade.[102] The middle ages were conclusively identified as a crucial stage in the development of modern European society, in the progress towards civilisation, and in the emergence of the nation state. In all these transformations, the Italian city states had a very particular role to play, and amongst British travellers, it was Florence where these historiographical developments had the clearest influence.[103]

Of more particular concern here, however, was the re-evaluation of the period's art and literature and a recognition of its inherent interest as an era of singular cultural development and achievement. Symptomatic of these changing attitudes was William Roscoe's best seller *The Life of Lorenzo de' Medici*, first published in 1795, which in itself was responsible for enthusing a whole generation of British travellers with admiration for the achievement of Lorenzo de' Medici and Florence.[104] The influence of Roscoe's volume may have been overrated, but it was certainly representative of changing cultural values amongst those who travelled to Italy. Roscoe was dazzled by the character and style of *il Magnifico*, but he also contributed to, and helped to reify, a perceptual

---

[100] On the historiographical developments in this period, see Karen O'Brien, *Narratives of Enlightenment. Cosmopolitan History from Voltaire to Gibbon* (Cambridge, 1997), and J. G. A. Pocock, *Barbarism and Religion, vol. II: Narratives of Civil Government* (Cambridge, 1999).

[101] William Robertson, *The History of the Reign of the Emperor Charles V: With a View of the Progress of Society in Europe, from the Subversion of the Roman Empire to the Beginning of the Sixteenth Century*, 3 vols. (1769), I, 36.

[102] Ibid., I, 135.

[103] William Forbes observed that 'Every reader of History knows that during that period of darkness & confusion, known by the name of the Middle Ages, the Chief Cities of Italy, particularly in Lombardy & Tuscany, taking advantage of the times, became independent States of Italy.' Forbes journal NLS MS 1540, fol. 284.

[104] William Roscoe's, *The Life of Lorenzo de' Medici, Called the Magnificent*, 2 vols. (Liverpool, 1795) had been translated into Italian, German and French by 1799 and reached its tenth edition in English by 1851. In his recommendations for preparatory reading John Chetwode Eustace assumed that his readers would already be familiar with Roscoe's volumes on both Lorenzo and Leo X: 'they have long since attracted the attention of every candid and reflecting mind'. *Classical Tour*, I, xxiii. William Forbes copied long passages from Roscoe's *Life of Lorenzo de Medici* into his own account of Florence: Forbes journal NLS MS 1540, fols. 286–91.

shift in the image of Florence, away from the Medici dukes to the Medici bankers of the fifteenth-century republic: a republic with a flourishing cultural life based upon wealth derived from manufactures and commerce.[105] Roscoe did not himself draw direct comparisons between Florence and Liverpool, although he was one of the prime movers in attempting to develop the artistic and cultural reputation of his native city. But the parallels were there to be drawn in the nineteenth century.[106]

Abolitionism aside, William Roscoe is also notable for having shown a precocious taste in the collection of Italian primitives; an interest which stemmed not so much from an aesthetic appreciation of their distinctive qualities as from an ambition to illustrate the rise and progress of the arts.[107] Not that he was the first to show this kind of interest: in the last three decades of the eighteenth century, a number of connoisseurs were beginning to direct attention towards the historical evolution of painting from the first 'revival' to what they perceived as the perfection of the cinquecento, and were building up collections accordingly.[108] This new direction in interest can be seen in part as a response to Winckelmann's historical analysis of the stylistic development of Greek art: its rise

---

[105] See, for example, James Barry, *A Letter to the Dilettanti Society, Respecting the Obtention of Certain Matters Essentially Necessary for the Improvement of Public Taste* (1798), 28: 'Looking back, for a moment, upon this early progressional state of things, once cannot help remarking . . . that the whole entire growth of art is peculiarly and exclusively to be ascribed to the laborious, generous, successful culture of the citizens of the little Republic of Florence.' This new appreciation of Florence's republican past was not exclusive to the British; it was also present in Mme de Staël's *Corinne* (1807), for example, where the eponymous heroine exclaims that the 'fine arts in Florence are still very republican'. The influence of de Staël's friend Sismondi on the novel is evident. *Corinne, or Italy*, transl. Sylvia Raphael (Oxford, 1998), 354. On de Staël's medievalism see Barbara G. Keller, *The Middle Ages Reconsidered: Attitudes in France from the Eighteenth Century through the Romantic Movement* (New York, 1994).

[106] For an overview of Florentine influence upon urban culture in British cities of the nineteenth century, see Tristram Hunt, *Building Jerusalem: The Rise and Fall of the Victorian City* (2005), 205–26. See also Arline Wilson, ' "The Florence of the north"? The civic culture of Liverpool in the early nineteenth century', in Alan J. Kidd and David Nicholls (eds.), *Gender, Civic Culture and Consumerism: Middle-Class Identity in Britain, 1800–1940* (Manchester, 1999), 34–46.

[107] Roscoe, *Life of Lorenzo de' Medici*, II, 175–227, offered a detailed discussion of the artists of the *trecento* and *quattrocento* (largely drawn from Vasari), presenting them in a more positive light than had traditionally been the case.

[108] These included Thomas Patch, author of *The Life of Masaccio* (Florence, 1772); Ignazio Hugford (see John Fleming, 'The Hugfords of Florence (Part II): with a provisional catalogue of the collection of Ignazio Enrico Hugford', *Connoisseur*, 136 (1955), 197–206); Charles Townley; George Ashburnham, Viscount St Asaph; and the Earl of Bristol (see Ingamells (ed.), *Dictionary of British and Irish Travellers*, 946–8, 834–5, 126–30, for biographical details) and William Young Ottley (see Brigstocke, Marchant and Wright, *John Flaxman and William Young Ottley*, 353).

to perfection and subsequent decline.[109] There were also parallels with the antiquarian movement within Great Britain, with its interest in the developments of gothic art and architecture, which had likewise been regarded by the majority as rude and barbaric.[110] This shift in attitude was complemented and encouraged by renewed efforts on the part of Florentines to assert the importance of Florence in the historical development of the arts. In 1775, for example, Leopold had a room in his gallery hung with specimens of the first restorers of art arranged in chronological order: the *Gabinetto de Antichi Quadri*. As successive editions of the Florentine guides became more and more detailed, one of the areas where additional information was most likely to be found was on the early renaissance paintings and the central role played by Florence in the revival of arts and learning. Civic patriotism, which was beginning to blossom once more under the benign authority of Leopold, drew strength from the traditions of Florence's artistic heritage in the centuries before the establishment of the Medici dukedom.[111]

These changes are visible too in the comments of travellers in the later eighteenth and early nineteenth centuries. The *Gabinetto de Antichi Quadri* was often remarked upon as an illustration of the revival of the arts, even if the paintings themselves found little favour.[112] Greater interest was shown in the precursors to Michelangelo and Leonardo da Vinci, such as Uccello, Ghirlandaio, Lippi and Botticelli. Qualities were recognised that had been invisible to previous generations of tourists: the Masaccio frescos in the Brancacci chapel at Sta Maria del Carmine, for example, began to feature more regularly in visitors' comments – due not least to the fact that Reynolds had highlighted their influence upon Michelangelo in his *Discourses*.[113]

---

[109] J. J. Winckelmann, *Reflections on the Painting and Sculpture of the Greeks*, trans. Henry Fuseli (1765).

[110] Sweet, *Antiquaries*, 238–76.

[111] This trend had become even more pronounced by the early nineteenth century: see, for example, L. F. M. Gargiolli, *Description de la ville de Florence et de ses environs précedée d'un abrége d'histoire Florentine*, 2 vols. (Florence, 1819). See also L. Lanzi, *Storia pittorica della Italia* (Florence, 1809). An English translation of the latter, by Thomas Roscoe, *The History of Painting in Italy*, appeared in 1828.

[112] Smith, *Sketch of a Tour*, I, 296; Eustace, *Classical Tour*, II, 199; Forsyth, *Remarks on Antiquities*, 39–40. Abbot journal TNA PRO 30/9/41, 182.

[113] It is likely that it was Thomas Patch who drew Reynolds' attention to the Masaccio frescos in the Brancacci chapel at Sta Maria del Carmine when Reynolds was in Florence in the 1750s. Reynolds singled the frescos out for particular praise and noted their influence on Michelangelo in his twelfth discourse on art delivered to the Royal Academy in 1784 and published in 1785. Thereafter a visit to the Brancacci chapel became a regular feature of the tourist itinerary, although prior to the 1780s it was rarely noted: not even Richardson had mentioned the frescos. Very few British observers, however, noted that the cycle of frescos was not the work of Masaccio alone, but a joint effort with Masolino, as Anon., *L'Antiquario fiorentino*, 218, pointed out.

They prompted Robert Finch to observe that Masaccio had made rapid steps towards carrying the art of painting to perfection.[114] In Rome, Finch would also seek out Masaccio's fresco cycle of the life of St Catherine in San Clemente, commenting that 'the drawing and the air of the heads is admirable'. But his observations on these, and other examples of *quattrocento* art in Rome, made no reference to their value as evidence of the revival of the arts: this was a narrative that was still exclusive to Florence.[115] Ghiberti's bronze doors had long been objects of note – and admiration – largely due to the fact that, thanks to Vasari, Michelangelo was known to have admired them as the gates of Paradise. But Ghiberti's name was seldom mentioned, let alone the period in which he lived. By the early nineteenth century, however, the doors and their creator were no longer detached from their context; rather, they were pointed out as proof of the fact that in Florence the arts had flourished, even during a period when Europe was supposed still to have been lingering in a dark period of ignorance and barbarism.[116]

Architectural observation of late medieval and early renaissance architecture likewise became more perceptive and acute. This is not to say that there was a rejection of the aesthetics of classicism, but tourists became somewhat more discriminating in their vocabulary of architectural description, more attentive in their description and more precise with regard to dates, architects and patrons. The study of architecture and its historical development had become increasingly sophisticated over the eighteenth century (as we shall explore more fully in Chapter 6) and travellers were more likely to be familiar with not just the language of classicism, but a familiarity with the elements of the gothic style.[117] Sir Richard Colt Hoare, visiting Florence in 1789, delighted in the 'simplicity and grandeur' of the gothic architecture and the slender arches which were 'so far asunder that they appear scarce strong enough to support their weight'.[118] Robert Finch was less appreciative of the aesthetic qualities of the duomo, describing it as awkward, squat and clumsy, but nevertheless devoted considerably more attention to describing the component parts of the building and identifying the different styles in which it had been built than had any of his eighteenth-century predecessors. Moreover, visitors

---

[114] Finch journal Bodl. MS Finch e. 15, fol. 30r.
[115] Finch journal Bodl. MS Finch e. 15, fol. 157v.   [116] Eustace, *Classical Tour*, II, 190.
[117] On the mediation and popularisation of knowledge of gothic architecture and antiquities in this period, see Sweet, *Antiquaries*, 309–43.
[118] Sir Richard Colt Hoare, 'Notes on paintings', CUL Add. MS 4155, fol. 82.

began explicitly to associate a particular style of architecture with the republican period, rather than merely as undistinguished specimens of an unenlightened age.[119] Henry Coxe described the Palazzo Vecchio as 'massive' and 'melancholy', but noted that it had been built at the end of the thirteenth century 'as a centre of republican dignity'; and although he found the black bricks of Sta Croce unattractive, he insisted that it was worthy of notice, having been built by the famous architect of the Florentine Republic, Arnolfino.[120] The private dwellings of the Medici and the Strozzi, claimed Sydney Morgan, were 'strong testimonies of the superiority of civilization in Italy in the middle ages, over that of the ancients'.[121] The contemporary Florentine interest in their own republican past was clearly a factor here, but it is also important to remember that at this time the British reading public – precisely the sorts of people who could afford to go to Italy – were becoming much better informed about the gothic style of architecture, its historical evolution and the debates over its origins because of its importance for their own national past.[122]

This interest in the art and architecture of the middle ages – the term 'renaissance' was not yet in usage – was also manifest in a more informed interest in Florence's claims to be the cradle of the revival of literature as well as painting, sculpture and architecture. Florentine pride in the city's literary heritage had always been closely linked to the origins of the artistic revival through the friendship between Dante and Giotto made famous in Vasari's *Lives of the Artists*. But amongst British travellers, interest in Dante had been muted to say the least. Of those who had read Dante's verse there were many who could not overcome their aversion to what they perceived as his barbarism and impropriety.[123] Interest in Dante, and also Boccaccio, was largely antiquarian: one author of a guide to Italy published in 1766 thought it necessary to explain to his readers that Dante was an 'old poet' considered as the 'Ennius, or Chaucer' of Florence.[124] Petrarch, by contrast, had always commanded more respect due to his efforts to revive classical antiquity, his composition of Latin verse and his invention of the Petrarchan

[119] Joseph Trapp's English translation of Archenholz's *A Picture of Italy Translated from the Original German of W. De Archenholz*, 2 vols. (1791), 159, described the duomo as a 'worthy monument of republican splendour'.

[120] Coxe, *Picture of Italy*, 381.   [121] Morgan, *Italy*, II, 44.   [122] See Chapter 6.

[123] Oliver Goldsmith, *Enquiry into the Present State of Polite Learning* (1759), described Dante as little better than a barbarian who 'addressed a barbarous people in a method suited to their apprehensions' (cited by Paget Toynbee, *Dante in English Literature from Chaucer to Cary c. 1380–1844*, 2 vols. (1909), I, xxxii). See also Marshall, *Italy in English Literature*.

[124] Northall, *Travels through Italy*, 87.

sonnet.[125] Yet, around mid-century, interest in Dante and his near contemporaries began to revive, with a noticeable quickening amongst the broader reading public from the 1780s.[126] The poetry of Dante, in particular, was made more accessible through translation and given greater immediacy through texts such as Thomas Warton's *History of English Poetry* (1774–81), which discussed Dante's influence on English poets from Chaucer to Milton.[127] Dante's poetic debt to the troubadours of Provence meant that he could be rediscovered as a poet of the age of chivalry and as such, an enthusiasm for Dante was part of the more general European discovery of the chivalry and romance of the middle ages. The poet's sublimated love for Beatrice, and also that of Petrarch for Laura, particularly appealed to the widely held view of the middle ages as a period of chivalry, gallantry and courtly love.[128] In 1778, Philip Yorke was eager to tell his uncle that his Italian master, Abbé Pellori, had set him on reading the *Inferno*, well aware that this was a demanding and unusual text to study. A year later, Sir James Hall was searching out 'Simon Sanese's' portrait of Petrach's Laura at Sta Maria Novella.[129] It was not until 1782 that the first full English translation of the *Inferno* was published, to be followed by another in 1785 by Henry Boyd, who thereafter produced the first complete translation of the *Divine Comedy* in 1802. These translations were discussed and reviewed in literary periodicals and journals such as the *Monthly Review* and the *Annual Register*. Consequently, more travellers were at least familiar with the tenor of the *Divine Comedy* and the broad outlines of its narrative, even if they were hardly Dante scholars. This much is apparent in the comments of visitors and in the tour guides themselves – references to set pieces from the *Inferno* such as the

---

[125] Petrarch was more widely read in the early eighteenth century, but there was similarly a quickening of interest in the last third of the century. See, for example, Susannah Dobson's translation of J. de Sade's *The Life of Petrarch*, 2 vols. (1776).

[126] Thomas Penrose, *A Sketch of the Lives and Writings of Dante and Petrarch* (1790).

[127] The development of interest in Dante and his influence upon English literature was surveyed by Toynbee, *Dante in English Literature*. See also V. Tinkler-Villani, 'Translation as a metaphor for salvation: eighteenth-century English versions of Dante's *Commedia*'', *Journal of Anglo-Italian Studies*, 1 (1991), 92–101.

[128] Richard Hurd, *Letters on Chivalry and Romance* (1762); J-B. de la Curne de Sainte-Palaye, *Mémoires de l'ancienne chivalerie* (Paris, 1779) and *Histoire des troubadours* (Paris, 1784), both of which were later translated into English by Susannah Dobson. On Curne de Sainte-Palaye, see Lionel Gossman, *Medievalism and the Ideologies of the Enlightenment: The World and Work of La Curne de Sainte-Palaye* (Baltimore, 1968). For a recent overview of the influence of medievalism on English literature, see Michael Alexander, *Medievalism: The Middle Ages in Modern England* (New Haven and London, 2007).

[129] Yorke to his uncle, 22 Sept. 1778, BL Add. MS 35378, fol. 241; Hall journal NLS MS 6326, fol. 187.

story of the doomed love affair of Paolo and Francesca, as well as the macabre horror of Count Ugolino's cannibalism (made yet more famous by Reynolds' painting exhibited in 1773) become increasingly common. Dante's portrait in the duomo was pointed out with greater frequency; and the white stone where he used to sit in the Piazza del Duomo became a site of reflection and veneration.[130]

Conclusion

In 1819, the poet Samuel Rogers travelled from Florence to Rome: it was both a physical and historical journey, and one which took him from the world of Lorenzo de' Medici to that of antiquity. Rogers, like so many other early nineteenth-century travellers to Italy, was familiar with Roscoe's idealisation of Medicean Florence: a city where a spirit of industry, the pursuit of wealth and the extension of commerce were fully compatible with the cultivation of literature, the arts and philosophy; where the favourable effects of freedom had strengthened the mind and allowed the arts to flourish.[131] The Florentine history of internal dissentions, far from being evidence of fatal factionalism which would open the way for Medici tyranny, was now presented rather as the active spirit of liberty.[132] Roscoe's evocation clearly influenced Rogers' own perceptions as the latter observed: 'at Florence we thought only of Modern Italy & of its golden age – As we approach Rome, Antient Italy rushes on the Imagination. Italy has had two lives! Can it be said of any other Country?'[133] This reference to Italy's 'two lives' recognized the fifteenth century, and its physical embodiment in the city of Florence, not as a pale shadow of antique grandeur, but as a vibrant, dynamic and creative era which could command admiration and inspire emulation in its own right. The priorities of the Italian tour were being transformed: for those whose interests lay in the middle ages, 'Florence becomes all that Rome is to the classic tourist'.[134] The subsequent Victorian idealisation of Florence and the civilisation of the Florentine Republic was already being anticipated in the early nineteenth century.[135] This sense of special

---

[130] Forsyth, *Remarks on Antiquities*, 65; Starke, *Letters from Italy* (1880 edn), I, 268; Coxe, *Picture of Italy*, 384; Finch journal Bodl. MS Finch e. 15, fol. 53r.

[131] Roscoe, *Life of Lorenzo de' Medici*, I, 5–6. On Roscoe, see Donald A. Macnaughton, *Roscoe of Liverpool: His Life, Writings and Treasures 1753–1831* (Birkenhead, 1996), and Bullen, *Myth of the Renaissance*, 40–52. The most recent study is Arline Wilson's biography, *William Roscoe: Commerce and Culture* (Liverpool, 2008).

[132] Roscoe, *Life of Lorenzo de' Medici*, I, 1.

[133] Hale (ed.), *Italian Journal*, 206.   [134] Morgan, *Italy*, II, 142.

[135] Bernd Roeck, *Florence 1900: The Quest for Arcadia*, trans. Stuart Spencer (New Haven and London, 2009).

affinity with Florence, to which commercial and manufacturing cities such as Liverpool or Manchester would later make claim through their architecture and their cultural ambition, was a distinctive nineteenth-century phenomenon, but one which can only be understood fully in terms of the particular admiration and favour with which Florence was regarded in the eighteenth century.

Perceptions of Florence underwent a significant re-orientation during the long eighteenth century. The reasons behind these change are not easily disentangled although this chapter has suggested some key factors. The changing composition of the travelling public, itself reflective of the growing prosperity and increasing cultural ambition of those beneath the landed elite, allowed for the articulation of rather different questions and a shift in perspective towards the achievements of Florence's commercial past. British confidence in the mutually beneficial relationship of liberty, trade and commerce, however, predisposed some to see in Florence the anticipation of the cultivated prosperity of their own country. When Henry Boyd, a clergyman, wrote the introduction to his translation of the *Inferno*, he offered a riposte to Edward Gibbon, arguing that, rather than being destructive of the arts and learning, the religious disputes between the Holy Roman Empire and the papacy in the middle ages had liberated minds and led to a revival of learning. But Boyd also placed considerable emphasis upon the Florentine Republic as an oasis of liberty; on its prosperity which had arisen from trade; and how this, in turn, had provided the conditions in which the arts could flourish.[136] Florence was also the beneficiary of the European-wide interest in establishing the progressive refinement of the arts from their 'rediscovery' in the fourteenth century, which steadily developed in the second half of the century. The growth of interest in the 'middle ages' amongst the British will be explored more fully in Chapter 6, but Florence's importance as the cradle of the 'renaissance', was not the sole discovery of the British. Indeed, their understanding of this period of Florence's history was heavily dependent on Italian and French authorities. But the re-orientation of European culture towards the early renaissance as a formative period in the renewal of European civilisation ensured that the Florence of Dante, Giotto and Petrarch assumed much greater significance for both the British travelling public as well as for those who represented the city to them as guides or hosts. The point of continuity was that Florence occupied a special place in the affections of the British and was a city with which they felt a strong sense of

---

[136] Henry Boyd, *A Translation of the Inferno of Dante Alighieri, in English Verse* (1785), 118–48.

compatibility, even identity. But the specific reasons why it was found so 'cheering to the English eye' were not immutable, rather, they evolved as the priorities of the travellers themselves shifted and were reconfigured to match the interests of an increasingly bourgeois travelling public.[137]

---

[137] On the British relationship with Florence in the 1820s see O'Connor, *Romance of Italy*, 37, 51–2. The special affinity she identifies, however, was a continuation of eighteenth-century patterns, rather than a distinctively new configuration in Anglo-Florentine relations.

3   Rome ancient and modern

Navigating Rome

Most travellers approached Rome with intense anticipation, recording the first glimpse of the gleaming dome of St Peter's with exultant delight: John and Ann Flaxman sang 'Huzza' and 'welcomed themselves to the Mistress of the world'.[1] Others claimed nights of sleepless excitement as they approached the longed-for destination.[2] The Flaxmans, like most visitors, arrived from the north, along the Via Flaminia, entering through the imposing Porta Flaminia (as it was then called). The wide expanse of the Piazza del Popolo, dramatically reshaped for Alexander VII, opened up before the new arrivals and invariably made a positive first impression – as it was intended to do (see Figure 5).[3] It was, as one traveller remarked, 'prodigiously striking'.[4] The visitor encountered a vast open space, flanked by two identical domed churches, from which three long, straight roads, the *tridente*, radiated out into the city of Rome, each one lined with grand and imposing palazzi. In the centre of the piazza was the obelisk, engraved with hieroglyphs, which Sixtus V had had erected in 1589. Viewed from the Corso, it gave the extraordinary impression of standing over the middle of the gate, with the 'sweep of the arch for its basis'.[5] The impact was unequivocal – there were no public spaces even in London that could match this kind of grandeur: 'It must be confessed', explained Blainville to his readers, 'that on entering *Rome* by this Gate, the Prospect which presents itself, gives a very high Idea of the City.'[6]

---

[1] Flaxman journal BL Add. MS 39787, fol. 38.
[2] Lemaistre, *Travels after the Peace of Amiens*, I, 357.
[3] Dorothy Habel, *The Urban Development of Rome in the Age of Alexander VII* (Cambridge, 2002), 63–95; Richard Krautheimer, *The Rome of Alexander VII, 1655–1667* (Princeton, 1985).
[4] Gray to his mother, 2 Apr. 1740, in William Mason (ed.), *The Works of Thomas Gray*, 2 vols. (3rd edn, 1807), I, 229.
[5] John Breval, *Remarks on Several Parts of Europe Relating Chiefly to the History, Antiquities and Geography of those Countries*, 2 vols. (1726), II, 242.
[6] Henry de Blainville, *Travels through Holland, Germany, Switzerland and Other Parts of Europe; but Especially Italy*, 3 vols. (1767), II, 452.

Figure 5 'Veduta della Piazza del Popolo', from Giovanni Battista Piranesi, *Vedute di Roma*, 2 vols. (Rome, n.d.).

For those who had failed to invest in the necessary passports, *lascia passare*, or who baulked at bribing the officials, the first stop was the customs house in the Piazza di Pietra. This building, converted by Carlo Fontana in the seventeenth century from the Temple of Hadrian, offered them their first example of a Roman structure adapted to modern use. Yet, despite the impressive façade of eleven 15 metre Corinthian columns, it rarely excited much comment from British travellers: its prosaic and (for visitors) irritating modern function overshadowed its claims to antique grandeur. It never became an iconic set piece on the tourist itinerary.[7] In addition to the customs officials searching one's luggage and demanding bribes, unemployed *valets de place* and touts for accommodation loitered around the customs house, attaching themselves to new arrivals who knew no better.[8] The customs house was the point at which exploration of the city began. Travellers were not recommended to resort to such *ad hoc* arrangements, however, and were strongly advised to make arrangements beforehand. For Rome was a city which demanded a guide. The sheer extent of the ancient city (and the amount that had been written about it) was in itself intimidating: the city walls' circumference, regularly measured by visiting British, extended for around fifteen miles. Beyond the inhabited area of the modern city were the vast expanses of the *disabatio*, where gardens, vineyards, grazing and wasteland were littered with ruins. There was much that was illegible or unrecognisable, which required the expertise of the *cicerone* or antiquary to give it meaning.

Discrimination rather than comprehensiveness was therefore the key in viewing the city. Rome could not be explored as an unknown quantity, waiting to be discovered: it was viewed, as we shall see, as the exemplification of knowledge, attained through preparatory reading and through the knowledge disseminated by the expert guide. Thus, employing one of the established *ciceroni* or an 'antiquarian' was both a practical measure and a statement of one's seriousness as a student of antiquities and correct taste. The young Roger Robertson, ever conscious of the need to use his father's money responsibly, explained that he had hoped to save himself the expense of an antiquarian, 'but upon mature consideration realised it was necessary to employ one to see the best things and most efficiently'.[9]

---

[7] Ann Flaxman referred to it as the ancient basilica of Antoninus Pius and noted the eleven Corinthian columns, but this was a rare observation: Flaxman journal BL Add. MS 39787, fol. 38v. Jane Waldie saw the reuse of the building as a customs house as yet another instance of the Romans' cavalier disregard for their heritage, *Sketches Descriptive of Italy*, I, 324.

[8] Smith, *Sketch of a Tour*, I, 340.

[9] Robertson to his father, 29 Dec. 1751, NLS Acc 12244.

Similarly, Sir William Forbes found himself 'confused and bewildered' by the multiplicity of objects to be seen in Rome, despite his diligent study of the guidebooks. He availed himself, therefore, of the services of the antiquary Patrick Moir for six weeks. Forbes's reasoning was that it saved him time and, more importantly, enabled him to learn a 'proper discrimination' of what was regarded as of 'superior value' and what 'may be only very well to take notice of'.[10] Thomas Jones, by contrast, who travelled to Italy as an artist rather than to 'make the tour' as a gentleman, was unable to afford such a guide, but his experience of wasting time in 'wearisome and unsatisfactory perambulations' confirms both the extent to which the British depended on being *shown* the city and the significance of employing an antiquary as an expression of wealth.[11] The gratuity for a 'course' of antiquities (which would also comprise the collections of antiquities and paintings in the modern city) with a guide such as James Byres or Colin Morison was said to be twenty sequins (the equivalent of around £10).[12] Sarah Bentham paid her guide six sequins a month – as much as the cost of her accommodation, whilst Thomas Pelham paid his antiquary £20 for a two-month course.[13] But one had also to exercise discrimination in the choice of antiquary: as many travellers warned their readers, it was pointless to waste money on such antiquaries as could only repeat what might be learnt from a book. Stories of the deceitful and greedy Italian *abbati* who fleeced their clients and gorged themselves at their employers' expense abounded in some of the more Italophobic travel literature.[14] Philip Francis claimed to have 'been taken possession of' by the Roman abbé whose services he had retained. This individual dragged him and his travelling companion 'like tame bears' to see the Capitol, and even turned up to breakfast at nine in the morning in the pouring rain when an antiquarian excursion

---

[10] Forbes journal NLS MS 1543, fol. 155.

[11] Oppé (ed.), *Memoirs of Thomas Jones of Penkerrig*, 53.

[12] William Patoun, 'Advice on travel in Italy', in John Ingamells (ed.), *A Dictionary of British and Irish Travellers in Italy, 1701–1800* (New Haven and London, 1997), xlv.

[13] Bentham journal TNA PRO 30/9/43, 216, and Thomas Pelham to his father, 23 Aug. 1777, BL Add. MS 33127, fol. 300. On the careers of James Byres and Thomas Jenkins, see Brinsley Ford, 'James Byres: principal antiquarian for the English visitors to Rome', *Apollo*, 99 (1974), 46–61; Brinsley Ford, 'Thomas Jenkins: banker, dealer and unofficial English agent', *Apollo*, 99 (1974), 416–25; and Ilaria Bignamini and Clare Hornsby, *Digging and Dealing in Eighteenth-Century Rome*, 2 vols. (New Haven and London, 2010), I, 209–21, 246–8.

[14] Abbati, or abbés, could be in clerical orders (regular or secular) or laymen, who dressed in clerical garb as part of their work. Visitors frequently commented on the custom amongst Roman men to adopt the sober black dress of the clerical profession, regardless of whether they were ordained or not, and tended to use the terms abbate and abbé somewhat indiscriminately.

was out of the question. 'For cool deliberate Impudence', he wrote, 'commend me to a Roman Abbé.'[15] A more economical strategy was to rely on the *valet de place* to guide one around: this would cost only three to four pauls a day for the valet's hire, plus the price of a guidebook. Dispensing with the services of an antiquary altogether, was nevertheless clearly an economy measure as well as a statement of independence.

It was an economy measure, however, that became common in the latter part of the century as the numbers of travellers coming to Italy with more limited means at their disposal grew. The guides published in Rome, such as those by Vasi, Magnan, Venuti and Manazzale, that divided the city up into *giornate* of sightseeing, with detailed information on what to view for each subsection, grew in popularity with English speaking visitors who were increasingly disinclined to subject themselves to the opinions and expense of a *cicerone*.[16] William Patoun recommended that Lord Brownlow should prepare for each day's tuition with his antiquary by reading the relevant chapter of Venuti's *Antichità di Roma* the night before.[17] But Anne Miller favoured the same volume as it enabled her and her husband to plan an itinerary without depending on an antiquary: 'by following his directions', she explained, 'it is easy to calculate how much may be seen in a morning'.[18] There was no question of placing themselves in the hands of a *cicerone* here. Similarly, 'Magnani's [sic] guide', claimed James Edward Smith, 'easily directed' him and his companions to any object that they wished to see and they were 'soon as much at home as in London': indeed, the text was

---

[15] Francis journal BL Add. MS 40759, fol. 16v; Italian guides, claimed George Ayscough, were a duplicitous and scrounging 'set of scurvy abbatis', who gorged themselves at their employers' table and took them to all sorts of spurious antiquities in order to prolong their employment. George Ayscough, *Letters from an Officer in the Guards to his Friend in England* (1778), 164. Lord Herbert made a similar complaint, telling his father that he hoped to see Rome 'without loosing [sic] my time at trifling objects, which would neither instruct or amuse me, but which Antiquarians always carry People to for the sake of prolonging the time'. Herbert (ed.), *Henry, Elizabeth and George*, 262. On *abbati* in Rome, see Susan Vandiver Nicassio, *Imperial City: Rome under Napoleon* (Chicago, 2005), 67–70.

[16] Giuseppe Vasi, *Itinerario istruttivo diviso in otto stazioni o giornate per ritrovare con facilità tutte le antiche e moderne magnificenze di Roma* (Rome, 1763); Ridolfino Venuti, *Accurata, e succinta descrizione topografica delle antichità di Roma dell'Abate Ridolfino Venuti Cortonese*, 2 vols. (Rome, 1763); Dominique Magnan, *La ville de Rome ou description abrégée de cette superbe ville*, 4 vols. (Rome, 1778); André Manazzale, *Rome et ses environs*, 2 vols. (Rome, 1798); André Manazzale, *Itinéraire instructif de Rome et de ses environs*, 2 vols. (Rome, 1802); A. Dalmazzoni, *The Antiquarian or the Guide for Foreigners to go the Rounds of the Antiquities of Rome* (Rome, 1803). For full bibliographical details and the different editions, see Ludwig Schudt, *Le guide di Roma: Materialen zu einer Geschichte der Römischen Topographie* (Vienna, 1930).

[17] Patoun, 'Advice on travel in Italy', xlv.   [18] Miller, *Letters from Italy*, II, 390.

explicitly designed to enable the tourist to find his or her way about the city without additional guidance.[19] In many cases travellers purchased the Italian editions of these guidebooks: Tobias Smollett got by with a *valet de place* and copies of Vasi and Venuti whilst the Flaxmans happily found their way round Rome in 1781 with only an edition of Vasi to guide them.[20] Those who could not read Italian could choose the French guides by Magnan or Manazzale and latterly English translations of Vasi or Angelo Dalmazzoni.[21] Joseph Forsyth, who was in Rome in 1802, asserted his superiority over the common run of tourists who depended on such volumes by declaring Vasi and Manazzale to be superficial and incoherent, suitable only for the visitor with little time to spend. Rather, like Anne Miller, he recommended Venuti, who, he explained, had 'sifted this farrago' of previous antiquarian scholarship and ground it down into a 'clean and digestible a mass' which would provide a properly informative guide to the city.[22] But Forsyth himself received his comeuppance in Byron's contemptuous dismissal of English tourists in 1823: 'the second-hand Society of half-pay economists – no pay dandies – separated wives, unseparated *not* wives – the Starke – or Invalid – or Forsyth – or Eustace or Hobhouse travellers – as they are called according to their Manual'.[23]

Visitors to a city now will generally rely on maps to negotiate their way around. In the eighteenth century, maps were always collected by travellers: they were aesthetically attractive and intended for display rather than for navigation, or as a souvenir and aide-mémoire of the appearance and location of the important sights and antiquities. Indeed, productions such as Nolli's 1748 giant map of Rome could not be used for any other purpose. John Chetwode Eustace's advice to would-be travellers in his *Classical Tour* is revealing: maps were part of the 'traveller's furniture', but those that he recommended were all of regions (such as the patrimony of St Peter's or Latium) rather than town plans and were praised for the quality of their execution and their beauty rather than their practical utility.[24] When Richard Colt Hoare published his *Hints to*

---

[19] Smith, *Sketch of a Tour*, I, 343.
[20] Smollett, *Travels through France and Italy*, II, 89–90; Flaxman journal BL Add. MS 39787, fol. 39.
[21] See n. 16 above; a French translation of Vasi appeared in 1773 and an English version in 1819.
[22] Forsyth, *Remarks on Antiquities*, 130.
[23] A. Nicholson (ed.), *Lord Byron. The Complete Miscellaneous Prose* (Oxford, 1991), 191, quoted in Timothy Webb, ' "City of the soul": English romantic travellers in Rome', in Michael Liversidge and Catherine Edwards (eds.), *Imagining Rome: British Artists and Rome in the Nineteenth Century* (Bristol, 1996), 22.
[24] Eustace, *Classical Tour*, I, xxxvi.

Travellers in Italy in 1815, he advised his readers to purchase a 'general' map of Italy as a whole, unless they had particular antiquarian interests, in which case they might prefer to purchase maps of a particular district.[25] Colt Hoare had no concept of using a map to find one's way in a particular place: in his view, maps were principally a medium for the representation of antiquarian knowledge – the location of ancient sites and settlements – rather than a means of articulating modern urban space.[26] Colt Hoare's continental travelling had been done in the 1780s, however, and his attitude to the purpose and function of maps was, by 1815, an increasingly outmoded one. Dominique Magnan's 1778 guide to Rome had been published with street plans so that visitors might 'conveniently see' all that interested them in Rome: the text contained references to the plans, and individual buildings were identified with a numbered key, the purpose being to enable readers to orientate themselves and find their own way around the city. Similarly, Magnan's use of street names to locate monuments or churches and the instructions he provided on how to get from one sight to the next implied the complementary use of a map.[27] Giuseppe Vasi followed suit, publishing functional plans of each *rioni* in his series of guidebooks. J. Salmon's English version of Vasi, *An Historical Description of Ancient and Modern Rome*, published in 1800, contained the same street plans to accompany each section and as such was the first English language guide to include maps in this way.[28] The new importance of maps as an aid to navigation, rather than as a souvenir or prompt to memory is reflected in Robert Gray's description in 1794 of his guide as a 'perfect walking map' of the city.[29]

At the same time, the introductory instructions to travellers provided by many of the guidebooks started to offer recommendations of where to acquire street maps, as well as the more traditional tourist purchases of prints and engravings.[30] English guides also began to assume that

---

[25] Richard Colt Hoare, *Hints to Travellers in Italy* (1815), 4, 30–1.

[26] Frank Brady and Frederick Pottle (eds.), *Boswell on the Grand Tour: Italy, Corsica and France 1765–1766* (1955), 63: Boswell recorded that he went to the Capitoline with Mr Morison: 'We climbed on the roof of the modern Senate, from which Mr Morison pointed out ancient Rome on its seven hills. He showed me a little map of it, and read me a clear summary of the growth of this famous city to its present extent.'

[27] Magnan, *La ville de Rome*, I, 1.

[28] J. Salmon, *An Historical Description of Ancient and Modern Rome*, 2 vols. (1800), was heavily derivative of Vasi's *Itinerario istruttivo*.

[29] Gray, *Letters during the Course of a Tour*, 353. Travellers looking down on Naples from a raised elevation also described it as 'laid out like a map', Forbes journal NLS 1542, fol. 49; Lewis Engelbach, *Naples and the Campagna Felice in a Series of Letters Addressed to a Friend in England in 1802* (1815), 17.

[30] Martyn, *Gentleman's Guide*, xviii; Coxe, *Picture of Italy*, xxxix; Eustace, *Classical Tour*, I, xxxvii–viii.

the reader would be viewing Rome independently, rather than under the guidance of a *cicerone*, and provided increasing amounts of information on the logistics of sightseeing and in doing so acquired more of the semblance of modern guidebooks. Such information included more precise directions as to where to go on arrival and advice on how to find one's way around the city for travellers who were unused to navigating the streets on their own. When Charles Burney was in Rome in 1770 he became disorientated after he had dismissed his unsatisfactory *valet de place* and was forced to find his own way from his lodgings to St Peter's: it was only then that he realised that he had 'never tried to find a street alone before'.[31] Street names, distances and directions were provided in the later guidebooks, creating a verbal spatial framework for the city which would have been unnecessary for an earlier generation of travellers who relied upon being shown around a city.[32] They also offered advice on such matters as fees, tips and opening hours. In the case of Mariana Starke's *Letters from Italy* (1800), a system of exclamation marks to indicate to the uninitiated the relative interest or importance of particular works of art or antiquity was also introduced.[33] These developments were not confined to Rome (or to British visitors): one can trace them in other cities also. However, given Rome's size and the emphasis when in the city on viewing its buildings and monuments – as opposed to simply art collections in Florence or the atmosphere of the streets in Naples – the trend was particularly apparent. This kind of advice was indicative of a way of seeing that was becoming more self-reliant and less dependent upon the assistance of the *cicerone*; it was also one which allowed greater scope for personal observation and discovery rather than deference to antiquarian authority and a prescriptive itinerary – although there were always those travellers who adhered equally obediently to the authority of the guidebook.

The anecdotal evidence of diaries and journals also shows how later travellers were attempting to use maps to find their way around: John Mayne, for example, described how he and his sister lost themselves on the first day in Rome but on consulting the map in their copy of Vasi upon their return to their lodgings found that they had been in the forum,[34] and in 1826, Anna Jameson described how she had

[31] Percy A. Scholes (ed.), *An Eighteenth-Century Musical Tour in France and Italy*, 2 vols. (Oxford, 1959), I, 215.

[32] Magnan, *La ville de Rome*; Coxe, *Picture of Italy*, 179–84.

[33] Moore, *View of Society and Manners*; Martyn, *Gentleman's Guide*; Starke, *Letters from Italy* (1800 edn).

[34] Waldie, *Sketches Descriptive of Italy*, I, 339.

'perambulated' around Rome guided by an 'excellent' plan.[35] Using a guidebook, following directions and consulting a map altered the way in which the city was understood: it made the spatial relationship between different buildings more explicit and the routes to be travelled more significant and memorable than if one was simply riding with a guide in a carriage, or following the *cicerone* on foot. Increasingly, both guidebooks and private journals would describe the routes taken between different places on the itinerary, rather than just the destination itself. Robert Finch's manuscript journal written in 1815 has the map of each of the *rioni* pasted into the journal opposite his own notes on what he saw in that area: notes which detailed the location of buildings on particular streets, the routes that he walked connecting different monuments. Such a marriage of cartography and text is unusual for the period but it is indicative of a paradigmatic shift in the way in which people conceptualised their own knowledge and spatial awareness of a city. The emphasis on walking around the city, which we see both in the directions given to travellers and the way in which they recorded their own experiences, reflects also a change away from one mode of seeing the city inherited from the traditions of renaissance antiquarianism towards one that viewed the city, and Rome in particular, as an organic entity, a product of historical changes rather than simply a collection of isolated monuments – a development to be discussed at greater length later in this chapter.

Ancient Rome

In Rome, more than any other city, travellers tended to abandon their efforts to describe all that they saw: the task was too daunting and the published authorities more than adequate in supplying the deficiencies of their powers of recollection and description. Most, however, made some distinction in recording their impressions between the ancient and modern city, and between collections of antiquity or modern works of art. Ironically, it is often easier to establish what visitors saw and in what order when the visit to Rome was short – a matter of days and weeks, rather than months. Those who stayed for extended periods in Rome frequently wrote up their impressions as observations on different types of antiquity, or on paintings, for example, drawing on the information provided by *ciceroni* and published volumes, rather than recording a day by day account of what they had seen. Others, who were only able to stay for a week or two, were more likely to summarise a list of what had been seen on a daily basis.

[35] Colles (ed.), *Journal of John Mayne*, 168; see also Anna Jameson, *Diary of an Ennuyée* (1826), 135.

There was a predictable range of highlights which almost every visitor saw, however briefly, comprising the best-preserved and monumental ruins of Rome: the forum and its temples; the Arches of Severus, Titus and Constantine; the Trajan and Antonine Columns; the obelisks; the Coliseum; the Baths of Titus, Diocletian and Caracalla; the Capitol with the Tullian prison and the Tarpeian Rock; the theatre of Marcellus; and the Pantheon. For many travellers, however, comparatively little time was spent studying these architectural remains, as opposed to the collections of statues, bas reliefs, medals and coins that were housed in the museums and private collections of Rome such as that of Cardinal Albani, or indeed the Roman columns that had been preserved in the fabric of Christian churches. A 'course of antiquities' was as much about viewing the specimens preserved in the palazzi and churches as it was about viewing the buildings or excavations. The antiquities outside were often crammed into two or three days' sightseeing, leaving the visitor, as Peter Cowling put it, 'devilishly fagg'd' and also somewhat confused. His state of fatigue is hardly surprising, given that in a single day he had visited the Temples of Vesta and Fortuna, the Baths of Caracalla, the Aventine Hill and the Circus Maximus, the mausoleum of Caecilia Metella, the 'Latin Gate', the gate and the church of St John Lateran, the Baptistery of Constantine and the 'Holy Stair case', returning home via the Coliseum, the Arch of Titus, the forum and the Capitol.[36] The contents of museums and collections could be taken at a more leisurely pace, with repeat visits where necessary.

Visitors who were familiar with the descriptions and engravings of topographical and antiquarian literature, where all was named and nothing was in doubt, were not prepared for how much of the ancient city was apparently nondescript and anonymous. There was little interest in viewing antiquities for which there was no corroborating literary evidence. Stand-alone monuments such as the Pantheon or the Coliseum needed little or no explanation or interpretation to visitors who were already well versed in Roman history. Other ruins were far more obscure and illegible. The disappointed surprise felt by Louisa Countess of Pomfret when she found herself confronted by 'old walls, with quantities of bricks, arches etc' which could not be identified was shared by numbers of other visitors.[37] They were daunted by the sheer profusion of antiquities and were confused by the conflicting and often highly implausible identifications that the Italian antiquaries had made. Most British visitors knew what they wanted to see and were not interested in

---

[36] Cowling journal CUL Palmer MS c. 5, 67.   [37] Phillips (ed.), *Correspondence*, III, 95.

speculative inquiries as to what might have stood in a given spot or in the rival debates over the identification of a specific antiquity. This kind of discussion tended to hinge upon what was often regarded as antiquarian pedantry, and threw into sharp relief the very flimsy foundations upon which some of the attributions were made. Thomas Pelham, like many others, found the situation exasperating: 'with regard to the particular Names & Situations of the [sic] some of the Building I pay very little Attention as I find all the Antiquarians so much divided in their Opinions as to make one despair of the Truth'.[38]

Whether or not one could afford to engage an antiquarian guide to Rome, any British visitor to the city in the first half of the century viewed the city primarily as an illustration to ancient history and classical literature.[39] A visit to Rome, as we have seen, was the summation of an education which drew directly upon the traditions of renaissance humanism through which a deep familiarity with the literature and history of antiquity had been acquired. As Joseph Addison, whose *Remarks on Several Parts of Italy* accompanied generations of British travellers to Rome, observed 'a man who is in Rome can scarce see an object that does not call to mind a piece of a Latin Poet or Historian'.[40] It was this that constituted the principal source of satisfaction and delight for visitors such as Joseph Spence, who tried to describe to his mother his constant pleasure in seeing the very spot of ground 'where some great thing or other was done, which one has so often admired before in reading their history'.[41] The monuments of Rome acquired meaning and interest principally from the events or personages with which they were associated. Rome's antiquities were as much intellectual prompts as objects of curiosity in their own right. The purpose of viewing them was to recall the piece of poetry or historical event with which they were associated, rather than to understand them as buildings, objects or constituent parts of a city. Travellers consequently sought out antiquities which would confirm or illuminate the history and the poetry with which they were familiar. Antiquities in the collections of the Vatican and in the nobility's palazzi (the busts, statues, bas reliefs, medals and inscriptions), therefore, were often more rewarding objects of contemplation than those anonymous ones scattered outside round

[38] Pelham to his mother, 23 Apr. 1777, BL Add. MS 33127, fol. 229v.
[39] This was a long-established tradition. See, for example, Amanda Claridge, 'Archaeologies, antiquaries and the *memorie* of sixteenth- and seventeenth-century Rome', in Ilaria Bignamini (ed.), *Archives and Excavations*, Archaeological Monographs of the British School at Rome 14 (2004), 33–54.
[40] Addison, *Remarks on Several Parts of Italy*, 301–2.
[41] Klima (ed.), *Letters from the Grand Tour*, 115.

about the city. Statues offered insight into character; medals offered confirmation of dates; bas reliefs illustrated scenes imperfectly understood from poetry and mythology. It was for this reason that Gilbert Burnet suggested that no antiquity was more useful or 'more glorious' than the tables of the consuls in the Capitol and none more valuable than the inscription on the Columna Rostrela, which dated from the first Punic war.[42] Given that visitors, as we have seen, tended to become impatient with antiquarian debate and uncertainty, the appeal of collections in which the majority of the items could be identified (or at least had been given an attribution) and which provided the opportunity for the exercise of aesthetic judgement and taste, is self-evident.

The exercise of the imagination was an essential part of the experience of viewing Rome and its collections, but it had to be rooted in the literary text: Rome, as Lord Percival enthused, was a city that 'gives an unexpressible pleasure when considered with a Book in one's hand'.[43] Indeed, with a book in one's hand or simply recalled to memory, it was not even necessary for the physical buildings to exist: it was sufficient only to be in the same place in which famous events and exploits had taken place.[44] Hence the pleasure and excitement felt by many travellers at standing upon the Tarpeian Rock, which in the eighteenth century represented a disappointingly shallow leap. The artist James Russel, who also offered his services as a *cicerone* to the English, told his father how he had observed some visitors

stand upon the same spot of ground for a good while, as it were in deep contemplation, where there was no appearance of any thing very remarkable or uncommon. Tho' such a one might be thought, by those who saw him, to be *non compos*, he might probably from his knowledge in history, be then calling to mind some brave action, performed upon that very spot; and enjoying a pleasure, not to be felt by any one, confined within the walls of a study, or a chamber.[45]

It was in the forum in particular that visitors were wont to conjure up the shades of Cicero and Cato and the traditions of Roman oratory, only to admit, as did William Forbes fifty years after Russel, that 'nothing survives of this interesting spot [the rostrum] except some massy walls'.[46] Rome was a city where the delight was chiefly in the exercise

[42] Gilbert Burnet, *Some Letters Containing an Account of what Seemed Most Remarkable in Switzerland, Italy, etc 1686* (repr. Menton, 1972), 238–9.
[43] Percival to Edward Southwell, 12 Mar. 1725/6, BL Add. MS 47031, fol. 115v.
[44] Edward Burton, *A Description of the Antiquities and Other Curiosities of Rome* (Oxford, 1821), 47: 'If we must have visible objects, on which to fix our attention, we have the ground itself, on which the Romans trod.'
[45] Russel, *Letters from a Young Painter Abroad*, II, 180.
[46] Forbes journal NLS MS 1543, fol. 164.

of imaginative powers well stocked with reading, rather than the immediate sensory experience. These pleasures of the imagination, however,
were to be distinguished from the fantastical conjectures of Piranesi, for
example, whose attempts to recreate the appearance of ancient Rome
based upon his antiquarian and archaeological investigations Forbes
dismissed as imaginative fancy.[47]

The antiquities of Rome were valued for the imaginative associations
to which they gave rise (and the consequent opportunity they offered to
display one's erudition) and as objects of aesthetic beauty; but they were
also something to be collected in the seventeenth-century virtuoso tradition. This was a mode of viewing that was particularly evident in the first
half of the century. Just as a virtuoso or antiquary might build up a
cabinet of coins and compile a catalogue, travellers to the city would
enumerate the statues or count the marble columns, specifying the
different types of marble and granite, their colour and their country of
origin.[48] This process of identification and enumeration was a form of
virtual appropriation: the columns thus counted could be listed and
categorised in the same way as a collection of coins or inscriptions would
be ordered and itemised. Furthermore, this approach to antiquities had
a discernible effect upon the way in which the city and its contents were
conceptualised as objects to be described: the city was simply the sum of
the constituent antiquities. Descriptions of Rome were not organised in
terms of the city's chronological development, or even by geographical
region, but under headings according to the type of antiquity: temples,
aqueducts, columns and baths. Buildings were not described in terms
of their architectural style or the period in which they were built, but
were rather reduced to a simple head count of pillars, and notes on the
type of marble used. At Sta Maria Maggiore in 1722, Edward Wright
found that

. . . among all the Remains of Antiquity scarce any thing I think is more
entertaining than the Columns, of an incredible Variety of Marbles, (if by that

---

[47] '[Piranesi] wishing to give a complete view of the whole [the forum] has formed a
topographical plan of this celebrated spot, in which he has crowded together so great a
number of edifices as it is scarcely possible to suppose were stood on the same ground. It
must be considered, therefore, very much as a work of his own imagination.' Forbes
journal NLS MS 1543, fol. 186. Smollett similarly observed that Piranesi was 'apt to
run riot in his conjectures and has broached some doctrines in regard to the arts of
antient Rome which he will find it very difficult to maintain', *Travels through France and
Italy*, II, 92.

[48] Sir Richard Colt Hoare noted in his journal that one of the Italian antiquaries had forty
years earlier counted 11,000 pillars in Rome: CUL Add. MS 3555, fol. 12v. Edward
Wright recorded that Ficoroni had claimed to have counted 11,400: *Observations*,
I, 343.

general Name we may call all those beautiful Stones,) which were collected from all parts of the Universe, when the Roman Empire was in its fullest Extent and greatest Glory.[49]

The fact that the columns were no longer in their original position, that they were divorced from their rightful context and could not be understood as part of the structure from which they came, was not an issue for visitors in this period. The interest and value of these monuments resided in the material quality of the marble and the workmanship, the illustration that they provided of Rome's imperial might and the technical prowess of her craftsmen rather than in the evidence that they offered of the form and physical appearance of ancient Rome, the city. Rome's ancient history was undifferentiated: lists of baths and triumphal arches from the later empire sat alongside notes on the Cloaca Maxima. This way of seeing and describing Rome influenced all accounts of the first half of the century, and in many cases beyond, whether they were personal observations, guidebooks or the lengthier books of travels and antiquarian treatises. Again, it drew heavily on long-established models of antiquarian topography in Rome itself. The most important of which was Palladio's *Antichità di Roma* which had been structured around an enumeration of the various types of monument or antiquity: arches, gates, pillars, temples.[50] Addison's account of Rome was a similarly disjointed exercise in describing individual antiquities (statues, bas reliefs, coins, pillars, arches and obelisks) which could illustrate literature or corroborate the facts of history.

The practice of describing Rome according to different 'types' of antiquity continued to inform accounts of the city throughout our period: there was an irreducible core of antiquarian knowledge that persisted through to the nineteenth century. But the framing of Rome's antiquities in travellers' descriptions underwent substantial change as travellers in the later eighteenth century arrived in Italy with a different

[49] Wright, *Observations*, I, 220. See also Addison, *Remarks on Several Parts of Italy*, 364: 'It is almost impossible for a man to form, in his imagination, such beautiful and glorious scenes, as are to be met with in several of the *Roman* Churches and Chappels [sic]; for having such a prodigious stock of ancient marble within the very city.'

[50] This was a format which went back to some of the earliest guides to the antiquities, see for example Andrea Palladio, *L'antichità di Roma di M. Andrea Palladio, raccolta brevemente da gli auttori antichi, & moderni* (Rome, 1554), or Pirro Ligorio, *Libro di M. Pyrrho Ligori Napolitano, delle antichità di Roma, nel quale si tratta de' circi, theatri, & anfiteatri* (Venice, 1553). See Vaughan Hart and Peter Hicks (eds.), *Palladio's Rome* (New Haven and London, 2006), xvi.

set of expectations. Increasingly, they were educated in the language of picturesque tourism which allowed them to articulate a different set of responses to what they saw. Those who found the antiquarian approach dry and indigestible were able to discover beauty in ruins and decay. They could appreciate the poignant contrast between antiquity and modernity that confronted them at every turn: in the vines that covered the ruins of the Palatine; in the hermit who inhabited the Coliseum; or in the cattle in the Campo Vaccino (recalling perhaps the lowing cows by Evander's house on the site of the future forum in Book 8 of the *Aeneid*).[51] Antiquities could be admired for their intrinsic aesthetic properties, rather than simply their historical associations. Whereas previously monuments had been described as if in their pristine perfection and divorced from the accretions of subsequent generations, the evidence of time's dilapidations and the prosaic purposes to which former magnificence was now reduced were equally the object of notice and careful portrayal in both published and unpublished accounts. Even John Chetwode Eustace, author of *A Classical Tour*, evoked Ossianic melancholy in his description of the Palatine Hill.[52] This sensitivity to the passage of time and processes of decay invited travellers to consider the fate of Rome subsequent to its fall and not just at the height of its glory, as they stood like Robert Harvey, amidst the ruins 'with pensive mood and folded arm'.[53] This was a conceptual leap they were able to accomplish with considerably greater ease following the publication of Gibbon's *Decline and Fall* which offered the traveller a narrative framework through which to understand the city's history in periods with which they were otherwise unfamiliar.

The picturesque – as antiquaries frequently complained – lacked precision and a true understanding of form, placing a higher priority on superficial appearances. But there were also more meticulously antiquarian influences at work which helped to change the way in which the city was perceived. The antiquary of the early eighteenth century, as we have seen, looked upon Rome's antiquities as the illustrations to literary texts, and as items to be grouped according to type or material, rather than arranged in chronological series, for example. By the 1770s, architects and antiquaries such as James Stuart and Charles Cameron, who visited Rome for professional purposes as opposed to acquiring the gentlemanly polish of taste and virtù, were employing more rigorous

---

[51] 'Talibus inter se dictis ad tecta subibant/pauperis Evandri, passimque armenta videbant/ Romanoque foro et lautis mugire Carinis', *Aeneid* 8.359–62.
[52] Eustace, *Classical Tour*, I, 216.   [53] Harvey journal NRO MS 20677, 170.

and accurate modes of measurement and representation. They were also excavating certain sites, such as the Baths of Trajan (believed by Cameron to be the Baths of Titus) and parts of the Domus Aurea, for the first time. This approach, studying buildings through excavation, rather than through inherited textual traditions going back to Vitruvius, marked a distinctive break with tradition and was chiefly driven by a desire to understand Roman architecture more fully in order to be able to build in the classical style in Britain.[54] Architects were not representative of the majority of British travellers, but the shift away from an exclusive reliance on a textually driven approach to the study of Rome to one which was able to incorporate information derived from antiquarian or archaeological observation was not restricted to these specialists, and can be traced in the works of British antiquaries and the publication of the Society of Antiquaries of London. Antiquarianism in Britain and Europe was turning increasingly towards the study of the object as well as the written text.[55] This trend towards what we would now call a more archaeological approach was apparent in both published and unpublished accounts of Rome by the end of the century and exercised an ever clearer influence in the period immediately following the end of the Napoleonic Wars.

One of the most obvious changes to the way in which travellers described the city was that closer attention was given to locating the historical moment at which buildings or monuments were constructed or erected. Given most travellers' familiarity with the narratives of ancient Rome, the apparently atemporal descriptions would have been more firmly rooted in an implicit understanding of Rome's history than they appear today, but nevertheless there was still a tendency to treat antiquity as a largely undifferentiated continuum. In the later eighteenth century, however, chronology was much more explicitly articulated in terms of the overall approach to viewing the city. The basic written structure of guidebooks, tours and manuscript accounts, however, still

---

[54] Frank Salmon, 'Charles Cameron and Nero's Domus Aurea: "una piccola esplorazione"', *Journal of the Society of Architectural Historians*, 36 (1993), 69–93, and Frank Salmon, 'Stuart as antiquary and archaeologist in Italy and Greece', in Susan Weber Soros (ed.), *James 'Athenian' Stuart: The Rediscovery of Classical Antiquity* (New Haven and London, 2007), 103–45.

[55] Chantal Grell, *Le dix-huitième siècle et l'antiquité en France 1680–1789*, 2 vols. (Oxford, 1995); Thomas DaCosta Kaufmann, 'Antiquarianism, the history of objects, and the history of art before Winckleman', *Journal of the History of Ideas*, 62:3 (2001), 523–41; Alain Schnapp, *The Discovery of the Past: The Origins of Archaeology*, trans. Ian Kinnes and Gillian Varndell (New York, 1997); Sweet, *Antiquaries*; on Rome specifically, see Tamara Ann Griggs, 'The changing face of erudition: antiquaries in the age of the Grand Tour', Yale University Ph.D. thesis (2003).

tended to be ordered according to particular areas of the city, or by the *giornate*, if one was using Vasi. The practicalities of sightseeing meant that following a chronological tour through the city was far less easy to follow consistently than adopting a geographical approach, but both English and Italian guides increasingly stressed the importance of taking a panoramic view of the city at first in order to understand its historical growth and to discuss the evolution of the city in terms of its historical development.[56] Even the Vasi guidebooks, by this stage, included three different plans marking Rome its successive stages of development. The greater importance that was now attached to identifying the historical growth of the city was also manifested in the higher levels of precision and consistency given to providing the date of construction of particular buildings (although this was obviously not a development that was confined to accounts of Rome alone). Descriptions of buildings generally became more specific in the identification of the architectural style in which they were built; styles were identified with particular periods, and dates of construction were more likely to be provided. As we have seen, such descriptions had formerly been highly formulaic, consisting of notes on the dimensions, the type of marble used and an itemisation of the main physical elements, rather than any qualitative judgement upon the workmanship or even the style in which it was executed. Verdicts were summed up in the use of generic adjectives such as 'fine', 'magnificent' or 'beautiful'.

On one level, this simply reflected the conventions of architectural description of the time, but it was also symptomatic of the prevailing assumption that these buildings were 'beautiful' simply by virtue of having been built in the period of classical antiquity – just as buildings of the middle ages were barbarous, coarse and ugly because they neither conformed to classical rules nor were they the products of classical civilisation or its revival. But by the end of the eighteenth century, thanks to the efforts of architects and antiquaries such as Stuart and Cameron, a more discriminating approach to the study of architecture had evolved and started also to influence the less specialist accounts which were often far more detailed – and also critical. To pursue a degree of accuracy down to a thousandth of an inch was still

---

[56] Joseph Forsyth advised his readers to trace first the outline of the city under the Republic, then the city as it was under Nero before the great conflagration, then the later imperial city, and was rigorous in identifying the historical progression and decline of art and architecture through the monuments and antiquities, Forsyth, *Remarks on Antiquities*, 154. See also Guiseppe Antonio Guattani, *Roma descritta ed illustrata*, 2 vols. (Rome, 1805), I, 3.

regarded as otiose by most,[57] but the vocabulary of architectural description which tourists and writers of travel literature were using by the end of the century was more sophisticated and more analytical; it showed the gradual dissemination of a kind of architectural literacy which made the traveller better able to interpret the physical environment as a historical document.

By the 1820s, these trends were more clearly marked, as is evident in a publication such as Edward Burton's *A Description of the Antiquities and Other Curiosities of Rome*, which was published in 1821. Burton deliberately distanced himself from those sentimental travel writers who sought only to convey the 'impressions' made upon them by the various antiquities, choosing instead to record something of the history of the antiquities that he described.[58] Thus, his portrayal was one that presented Rome as the product of continuous historical development to be read through its buildings rather than simply a collection of monuments divorced from their temporal context. He explained that

Rome, though frequently overthrown has never been deserted. It stands as a link in the chain, which connects ancient and modern history; and in this part the continuity has never been broken. Even if contemporary accounts were silent, we might learn from recent excavations how overwhelming were the calamities which befell this unhappy city.[59]

Burton was articulating a vision of how Rome had evolved over time, how its appearance and physical extent had changed; how the modern city related to the ancient one.

It is also evident that the British were showing a greater appreciation of the value of what would now be called archaeological evidence. The arguments of Italian antiquaries and 'proto'-archaeologists which had formerly been ignored or dismissed by all but the most studiously antiquarian visitors, started to attract greater interest and to be taken more seriously. Andrew Lumisden, for example, whose *Remarks on the*

---

[57] Stephen Weston, *Viaggiana: Or, Detached Remarks on the Buildings, Pictures, Statues, Inscriptions etc of Ancient and Modern Rome* (1776), 28, commented on the remains of an ionic capital on the Palatine: 'It must be observed, however, that one volute is an inch broader than the other, which may serve to show how little important it is to spend any length of time in measuring a pillar, or any other relique of antiquity, to that thousandth part of an inch, that may not be found perfect after all.'

[58] Burton, *Description of the Antiquities*, v.

[59] Ibid., 146. This kind of interpretation of Rome's historic fabric had been anticipated by Italian antiquaries at least one hundred years earlier, see in particular Ficoroni, *Le vestigie e rarità di Roma*, and Francesco Eschinardi's posthumously published description in Ridolfino Venuti, *Descrizione di Roma e dell'Agro Romano, fatta gia ad uso della carta topografica del cingolani dal padre Francesco Eschinardi della Compagnia di Gesù* (1750).

Antiquities of Rome (1797) represented the fruition of a long career as
a guide and antiquarian advisor to British visitors to Rome referred
frequently to earlier antiquaries such as Famiano Nardini, author of
Roma antica (1666) and Giuseppe Bianchini as well as the more recent
Venuti and Piranesi. (Bianchini was otherwise only ever mentioned in
reference to his meridian line in Sta Maria Maggiore.)[60] Lumisden
maintained an intransigently sceptical stance, accusing both Bianchini
and Piranesi of fertile invention, but he did at least recognise that their
attempts to trace the plans of buildings that were no longer standing, for
example, could be productive of useful knowledge.[61] After 1815, the
insights derived from the archaeological excavations undertaken during
French occupation began to find their way into descriptions of the city.
They were strikingly illustrated in *The Architectural Antiquities of Rome*
(1821) published by Edward Cresy and George Taylor, a pair of architects
who took advantage of the spate of excavations and the unprecedentedly
cooperative attitude of the Roman authorities in the post-Napoleonic era
to offer strikingly different images of familiar monuments. The Temple of
Jupiter Stator (Castor and Pollux), for example, was depicted looking
into the excavation pit that had revealed the full extent of the pillars and
the travertine base on which they stood (see Figure 6). Similarly, the
standard image of the exterior of the Coliseum was followed by a view of
its interior displaying the recently excavated network of subterranean
walls and chambers, while the Arch of Titus was shown newly denuded
of its medieval accretions. (see Figure 7).[62]

[60] Few tours referred to Bianchini by name, but see Blainville, *Travels through Holland, Germany, Switzerland*, III, 13; Johann Georg Keysler, *Travels through Germany, Bohemia, Hungary, Switzerland, Italy and Lorraine*, 4 vols. (1756), II, 104, and Martyn, *Gentleman's Guide*, 184, all of whom referred only to his meridian line at Sta Maria Maggiore. On Bianchini's antiquarianism and his influence on Piranesi, see Susan M. Dixon, 'Piranesi and Francesco Bianchini: *capricci* in the service of pre-scientific archaeology', *Art History*, 22:2 (1999), 184–213, and Susan M. Dixon, 'The sources and fortunes of Piranesi's archaeological illustrations', *Art History*, 24:4 (2002), 469–87.
[61] Andrew Lumisden, *Remarks on the Antiquities of Rome and its Environs* (1797), 105, 158, 161, 198, 252, 303, 347, 371–2. Lumisden had been resident in Rome since the 1750s as secretary to both the Old and the Young Pretender. William Forbes made extensive use of Lumisden's *Remarks on the Antiquities of Rome* when he came to write up his own travel journals. On Lumisden's debt to Piranesi, see Michael McCarthy, 'Andrew Lumisden and Giovanni Battista Piranesi', in Hornsby (ed.), *The Impact of Italy*, 65–81. Forsyth similarly made reference to a much wider range of Italian antiquarian works, including volumes by Marliani, Nardini, Panvinio and Bianchini, and included a brief discussion of the latter's excavations on the Palatine Hill. He was unconvinced, however, by the detail of Bianchini's efforts to reconstruct the imperial palace, *Remarks on the Antiquities*, 141.
[62] Edward Cresy and G. L Taylor, *The Architectural Antiquities of Rome*, 2 vols. (1821), II, plates XCI and CXV; Frank Salmon, *Building on Ruins: The Rediscovery of Rome and English Architecture* (Aldershot, 2000), 65–72.

TEMPLE OF JUPITER STATOR, ROME.
View showing the Excavation.

Figure 6 'Temple of Jupiter Stator, Rome, showing the excavation', from Edward L. Cresy and G. L. Taylor, *The Architectural Antiquities of Rome*, 2 vols. (1821).

COLOSSEVM, ROME.

Interior View looking west, taken at the time the Arena was excavated.

Figure 7 'Interior view of the Coliseum, showing the excavations', from Edward L. Cresy and G. L. Taylor, *The Architectural Antiquities of Rome*, 2 vols. (1821).

The two-volume folio publication that resulted in 1821 was an item
for the collector and the connoisseur rather than the average tourist, but
archaeological insights were already being integrated at a broader level
and were adopted even by those who deliberately distanced themselves
from what they considered to be the futile speculation of antiquaries.[63]
With Nardini as her guide, Charlotte Eaton explored Rome in 1817,
attempting to detect the remains of Servius Tullius' wall or the traces of
the praetorian camp near Sta Croce which were evident in the superior
quality of the masonry and the bricks. Antiquarians, she claimed, ruined
one's enjoyment of the city, but she was nevertheless prepared to learn
from them when it came to understanding the physical remains of the
city that she encountered on a daily basis.[64] Similarly, from the 1790s
we find more references amongst English visitors to the evidence of the
forma urbis Romae as a source of information. The fragments of the
marble plan displayed on the wall of the Capitoline had always attracted
the attention of visitors but as a curiosity and a piece of antiquity, rather
than for the clues it held regarding the topography and appearance
of ancient Rome. When Edward Wright was visiting the city in 1721,
he had simply observed that it was 'now to be seen in several Pieces, not
regularly put together, in the *Farnese* Palace on one of the floors'. But by
the end of the century, even Adam Walker, whose *Ideas Suggested on the
Spot* (1790) was anything but an antiquarian treatise, noted that it
showed that the houses of old Rome had arcades in the lowest storey
as they did in modern Rome.[65]

This shift in perspective, away from the monumental, has to be seen
in the broader context of the emergent interest in the history of 'everyday
life' and domesticity, itself the natural consequence of the historical
study of manners and customs as the index to the development of
civilisation, which characterises the historical thought of the eighteenth
century.[66] But clearly, it also owed much to the discoveries at Pompeii –
not just in terms of material evidence, but because the excavations
brought the visitor face to face with a very different version of Roman
history to that which was conventionally rehearsed around the ruins of
Rome. In Rome, the Earl of Winchilsea had enthused to his mother over
the scale, grandeur and workmanship of Roman architecture that had
'exceeded' all his expectations. But in Pompeii, he confronted a more
prosaic version of Rome, telling her that 'I believe the common opinion

[63] Ronald T. Ridley, *The Eagle and the Spade: Archaeology in Rome during the Napoleonic Era* (Cambridge, 1992).
[64] Eaton, *Rome in the Nineteenth Century*, I, 190, 193.
[65] Walker, *Ideas Suggested on the Spot*, 279.   [66] Phillips, *Society and Sentiment*, 129–89.

is that except their Palaces, Temples &c the Romans lived in a very dirty, & uncomfortable manner.'[67] The implications of this new awareness of urban antiquity and the different approaches and questions that it provoked can be seen in Lumisden's *Remarks on the Antiquities of Rome*. Lumisden began his discussion with a description of Rome's original irregular layout, with narrow streets and tall houses, so tall that they often fell down, hence necessitating legislation to restrict the height of houses and stipulating a minimum gap between them. This, he explained, was the origin of the insulae, the high-rise tenements which had housed most of the population of Rome. The practicalities of domestic housing had not been something that British visitors to Rome had ever engaged with before; on the contrary, they passed over it quickly with little comment. Lumisden also enlightened his readers – by now used to the building regulations enforced in the wake of the Fire of London – with regard to the laws of Constantine and Theodosius, which had stipulated the minimum distance to be maintained between private houses and public buildings.[68] His authorities included traditional sources such as Vitruvius but also the evidence of finds at Herculaneum and Pompeii, from which he argued that the Romans had used glass in their windows. If only, he observed, the Italians had made a better job of excavating these sites, 'we should have seen the disposition of the streets, houses, temples &c., we should have seen the interior of the houses and a thousand curiosities we are now deprived of'.[69] This kind of approach was picked up by other writers in the early nineteenth century, as when Cornelia Knight discussed the internal arrangements of Roman houses in her *Description of Latium* or when Charlotte Eaton speculated whether Romans had enjoyed the benefit of windows or not, and if so what they used to glaze them.[70]

The awakening interest in archaeology, therefore, predated the French excavations of the forum. The news of the discoveries at Herculaneum (1738) and Pompeii (1748) caused great excitement, even amongst

[67] Winchilsea to his mother, 25 May 1773, ROLLR Finch MSS DG 7/4/12 box 4953 bundle 32.

[68] Lumisden, *Remarks on the Antiquities of Rome*, 12–14. The comparison between post-fire building regulations and urban improvement in Rome and London had been made directly over twenty years before in descriptions of London: see [James Stuart], *Critical Observations on the Buildings and Improvements of London* (2nd edn, 1771), 20–2.

[69] Lumisden, *Remarks on the Antiquities of Rome*, 477. Lumisden, it should be noted, was only following here lines of inquiry that Italian antiquaries such as Ridolfino Venuti had mapped out many years previously.

[70] Cornelia Knight, *Description of Latium; or, La Campagna di Roma* (1805), 35–7; Eaton, *Rome in the Nineteenth Century*, I, 220; James John Blunt, *Vestiges of the Ancient Manners and Customs, Discoverable in Modern Italy and Sicily* (1823), 224–35.

those who never travelled to Italy, and was widely reported in the British press. Archaeological excavation had already become something of a fashionable pastime in Britain – unearthed mosaics were a popular attraction regularly reported in newspapers, and the opening of barrows always attracted a crowd.[71] But the impact of the excavations in the forum and the Coliseum, as well as those of Pompeii, certainly crystallised awareness that there was much more to be learnt from the material remains than was possible in an approach which was defined by what could be known from literary sources.[72] John Cam Hobhouse could appreciate the significance of what had been uncovered, comparing its transformation to the wonders revealed at Pompeii. The remnants were, he observed, 'sufficient to shew what must be the subterranean riches of Rome', but he nevertheless retained the English tradition of scepticism regarding the rather bolder claims of the Italian antiquaries: the attempt of Carlo Fea (the papal antiquary) to establish the course of the triumphal way through the forum up to the Capitoline seemed a hopeless ambition to him.[73] But irrespective of whether or not the triumphal way was discovered, excavating the true ground level of the forum allowed accurate measurements to be taken of buildings in their entirety for the first time, thereby focussing attention on their dimensions, proportions and their spatial relationship to each other, rather than simply upon their literary and historical associations. This had a discernible effect on the way in which the city was represented to visitors in a number of topographical guides.[74] It heralded a different approach to seeing Rome – one which was more interested in understanding how the ancient city had operated as an entity, as opposed to viewing its antiquities simply as a prompt to literary recollection or philosophical reflection.

The combined effect of these changes was that the rigidly textual approach to ancient Rome, which focussed on the monuments associated

---

[71] See, for example, Richard Fenton, *A Historical Tour through Pembrokeshire* (1810), 192–3.

[72] On the excavations see Ridley, *The Eagle and the Spade*, 53–61. Ridley notes the absence of interest on the part of many British visitors in the period during and immediately after the French occupation, citing, for example, Eustace's laconic observation that the French 'have commenced several excavations, and of course made some discoveries' (ibid., xxi). (His firm francophobia should be acknowledged here.) When Eustace did urge excavation, it was purely in the hope that additional specimens of statuary would be uncovered: 'What precious remnants of ancient art and magnificence might we find, if all the streets of this *subterraneous* city (for so these *thermae* may be called) were opened, and its recesses explored!' *Classical Tour*, I, 223.

[73] J. C. Hobhouse, *Historical Illustrations of the Fourth Canto of Childe Harold: Containing Dissertations on the Ruins of Rome and an Essay on Italian Literature* (1818), 222–3, 243–4. See also the account of the 'French improvements' provided by Coxe, *Picture of Italy*, 187.

[74] Cecelia Powell, *Italy in the Age of Turner: 'The Garden of the World'* (1998), 25.

with famous people, events and literary texts, began to be broken down. In its place was a sharper awareness of the importance of what remained buried in Rome as well as what was still visible. Excavation might reveal not just statuary to add to the country house collections of English gentlemen, but information concerning the function, identity and location of buildings within the city. This encouraged a tendency on the part of some observers to try to interpret and understand Rome as a functioning urban centre inhabited by people, not just by the Roman Senate or emperors and their armies; a city whose growth, glory and decline could be traced through its physical remains. Burton's *Description of the Antiquities and Other Curiosities of Rome*, for example, attempted to convey a sense of the appearance and lived experience of the ancient city, reducing it to a human, rather than a monumental, scale. Like Lumisden, he raided Tacitus, Suetonius and also Livy for comments which conveyed a sense of the closely packed, densely built environment of Rome and showed that for all its magnificence – like any other city – it had its areas of human squalor and misery. Even the temples, he suggested, were not necessarily as magnificent as subsequent generations had liked to make out.[75] The Romans themselves were called to account: he found fault with their architecture as a debasement of the Greek original, and concluded that the Romans 'were not naturally a people of taste'.[76]

Burton's damning dismissal of the taste of the Romans is in itself indicative of a sea change in the way the nineteenth-century visitor approached Rome. His comments reflected the impact of the late eighteenth-century Greek revival which had established Rome's cultural debt – and inferiority – to Greece, placing greater value on the purity, simplicity and authenticity of Greek art and architecture (he consistently compared the antiquities of Rome unfavourably to those of Athens). The 'discovery' of Paestum in the 1750s reinforced the gathering sense that Rome's greatness was cyclical and not unique: the temples at Paestum, noted one traveller, had been built 'at a period when Rome consisted of thatched hovels'.[77] Taking his cue from Winckelman, Joseph Forsyth was similarly damning of many of the monuments that had formerly provoked such profuse praise from earlier travellers.[78] The Romans had corrupted the ancient purity of Greece; their architecture and their

[75] Burton, *Description of the Antiquities*, 19.

[76] Ibid., 20; see also Forsyth, *Remarks on Antiquities*, 140, on the decline of arts under the Empire.

[77] Lord Palmerston writing in 1764, cited by Black, *Italy and the Grand Tour*, 13.

[78] Forsyth, *Remarks on Antiquities*. The best introduction to the Greek revival and its values remains J. Mordaunt Crook, *The Greek Revival: Neo-Classical Attitudes in British Architecture, 1760–1870* (1972).

statuary was derivative and inferior. Even Trajan's Column, conventionally one of the descriptive set pieces of the Grand Tour, was not immune
from his criticism: Forsyth found fault with its failure to conform to any
single order of architecture, with its Tuscan base and capital, Doric shaft
and Corinthian mouldings on the pedestal. By the end of the Napoleonic
Wars, this increasingly critical tenor to comments on imperial Rome was
becoming more pervasive, and was repeated, with varying degrees of
condemnation, by many travellers of the early nineteenth century.[79]

The tendency to fault finding may also be understood as the consequence of a re-imagining of Britain's relationship to Rome and its own
national past. Rome was to be admired and emulated but could also be
subjected to a measure of criticism in order to assert the superiority
of modern Britain. In 1766, for example, the architect John Gwynn
(who had never been to Rome) could claim in his plan for the rebuilding
of London that the English 'are now what the Romans were of old,
distinguished like them by power and opulence, and excelling all other
nations in commerce and navigation. Our wisdom is respected, our laws
are envied, and our dominions are spread over a large part of the globe.'[80]
Gwynn believed that the modern English could equal the Romans; by the
end of the century, it was clear that in some areas at least, they could
surpass them. It was no longer a relationship of straightforward inferiority
and imitation. In 1775, John Entick, author of dictionaries and histories,
triumphantly pronounced the superiority of the British Empire over Rome
with respect to 'Constitution, Dominion, Commerce, Riches or Strength'.[81]
From the later eighteenth century, Britons travelled in the knowledge that
the British Empire, founded on commerce and liberty, now exceeded the
territorial empire of Rome, which had arisen on the basis of slavery. Britain,
as Gibbon put it, had been the first nation to succeed in uniting 'the
benefits of order with the blessings of freedom'.[82] Whilst the Roman
Republic could and did continue to command admiration, attitudes
towards the later imperial period became increasingly critical.[83] For the

---

[79] Sydney Morgan was similarly critical of the monuments of imperial Rome, although
from a rather different perspective, as a critic of both Roman and British imperialism.
Morgan, *Italy*, II, 184–7.
[80] John Gwynn, *London and Westminster Improved* (1766), xv.
[81] John Entick, *The Present State of the British Empire*, 4 vols. (1775), I, 1–3.
[82] Cited in Roy Porter, *Edward Gibbon: Making History* (1988), 152.
[83] Frank M. Turner, 'British politics and the demise of the Roman Republic: 1700–1939',
H J, 29:3 (1986), 577–99; Norman Vance, *The Victorians and Ancient Rome* (Oxford
1997); on the use of analogies with the Roman Empire in debates over territorial
conquest in Parliament, see Jeremy Black, 'Gibbon and international relations', in
Rosamund McKitterick and Roland Quinault (eds.), *Edward Gibbon and Empire*
(Cambridge, 1997), 217–46.

British, it exemplified the corruption of political virtue through luxury and excess: Roman imperial decadence could be contrasted with the principled integrity of Britain who avoided territorial conquest. The experiences of the French Revolution and the subsequent collapse of the Napoleonic Empire, with its deliberate evocation of republican Rome, only served to emphasise the fragility of temporal power.[84] 'Empire', Eustace warned his readers, 'like the sun, has hitherto rolled westward ... it now hovers over Great Britain; but it is still on the wing.'[85]

The increasingly critical stance taken towards later imperial Rome, combined with a more rigorously historical approach to the architecture and antiquities, engendered amongst some travellers rather different responses to the set pieces of Roman tourism towards the end of the eighteenth century. Forsyth's objections to Trajan's Column have already been noted, but nor did other monuments escape censure. The Coliseum, for example, assumed a more ambiguous status: its monumental size and design could not be gainsaid, and its picturesque qualities, particularly by moonlight, were widely celebrated. But it was symptomatic of what British tourists saw as a decline in the standards of morality and public virtue of late imperial Rome. Like the huge complex of the Baths of Caracalla, the Coliseum symbolised the excess and luxury of the later empire and the moral corruption that accompanied it, provoking not only nocturnal meditations on the fragility of sublunary power but diatribes against the barbaric excesses of gladiatorial combat under the Roman emperors. John Moore found his admiration of ancient Rome tempered with disgust as he recalled the cruelty and mindless depravity of the gladiatorial combat that took place in the Coliseum.[86] Joseph Forsyth was equally offended by the sadistic cruelty that it embodied: 'here sate the conquerors of the world, coolly to enjoy the tortures and death of men who had never offended men'. Two aqueducts were scarce enough to carry off the human blood from a few hours of sport.[87] Even the size of these structures – the Coliseum, the Circus Maximus and the Baths – bore witness to dissipation of the Roman people. William Forbes calculated that the Circus Maximus must have held at least 10 per cent of the population of Rome when full, but not even Paris on the eve of the Revolution (the eighteenth-century centre of luxurious decadence on the verge of its downfall) could have housed such a high proportion of its inhabitants in all its theatres combined. The Romans, he concluded,

[84] Webb, ' "City of the soul" ', 20–37.   [85] Eustace, *Classical Tour*, I, xxxii.
[86] Moore, *View of Society and Manners*, I, 418–25.
[87] Forsyth, *Remarks on Antiquities*, 144, 147.

had been the 'idlest and most dissipated people that ever existed'.[88] This oscillation between admiration for a monument and revulsion at the social mores and customs that it represented (as well as the implied assumption of British superiority in this respect) featured in a number of other accounts of the early nineteenth century and contributed to an increasingly ambivalent response to the antiquities of ancient Rome.[89]

Although the period of republican Rome was by far the most familiar to Britain's travelling public, and also the best documented in literary terms,[90] by the end of the eighteenth century the attentive visitor was ever more aware of the fact that very little of what he or she saw in Rome actually belonged to that period in which they were principally interested.[91] The closer scrutiny of the material fabric of the city that characterised many of the accounts of this period highlighted more clearly how many of the most iconic antiquities dated from the later periods of the history of ancient Rome. They represented not so much the values of public service and political virtue with which a gentleman was expected to identify, but the vainglorious display of conspicuous consumption through which a succession of Roman emperors sought to advertise their power and assert their arbitrary authority over the population. But as criticism of the ruins of the later empire became more strident, the monuments of republican Rome, which were less visible and less physically impressive, accordingly attracted more attention and positive evaluation. An old wall-end, admitted J. B. S. Morritt, 'grows into some estimation with me when some glorious names of the Republic are tacked to it, and I have some pleasure in seeing the works of a virtuous and free nation'.[92] By the early nineteenth century, the solid simplicity

---

[88] Forbes journal NLS MS 1543, fols. 201–2.
[89] See Eaton, *Rome in the Nineteenth Century*, II, 71: 'beautiful as it is we must regard it with mingled admiration and horror'; Morgan, *Italy*, II, 187: 'it is so beautiful in ruin, that taste and feeling can send back no regrets for its former state of perfectness. This is the Coliseum – the last and noblest monument of Roman grandeur, and Roman crime – erected by the sweat and labour of millions of captives, for the purpose of giving the last touch of degradation to a people, whose flagging spirit policy sought to replace by brutal ferocity.' See also the review of Eustace in *Edinburgh Review*, 21 (1813), 396.
[90] Gareth Simpson, 'The rise and fall of the Roman historian: the eighteenth century in the Roman historical tradition', in James Moore, Ian Macgregor Morris and Andrew J. Bayliss (eds.), *Reinventing History: The Enlightenment Origins of Ancient History* (2009), 187–218.
[91] Colston, *Journal of a Tour in France*, 192–3: 'The fact is, that the Roman people were morally greatest, when least surrounded by the pomp of external grandeur, during the time of their Republic, – and at this period, the arts were scarcely known; and their buildings, publick and private, accorded with the moderation of their ideas.' Morgan, *Italy*, II, 181, complained that all the surviving monuments were imperial ones.
[92] J. B. S. Morritt, *A Grand Tour: Letters and Journeys 1794–96*, ed., G. S. Marindin (1985), 299.

of pre-Augustan architecture and engineering was being portrayed as the embodiment of the disinterested virtue associated with that era.[93] The Cloaca Maxima, for example, had always been on the tourist itinerary, not least because Pliny the elder had described it at length, but it had never elicited from eighteenth-century travellers much more than recognition of its sturdy and functional qualities – it was, according to one authority, simply 'a common gutter for the Conveyances of dirt and Filth'.[94] By the nineteenth century, however, its value in the eyes of British visitors had been greatly enhanced: it represented a concern for urban order and the public good which appealed directly to the priorities of the increasingly urban and middle-class travelling public. The Cloaca Maxima, enthused Edward Burton in 1821, 'is one of the most wonderful works, which any people ever constructed'.[95]

Burton had similarly noted the sparsity of antiquities from the era of the Roman Republic. But, he argued, those who could conjure up the shades of Cicero or Caesar or feel pleasure in treading upon the same ground upon which those events had taken place 'need not complain that there are no monuments of the time of the Republic'.[96] Burton's comment alludes, of course, to the importance of the traveller's ability to evoke the appropriate imaginative associations – the mark of the civilised and educated traveller – but also responds to a sense of disappointment and anti-climax that was expressed by travellers with greater frequency from the second half of the eighteenth century. Earlier in the eighteenth century, the talk was invariably of the delight to be found in retracing the steps of famous heroes, of visiting scenes so familiar from childhood and of the feelings of admiration and awe that such monuments inspired. Failure to experience the requisite emotions of pleasure and delight could not easily be expressed within the conventions of the travel literature of the time and, moreover, would have reflected badly upon the philosophical and imaginative powers of the traveller in question, as James Russel's analysis of the disappointment experienced by some of his clients illustrates very clearly. In a letter to his father written in 1748,

[93] Joseph Wilcocks, *Roman Conversations* (1792); Piozzi, *Observations and Reflections*, 193–4; Hobhouse, *Historical Illustrations*, 195–6; Morgan, *Italy*, II, 260.

[94] Basil Kennett, *Romae antiquae notitia: Or, the Antiquities of Rome in Two Parts* (10th edn, 1737), 58.

[95] Burton, *Description of the Antiquities*, 22. Enthusiasm for the drain continued to grow: a guidebook of 1841 described it as 'the most extraordinary structure' in Rome and praised the Romans' attention to health and cleanliness that it embodied, a view that was no doubt influenced by the Victorians' growing appreciation of the importance of adequate drains for the urban infrastructure. T. H. White, *Fragments of Italy and the Rhineland* (1841), 90.

[96] Burton, *Description of the Antiquities*, 48.

Russel, who supplemented his earnings as an artist by offering his services as a *cicerone*, commented ruefully on the frequency with which travellers left Rome dissatisfied – a feeling, he suggested, that was 'occasioned by the great ideas they have formed to themselves, either from reading, or from oral relations, having seen and heard the most ancient curiosities magnified too much'. They expected to find buildings such as the Capitol standing intact 'in their old magnificence'. Their ideas had been formed by prints and engravings which had given rise to entirely unrealistic expectations based on the pristine perfection of Desgodetz or the exaggerated scale and monumentality of Piranesi. But their disappointment was their own fault because they had failed to consider 'the many sackings, burnings, and ravages, which they have from time to time undergone'.[97] Had they reflected upon such matters, he implied, they would have experienced rather different sentiments.

It was precisely this failure of imagination that John Mayne felt himself to be suffering when he visited Rome in 1814: 'During the first hour after I arrived I could not help constantly repeating to myself, "Am I indeed in Rome?" and the difficulty of raising my imagination to feel the full force of my situation only served to depress me the more.'[98] Edward Burton was similarly 'mortified' on his arrival in Rome by a sense of unfulfilled expectations. Whilst Mayne did not analyse the reasons for his disappointment, Burton recognised for his part that it was a consequence of having allowed himself to 'anticipate so much' combined with the disappointing dreariness of the approach to Rome.[99] In general, this sense of anti-climax was a response not just to the absence of republican era monuments or the confusing anonymity of what had survived, but to the prosaic reality of antiquities surrounded by the paraphernalia of everyday life – sheds, shops, market stalls, washing lines, rubbish and animals. Joseph Forsyth began his account of Rome by predicting that anyone used to engraved images of Rome would be badly disappointed by the scenes that confronted them, and proceeded to elaborate upon the dirt and the lack of street lighting: 'The objects which detain you longest, such as Trajan's Column and the Fountain of Trevi, etc are inaccessible from ordure.' Further, in a particularly telling comparison between the ancient and modern city, which highlights a new criterion by which the British were judging foreign cities, he informed his readers that: 'Ancient Rome contained 144 public necessaries, plus the sellae patroclianae – the modern city has none of these conveniencies.'[100]

[97] Russel, *Letters from a Young Painter*, II, 178.
[98] Colles (ed.), *Journal of John Mayne*, 162.
[99] Burton, *Description of the Antiquities*, 3–4.   [100] Forsyth, *Remarks on Antiquities*, 124.

Forsyth's outburst was not untypical for his time, but could not have been articulated a century earlier. This is not to say that travellers were never disappointed before this time, but they did not express it in the same way: when they found fault it was with modern Rome (the taste of the architecture, for example) and modern Romans, not the ancient city. The later eighteenth-century emphasis on the subjective, personal experience of travel allowed greater opportunity to record the impressions formed, rather than simply to document the existence of a monument, and thus also enabled travellers to own up to feelings of frustration, discontent and disappointment, as well as delight and excitement.[101] On one level, as Buzard has argued, this kind of rhetoric was part of a quest for authenticity: by describing the depressing reality of decay and detritus and recording a sense of disappointment, the traveller was demonstrating the truthfulness of his or her account and distancing him or herself from the well-worn conventions of earlier topographical literature.[102] But this shift in tone was also a consequence of the changes in the relationship with antiquity noted above. Burton's admiration for ancient Rome was tempered with an awareness of its limitations – which allowed him to examine the antiquities with a more critical eye, one that was prepared to acknowledge their shortcomings and see their decay. For Burton, the city was not just a prompt to his imagination but was an artefact to be studied. He therefore observed the mundane surroundings in which the ancient monuments survived and was also prepared to find fault with the antiquities themselves.[103] Thus, he complained that the Pantheon – so often held to be irreproachable by earlier travellers – was 'decidedly ugly' in its 'round part' and stood in a dingy part of the city surrounded by houses.[104] The nineteenth-century vision of ancient Rome was increasingly one which embraced an appreciation of the city as the product of historical change, whether from Republic to Empire, or from antiquity, its destruction and its modern recovery.

Modern Rome

Roma antica provided the primary justification for British travellers to visit Rome, but *Roma moderna* exercised an almost equal fascination,

---

[101] Spacks, 'Splendid falsehoods'.   [102] Buzard, *The Beaten Track*, especially 173–4.
[103] The perspective views of the monuments depicted by Cresy and Taylor in *Architectural Antiquities of Rome* also highlighted the monuments' state of decay – the iron cincture holding the pillars of the Temple of Jupiter Stator upright, for example – and the buildings' location amongst the houses, lines of washing, muddy roads and daily life of Rome.
[104] Burton, *Description of the Antiquities*, 150.

even for those who were not drawn to it for reasons of pilgrimage. The modern city was epitomised by St Peter's basilica. Its gleaming dome was the first glimpse of the city to catch the traveller's eye on the approach from the north and many travellers went straight to St Peter's and the Vatican on their first arrival – and returned frequently thereafter – rather than to the Capitol or any of the monuments of antiquity.[105] Its fame was as widespread and its appearance as familiar as that of the Coliseum or the Pantheon. St Peter's was not, however, the sole attraction of the modern city, for all that it consumed a disproportionate amount of travellers' attention: the churches, palaces and museums were also an essential part of the tourist itinerary. The glory of modern Rome resided in the baroque splendour of the Catholic church and the Roman nobility and the paintings that were housed in the churches and palazzi. *Ciceroni* were expected to take their clients around the collections of art, as well as antiquities, and many doubled up as picture dealers on the side. Just as there was an itinerary of set pieces of antiquities to be seen, so too there was a hierarchy of paintings that the traveller had to view to establish his or her credentials as a person of taste. The four 'best' paintings in Rome were said to be Raphael's *Transfiguration*; the *Communion of St Jerome* by Dominichino; Andrea Sacchi's *Vision of San Romualdo* and Volterra's *Deposition*. In addition to these, there were the cycles of frescos by the Carracci in the Palazzo Farnese and Guido Reni at the Palazzo Ruspigliosi, and, most importantly, the glories of the Sistine Chapel and the Vatican. Here, the Raphael *Stanze* attracted more consistently favourable comment than the Sistine Chapel ceiling or the *Last Judgement*. Rome, for the British, was primarily Raphael's city; Michelangelo won rather more qualified admiration and came in for a considerable amount of criticism, particularly for the *Last Judgement*.[106] Just as much as with ancient Rome, therefore, the comments that were made regarding the modern city displayed a considerable degree of repetition and continuity over the century, but they likewise showed a tendency to become more critically evaluative and for travellers to express more qualified admiration by the end of the period.

[105] Mitford journal GA D 2002/3/4/1, vol. 3, 6–7: 'As the remains of the ancient magnificence of Rome have been the great sources whence the power & riches of the ecclesiastical government of this country have drawn the peculiar splendour of the modern city, those remains would become the first object of the traveller's curiosity if the reputation of the church of St. Peter, & the immensity of it's dome which caught his eye long before he reached the city, did not insensibly draw him first to take a view of that superb edifice.'

[106] The art-world of eighteenth-century Rome and the views of connoisseurs on art in Rome is too large a topic to enter into here, but for an overview, see Edgar Peters Bowron and Joseph J. Rishel (eds.), *Art in Rome in the Eighteenth Century* (2000).

As we have seen, perceptions of ancient Rome were overwhelmingly influenced by the inherited traditions of humanist scholarship and anti-quarianism. Descriptions of the modern city were also heavily deter-mined by an established corpus of literature over and above that of humanism: the tradition of pilgrimage guides, for example, had set out a sacred itinerary around the city's churches, which, whilst it was not followed in spiritual terms, still determined which churches featured in the local guidebooks, and therefore indirectly structured the experience of even the Protestant British tourist.[107] More overt in their influence were the publications devoted to the modern city that celebrated the remodelling and rebuilding of the city which had taken place under papal authority since the fifteenth century and which recorded the artis-tic patronage of the Roman nobility and the church.[108] These included guides which were aimed at the educated visitor, whose interests were not so much spiritual as artistic or antiquarian, such as Totti's *Ritratto di Roma moderna*; Titi's *Nuovo studio di pitture* reprinted until 1789; Rossini's *Mercurio Errante* reprinted until the mid-eighteenth century in various guises; and Martinelli's *Roma Ricercata* first published in 1644 and reprinted until 1771.[109] Given that much of the time that any British visitor stayed in Rome was taken up with viewing the collec-tions of paintings in the churches and the palazzi that had been amassed in the sixteenth and seventeenth centuries, these guides were essential reading and, along with the more substantial publications such as those by Vasi and Venuti, featured frequently in the notes of both published tours and in unpublished journals. They clearly exercised considerable influence over both what was seen and the comments that were made.

British visitors evidently accepted much of what they were told about the modern city: travellers in the first half of the eighteenth century echoed the praise for Sixtus V, 'that miracle of a man' who had done so much to give the city its modern appearance, preserving the remains of antiquity and making the streets regular and straight.[110] But this was not just uncritical repetition: baroque Rome was an impressive sight, and the more so in the earlier eighteenth century, at a time when British towns had yet to embark upon wide-scale urban improvement and expansion. The size and scale of the stone-built palazzi and the spacious

---

[107] See, for example, Nugent's *Grand Tour* in which the only churches discussed in detail were the seven basilicas.

[108] Habel, *Urban Development*; Krautheimer, *Rome of Alexander VII*.

[109] Rose Marie San Juan, *Roma. A City out of Print* (Minneapolis and London 2001), especially 57–94; Schudt, *Le guide di Roma*.

[110] Wright, *Observations*, I, 196–7; Drake journal MCO MS MC F15 vol. 1, 67, 101; Thomas to Jeremiah Milles, 23 Sept. 1773, BL Add. MS 19941, fol. 21r–v.

piazzas with their fountains and obelisks commanded awe and admiration. 'There is a Magnificence in the Town', enthused one traveller, 'that you do not see in any other; what gives that is the immense Number of fine Palaces, Squares & the profusion of fountains & water.'[111] But awe and admiration did not necessarily result in detailed descriptions and the accounts of British travellers are remarkably uninformative regarding the ongoing programme of building and improvement carried out by successive popes.[112] As with other destinations, visitors resorted to brief generalisations (straight streets, noble palazzi, elegant fountains) and saved the detail for itemising the collections of paintings and antiquities or calculating the value of the precious stones and silver plate decorating the church interiors. Even the modern city was a place to be viewed in the past – a place that had been beautified and improved but was now, in the perception of British travellers at least, essentially unchanging.[113] Recent buildings, restorations or alterations, such as Pius VI's erection of the obelisk at Montecavallo in 1786, were rarely even noted as such: the city's modern history was simply defined by its juxtaposition to antiquity.[114]

Rome was a city for walking. The various monuments were widely dispersed across the inhabited city and the *disabatio*; the Borghese gardens lent themselves to the kind of exercise to which the British were accustomed at home; whilst the Corso offered the opportunity for promenading and social display in the evening – even if most of the Italians remained resolutely in their carriages. But visitors to Rome did not stroll in the streets to capture the atmosphere as they did in Naples, or sit in the piazzas watching the life of the city pass by as was the custom in the Piazza San Marco. The *cantastoria*, who recited stories to the accompaniment of a guitar in the Piazza Barberini, or

---

[111] Winchilsea to his mother, 26 Apr.1773, ROLLR Finch MSS DG 7/4/14 box 4953 bundle 32.

[112] On papal improvement projects see Bowron and Rishel (eds.), *Art in Rome*, 17–33; Jeffrey Collins, *Papacy and Politics in Eighteenth-Century Rome* (Cambridge, 2004); and Christopher M. S. Johns, *Papal Art and Cultural Politics: Rome in the Age of Clement XI* (Cambridge, 1993).

[113] David Jefferies, *A Journal from London to Rome, by Way of Paris, Lyons, Turin, Florence, etc and from Rome back to London, by Way of Loretto, Venice, Milan* (2nd edn, 1755), offers a telling contrast to most English language accounts of Rome in that he was one of the few British observers specifically to highlight the achievements of Clement XII: the construction of the Capitoline Museum, the revamping of the Lateran church and of the Corsini chapel, the restoration of the Arch of Constantine and the unfinished Trevi fountain. Jefferies' sympathetic stance towards the papacy may be explained by the fact that he was a Catholic.

[114] On the erection of the obelisk and Pius VI's programme of urban improvement, see Collins, *Papacy and Politics*, esp. 193–8.

the high wire acts and magic lantern shows, which entertained the
Romans in Piazza Navona, never featured in the descriptions of British
travellers.[115] The brief carnival preceding the onset of Lent attracted
visitors, who watched the riderless horses race down the Corso, but in
most accounts it was a shortlived affair compared to those in Naples and
Venice. With so much else to see and record in Rome, the description of
'manners and customs' never dominated in the way that such set pieces
did for other urban centres, where the experience of the city was not
determined so narrowly by the lists of buildings and collections to be
viewed or by the necessity of engaging with imaginative reflections upon
the city's history. Indeed, the city's inhabitants were often invisible – many
travellers were able to describe Rome with only a passing mention of 'the
people', that is, those who lived and worked in the city as opposed to
the elite of Roman society with whom the British mixed in a *conversazione*.
Piozzi, for example, who commented at some length on street life and the
lazzaroni in Naples, simply noted the 'air of cheerfulness' amongst the
poor in Rome, and their propensity to quarrel without the aggravation of
inebriation.[116] As she herself explained, 'in this town, unlike to every
other, the *things* take my attention all away from the people'.[117] In the
early nineteenth century, when depictions of the 'people' – both graphic
and literary – were gaining in popularity, Rome continued to be rendered
depopulated in many accounts – for, as Timothy Webb has argued, the
romantic view of Rome was one that marginalized contemporary Rome in
order to 'find solitude and space for imaginative engagement with the
spirit of the city and its history'.[118]

Comments on the 'people' were almost always confined to the
Trastevere area – partly because the people themselves claimed unique
descent from the ancient Romans and maintained a distinctive way
of life, but partly because Trastevere was relatively poor in antiquities,
enjoying a very insignificant profile in the traditional tourist itinerary –
as Ann Flaxman explained to her father, it was a quarter that few people
visited except to see the two or three churches.[119] The inhabitants,
therefore, were not in competition with buildings or antiquities; nor

[115] Hanns Gross, *Rome in the Age of Enlightenment: The Post-Tridentine Syndrome and the Ancien Regime* (Cambridge, 2002), 298. Adam Walker, author of *Ideas Suggested on the Spot*, did not describe such characters but did make passing reference to the wretch 'strumming his mandolino' upon the place where a 'virtuous' father had killed Virginia, his daughter, rather than see her made the 'handmaid of an Emperor's lust', 318.

[116] Piozzi, *Observations and Reflections*, 218.   [117] Ibid., 208.

[118] Webb, ' "City of the soul" ', 4. As Webb also points out, it should be remembered that Italian guidebooks did not have sections on manners and customs either and simply repeated the urban myth of the Trasteverini's descent from ancient Romans.

[119] Flaxman journal BL Add. MS 39787, fol. 82v.

did they in turn detract from the objects of virtù which the visitor would otherwise seek out. Thus, comments on 'the people' and their manners and customs could be tidily contained within observations on Trastevere, and the inhabitants of the rest of Rome remained unidentified and unremarked. The Trasteverini's character was represented as rude, uncivilised and even savage – the more to emphasise the contrast with the monuments of antique civilisation and refinement that surrounded them. Flaxman told her aunt that they retained their 'ancient rudeness and ferocity' whilst Charlotte Eaton described them as ferocious and passionate, prone to jealous rages and revenge, and the men were strong and vigorous (despite the unhealthy situation). She dutifully repeated their claim to be the true descendants of the ancient Romans and traced in their game of *morra* elements of the Roman game of *micare digitis*, in the same way that visitors to Naples saw echoes of the Pompeian wall paintings in the manners and customs of the modern day Neapolitans.[120] Eaton's representation of the Trasteverini may have been influenced by the etchings of Pinelli, himself a native of Trastevere, whose *Raccolta di cinquanta costumi pittoreschi* had appeared in 1809 and proved extremely popular amongst tourists (the game of *morra* was one of the scenes that he chose to illustrate).[121] The popularity of Pinelli's scenes and the interest in the popular manners and customs amongst travellers that they reflect is also evident in the fact that they were chosen to illustrate Henry Coxe's *Picture of Italy* (1815).

The Trasteverini's propensity to violence that Eaton and others noted was notorious: their jealousy, which was easily inflamed, was particularly dangerous due to their custom of carrying knives (a practice which, providing further evidence of their barbarity, was shared by the women). They would descend into fighting as soon as they met with inhabitants from another part of the city, claimed another traveller.[122] At one level, this kind of commentary operated as an indictment of the inadequate street lighting and what travellers considered to be the poor civil order and police in Rome.[123] The ubiquitous right of asylum for any criminal

---

[120] Eaton, *Rome in the Nineteenth Century*, II, 343–6.
[121] Bartolomeo Pinelli, *Raccolta di cinquanta costumi pittoreschi* (Rome, 1809).
[122] William Otter, *The Life and Remains of the Rev. Edward Daniel Clarke* (1824), 154–5. Clarke also noted their claim to be the true descendants of the ancient Romans. See also Ann Flaxman to her aunt, 16 June 1788: 'The city abounds with venomous creatures the worst of which are the signorie – the Italian men – especially those in low life, who play together at ball for 5 mins, the next 5 mins they quarrel and the next they kill.' BL Add. MS 39780, fol. 175; Morgan, *Italy*, II, 261, devoted a lengthy footnote to the Trasteverini, but suggested that since the practice of carrying stilettos had been outlawed, levels of violence had considerably diminished.
[123] Moore, *A View of Society and Manners*, II, 460.

in the city's churches and the ease with which absolution might be obtained afterwards were widely blamed for encouraging criminality.[124] But the comments also drew upon the longstanding caricature of the hot-blooded and violent Italian male that had been circulating in English accounts of Italy since the seventeenth century and earlier: qualities which were the more evident in the lower orders who lacked the restraint of civility and whose masculinity had been less compromised by the excesses of luxury that afflicted the elite.[125] Yet, whereas in Naples and Venice the dangers posed by the *lazzaroni* or the *gondolieri* appear to have been largely diffused by the end of the century, to be replaced by a perception of the lower orders as charming and unthreatening, in Rome this kind of transformation was much less apparent. Fears were still expressed over their propensity to violence and their predilection for the stiletto in the nineteenth century.[126] As the embodiment of mal-government and disorder in Rome they continued to represent a threat.

The spaces and contexts of everyday life in Rome were rarely described. The Campo di Fiore was central to the life of Rome on account of the horse fair and the markets that were held there. It was also the location for the punishment of those found guilty by the Inquisition. Yet, one rarely finds a mention of it as a space in British writings, despite the fact that those who followed Vasi's directions would have known of it, both from the description and the accompanying illustration, complete with gibbet.[127] The Piazza Navona, by contrast, was widely praised by visitors, but the fact that it played host to a weekly market was not worthy of comment – unless to complain of the rubbish left behind. The much rarer annual flooding of the piazza in August, however, the pseudo-naumachia,

---

[124] Anon., 'Remarks', Bodl. MS Douce 67, 236–7; Gibbes journal TNA PRO 30/9/7/10, 21 Nov. 1789: '& yet such are the mischievous effects of the right of asylum, the ease with which absolution is obtained upon the confession of the crime, & the prejudice which exists among the lower orders of the people in favour of the practice, that during the first 13 years of the reign of the present Pope no less than 30,000 murders were committed. This fact is ascertained by the register which is kept of deaths throughout the papal dominions.'

[125] Andrew M. Canepa, 'From degenerate scoundrel to noble savage: the Italian stereotype in eighteenth-century British travel literature', *English Miscellany*, 22 (1971), 107–46.

[126] Coxe insisted that the better system of police introduced by the French, and in particular the end to sanctuary offered by the churches and improved street lighting, had significantly reduced levels of crime: *Picture of Italy*, 177. Coxe offered a consistently positive evaluation of the impact of the French on Rome; his assessment of the crime situation was not shared by other visitors.

[127] Giuseppe Vasi, *Itinerario istruttivo per ritrovare con facilità tutte le Magnificenze artiche e moderne di Roma* (Naples, 1770), 294. By 1791, the description had been reduced to one sentence's worth and the illustration showing the gallows set in the centre of the Campo had disappeared.

when all the nobility of Rome paraded in their carriages, was regularly recorded in print and graphic form. Similarly, whilst the British deplored the despoliation of the Coliseum to build the Palazzo Farnese, the fact that Clement XI had used masonry from a collapsed arch to build the new Ripetta, with its elegantly curved staircase, was never mentioned.[128] The riverine trade (a muted, but visible, element of a guidebook like Vasi's) and papal efforts to improve it by clearing the Tiber, were of no concern. The papacy's failure to dredge the river in search of antiquities – supposed to have been thrown in there during the various sacks of Rome – was frequently berated, as we have seen, but the negative consequences of this inaction were never considered in terms of the trading potential of the city.[129] Efforts to stimulate the manufacturing economy, such as the tapestry works at the Ospedale di San Michele and the calico works which Clement XIV had established in the Baths of Diocletian in 1774, were similarly invisible and rarely recorded.[130] The first guidebook which actually included a section on the commerce of Rome was Henry Coxe's *Picture of Italy* (1815) but this was simply because the author used the same subheadings to divide his material for each city he described. The substantive information conveyed on Rome's commerce was minimal and consisted chiefly of observations on the supply of grain to the capital.[131] Otherwise, it was only visitors such as the merchant Robert Harvey, whose tour of Italy was part business part pleasure, who noted the presence of a paper manufactory by the Cloaca Maxima and who commented upon the shops and commercial activity on the Corso.[132]

However much the eighteenth-century popes, like any other enlightened ruler, may have been attempting to stimulate the Roman economy and relieve poverty and unemployment, the British resolutely declined to acknowledge this. Comments on the charitable foundations in

[128] Venuti, *Accurata, e succinta descrizione topografica di Roma*, 28; Ficoroni, *Le vestigie e rarità di Roma*, 39. On the building of the port by Specchi, see Johns, *Papal Art and Cultural Politics*, 184–5.
[129] See, for example, Drake journal MCO MS MC F15 vol. 1, 144; John Owen, *Travels into Different Parts of Europe*, II, 31.
[130] Unusually, Mary Berry recorded a visit to the pope's manufactory of printed linen (although she did not specify that it was located in the Baths of Diocletian) and observed that it was failing to make a profit and would be given up. Lewis (ed.), *Extracts of the Journals and Correspondence*, I, 111.
[131] Coxe, *Picture of Italy*, 263–5. The trade and commerce of Rome was discussed in other publications, however, such as Thomas Denham, *The Temporal Government of the Pope's State* (1788); Walker, *Ideas Suggested on the Spot*, 233, 236, documented the *absence* of any significant manufactures or trade within Rome, chiefly in order to affirm the superiority of Britain over the modern Romans.
[132] Harvey journal NRO MS 20677, 174.

Trastevere were as rare and as limited as those on the economy, in contrast to comments in Genoa, for example, where the Albergo dei Poveri was widely admired and frequently merited an extended description.[133] Instead, they maintained a view of Rome as a city that survived on the wealth of tourists and the revenues of the Catholic church. Indeed, it is noticeable that successive editions of, for example, Vasi's guide, were evidently being tailored to meet the tastes of the visitor market, and gradually dropped whatever material the earlier editions had included on the day to day life of the city such as the markets in the Campo di Fiore or the public executions that traditionally took place there; the trade at the Porta di Ripetta; the accounts of charitable foundations in Trastevere; or the lesser churches with their relics. These elements were gradually squeezed out of Vasi's tour, and in their place more and more information on the paintings, statues and antiquities to be found in palazzi and churches was included, with a liberal sprinkling of the adjective 'pittoresco' to cater to the new aesthetic tastes of travellers, where none had existed before.[134] Thus, even in the Roman guidebooks, representations of the contemporary city were being revised to suit the agenda of the travelling public.

Those who professed affection for or delight in Rome tended to be the travellers who were self-consciously preening themselves as devotees of antiquity, taste and virtù. Edward Thomas, whose earnestness of purpose betrayed itself regularly in his letters to Jeremiah Milles, described Rome as 'the chief repository of all virtu' and 'that charming and amusing place' where he had spent the six 'happyest and most entertaining months of my life', delighting in the antiquities, music, public shows, spectacles and paintings.[135] The equally earnest Thomas Gray similarly found much to delight him in the collections of art and antiquities: it was the insistence of his travelling companion, Horace Walpole, that they should return to what the latter found to be the more congenial environment of Florence that contributed to the breakdown in their friendship.[136] But for those travellers less intent on the cultivation of the fine arts, Rome was not so much a place to enjoy oneself or

[133] In the early eighteenth century the *Albergi dei Poveri* in various cities attracted attention from several travellers, presumably because of the topicality of workhouses in current debates over poverty, see, for example, the comments of Andrew Mitchell in his journal of 1734 BL Add. MS 58319, fos. 54–5, or Walter Bowman in 1737, St Andrews University Library Special Collections MS 3671/6, fol. 26.

[134] The adjective 'pittoresco' is not found in the earlier editions of the Vasi guidebook, but see, for example, Mariano Vasi, *Itinerario istruttivo di Roma antica e moderna* (Rome, 1804), 119, 239.

[135] Thomas to Jeremiah Milles, 3 Mar. 1751, BL Add. MS 19941, fol. 35.

[136] Robert L. Mack, *Thomas Gray: A Life* (New Haven and London, 2000), 249–51.

be entertained than a place of demanding and gruelling edification. Robert Harvey found that his brain had become 'a compound of pictures & antiquities well pounded together'.[137] Another spoke of the 'positive pain' and exhaustion induced by the endless collections of objects and places to be seen.[138] Roger Robertson, mindful of the reasons why his father had sent him to Italy, was careful to reassure him that no one enjoyed the experience of studying virtù more than he did. But, in a letter to his younger sister, where a greater degree of honesty was possible, he confessed that Rome was not such a sociable place as Naples, and that after studying antiquities all day time could lie rather heavy in the evening.[139] The potential tedium of this austere diet of art and antiquities was compounded in these visitors' view by the lacklustre social scene: the 'resources of Rome' as William Patoun tactfully warned Lord Brownlow, 'are to be derived more from the place than the inhabitants'. The conversazioni, he continued, 'are the dullest things in the world'.[140] In other cities, the social and cultural life was a principal attraction, but few visitors claimed to love Rome for its sociability. In the absence of an official representative of the British state – such as Sir Horace Mann in Florence or Sir William Hamilton in Naples – the social lives of the British visitors lacked an obvious focal point and there was no official channel through which to introduce them to Roman society. From 1718, when the Pretender established his court at Rome, British visitors had to be wary with whom they mixed to avoid provoking the suspicions of the network of spies employed by the British government.[141] The Pretender's acolytes were reported to use tricks and deception to ensnare unsuspecting British visitors and affiliate them to the Jacobite cause. However, in practical terms, the Stuart court provided essential services – passports, diplomatic protection, an Anglican chapel and social introductions – of which Protestants as well as Catholics readily availed themselves.[142] By the later eighteenth century, when the Young Pretender had declined into a drunken curiosity, the gap in hospitality was to a great extent filled through the offices of other

---

[137] Harvey journal NRO MS 20677, 202.
[138] Colles (ed.), *Journal of John Mayne*, 189.
[139] Robertson to Babie Robertson, 29 Dec. 1751, NLS Acc 12244.
[140] Patour, 'Advice on travel in Italy', xlvi.
[141] Lesley Lewis, *Connoisseurs and Secret Agents in Eighteenth-Century Rome* (1961); Daniel Szechi, 'The image of the court: idealism, politics and the evolution of the Stuart court, 1689–1730', in Edward Corp (ed.), *The Stuart Court in Rome: The Legacy of Exile* (Aldershot, 2003), 49–64.
[142] Edward Corp, *The Stuarts in Italy 1719–66: A Royal Court in Permanent Exile* (Cambridge, 2011), 3–8, 125; see also the comments of Jefferies, *Journey from London to Rome*, 52–3.

long-term British residents, such as the banker Thomas Jenkins. Jenkins performed many similar functions to those of Mann and Hamilton: arranging accommodation, assisting with passports, providing advice on what to see and offering hospitality and banking facilities. But Jenkins did not have the social status or position to assert such a dominant role in Roman life and his influence declined after the death of Clement XIV.[143]

These factors may have reinforced the British tendency to mix only amongst themselves, noted by numerous contemporaries. Such insularity was due in part to British unease with the Italian language, however, there were others who attributed it much more prosaically simply to the want of good company amongst the Romans.[144] Robert Harvey, with his over-taxed brain, was unimpressed at what he encountered: 'They do not know the joy of society ... Thanks to ye Gods, I was not born a roman.'[145] But it was also a reflection of the fact that, as in other Italian cities, the British found only a limited number of Italian families willing to receive them.[146] Thomas Pelham complained to his father of the difficulties in making the acquaintance of the Italian nobility, but allowed that this was hardly surprising given how many strangers were constantly passing through: 'they grow very indifferent about it', he concluded.[147] Those members of the nobility who were prepared to receive foreign visitors were generally those who had been close to James III and often had English connections, such as Prince Giustiniani, who had married the daughter of Englishwoman, Cecilia Mahony,[148] or the Princess Sta Croce, wife of the Spanish ambassador, whose *conversazioni* the British regularly attended,[149] or the Marquis Torlonia, who had

---

[143] Ford, 'Thomas Jenkins'.

[144] Paul Mellon Centre, Brinsley Ford Archive, extracts of correspondence between Richard and John Newdigate, letter dated 24 Jan. 1740; see also the comments of John Andrews, *Characteristical Views of the Past and Present State of the People of Spain and Italy* (1808), 220–1.

[145] Harvey journal NRO MS 20677, 202.

[146] On the trials of becoming accepted in Roman society, and the limits of Roman sociability, see Lady Elliott-Drake (ed.), *Lady Knight's Letters from France and Italy 1776–95* (1905).

[147] The *conversazioni* in Rome, Thomas Pelham informed his mother, 'are not entertaining', BL Add. MS 33127, fol. 218v, 8 Apr. 1777; Philip Yorke told his uncle that he attended the *conversazioni*, but that it was very difficult 'to make acquaintances of any intimacy with the Romans because such a number of strangers are continually passing through here that they grow very indifferent about it', 18 Nov. 1778, BL Add. MS 35378, fol. 270.

[148] Cecilia Mahony was the daughter of Count James Joseph Mahony who was in the Neapolitan service and Lady Anne Clifford, see Ingamells (ed.), *Dictionary of British and Irish Travellers*, 629. See also Corp, *Stuarts in Italy*, 6.

[149] Ernest Taylor (ed.), *The Taylor Papers: Being a Record of Certain Reminiscences, Letters and Journals in the Life of Lieut-Gen Sir Herbert Taylor* (1913), 11.

become the principal banker to the British by the end of the century. Sarah Bentham's journal, which provided a blow by blow account of her social engagements in Rome, bears witness to the very limited extent to which the British and Italian social circles intermeshed. During the months of January to March 1794, for example, she attended a series of twelve concerts held at the palazzi of the leading Roman nobility – an unprecedented arrangement necessitated by the fact that the pope had closed all the theatres in response to the execution of Louis XVI. These concerts aside, however, the social events which she attended were mostly organised by her countrymen or by other non-Roman establishments such as the Cardinal de Bernis or the Venetian ambassador. The only Roman *conversazioni* to which she was invited were those held by the Princess Sta Croce, Princess Doria and the Princess Borghese: and these were events that were dominated by French and English visitors – resident Italians were in the minority, and Italian ladies in particular were few and far between.[150] Similarly, Sir William Forbes, who was in Rome the preceding winter, recorded a far less active social scene than that in which he and his family had participated in Naples. Instead of regular dinner parties, suppers and balls, there was only a succession of *conversazioni* and sedate card parties, at which, he complained, nobody played for money.[151] Even the entertainments that the British enjoyed in other cities were more circumscribed in Rome – theatres there were, but they were open only for the few weeks between Christmas and Lent. British audiences, discomfited by the presence of male actors taking the parts of women, were predisposed to find fault with the quality of the performances and the state of the decor. Rome lacked that air of 'cheerfulness and gaiety' which was so often identified in Florence and Naples.[152]

Tobias Smollett refused to be impressed by modern Rome on principle. His disgusted description of the 'depositories of nastiness' to be found in the most elegant palaces, that smelled as strong as 'spirit of hartshorn', may be taken as representative of a new tone of criticism that was creeping into descriptions of Rome in the latter part of the eighteenth century, but it was a critique that affected his descriptions of almost any town that he described. His outspoken xenophobia played a part, but so too did his anti-urban misanthropy: he was equally

---

[150] Bentham journal TNA PRO 30/9/43; Elizabeth Gibbes' social diary was similarly restricted in terms of the level of interaction with the Italian nobility for the winter and spring of 1789/90: TNA PRO 30/9/7/10 and 11.

[151] Forbes journal NLS MS 1540, fols. 374, 377.

[152] Milford, *Observations, Moral, Literary and Antiquarian*, II, 122.

vehement in his denunciation of the dirt and pollution of Bath and London in *Humphry Clinker*.[153] More broadly, however, observations on the lack of cleanliness in Rome began to feature with greater frequency in both published and unpublished sources by the end of the eighteenth century. Earlier travellers had occasionally remarked upon the dirty floors of a palazzo or the rubbish in the Campo Vaccino, but it had not been a major theme in the commentary on Rome, as it was in remarks on Venice, for example.[154] This changed, however: in the later eighteenth century, visitors made much more frequent reference to dirt in the streets; to the insalubrious state of the palazzi; to the filth which surrounded the various monuments and to the general nastiness in passageways, streets and entrances. The day to day detritus of contemporary Rome, and even the Roman habit of urinating in public spaces, all became more prominent in visitors' accounts.[155] Most noticeably, there was a new emphasis on smell. In 1815, Robert Finch walked along the Tiber from the Castel San Angelo to the Temple of Vesta and found his nose 'unremittingly assailed by a most overpowering essence of combin'd stinks'.[156] As Alain Corbin has argued, the second half of the eighteenth century saw the emergence of a more refined attitude to odour and diminished tolerance amongst the European elite towards the dirt and pollution that generated offensive smells and posed a risk to health.[157] Whereas formerly it was rare to complain about the filth of the streets or the presence of foul-smelling drains, increasingly this became a criterion by which towns and cities were judged. (Joseph Forsyth's unfavourable comparison between the ancient and modern city with respect to the provision of public conveniences has already been noted.) Paving, which in the wake of urban improvement in Britain had become the mark of civilized urbanity, was valued not simply for its practical benefits or because of its allusions to the pavements of ancient Rome, but because the paving stones sealed off the filth of the underlying soil and the noisomeness of underground water.[158] Comments about odours, stenches and effluvia, as well as the quality of pavements and drains, therefore became a consistent element of travellers' observations

[153] Smollett, *Travels through France and Italy*, II, 95; Tobias Smollett, *The Expedition of Humphry Clinker* (1771).

[154] Phillips (ed.), *Correspondence*, I, 94–5; Wright, *Observations*, I, 198.

[155] Hale (ed.), *Italian Journal*, 88. Henry Matthews similarly found the Piazza di Spagna 'a little less nasty than the other piazzas in Rome, because the habits of the people are in some measure restrained by the presence of the English', *Diary of an Invalid*, 64.

[156] Finch journal Bodl. MS Finch e. 16, fol. 36r.

[157] Alain Corbin, *The Foul and the Fragrant: Odor and the French Social Imagination* (Leamington Spa, 1986).

[158] Ibid., 90; Sweet, 'Topographies of politeness'.

in this period.[159] This new olfactory sensibility meshed with the shift away from the mode of objective description, which enumerated columns and listed the measurements of buildings, to the subjective experience of the sentimental traveller who could respond to the sensory stimuli of the streets.

But the emphasis on the dirt and decay in the streets of Rome that we find from the later eighteenth century also played to other agendas. On one level, it was related to the influence of the picturesque already noted – it was an inseparable element of the irregularity and deformity that this aesthetic prized.[160] It was also a way of highlighting the 'degeneracy' of modern Romans and their failure to safeguard the heritage which had been entrusted to them and to which the British now saw themselves as the heirs in spirit.[161] Complaints about the piles of rubbish surrounding the antiquities and the wretched houses built up against them brought into focus the contrast between the ancient and the modern city (the 'upstart structures of degenerate days', as Charlotte Eaton dismissed them) and the irresponsible stewardship of modern Romans.[162] Yet, those writing for a less public audience, such as Ann Flaxman or Mary Berry, who recorded their experiences in journals and letters home without a view to publication, adopted a more pragmatic tone; one that highlights the rhetorical function of dirt in the other publications. Flaxman was certainly disgusted by the slovenly and dirty habits of the Romans, but her disgust was provoked by concern for domestic comfort, not because of the implications of noisome smells for health or the implied commentary on public virtue. Her principal preoccupation was actually with the fleas that flourished in the infested streets and 'plagued' her as soon as she stepped out of doors. It was the vermin, not the smells, that were the overriding cause of discomfort.[163] Mary Berry, by contrast, seems not to have been overly troubled by the cleanliness or otherwise of Rome, although she did remark that the steps at the base of Trajan's Column were 'neither dark nor dirty'.[164] This was in 1783. Yet, less than ten years later, John Owen found the column 'scarcely accessible because of filth around it'.[165]

---

[159] David Inglis, 'Sewers and sensibilities: the bourgeois faecal experience in the nineteenth-century city', in Alexander Cowan and Jill Steward (eds.), *The City and the Senses: Urban Culture since 1500* (Aldershot, 2007), 105–30.

[160] Malcolm Andrews, 'The metropolitan picturesque', in Stephen Copley and Peter Garside (eds.), *The Politics of the Picturesque: Literature, Landscape and Aesthetics since 1770* (Cambridge, 1994), 282–98.

[161] Andrews, *Characteristical Views*, 217.

[162] Eaton, *Rome in the Nineteenth Century*, I, 140.

[163] Flaxman journal BL Add. MS 39787, fol. 176.

[164] Lewis (ed.), *Extracts of the Journals and Correspondence*, I, 65.

[165] Owen, *Travels into Different Parts of Europe*, II, 30.

Either conditions had deteriorated badly in the interim, or Owen's emphasis on dirt was performing another function – specifically contributing to a rhetoric that established the superiority of Britain over modern and ancient Rome. Dirt was the signifier for the fallen condition of the Roman state and its modern inhabitants.

Owen was not the only traveller who used comments about the dirt and the smells of Rome to assert British superiority and to demonstrate the degeneracy of the modern city.[166] 'Nothing resembling such a hole as this [the Piazza della Rotonda] could exist in England', exclaimed Charlotte Eaton, 'nor is it possible that an English imagination can conceive a combination of such disgusting dirt, such filthy odours and foul puddles, as that which fills the vegetable market in the Piazza Della Rotonda at Rome' (see Figure 8).[167] The fountains, it was pointed out by several tourists, were dirty and polluted with vegetable waste. They provided an abundance of water, but none of it was used to clean the filthy streets.[168] As Eaton observed with deliberately hard-nosed pragmatism, had the popes built more baths and fewer churches, using some of the water that was wasted with such profligacy in the fountains, 'his subjects would have cleaner bodies and no worse souls'.[169] Cleanliness was certainly not next to godliness in Rome. These fountains represented the corruption of the virtues of antiquity in the taste of modern Italians for conspicuous consumption and wasteful display instead of utility and true beauty. Similarly, visitors were increasingly offended by the juxtaposition of grandiose noble palazzi with mean hovels and the overt manifestation of poverty. In the eighteenth century, this contrast was simply represented as an incongruity; by the nineteenth century, the travellers were far more aware of the rickety reality behind the façade of wealth and grandeur that the palazzi represented. Complaints about dirt were the principal means through which the British asserted their superiority over the deluded pride of the Roman nobility: their palazzi were splendid, but they lived in squalor and poverty. Their indigence was such that they were reduced to selling their collections and leasing their palazzi to the visiting British. Hester Piozzi's observations on the nastiness within and without the palazzi are probably the most detailed to have come down to us, but she was simply elaborating upon a theme rehearsed at greater or lesser length by many other

---

[166] See also pp. 75–6 on Florence and 220–1 on Venice.
[167] Eaton, *Rome in the Nineteenth Century*, I, 329.
[168] Smollett, *Travels through France and Italy*, II, 95; Spacks, 'Splendid falsehoods', 210; Piozzi, *Observations and Reflections*, 219; Smith, *Sketch of a Tour*, II, 4.
[169] Eaton, *Rome in the Nineteenth Century*, II, 76.

Figure 8 The Piazza della Rotonda, from Giovanni Battista Piranesi, *Vedute di Roma*, 2 vols. (Rome, n.d.).

tourists.[170] The disgust expressed by Sydney Morgan, the novelist and Irish patriot, who visited Rome in 1819, formed part of her broader critique of the corruption of papal government, its negative influence over the well being of the people of Rome, and its inability to preserve the antique heritage in its midst. Her account of Rome functioned as a platform from which to denounce the temporal power of the papacy and to espouse the cause of republicanism. Again, her comments were directed at the Piazza Rotonda, which presented a stark contrast between the perfection of antiquity and the detritus of modern urban living: 'The senses are every where assailed; and the pavement, sprinkled with blood and filth, exhibits the entrails of pigs, or piles of stale fish, sold almost within the pale of that miracle of art, which Phidias might have gloried to have raised, and which Michael Angelo was proud to copy.'[171]

The grandeur of Sixtus V's town planning or set pieces such as the Strada Felice were likewise brought into question: Morgan accused Sixtus V, so much admired by Edward Wright, of being a 'bustling tyrant' who threw down streets and houses in order to clear spaces in which to build his palaces.[172] But she was not the only one who found the urban planning of renaissance and baroque Rome less impressive than the travellers of the earlier eighteenth century. The standards by which British visitors judged the modern city had undergone substantive change since the early eighteenth century: paved streets, elegant squares, magnificent public buildings were a feature not just of London, but of many provincial towns. Rome had nothing to match the developments of Edinburgh New Town, London's West End, Bath, Dublin or even Liverpool. 'I never was more disappointed than at Rome', John Patteson told his mother, 'I carried the ideas of a London with me, which is infinitely superior to it as a city.'[173] Robert Finch looked in vain for the neatness, taste and symmetrical regularity in the streets and squares that he claimed one could expect to see in London.[174] Edward Burton, whose attitude to the Catholic church was far more moderate than Morgan's, similarly abandoned the tone of uncritical praise that had characterised so many accounts in the eighteenth century: the Piazza del Popolo, that had made such a powerful impression on earlier visitors, failed to impress him. The Porta del Popolo (Porta Flaminia), he wrote, opened into an 'irregular space' with, he implied, little to recommend it beyond the fact that it was the first part of Rome that any visitor actually saw.[175]

---

[170] Piozzi Observations and Reflections, 212–13.   [171] Morgan, Italy, II, 181.
[172] Ibid., 225.   [173] Cubitt, Mackley and Wilson (eds.), Great Tour of John Patteson, 289.
[174] Finch journal Bodl. MS Finch e. 16, fol. 79r.
[175] Burton, Description of the Antiquities, 7.

The monumentality of modern Rome was never challenged outright, but it now commanded a more qualified admiration, and fault finding became an increasingly important element of travellers' commentaries, and not just in Rome. The focus upon dirt and the state of the streets was part of the more general shift, already noted, towards describing the city as a whole, rather than as a disconnected series of antiquities, buildings and collections. Rather than listing individual buildings, travellers who were finding their way around Rome with the aid of maps and plans started to record their experience of the streets and the environment through which they passed. They described the paths they took in viewing the city and commented upon the insalubrious environs in which St Peter's was located; the filthy alleyways through which one had to walk to reach it and the shabby buildings that crowded around it.[176] The city was being imagined as a space, rather than simply a collection of buildings.

These changes were also related to the shift in the way that the British conceived of their own relationship to the city, already noted above. By the time of the Napoleonic Wars, and Rome's capitulation to the French, there was a much clearer sense amongst the British of their own prosperity and superiority, not only vis à vis ancient Rome, but also the modern Romans, whose economic and political fortunes had declined steadily over the eighteenth century. The British had acquired some of the choicest specimens of art and antiquity from the collections of the Roman nobility and saw themselves as the new leaders of enlightened and cultivated patronage of the arts. The poverty of the Roman nobility – and their dependence on the income that British tourists brought – was proof that the vigour and might of Rome had long since passed elsewhere. The Roman economy – heavily dependent on catering to visitors, producing paintings and statues, selling cameos and fans – barely merited discussion, let alone admiration. The ease with which Napoleon, the self-styled Caesar of the modern age, had entered Rome was further proof of the supine degeneracy of the modern Romans. Whilst Venice's loss of its ancient independence in 1797 was looked upon with regret, few British travellers bemoaned the presence of the French, beyond the temporary inconvenience of so many choice antiquities and works of art having been transported to Paris. Rather, it was accepted that the French had done much to improve Rome – not only had they excavated the forum, but they had brought better order to the streets and considerably improved the

---

[176] Finch journal Bodl. MS Finch e. 15, fol. 61v; MS Finch e. 16, fol. 252v; Eaton, *Rome in the Nineteenth Century*, I, 111.

manners of the people.[177] London, in the meantime, the hub of Britain's commercial empire, had steadily grown in wealth, size and magnificence.

These changes, combined with the evolution in the genre of travel writing towards a record of sensory impressions and personal experience, allowed travellers to explore a much greater range of themes in their descriptions of the city. The listing of emblematic antiquities or itemising of collections that characterised so many of the late seventeenth- and early eighteenth-century descriptions was gradually giving way to a mode of description that offered greater scope for the elaboration of a sense of place and its historical development. The antiquarian paradigm through which Rome was viewed had been substantially modified; parts of Rome were now becoming visible in travellers' accounts that had hitherto gone largely unnoticed. One area in which these developments were particularly evident was the treatment given to Christian Rome.

Christian Rome

Modern Rome, as visitors were well aware, was essentially the product of papal power and as such was a reflection of the wealth and authority of the Catholic church. In the late seventeenth century, when Protestant suspicions of the papacy and Catholicism were still acute, the descriptions provided by travellers such as Gilbert Burnet or Maximilien Misson were effectively exercises in censuring the superstition and priestcraft of the Catholic church. The relics and miracles of the sacred itineraries were held up for ridicule and denunciation; the richness of the churches were an indictment of the worldly greed of the papal camera. The Lenten penance of self-flagellation in particular excited an almost prurient fascination amongst British travellers which continued well into the eighteenth century.[178] Miracles, relics and patronal dedications were largely ignored, except by those like the non-juror Richard Rawlinson or the future Bishop of Meath, Richard Pococke, who had a professional and antiquarian interest in such matters. Yet, in the course of the century, the militant anti-Catholicism of the earlier period became more muted. Most British Protestants shared the scepticism of the seventeenth-century travellers regarding Catholicism, but the tone of their critiques became more measured as their fear of the papist threat receded. Indeed, Misson and Burnet were taken to task by a later traveller for their

---

[177] See, for example, the chapter on 'French improvements' in Coxe, *Picture of Italy*.
[178] See, for example, Wright, *Observations*, I, 189–90, and Northall, *Travels through Italy*, 66. Tellingly, 'The pious flagellator' was selected as the frontispiece for Anon., *The Polite Traveller*, 4 vols. (1783), a book of travels aimed at a more popular readership.

excessive anti-Catholic zeal which led them 'into absurdities'.[179] The majority of the educated elite who came to Rome in the eighteenth century viewed Catholicism less as a potent danger to true religion or the Protestant interest than as a system of corruption and abuse which owed more to paganism than to the teachings of Christianity. The influence of works such as Conyers Middleton's *Letter from Rome: Shewing an Exact Conformity between Popery and Paganism* (1729) and Joseph Spence's *Polymetis* (1747) was palpable in the way that travellers drew analogies between Catholic saints and pagan deities, or identified traces of pagan rituals and superstition in the devotional practices of modern day Catholics into the nineteenth century.[180] This rather more tolerant attitude to Catholicism on the part of most travellers would have an obvious bearing upon the way in which the city was perceived and described.[181]

Given the dependence of British travellers and tour writers upon the Catholic guides to the city, the structural components of pilgrimage guides – the list of seven principal churches, for example – continued to determine the church-visiting itinerary of many travellers. But the churches themselves were represented less as places of worship, or even superstition, than as repositories of art and specimens of architecture. They were described in one guide as 'theatres' for the exhibition of architecture, painting and sculpture.[182] This was a view that was reflected in many other descriptions as travellers focussed, for example, upon the theatrical damask draperies and curtains that decorated so many Italian churches or compared them to secular buildings such as the Assembly Rooms at York.[183] When religious ceremonies were observed, they were discussed in terms of 'manners and customs' or as a theatrical performance rather than Christian observance. 'The

---

[179] Drake journal MCO MS MC F15 vol. 1, 95.

[180] Phillips (ed.), *Correspondence*, I, 209; Breval, *Remarks on Several Parts of Europe* (1726 edn), II, 253; Gray, *Letters during the Course of a Tour*, 356; Matthews, *Diary of an Invalid*, 90–1; Piozzi, *Observations and Reflections*, 255; Blunt, *Vestiges of the Ancient Manners and Customs*, 91.

[181] Colin Haydon, *Anti-Catholicism in Eighteenth-Century England: A Political and Social Study* (Manchester, 1993), 164–203, on the later eighteenth-century softening in attitude towards Catholics. Clare Haynes has recently challenged the view that anti-Catholicism became less strident amongst the travelling elite and argues that it continued to represent an important dimension of the Protestant identity of British travellers: Clare Haynes, 'A trial for the patience of reason? Grand tourists and anti-Catholicism after 1745', *Journal for Eighteenth-Century Studies*, 33:2 (2010), 195–208.

[182] Northall, *Travels through Italy*, 294.

[183] Piozzi, *Observations and Reflections*, 326, complained of the folly of 'hanging churches with red damask' which gave them the 'air of a tattered theatre'. See also Mary Berry's comments in Lewis (ed.), *Extracts from the Journals and Correspondence*, I, 61, 122.

Functions in Lent and in the holy Week', wrote William Patoun, 'are the great Shew [sic] at Rome.'[184] In 1815, Henry Coxe made precisely the same assessment: what Rome lacked in theatres and other forms of entertainment, he told his readers, it made up for in religious pageantry and spectacle.[185] Relatives back home in England were often more apprehensive of the dangers posed by exposure to so much popery than the travellers themselves. Martha Patteson's letters to her son betray a constant flutter of anxious agitation: 'excuse my, dearest life if I again say beware of religion, politicks and intrigues'.[186] But, tellingly, Anne Miller urged her anxious mother to put away all thought of superstition and priestcraft and to think of the churches simply as collections of painting and sculpture.[187] As such, irritation might even be expressed that churches were unavailable for sightseeing on Sundays, when services were being held.[188] And, as in Florence or Bologna, there was a well-established itinerary of art to be viewed and admired, which few tourists ever challenged outright.

The institution of the papacy itself had similarly lost some of its power to shock or provoke the British. The popes of the eighteenth century, as the British knew full well, were not just politically impotent but also financially dependent upon the money brought into the Roman economy by *milordi inglesi*.[189] It was therefore widely assumed amongst the British that the pope, whose worldly acumen they were never slow to detect, would be reluctant to alienate or antagonise those who represented such a valuable source of revenue, and who were also, after 1763, the representatives of the most powerful navy in the Mediterranean. In Rome, explained Edward Wright, no one expected the British to genuflect or fall in with Catholic devotions as everyone was well aware of the value of heretics' money.[190] Some of the more doggedly Protestant writers, such as Sacheverell Stevens or Samuel Sharp, suggested that heretics were still in danger in Rome and that discretion needed to be

---

[184] Patoun, 'Advice on travel in Italy', xlvii.   [185] Coxe, *Picture of Italy*, 244–5.
[186] Cubitt, Mackley and Wilson (eds.), *Great Tour of John Patteson*, 184. Black, *Italy and the Grand Tour*, notes that Lady Harcourt was anxious that her son, Viscount Nuneham, should not have an audience with the pope when he visited Rome in 1755–6 (169).
[187] Miller, *Letters from Italy*, I, 293.
[188] Herbert (ed.), *Henry, Elizabeth and George*, 272.
[189] On the eighteenth-century papacy and European politics, see Owen Chadwick, *The Popes and European Revolution* (Oxford, 1981).
[190] Wright, *Observations*, I, 204. Such comments should be contrasted with John Swinton's shocked reaction to the desecration of the English burial ground at Leghorn, done, he claimed by the natives who bore 'an implacable hatred to the English on account of their religion ... in which they are encouraged by their ignorant and zealous priests'. Swinton journal WCO Wadham MS A11.5, 15 Feb. 1731.

exercised in coffee houses and other public spaces where the spies of the Inquisition might be located, even in the 1760s.[191] Such paranoia was inspired as much by the political implications of associating with known Catholics and Jacobite sympathisers back home as from hostility to popery per se, and as the Jacobite threat receded post-1746 and Benedict XIV distanced himself from the Pretender's court, this kind of fear-mongering gradually ceased to feature in descriptions of the city.[192]

More commonly, commentary on the pope emphasised his unthreatening impotence and harmless affability. He was presented as another curiosity, one of the sights to be seen. British travellers made no great effort to distinguish between the successive incumbents of the papal see: regardless of which pope they met, the general impression seems to have been of a venerable and kindly figure, who cheerfully welcomed the British and even extended preferential treatment to them as they lined up for an audience to kiss the papal toe. In 1717, one anonymous traveller described Clement XI, whom he was determined to see before leaving Rome, as very civil and courteous. Benedict XIV whom Edward Thomas met in 1751 made a similarly favourable impression – Thomas found him a 'fine, venerable old man' and 'no Bigot'. Lord Kildare reported that Clement XIII was 'a very agreeable old man', and kissed his toe.[193] Clement XIV similarly was particularly renowned for his affability to the British.[194] The fact that he had dissolved the Jesuit Order could only endear him to Protestant sensibilities. Pius VI was admired for his dignified and handsome persona and was likewise welcoming: Robert Harvey remembered a friendly and genial person who greeted him and the other English who had been granted an audience by pulling them on the cheek, whilst Thomas Watkins engaged him in conversation on the differences between English and Italian hunting.[195]

---

[191] This was despite the fact that Clement XIII had distanced himself from the Pretender's court, establishing a rapprochement with the Hanoverian monarchy.

[192] On papal involvement with the Jacobite court, see Lewis, *Connoisseurs and Secret Agents*, and Corp, *Stuarts in Italy*.

[193] Lord Kildare to Duchess of Leinster, 4 Apr. 1767, in Fitzgerald (ed.), *Correspondence*, III, 463. Clement's standing with the British had undoubtedly been improved by his open espousal of the Hanoverian dynasty when he entertained the Duke of York who visited Rome in 1763 and would be confirmed by his decision not to recognise Prince Charles as the legitimate king of Great Britain and Ireland in 1766.

[194] Francis journal BL Add. MS 40579, fol. 17v, and Philip Yorke to his uncle, 5 Dec. 1779, BL Add. MS 35378, fol. 282.

[195] Watkins, *Travels through Switzerland, Italy, Sicily*, II, 93; John Mitford described him as 'a tall majestic figure with a handsome countenance and an air of high dignity', Mitford journal GA D 2002/3/4/1, vol. 4, 8; Harvey journal NRO MS 20677, 181; see also Abbot journal TNA PRO 30/9/41, 223, and Moore's much quoted description, *View of Society and Manners*, II, 43.

Whatever the deficiencies in the governance of Rome and the Papal States – and the British saw many – it was rare to hold the popes themselves personally responsible for such evils: they were seen as hapless cogs in a system that they were largely powerless to change.

But regardless of whether travellers viewed Catholic Rome with suspicion, distaste or condescension, the modern city was unequivocally dominated by the basilica of St Peter's (see Figure 9). St Peter's defined the perception of Rome as much as, or possibly even more than, any of the antiquities: the rather prissy Thomas Watkins complained to his father that many of the English whom he had met in Rome stayed no more than three weeks, with the intent solely of being able to tell their acquaintance in England that they had seen St Peter's.[196] The Italian guidebooks were, of course, full of superlatives in praise of the basilica, and for all the scepticism with which most British regarded such monuments to Catholic superstition and papal grandiloquence, the sheer size and scale of the building demanded their admiration – and it was for the most part given. Reactions varied, however, from the uncritically adulatory to a more grudging mixture of praise and fault finding, whilst a patriotic determination that Christopher Wren's St Paul's should not come off the worse in any comparison between the two ran throughout the eighteenth century and beyond. Some declared St Peter's the finest building in the world, a match for anything erected in antiquity. It was nearer perfection than any other building, according to Hester Piozzi. 'The grandest effort of human art in the world', agreed Thomas Jones.[197] The visitor could not but be impressed by the accumulated piety of so many countries and so many ages which it represented.[198] Others, however, took a more cynical approach and saw the riches of St Peter's as nothing more than the consequence of generations of superstition.[199] Ultimately, St Peter's could not be immune from criticism: the sheer quantity of effusive praise prompted many visitors to find fault, if only to distinguish their own observations from those who had come before them. They claimed to be offended by a lack of propriety in the ornamentation; were disappointed by the scale of the proportions; or, like Anne Miller, found fault with Bernini's colonnade in the piazza outside.[200]

Considerable ingenuity was required on the part of the British to allow St Paul's the advantage over St Peter's, given that it was undeniably built

---

[196] Watkins, *Travels through Switzerland, Italy, Sicily*, II, 90.
[197] Oppé (ed.), *Memoirs of Thomas Jones of Penkerrig*, 53.
[198] Drake journal MCO MS MCF 15, vol. 1, 40.
[199] Mitford journal GA D 2002/3/4/1, vol. 3, 8.   [200] Miller, *Letters from Italy*, II, 201.

Figure 9 View of St Peter's and the Piazza, from Giovanni Battista Piranesi, *Vedute di Roma*, 2 vols. (Rome, n.d.).

on a much smaller scale. Indeed, the width of St Peter's at the transept exceeded the length of St Paul's as a number of visitors pointed out – thanks to the marks in the nave which showed the comparative size of the other major churches in Italy and Europe. Because St Paul's arguably occupied an even more cramped location than St Peter's, superiority had to be located in the 'taste' of the ornamentation of the façade,[201] and in the fact that, measurements notwithstanding, St Paul's looked (it was claimed) more impressive from a distance.[202] If one were to forget about the arcade and the fountains, suggested Whaley Armitage, St Paul's would be reckoned the finer building and moreover it was not spoiled, as St Peter's was, by the irregular appearance of the Vatican palace behind it.[203] The frequency with which St Paul's was preferred over St Peter's seems to have increased in the later eighteenth century and in the nineteenth, fuelled, no doubt, by a sense of Protestant nationalism that had become more clearly defined as a consequence of war.[204] If the events of the Napoleonic era had conclusively demonstrated the weakness of the pope's power, the architectural superiority of St Peter's had also been rendered less invincible. St Peter's provided the model for St Paul's, but just as modern Britain surpassed the Roman Empire, so too for the patriotic British traveller the beauty of St Paul's transcended that of its progenitor.[205] 'Fifteen Architects constructed the Basilica of Saint Peter', concluded Robert Finch at the end of an extended account of St Peter's, 'Let England boast her unrivall'd glory in her metropolitan Cathedral being built by her Wren and in her dictionary compil'd by Johnson!'[206]

But there was also more interest amongst British travellers in Rome's history as the centre of the Christian church by this point. When eighteenth-century visitors hailed Rome as the 'Mistress of the World', it was not the authority of the Holy Mother Church to which they referred: the presence of the Catholic church, as we have seen, was acknowledged but was treated rather as a variation upon the paganism of antiquity than as the nurturing centre of Christendom. The efforts of the papacy in the eighteenth century to preserve and celebrate Rome's palaeochristian heritage – through the restoration of San Clemente or Sta Maria in Cosmedin for example – were not taken seriously by the British traveller, who scarcely noticed these renovations, let alone appreciated their

[201] Moore, *View of Society and Manners*, I, 399.
[202] Abbot journal TNA PRO 30/9/41, 226; Stevens, *Miscellaneous Remarks*, 165.
[203] Armitage journal TCC Add. MS a 226 37 (1), unfoliated MS, 19 Oct. 1790.
[204] The Catholic Eustace was a lone dissentient voice, emphatically arguing the case for the superiority of St Peter's over St Paul's: *Classical Tour*, I, 354.
[205] Coxe, *Picture of Italy*, 191.   [206] Finch journal Bodl. MS Finch e. 16, fol. 230v.

symbolic import.[207] Modern Rome's claims to be Ecclesia Triumphans fell on deaf Protestant ears, such that Benedict XIV's conversion of the Coliseum into a shrine to martyrs was welcomed simply as a means of ensuring that no further depredations were made upon it, rather than as a tribute to the suffering of the early Christians.[208] At the start of the eighteenth century, Joseph Addison had given a cursory dismissal of the Christian antiquities of Rome as unworthy of study and devoid of interest compared to those of antiquity: 'though of a fresher date', he remarked, '[they] are so embroiled with Fable and Legend, that one receives but little satisfaction from searching into them'.[209] This was an attitude which continued to shape responses to early Christian Rome throughout the eighteenth century. Thus, Edward Wright, for example, observed that the churches built at the time of Constantine were little worthy of note for their architecture; their only point of interest for the visitor were the very fine pillars taken from ancient heathen buildings.[210] Even before Gibbon pointed to the role of Christianity in bringing about the fall of Rome, the story of the early Christian church in Rome was represented by some as a regrettable assault upon the achievements of antiquity. Francis Drake complained that early Christians 'out of a spirit of resentment for their sufferings' or religious zeal had 'spoiled many ancient temples to build their churches'.[211] Drake, a clergyman himself, was not anticipating Gibbon's religious scepticism, but nevertheless the meaning of these monuments was unequivocally located in Roman antiquity; their subsequent fate and association with the Christian church of which he was a member was of little, if any, importance. Over fifty years later in a similar vein, the Unitarian James Edward Smith described the three small churches in the vicinity of the Ponte Rotto, which he noted were interesting for what they had been, that is classical temples, rather than 'for what they are now'.[212] The stories of Christian martyrdom with which so many churches were decorated were invisible to the eyes of British travellers, unless they had been painted by the hand of an acknowledged master. The British could see nothing edifying or of aesthetic value in them. If observed at all, they evinced distaste rather

---

[207] See Johns, *Papal Art and Cultural Politics*, esp. 94–131.
[208] Drake journal MCO MS MC F15 vol. 1, 226–7. John Mitford simply saw it as further testimony to Catholic superstition: Mitford journal GA D 2002/3/4/1, vol. 3, 26.
[209] Addison, *Remarks on Several Parts of Italy*, 301–2; a sentiment echoed in Conyers Middleton's equally influential *Letter from Rome*, 9–10. See also Haynes, *Pictures and Popery*, 22–5.
[210] Wright, *Observations*, I, 200.   [211] Drake journal MCO MS MC F15 vol. 1, 100.
[212] Smith, *Sketch of a Tour*, II, 41–2. The churches in question were Sta Maria in Cosmedin; Sta Maria del Sole or Temple of Vesta (i.e. Temple of Hercules Victor); and Sta Maria Egiziaca or Temple of Fortuna Virilis (i.e. Temple of Portunus).

than admiration, provoking Robert Harvey, for example, to protest against the 'most dreadful horrid fresco pictures' of the torments of primitive Christians that adorned the walls of San Stefano Rotundo.[213]

But by the early nineteenth century, some travellers, such as the clergyman Robert Finch, were showing a much greater interest in these churches and not simply because they preserved elements of antique temples. Churches which could claim early Christian origins, such as San Clemente, Santi Quattuor Coronati, Sta Sabiena, Sta Prasseda, San Pudentius, as well as the churches of Trastevere, all attracted his attention and his comments. Finch was a dedicated visitor of churches, seeking out even the most remote. He equipped himself with copies of the local guidebooks and perused them carefully, gleaning far more from them than most of his compatriots. The entries in his journal indicate that he was particularly interested in the fabric of the churches – not just their tombs or their paintings – and in their development over time, an issue which eighteenth-century tourists had generally ignored. His interest went much further than the simple recital of dates: he was one of those who was beginning to take note of instances of gothic architecture. Rome, it is true, did not have many specimens of the kind of 'pointed' gothic architecture with which the British were familiar from their own country or which they would have encountered in France and Germany on their journey south to Rome.[214] Nevertheless, Finch singled out the 'Gothick structure' of the basilica of San Paolo, complaining that it 'accorded ill with the Greek columns', and was intrigued by San Clemente, where the visitor entered a court 'through a portico supported by two rude Corinthian and two ionic pillars and a gothic attic'. He took particular note of the interior arrangements: the church was, he noted, in the Greek form, with an isolated high altar around which was arranged the choir, with two marble pulpits and three rows of seats.[215]

John Chetwode Eustace, who had been in Rome a few years earlier, went further. His *Classical Tour* was one of the most widely used guides of the early nineteenth century with eight editions between 1813 and 1841 and much of his text reappeared in other guides such as Coxe's *Picture of Italy*. Written for what was inevitably a largely Protestant readership, Eustace was carefully moderate in his defence of Catholicism and was evidently determined not to alienate his intended readers. (Nevertheless, the *Edinburgh Review* grumbled that he had included too much detail on churches at the expense of more 'valuable'

[213] Harvey journal NRO MS 20677, 168.
[214] This issue is discussed more fully in Chapter 6.
[215] Finch journal Bodl. MS Finch e. 16, fol. 164v; MS Finch e. 15, fol. 157r–v.

information.)[216] As a classicist, Eustace had little aesthetic sympathy for gothic architecture, clearly stating his preference for the open form of the basilica with its long perspective and uncluttered interior to the arrangement of gothic churches which were 'divided by screens, insulated by partitions and terminating in gloomy chapels'.[217] San Clemente was, he noted, one of the best models that still existed of the original form of Christian churches. Because it was so well preserved, it was possible to establish what the physical layout of the early Christian churches had been. On this basis, he suggested, one could attempt some conjectures concerning the form and practice of early Christian worship and arrive at a historicised understanding of its development. The extent to which both the built form and the specific rites were rooted in the traditions of pagan Rome allowed the visitor, he suggested, 'to judge how far the ancients may have thought proper to transfer the rules observed in civil assemblies to religious congregations'.[218] As a Catholic, Eustace's intent was not to provide additional opportunities for Protestants to highlight the uncomfortable proximity between Catholicism and paganism, but rather to offer a genuine historical inquiry into the nature of early Christian devotional practice. The guide was published with ground plans and cross sections of the more notable churches – a trend which had become more common since around 1800 – which showed those elements which were deemed 'original' and those which were subsequent additions. The architectural form, rather than simply the exterior appearance, of these churches was now being recognised as a matter of historical interest which had implications for understanding the practice of religious worship in the past.[219]

Buildings which had once been simply regarded as excrescences or encumbrances upon the classical fabric were acquiring a historical value and meaning in their own right. Structures, such as Sta Costanza or San Stefano Rotondo, which formerly had been assumed to be of Roman construction, were now correctly identified as Christian monuments from the fourth and fifth centuries.[220] The fact that a church had been used by the primitive Christians was now in itself a matter worthy of note, which even a traveller such as Charlotte Lindsey, who had no

---

[216] *Edinburgh Review*, 21 (1813), 380, 399.   [217] Eustace, *Classical Tour*, I, 305, 381.

[218] Ibid., I, 299–300. In taking this approach, Eustace was simply following the researches of Catholic scholars of the late seventeenth and early eighteenth centuries: see Johns, *Papal Art and Cultural Politics*, 96–7.

[219] Not all readers were persuaded by Eustace's approach. The *Edinburgh Review* protested that it was 'preposterous' that there were no drawings of churches but only ground plans: *Edinburgh Review*, 21 (1813), 399.

[220] Gunn journal NRO WGN2/2, 29.

special interest in such matters, might record.[221] Romanesque churches were no longer overlooked as specimens of poor taste, but were re-evaluated as evidence of the efforts of early medieval architects to imitate the rounded Roman arches they saw around them. In 1821, Edward Burton pointed out to his readers that the continuous presence of Christianity in Rome from its first arrival until the present day offered a chronological continuum of the development of ecclesiastical architecture visible throughout the city. His description of Rome, dominated by classical antiquities though it was, nevertheless offered visitors an alternative way of viewing Rome according to which the buildings were illustrative of different stages of the city's history.

We have here to take into account the changes in British religious culture which became particularly marked towards the end of the eighteenth century, with the rise of evangelicalism and a resurgence of moral reform.[222] The cynicism of Conyers Middleton, the worldly tolerance of Hume, the scepticism of Gibbon, were being replaced by a more overt, personally expressive piety which placed far more didactic and spiritual value upon the stories of early Christian piety and martyrdom which could be found in Rome and to which the churches in particular bore witness. Even Loreto, the town that had grown up around the shrine of the Holy House transported to Italy from Nazareth by angels and once regarded as the most egregious instance of Roman Catholic superstition, began to attract more sympathetic treatment as a site of admirable piety, not gross idolatry.[223]

This shift in religious sensibility was particularly apparent in the reactions to the catacombs, much revered by Catholics as the site of early Christian martyrdom, and also an apparently inexhaustible supply of holy relics with which to sustain counter-reformation piety.[224] No pilgrimage to Rome was complete without a visit to San Sebastiano and an excursion underground. For most of the eighteenth century, the

---

[221] Lindsey journal Bodl. MS Eng. c. 7052, fol. 20.

[222] On the moral reform movement see Joanna Innes, 'Politics and morals: the reformation of manners movement in later eighteenth-century England', in Joanna Innes, *Inferior Politics: Social Problems and Social Policies in Eighteenth-Century Britain* (Oxford, 2009), 179–26.

[223] James Edward Smith judged that 'from one perspective the madonnas and their mummery are beneath contempt but in another light they are not just symbols of spiritual tyranny but of piety and virtue', *Sketch of a Tour*, II, 312; Edward Clarke saw Loreto from afar and felt a 'momentary sensation of devotion': Otter, *The Life and Remains of the Rev. Edward Daniel Clarke*, 117.

[224] R. Gaston, 'British travellers and scholars in the Roman catacombs 1450–1900', *JWCI*, 46 (1983), 144–65; Wendel William Meyer, 'The church of the Catacombs: British responses to the evidence of the Roman catacombs, 1578–1900', University of Cambridge Ph.D. thesis (1985).

catacombs were regarded with deep suspicion and scepticism by the British. This was a tradition dating back to seventeenth-century tourists such as Gilbert Burnet, later Bishop of Salisbury, or the staunchly Protestant Maximilien Misson, whose travels were first published in English in 1695. Burnet disputed the claim that the catacombs had been secretly excavated by the persecuted Christians and that they were used by the primitive Christians as sites of worship or even burial grounds. Rather, he argued, they were the *putecoli*, heathen burial grounds for slaves and meaner sorts of people, although he did allow that they might have been used by Christians in the post-Constantinian era. This sceptical tone prevailed throughout the eighteenth century. Furthermore, the unhealthily close atmosphere of the tunnels; the overwhelming darkness and obscurity; and the ease with which one could get lost all operated on a metaphorical level as an illustration of the deceit and blindness of Catholicism. Henry de Blainville, who travelled as tutor to William and John Blathwayt of Dyrham Park, wrote a letter to the boys' father describing their experiences in the catacombs: at one point the guide had nearly lost them and was forced to tear up their linen shirts to burn as torches. They had only found their way back, he claimed, by accident. As a consequence, he had advised the guide always to take with him a ball of twine to mark the way and a flint for relighting candles in future. Unsurprisingly, perhaps, the younger boy, John, apparently refused point blank to go down into the catacombs again. [225] In the 1760s and 1790s, the popularity of the catacombs as a destination receded and many travellers do not appear to have entered the catacombs at all. (Those in Naples were often deemed to be of greater interest.)[226] It would seem that classically minded antiquaries such as James Byres did not consider them worthy of his or his clients' attention.[227] Other visitors, such as Anne Miller, started to introduce an element of gothic horror to their accounts, exploiting the potential for mystery and terror with heart-stopping stories of candles being suddenly extinguished.[228] There was, however, as Meyer suggests, also another strain of commentary which emerged towards the end of the century in certain travellers' accounts, which was much less dismissive of the early Christian traditions that the catacombs appeared to represent. Hester Piozzi, for example, who was more sympathetic than many British tourists to Italian

---

[225] Nora Hardwick (ed.), *The Grand Tour: William and John Blathwayt of Dyrham Park 1705–1708* (Bristol, 1985), 101. Blainville's published account in *Travels through Holland, Germany, Switzerland*, II, 541–5, similarly emphasised the dangers of losing one's way and one's life in the subterranean labyrinth.

[226] Wright, *Observations*, I, 159–63.   [227] Meyer, 'Church of the Catacombs', 56.

[228] Miller, *Letters from Italy*, III, 53–4, quoted by Meyer, 'Church of the Catacombs', 60.

sensibilities, found herself powerfully reminded of the 'melancholy lives, and dismal deaths' of those who had 'first dared at Rome to profess a religion inoffensive and beneficial to mankind'.[229]

When Robert Finch visited the catacombs in Rome in 1815, he was overwhelmed, not by the noxiousness of the air or the endless capacity of the Catholic church cynically to replenish its supplies of martyrs' relics, but by the monument to Christian piety that the catacombs represented:

How glorious will their second clothing be at the sound of the last trumpet; and how many will rise from these obscure and lowly vaults to put to shame the Princes and Great Ones of the earth. Insensate must he indeed be, who can spatiate in these obscure recesses without feelings of veneration and love for those noble spirits, who, when invested with mortality, were such patterns of virtue, who endured all things for the love of their Saviour, who hoped all things for the glory that shall never fade away![230]

Finch did not specify his sources; he was certainly aware of Eustace but never referred explicitly to his work. Eustace was, in fact, more muted than Finch in his response to the catacombs, although given that he was a Catholic, unsurprisingly he failed to embrace the traditional scepticism of the eighteenth century: it was impossible, he wrote, to enter the catacombs 'these walks of horror and desolation, without sentiments of awe, veneration, and almost of terror'.[231] The sense of reverence expressed by both Finch and Eustace anticipated a sentiment that fifteen years later was to become much more mainstream, and was echoed in, for example, Richard Burgess' *Topography and Antiquities of Rome* of 1831. Burgess was unequivocal in identifying the catacombs as the location of true Christian piety and martyrdom: 'Whatever we may think of the histories which tradition or fanaticism in later ages may have produced', he wrote, 'we are compelled to be serious when we enter these gloomy abodes, and witness those traces of persecution and mortality, and tread upon the ashes of those who suffered in such a cause.'[232] Above ground, at San Pudentius, Burgess described the recently excavated vaults, which he believed had belonged to the original church, and which in turn had been built upon other ruins. These early traces of Christianity, he observed, and the traditions of martyrdom with which they were associated, were 'by no means unedifying for the Christian'.

[229] Piozzi, *Observations and Reflections*, 289, quoted by Meyer, 'Church of the Catacombs', 58.
[230] Finch journal Bodl. MS Finch e. 16, fol. 153r–v.
[231] Eustace, *Classical Tour*, I, 313. Burton also suggested 'a little veneration' for the spot that had 'preserved the early professors of our religion', *Description of the Antiquities*, 484.
[232] Richard Burgess, *The Topography and Antiquities of Rome*, 2 vols. (1831), I, 116.

Far from being the subject of ridicule, they allowed one 'to reflect upon these earliest scenes of holy zeal and piety, and combine the little evidence there is left with probabilities'.[233]

Conclusion

Responses to Rome showed, in many respects, remarkable consistency. The key sights remained the same; the hierarchy of artistic masterpieces changed little; the combination of antiquarianism, connoisseurship and sociability, with an undercurrent of pilgrimage, continued to shape the experience of visitors from the late seventeenth to the early nineteenth centuries. But within this overarching scheme, the reactions of visitors, the comments they made and the ways in which they chose to write about the city underwent significant modification. Some changes, such as the influence of picturesque language or the evolution of antiquarian studies, were symptomatic of broader cultural trends common across the experience of travel in Italy as a whole as other chapters show; some were a consequence of the changing circumstances of the travellers, such as the increasing reliance on guidebooks for navigation, for example. But the stories told about Rome itself also changed, and with them the itinerary of sightseeing, such that the associative values attached to particular buildings, and the descriptive tropes that were used to impose meaning upon what was seen, could not remain the same either. Part of Rome's appeal lay in the fact that it had withstood so long the vagaries of time and human vicissitude, but whereas in the earlier period the phys-ical remains of the city had represented a finite body of antiquities that could be studied and comprehended, now these antiquities were simply a part of a greater whole that had yet to be fully recovered or understood. Similarly, the uncomplicated admiration that exalted ancient Rome above all other cities had been undermined and compromised: its history and its reputation were no longer unassailable. A greater awareness of ancient Rome's debt to Greece, of the city's fate subsequent to the Empire's fall, and of its centrality to the history of the early Christian church made the unquestioning admiration of antiquity that character-ised the descriptions of the earlier eighteenth century untenable, compli-cated the city's narrative meaning and enriched the ways in which it could be represented.

What were the factors that brought this about? The shift in the relative balance between Britain and both ancient and modern Rome played an

[233] Ibid., I, 208.

important role: with regard to modern Rome, as we have seen, anti-Catholicism still existed, but popery no longer embodied the menace of fifth columnists or Jacobite conspirators. The Catholic threat to Britain, such as it was, of the late eighteenth and early nineteenth century was home-grown and manifested itself in agitation for Catholic Relief rather than in conspiracies against the state or the monarchy. In the wake of the French Revolution, atheism and irreligion seemed to pose a greater national danger. Catholic churches and monuments such as the catacombs could be recognised as sites of religious veneration, rather than denying their presence by treating them as classical antiquities or spaces of artistic and theatrical display. For those travellers with a more pronounced sense of religious propriety, the espousal of a shared Christian identity and a common heritage of belief had become more important than rehearsing the evils of Catholic superstition and extortion. Anti-Catholicism did not disappear but it was replaced by a greater diversity in response and a greater willingness to recognise in the monuments of the Catholic church a record of piety and Christian observance that transcended doctrinal difference.

Attitudes to ancient Rome had also changed, due in part to developments in the understanding of antiquity and the history of Europe subsequent to Rome's fall which were common currency in western Europe. The elevation of ancient Greece as Rome's cultural superior and the greater interest in Europe's development from the 'dark ages' through to the renaissance were by no means confined to the British, who were part of a pan-European movement towards a more historicist approach to the past and a burgeoning interest in national history. In this context, interest in Italy's fate subsequent to the fall of Rome made an impact on travellers' perceptions not just of Rome, but other cities too, as we shall see in Chapter 6. With regard to Rome, it heralded the recognition that the city was not just a collection of antiquities but a place with a history that extended beyond classical antiquity or the story of its modern recovery in the renaissance. The greater sensitivity to the information that antiquarian or archaeological investigation might reveal, which we have noted in the later accounts of travellers, was as much a characteristic of Italian and French antiquaries as it was of British;[234] indeed what is more surprising is why British visitors were not more responsive to the insights of Italian antiquaries such as Ficoroni, Eschinardi, Venuti or even Piranesi, particularly in the earlier part of our period. Part of the answer lies in British scepticism regarding the

---

[234] Schnapp, *Discovery of the Past.*

bombastic claims of Italian antiquaries, but it stems also from the preconceptions with which they travelled to Rome, expecting to find the physical embodiment of texts with which they were already familiar. It was only when some of the expectations of travel changed in the later eighteenth century that we see greater receptiveness to a different view of Rome; one which went beyond the monumental and the familiar to include the domestic and uncertainty.

But attitudes also changed because of the way in which the British perceived themselves. In the years immediately after the Napoleonic Wars, Great Britain had not yet arrived at a position of imperial dominance from which comparisons with Rome and the decline consequent upon an over-extended land-based empire would become uncomfortably challenging. (The parable of fallen empire applied at this point to Napoleonic France, rather than Britain.) Although the fate of imperial Rome offered a warning which moralists might seize on, the British could still persuade themselves, despite the loss of the American colonies, that they were part of a maritime and commercial empire, based upon the extension of freedom and liberty still uncorrupted by the greed and luxury consequent upon conquest, as opposed to one which entailed the subjugation and oppression of subject peoples.[235] The Roman Republic continued to offer a role model for political virtue through figures such as Cicero, but the sense of Britain's divergent destiny became stronger, encouraging a greater willingness to question the traditional humanist mode of viewing the city.

Back at home, Rome was present in Britain too, imaginatively but also physically in the Roman roads, the Roman Wall, the material fabric of towns and cities and in the collections of antiquaries and numismatists. Knowledge of Italy and its Roman antiquities had helped to stimulate antiquarianism in Britain since the sixteenth century; during the eighteenth century much had been done to record and recover the Romano-British legacy.[236] However, antiquaries were also increasingly turning to the study of pre-Roman, Saxon and medieval antiquities as well.[237] By the later eighteenth century, they were no longer so eager to attribute Roman origins to all antiquarian finds, and less willing to admit the superiority of Rome over native British or Anglo-Saxon society. A new narrative of English achievement was emerging, which owed less to Rome and far more to native English

---

[235] Virginia Hoselitz, *Imagining Roman Britain: Victorian Responses to a Roman Past* (Woodbridge, 2007), 39–40.
[236] Ayres, *Classical Culture*, ch. 3; Sweet, *Antiquaries*, ch. 4.
[237] Sweet, *Antiquaries*, chs. 2, 5 and 6.

genius.[238] 'The works of the Romans are now mouldering into dust in their splendid city' wrote the author of *Londinium redivivum*, 'but the works of *our* Aborigines mock the efforts of Time, and will for ages after Rome has not a remnant left.'[239] And meanwhile in Rome, British travellers could be found expressing similar sentiments. 'Rome', pronounced John Owen, 'had her reign ... and Britain, once her vassal, looks down with proud contempt upon her ruins.'[240] For all the palpitations of excitement that John Cam Hobhouse claimed to have felt on approaching Rome, he nevertheless observed that the buildings of the newly excavated forum were crowded into a space 'not so considerable as one of our smallest London squares'.[241] Rome was now unequivocally being placed in historical perspective and cut down to size.

---

[238] Newman, *Rise of English Nationalism*, 227–44; Colin Kidd, *British Identities before Nationalism: Ethnicity and Nationhood in the Atlantic World 1600–1800* (Cambridge, 1999), 211–49.

[239] J. P. Malcolm, *Londinium redivivum; or, an Antient History and Modern Description of London*, 4 vols. (1802), III, 522.

[240] Owen, *Travels into Different Parts of Europe*, II, 32; see also Eaton, *Rome in the Nineteenth Century*, I, 297–8, and Engelbach, *Naples and the Campagna Felice*, 102.

[241] Hobhouse, *Historical Illustrations*, 43, 223; see also Adam Walker, who pointed out that Trajan's Column was smaller and narrower than the London Monument, *Ideas Suggested on the Spot*, 239.

4   Naples: leisure, pleasure and a frisson of danger

Introduction: the city and its setting

When Joseph Forsyth recorded his impressions of the city of Naples in 1803, he emphasised both its sensual allure and its danger to virtue and morality.[1] His verdict evoked two themes which dominated British reactions to Naples throughout the eighteenth and nineteenth centuries, and continue to do so today: a dangerous frisson combined with seductive beauty. The Bay of Naples has not lost its appeal, despite the oil refineries, and the activities of Cosa Nostra continue to give the city an additional 'edge' that is missing in the more sedate environs of Tuscany. The juxtaposition of beauty and danger provides a thread of continuity to travellers' accounts over the long eighteenth century, but the composition of the peculiar balance of menace and attraction was mutable and reflected the changing preoccupations and priorities of the travellers. Naples represented difference, not just in its physical appearance or even its climate, but in its atmosphere. Of all the cities of the Italian tour, Naples was the most clearly defined by its people, its ambience, its way of life, and this trope became increasingly dominant. By the nineteenth century, the representation of Naples had become ineluctably bound up with the idealisation of the carefree and romantic Italian south; an ideal which offered travellers from the colder northern climes the opportunity to escape familiar strictures and conventions, to transgress the morals and mores of their own society. For some, the challenge proved too unsettling and they retreated into a defensive criticism. Either way, Naples came to represent the antithesis of what many travellers believed to be defining attributes of their own society: it rarely evoked a lukewarm response.

In the late seventeenth and early eighteenth centuries many travellers had failed to make their way as far south as the Neapolitan kingdom: the place of Naples in the itinerary of the Italian tour was not securely established

[1] Forsyth, *Remarks on Antiquities*, 272–3.

until somewhat later in the century. In the eighteenth century, the kingdom was ruled by a viceroy, and Naples lacked the attraction of a royal court; the journey between Rome and Naples was dangerous and uncomfortable, and Naples itself was also intermittently engaged in warfare. All of these factors were disincentives to travel. However, with the discovery of the buried cities of Herculaneum (1738) and Pompeii (1748), the accession of Charles III (Carlo Borbone) in 1734 and the increasing interest in vulcanology stimulated by the obliging frequency with which Vesuvius erupted in this period, the kingdom of Naples became more and more attractive as a destination.[2] The 'discovery' of the Greek temples at Paestum at mid-century added a further incentive to draw travellers south.[3] In the second half of the century, few travellers omitted a visit to Naples from their itinerary.

The allure of Naples is in many respects self-explanatory. 'Vede Napoli e poi mori' was a cliché even before consumptive British travellers started arriving in Naples in the hope of a cure towards the end of the eighteenth century. Indeed, the beauty of Naples and its surrounding region was a commonplace which went back to antiquity and the majority of those who travelled to Italy were thoroughly familiar with the literature that extolled the region, even if only in translation. It is therefore no surprise to find visitors exclaiming upon the beauty of the Bay of Naples, quoting Ovid, Virgil and Horace and recommending the best vantage points from which to get a view of the bay. Some carried the intensity of this imaginative engagement with antiquity to self-parodic extremes: Thomas Watkins declared that he 'almost wished to be stung by those flies which Virgil notices as peculiar to his country'.[4] But even disregarding the poets of antiquity, Naples was accepted to be a place of great natural beauty, a beauty which would have been all the more keenly felt by visitors from a cold northern European climate, whose recent journey had been through the barren landscapes of the still undrained pontine marshes. After Terracina, the last town in the papal dominions, the countryside was transformed: it became thick with myrtle bushes, with aloes and orange groves in a delightfully mild and pleasant climate.[5]

---

[2] On interest in vulcanology, see Richard Hamblyn, 'Private cabinets and popular geology: the British audiences for volcanoes in the eighteenth century', in Chloe Chard and Helen Langdon (eds.), *Transports: Travel, Pleasure and Imaginative Geography 1600–1830* (New Haven and London, 1996), 179–205.

[3] G. Ceserani, 'The study of Magna Graecia: classical archaeology and nationalism since 1750', University of Cambridge Ph.D. thesis (2000), 79–96.

[4] Watkins, *Travels through Switzerland, Italy, Sicily*, I, 448.

[5] Forbes journal NLS MS 1540, fols. 413–14. The change in territorial overlordship was significant: the dead hand of papal government was rendered visibly manifest in many travellers' observations in descriptions of the poverty of the countryside and the backwardness of the agriculture.

Figure 10 View of Naples from the Chiaja, from Jean Claude Richard de Saint-Non, *Voyage pitoresque ou description des royaumes de Naples et de Sicilie*, 5 vols. (Paris, 1782–5).

What visitors relished was not so much the beauty of the city per se but the composite of the city, its balmy climate and its location in the bay set against the backdrop of the surrounding *campagna felix*. Tellingly, topographical artists tended to favour prospect views of the city rather than street scenes or views of buildings (see Figure 10).[6] In contrast to either Rome or Venice, where views of buildings and streetscapes were essential purchases as souvenirs, the comparative absence of anything but prospect views or scenes of the Chiaja (the promenade along the Bay of Naples) is striking: thus Roger Robertson explained to his father that Naples 'is the prettiest situation and almost every stranger orders a view of it to be done'.[7] Even the choice of souvenir maps was limited: Alessandro Baratti's perspective plan of the city, *Fidelissima urbis neapolitanae cum omnibus viis accurate et nova delineato*, first published in 1627, was not replaced until the publication of Giovani Carafa's giant *Mappa topografica della Città di Napoli e de' suoi contorni* in 1775.[8] Neither of these, of course, depicted individual buildings in any detail.

Descriptions instead tended to offer a verbal rendition of idealised landscapes by artists such as Vernet and Hackert, so popular amongst travellers. In these paintings, cheerful activity on the elegant promenade of the Chiaja was combined with the picturesque charm of a fertile hinterland, strewn with antiquities, and contrasted with a blue, and invariably placid, Mediterranean sea. But this was a landscape that also represented danger: the smoking crater of Vesuvius dominated almost every prospect view of the city and its surroundings, supplying a uniquely sublime element to the scenery, but also embodying an ever-present and unpredictable danger, which could erupt at any moment. It was not without reason, as Joseph Spence observed, that the ancients placed both their Hell and their Elysian Fields in the neighbourhood of Naples.[9] And so much fertility combined with such a benign climate held its own perils: the dangers of luxury, ease and lassitude. The area around Naples had been known as 'otiosa' since antiquity, but the connection between warmth, ease and lassitude was drawn all the more sharply in the eighteenth century in the wake of Montesquieu's analysis

---

[6] On depictions of Naples and its environs in the landscape art of the period, see Leonardo di Mauro, 'Naples and the South', in Ilaria Bignamini and Andrew Wilton (eds.), *Grand Tour: The Lure of Italy in the Eighteenth Century* (1997), 144–50; Silvia Cassani (ed.), *In the Shadow of Vesuvius: Views of Naples from Baroque to Romanticism, 1631–1830* (Naples, 1990).

[7] Roger Robertson to his father 13 Nov. 1751, NLS Acc 12244.

[8] Barbara Ann Naddeo, 'Topographies of difference: cartography of the city of Naples, 1627–1775', *Imago Mundi*, 56:1 (2004), 23–47.

[9] Klima (ed.), *Letters from the Grand Tour*, 105.

of the relationship between climate and national character. Montesquieu contrasted the vigorous activity necessitated by the cooler climes of the north with the passive indolence and ease of the south in *Esprit des lois* and it rapidly became a truism across Europe.[10] So fertile was the soil, there was barely any need to cultivate it; so mild the climate, there was no need to work. Idleness and inactivity were positively encouraged and the disciplined labour and busy activity of more temperate climes was simply uncalled for. Such sloth and indolence, it was said, accounted for the many conquests to which the Neapolitans had submitted throughout their history: they simply could not or would not exert themselves to self-defence. Venery flourished, whilst ease and luxury rendered the Neapolitans effeminate and supine.[11]

The beauty of the city and its region was all part of a wider discourse concerning the luxury of Naples, and one which had all the greater cogency because it was inherited from classical antiquity. Naples and the *campagna felix* had been where generations of wealthy Romans built their villas and went to relax and to enjoy the finest luxuries which money could buy. Travellers looked for, and found, continuity in such luxurious practices, matching the manners, customs and mores of modern Neapolitans with those of antiquity.[12] Henry Swinburne observed that 'From classic authors it seems that Neapolitans were a race of epicureans, of a soft and indolent turn, averse to martial exercises and fond of theatre, music and the refined arts and luxury, credulous and superstitious – some mixing of blood has taken place but modern inhabitants are very similar.'[13] This propensity was particularly notable amongst visitors to the museum of antiquities excavated from Herculaneum and Pompeii at Portici. Here, visitors liked to compare the dress of the modern peasantry with the costume depicted on the wall paintings and vases, or to see ancient domestic arrangements replicated in the houses of Portici and Naples.[14] Anne Miller was particularly pleased to

[10] Charles de Montesquieu, *The Spirit of the Laws*, 2 vols. (1750), II, 22–3. The Enlightenment debate on climate and its influence on physical and moral health is discussed by Jan Golinski, *British Weather and the Climate of Enlightenment* (Chicago, 2007), 173–91. See also Dror Wahrman, *The Making of the Modern Self: Identity and Culture in Eighteenth-Century England* (New Haven and London, 2004), 83–126.
[11] See, for example, Thompson, *The Travels of the Late Charles Thompson Esq*, I, 203; Stevens, *Miscellaneous Remarks*, 294.
[12] Wright, *Observations*, I, 147.
[13] Henry Swinburne, *Travels in the Two Sicilies in the Years 1777, 1778, 1779 and 1780*, 2 vols. (1783), II, 79.
[14] Gibbes journal TNA PRO 30/9/7/11 apropos of a visit to the museum at Portici, Elizabeth Gibbes noted that the custom of painting on walls was carried down to the present day.

identify what she took to be Roman moulds for ices and pastry cutters at the museum of antiquities at Portici – further evidence of the taste for luxury and self-indulgence amongst the Romans and one which lived on amongst the Neapolitans of the present day.[15] In Rome, by contrast, where travellers were looking for monuments of republican virtue or military glory, they were more likely to observe that modern Romans were degenerate and bore little relation to their illustrious counterparts.

The city of Naples

Whilst no one ever disputed the beauty of Naples' situation, the attractions of the city itself evinced rather more equivocal responses. This caused some irritation amongst the Neapolitan elite who were riled by the dismissive attitude of foreign visitors towards their city. The Neapolitan reformer, Ferdinando Galiano, complained to Antonio Cocchi in 1753 about the failure of foreign visitors to show any interest in the contemporary city:

They [tourists] come to a city in which the government, national character and political system are the only curious objects worthy of a man's study, and yet all they do is go and see four lumps of brick and marble at Pozzuoli and Portici, four fiery stones at the Solfatara and Vesuvius, a day at San Martino, an evening at the opera and in eight days they've done the lot.[16]

Visitors were, however, generally impressed by the size of the city and its streets – it was by far the largest city in Italy, and some contemporary estimates in the 1780s put the population at 600,000 although in reality its population was closer to half that figure, rising to 400,000 by the end of the century.[17] One of the differences between visitors' comments upon Naples and those relating to other cities such as Rome, Florence or Venice is the fact that very often remarkably little was said about the city itself – it was, as Galiano pointed out, primarily the base from which to explore Vesuvius and the sites of antiquity in the *campagna*.[18] Much of

---

[15] Miller, *Letters from Italy*, II, 261.

[16] Quoted in Anna Maria Rao, 'Antiquaries and politicians in eighteenth-century Naples', *Journal of the History of Collections*, 19:11 (2007), 166.

[17] Messrs Tracy and Detand were informed that the population was 500,000–600,000 in 1766: Bodl. MS Add. A 366, fol. 56; see also Pearce and Salmon (eds.), *Charles Heathcote Tatham in Italy*, 52. The 1707 census enumerated the population at 215,608 and by 1798 it had grown to 435, 903: Anna Maria Rao, 'The feudal question, judicial systems and the Enlightenment', in Girolamo Imbruglia (ed.), *Naples in the Eighteenth Century: The Birth and Death of a Nation State* (Cambridge, 2000), 97.

[18] Lemaistre, *Travels after the Peace of Amiens*, II, 16: 'because the countryside around affords much more interesting sights, travellers frequently concentrate on the country and pay very little attention to the sights in the town'.

the time that visitors spent in Naples was taken up with excursions out of the city, rather than remaining resident within the city itself. As a city, Naples had little to recommend it in terms of antiquities as few monuments had survived successive earthquakes and reconstruction; its buildings commanded little interest. Thus, the Earl of Winchilsea explained to his mother 'the town is nothing very extraordinary'.[19] There were nevertheless perfunctory comments to be made on the general appearance of this town, as there were of any other.

Some visitors did not even bother to record their impressions of the city at all, concentrating only on the sites they visited in the *campagna*.[20] More typically, travellers would make bland generalisations about the city's size and its magnificence; the streets paved with large slabs of lava from Vesuvius; the lofty stone-built houses with flat roofs and terraces furnished with pots of oranges, roses and jessamine.[21] The flat roofs were clearly intriguing to northern eyes used to the pitched roofs required in climates of heavy rainfall. The roof terraces had a hint of the exotic about them – not least because they were characteristic of a distinctive lifestyle in which evening sociability took advantage of the temperate weather, with company gathering in the evenings on the terraces.[22] Visitors commented too on the impressive sweep of the Strada di Toledo and the Chiaja where all of Neapolitan society congregated in their coaches in the evening, and most noted the three fortresses overlooking the city or made some reference to the hundreds of churches.

The responses to the built environment of Naples, limited though they are, reflected the changing currents of architectural taste in eighteenth-century Britain and offer some indication of how visitors responded to an unfamiliar urban space.[23] In the late seventeenth and early eighteenth centuries, the British had tended to be impressed by the manifestation of wealth in both the civil and ecclesiastical architecture, commenting on the size of the palazzi and in particular the ornamentation of the

---

[19] Winchilsea to his mother, 18 May 1773, ROLLR Finch MSS DG 7/4/12 box 4953 bundle 32.

[20] See, for example, Sir James Hall's journal NLS MS 6237.

[21] Blainville, *Travels through Holland, Germany, Switzerland*, III, 232. See also Northall, *Travels through Italy*, 191; Wright, *Observations*, I, 149; Nugent, *Grand Tour*, III, 391; Pearce and Salmon (eds.), *Charles Heathcote Tatham in Italy*, 52.

[22] Klima (ed.), *Letters from the Grand Tour*, 110.

[23] The shifts in taste outlined in the following paragraphs parallel those of French travellers, whose comments on art and architecture are discussed by Blunt, 'Naples as seen by French travellers 1630–1780'. Given how many British travellers relied on guidebooks such as J. Richard, *Description historique et critique de l'Italie*, 6 vols. (Dijon, 1766) and J. J. Lalande who had recorded this story in *Voyage d'un François en Italie, fait dans les années 1765 & 1766*, 8 vols. (Yverdon, 1769), there is a predictable similarity in many of the comments.

churches. One late seventeenth-century traveller, Thomas Twisden, who was in Naples in 1693, thought that their beauty exceeded even those of Rome.[24] Similarly, in 1721, George Parker told his father they were 'extraordinarily rich and beautiful' whilst his bearleader, Edward Wright, described them in his published tour as 'excessively rich and fine'.[25] Guidebooks such as Thomas Nugent's *Grand Tour* (1756) were similarly impressed by the wealth on display, but offered a catalogue rather than qualitative judgements, and computed the total value of plate in the Neapolitan churches at over eight million crowns.[26] But by mid-century, the prevailing taste for the order and regularity of Palladianism was coming to dominate architectural judgements and Neapolitan architecture, in all its baroque excess, was found wanting. Comments became more critical or were conspicuous by their absence – buildings which did not meet the criteria of good taste did not merit description and were rendered invisible in the texts. By the end of the century, as the preference for neo-classicism was beginning to give way to the purism of the Greek revival, the florid excess of Naples' churches appeared even more distasteful and attracted biting criticism. 'The prevailing taste [in architecture]', John Chetwode Eustace informed his readers, 'if a series of absurd fashions deserve that appellation, has always been bad'.[27] Out of 300 churches there was not one, he complained, which had a front or portico of any merit. The civil architecture was equally wanting in taste, being heavy and crowded with ornament: 'They delight in the crooked, the piebald, the gaudy, and push irregularity to its farthest bourn', carped Joseph Forsyth. 'Some of the modern churches', he allowed, 'are striking to the eye; but so is every monster.'[28] Marianna Starke, whose *Letters from Italy* was one of the most widely read guidebooks of the early nineteenth century, had found Naples captivating at first sight but this initial impression soon wore off, she complained, as one became more familiar with the 'extreme bad taste' which pervaded almost every building.[29]

Neither Neapolitan gothic nor baroque appealed to the British taste simply on aesthetic grounds, but architecture was never just a matter of proportion or ornament. It was also the embodiment of taste, virtue and ultimately, according to theorists such as the Earl of Shaftesbury, an

---

[24] Twisden journal Bodl. MS Eng. misc. c. 206, fol. 23r.
[25] Parker to his father, 18 Apr. 1721, BL Stowe MS 750, fol. 367; Wright, *Observations*, I, 149.
[26] Nugent, *Grand Tour*, III, 393. Nugent took this detail from Gilbert Burnet, but see also Thompson, *Travels of the Late Charles Thompson Esq*, I, 191 who put the value at £2 million.
[27] Eustace, *Classical Tour*, I, 482–3.   [28] Forsyth, *Remarks on Antiquities*, 271.
[29] Starke, *Letters from Italy* (1800 edn), II, 68.

expression of morality. Moreover, to Protestant eyes the florid extravagance of the Neapolitan baroque was expressive of not simply a perversion
of correct taste, but also of the corruption of the Catholic church. The
want of taste and the distortion of true belief that it represented were
inextricably combined in the view of the Protestant visitor and were
symptomatic of the power of the Roman Catholic church. Part of the
'dangerous' element to Naples lay in the fact that it was also notorious for
being a particular stronghold of Catholicism. Francis Drake described the
credulity, bigotry and superstition that he encountered as 'incredible';
twenty years later, Lord Winchilsea observed that 'the Superstition at
Naples is beyond any thing'.[30] The profusion of gilding and silver and
the ostentatious excess of ornamentation were self-evident confirmation
of both the capacity of the Catholic church to extort money from its
congregation and of the superstitious thrall in which the congregation
was held: a thrall that was so tight that the people willingly tolerated these
punitive exactions to support the corrupt and overblown display of popery.

In Rome, part of the attraction in visiting many of the churches
derived from their value as antiquarian curiosities; the pleasure lay in
seeking out and identifying those elements which were taken from earlier
Roman structures and in observing how Roman basilicas had been
converted into Christian churches. In the city of Naples (as opposed to
the surrounding *campagna*), there was less scope for that kind of activity,
or indeed any kind of antiquarian activity at all. Guidebooks and visitors
were quick to emphasise that the city had undergone so many revolutions and so many earthquakes that, despite its ancient foundation, there
was little of the physical fabric of antiquity to view: Sta Restituta was said
to be built on the site of a temple to Apollo and traces of the façade of the
Temple of Castor and Pollux were to be seen in San Paolo Maggiore.
Beyond that, as many travellers noted, the churches of Naples had had
little to attract the visitor who had already seen those of Rome. Even
John Breval's account, which was notably fuller on the city's ancient
history than most, was disdainful of the local antiquarians' pretensions
to be able to trace the ruins of the ancient cities of Parthenope and
Palaeopolis through the modern city.[31] Closer reference to

---

[30] Drake journal MCO MS MC F16 vol. 2, 31; Winchilsea to his mother, 3 June 1773,
ROLLR Finch MSS DG 7/4/21 box 4953 bundle 32.

[31] Breval, *Remarks on Several Parts of Europe* (1738 edn), I, 59: 'There are likewise in many
other Parts of the City, manifest Foundations of antient Edifices, insomuch that the
Virtuosi pretend to point out the certain Boundaries of *Palaeopolis* and *Parthenope*, which
two Cities became united into one about the End of the Consular Times; but the whole
was not wall'd in till the Age of *Augustus*, nor even then bore any Proportion to what
Naples is now, owing its *Eclat* in a great measure to the Neighbourhood of *Baiae*.'

contemporary guidebooks would have provided the visitor with considerably more information about the antique elements still discernible through the fabric of the city and its churches, but this was not an agenda which many British tourists chose to explore. Antiquarianism within the city of Naples rarely featured in the visitor's experience. 'A traveller', explained John Northall, 'in giving an account of this noble city, is obliged to confine himself to modern curiosities, such as castles, palaces, and especially religious houses, which abound here more than in any other Romish country. The consequence is, that a writer too often falls into tedious repetitions, as the same terms must necessarily be employed in describing buildings.'[32] Tedious and repetitive these descriptions may have been, but this was largely because the majority of British travellers had no interest in what these buildings were, their history or their meaning: they could not command the traveller's attention as could those of Rome.

Churches, as we have seen, were rarely regarded as sacred spaces by British tourists; rather, they were viewed and described as sites of antiquity or as arenas of connoisseurship or even sociability. Aside from the churches of Rome, where so many incorporated antique remains, their principal attraction lay in the paintings that were on display inside. But Naples was not, for most of the eighteenth century, a city where one went to view art as was the case in Florence, Rome, Bologna or even Venice. Part of the reason for the neglect amongst British travellers, at least until the 1760s, was the absence of any English guide which could direct them as to what to admire. Volumes such as Edward Wright's *Observations* or Thomas Nugent's *Grand Tour* listed the various paintings to be seen in the churches and palazzi of Naples, but beyond providing the name of the artists, and occasionally an indication of subject matter, they offered no advice on the quality of the painting. After the publication of the Richardsons' *An Account of Some of the Statues, Bas-Reliefs, Drawings and Pictures in Italy* (1722), the level of artistic connoisseurship amongst British travellers had started to increase, but Richardson junior never travelled as far as Naples and the city and its collections did not feature in their guide. The standard authorities on Italian art to which the British referred, such as Vasari or Bellori, devoted little if any attention to Neapolitan art: their focus was always upon the Tuscan, Bolognese and Roman schools. Neapolitan art was an also-ran. The authors of the Neapolitan guidebooks did their best to counteract this and puffed their artists as best they could – but they were unable to

[32] Northall, *Travels through Italy*, 219.

challenge the canon of taste and the hierarchy of artists that had been long established by the eighteenth century under the influence of the Tuscan Vasari. A handful of Neapolitan artists – notably Salvator Rosa and Luca Giordano – were admired, but Giordano was never held in the same high regard as, for example, Guido Reni, Guercino or the Carracci. In 1769, however, the Abbé de Lalande published his eight-volume *Voyage en Italie* with a comprehensive account of not just the churches but also the paintings of Naples: from now on it was possible for the assiduous tourist to take a more informed interest – and many did, parroting Lalande shamelessly, as they went through the churches and the contents of Capo di Monte which housed the King of Naples' art collection in the eighteenth century. But there never arose in Naples the kind of itinerary of highlights of paintings and statues that was established in Florence, Rome or Bologna, even after the choicest specimens of the Farnese collection had been brought from Rome to Naples in 1787.[33]

Indeed, there is an argument to be made that most visitors were all the more ready to write off the churches, palazzi and antiquarian heritage of Naples because they had already undergone, or had at least felt it necessary to make some pretence of undergoing, a strenuous course of antiquities and connoisseurship in Rome. Traditionally, most tourists went to Naples during Lent to escape the tedium of abstinence and sobriety in Rome, to experience the drama and pageantry of the Neapolitan carnival, to engage in sociability and pleasure and, implicitly, to have a break from rigorous antiquarianism and virtù. The readiness with which they decided that the churches were all inferior to those in Rome and scarcely worth the effort of visiting has to be seen as a reaction against the experience of visiting Rome. So, despite the quantities of information available in both standard guides such as Lalande or Keysler, as well as the locally published guidebooks, British visitors generally recorded visits to only a handful of the 300 churches. They lived in a 'lounging, idle style', as William Forbes candidly admitted when justifying to himself in his own journal his failure to record any impressions or descriptions of the city's churches, despite the directions he had been given on what to see by his *cicerone*, Mr Clarke.[34] Part of the attraction of Naples – part of its allure – was that there was no need to

---

[33] Francis Haskell and Nicholas Penny, *Taste and the Antique* (New Haven and London, 1981), 77, similarly note that the statues excavated from Herculaneum and Pompeii on display at Portici failed to make a comparable impact on the visual consciousness of Europeans to that made by those excavated from Hadrian's villa at roughly the same time.

[34] Forbes journal NLS MS 1542, fol. 231.

submit to a punishing regime of sightseeing like that which one was supposed to undergo in Rome or even in Florence in the Duke's Galleries. When the Norwich banker Hudson Gurney arrived in Rome, he engaged a *valet de place*, who whipped him round all the monuments and antiquities. Gurney listed these in chaotic order in his diary, observing drily that he was left in a state of 'confusion double confused'. When he reached Naples, however, he was content simply to 'lounge' away the morning, walking about the city with no specific agenda, and failed to record a single building that he had seen.[35] The emphasis placed by travellers upon the transformation of the countryside into a kind of earthly paradise as they passed into the Neapolitan kingdom was a well-established trope but it also reflected this sense of release from a regime of serious-minded antiquarianism and connoisseurship and symbolised the entry into an atmosphere of pleasure and relaxation.

There was, then, comparatively little interest in the physical fabric of the city or its history. This was despite the fact that perceptions of Naples were deeply influenced by its history and reputation in antiquity – first as a Greek colony and subsequently as a Roman city – and despite the fact that it was the starting point for some of the most important archaeological and antiquarian sights of the Grand Tour. Nor did the medieval history of Naples at this stage capture the imagination of the British public. Unlike Florence, Naples offered no lessons on the successful synergy of commerce, liberty and cultural achievement. Whilst William Robertson praised the commercial spirit of the Florentine Republic in his *History of the Reign of the Emperor Charles V* (1769), Naples presented the far less edifying example of a state where the frequent and violent revolutions in that monarchy had rendered the defects of feudalism even more intolerable.[36] Not even the presence of four castles within the city walls could draw more than passing interest in its medieval and early modern history. The succession of rulers and dynasties through the medieval and early modern period was, to most visitors, tedious and repetitive and further evidence of the Neapolitans' indolence in that they had simply allowed themselves to be conquered.[37] The Neapolitans' attempts to claim for their city a historical role in the revival of the arts, which the British would have encountered in guidebooks such as Galanti's, *Breve descrizione della città di Napoli e del suo contorno*, failed to

---

[35] Gurney journal SAL MS 677, fols. 48, 50; see also Morgan, *Italy*, II, 335: 'it is a relief, rather than a disappointment, to learn that Naples contains few of any of these objects, worthy to arrest that attention on which Florence and Rome have already so deeply drawn'.

[36] Robertson, *History of the Reign*, I, 135–6.

[37] Thompson, *Travels of the Late Charles Thompson Esq*, I, 203.

make any impression on the majority of visitors.[38] Although Sigismondo's
three-volume account of Naples, *Descrizione della città di Napoli e suoi
borghi* claimed that the cathedral had been designed by Niccolò Pisano,[39]
whose family had played such a key role in the early renaissance in
Tuscany, it was not possible to trace out the same gradual evolution of
art and architecture in Naples as one could at the Campo Santo in Pisa
or in Florence where the revival of the arts under Giotto, Cimabue,
Arnolfino and the Pisano dynasty could be documented through the city's
churches.[40]

Even the rapid sprawl of Naples in the late seventeenth and eighteenth
centuries, incorporating the suburbs and expanding over the countryside
(plainly visible in the Carafa map), failed to provoke comment until
after the Napoleonic era.[41] Gilbert Burnet had noted in 1687 that the
Catholic church, which had the right to purchase property where it lay
on either side of a religious foundation, was taking systematic advantage
of this privilege. Given the fact that there was a convent on almost every
street, he surmised that the church would soon buy the entire town. This
comment betrays the Protestant Burnet's visceral hostility to the power
of the Catholic church as an institution, but it also suggests an awareness
of, and interest in, the built form of the city which subsequent travellers
failed to echo – although they readily repeated his estimate of the value
of plate in the churches at 8 million crowns.[42] Similarly, visitors seldom
described the Bourbons' grandiose building schemes as such; specific
buildings such as the Teatro San Carlo or Fuga's monumental Albergo
dei Poveri, the largest poorhouse in Europe, might be mentioned individually but never in terms of a Bourbon re-edification or a programme
of urban improvement. They were taken as isolated buildings, representative of either Neapolitan sociability or of charity and philanthropy.
Naples was to be experienced in the present and chiefly through its
people and through social gatherings and organisations, rather than
through buildings, antiquities or art.

---

[38] Giuseppe Sigismondo, *Descrizione della città di Napoli e suoi borghi*, 3 vols. (Naples
    1788); Giuseppe Maria Galanti, *Breve descrizione della città di Napoli e del suo contorno*
    (Naples, 1792); and Jean Claude Richard de Saint-Non, *Voyage pittoresque ou description
    des royaumes de Naples et de Sicilie*, 5 vols. (Paris 1782–5), I, 94.
[39] Sigismondo, *Descrizione della città di Napoli*, 4.
[40] The responses of British visitors to Neapolitan gothic are discussed at greater length in
    Chapter 6. Starke offers a partial exception to this generalisation as she noted that the
    cathedral had been built by Niccolò Pisano (*Letters from Italy* (1800 edn), II, 86). This
    information may also have come from a reading of Sigismondo or Saint-Non, *Voyage
    pittoresque*, I, 73.
[41] Coxe, *Picture of Italy*, 305.   [42] Burnet, *Some Letters*, 195.

Society and the people

With the accession of Charles III in 1734 and the establishment of a permanent court at Naples, the social life of the city had taken an upward turn – under the Spanish viceroys it had been dull and lacklustre – and the city became a more established feature of the Italian tour. Like Venice, Naples acquired the reputation of being something of a hedonistic, pleasure-seeking city, although without the same reputation for gambling and organised prostitution. 'Rome appears very dull and melancholy after Naples', lamented one female traveller.[43] The buzz of social activity was scarcely even interrupted by war, as J. G. Lemaistre found when he visited Naples in 1803 during the lull in hostilities following the Peace of Amiens: 'The gaiety of this city is greatly superior to what I have witnessed in any other city of Europe.'[44] The pleasures of sociability became an increasingly important aspect of the Neapolitan experience, particularly during the period that Sir William Hamilton was British envoy to the King of Naples (1764–1800).[45] This was also the era when the social composition of British travellers became more mixed in terms of women and men with many married couples and family groups making the tour for health, pleasure and education: a change which fostered increased levels of sociability amongst the travelling community. Sir William Forbes, who was in Naples for the winter of 1792/3 with his wife and daughter, kept a particularly detailed record of their stay. He noted the names of the other 'English' visitors there, comprising thirty-five women (including daughters) and forty-four men, and maintained a strict record of their social engagements and his own expenditure on entertaining.[46] A year later the Countess Spencer recorded the names of a subscription got up amongst the British community to purchase flannel waistcoats for the sailors and soldiers at Toulon in December 1793. Of the 138 named subscribers, sixty-seven were women and children.[47] Sir William Hamilton's hospitality at the Palazzo Sessa was unquestionably important, and it was through him that the Countess Spencer, Forbes and their compatriots gained whatever limited entrée they had to Neapolitan society.[48]

---

[43] Derbishire journal NRO DCN 118/6, 86.
[44] Lemaistre, *Travels after the Peace of Amiens*, I, 410.
[45] On Hamilton's career in Naples, see Brian Fothergill, *Sir William Hamilton, Envoy Extraordinary* (1969); David Constantine, *Fields of Fire: A Life of Sir William Hamilton* (2001).
[46] Forbes journal NLS MS 1541, fols. 45–53.
[47] BL Add. MS 75743 unfoliated MS, list of subscribers for the relief of sailors.
[48] Patrick Brydone, *A Tour through Sicily and Malta*, 2 vols. (2nd edn, 1776), I, 12: 'This party [at Sir William Hamilton's], I think, constitutes one principal part of the pleasure we enjoy at Naples.'

Far more significant, however, was the regular round of card parties, suppers, dinners and balls staged by the British visitors themselves – in fact, so crowded was the social calendar during the Forbes' residence in Naples that on one occasion Mrs Parker's card party clashed with Lady Plymouth's supper: a potentially embarrassing situation was avoided by the English company agreeing to attend both events in succession.[49] The English gentlemen even created their own informal dining club, taking it in turns to entertain each other: when it fell to Forbes, he treated twenty-two of them to dinner at a total cost of £11 15s 8d, which, he noted with great satisfaction, was far less than it would have cost him at the Thatched House Tavern in London.[50]

Accordingly, when Forbes, and others, described the city of Naples, their descriptions focussed overwhelmingly on the spaces of sociability and entertainment: the theatre, the opera, the social parade on the Chiaja and the Strada di Toledo. Music and theatre in particular flourished, best symbolised by the construction of the Teatro San Carlo in 1737, which was the largest theatre in Europe at the time. The theatre was a key venue for travellers in any of the cities which they visited: it provided a focal point around which they could discuss the state of the arts through the quality of the performance and the interior décor. It allowed them to observe the manners and customs of local society as manifested through the behaviour of the audience and to pass comment on social order and police with respect to the cleanliness or otherwise of the theatre. Although theatre going was a common experience to every Italian city, it was frequently in Naples that travellers embarked upon an extended discussion of the character of Italian opera and drama, the appearance of the theatres, the behaviour of the audience and the quality of the performances.[51]

For Charles Abbot, a visit to the theatre was always the occasion for extensive notes in his journal, but after a visit to the Teatro San Carlo, his description was particularly full. He noted the horseshoe shape, the size and seating capacity of 1800, achieved through a truly impressive array of boxes in six storeys, as well as an extensive pit. Each box was fronted with looking glass in a gilt frame, and illuminated by three lights: the result was dazzling and magnificent, but also, he noted pragmatically, inconveniently hot. Although he acknowledged that the theatre exceeded those of London and Paris for size and splendour, he found the performance itself inferior, and was disgusted by the dirt on the staircases.

[49] Forbes journal NLS MS 1541, fol. 188.
[50] Forbes journal NLS MS 1541, fols. 194–5.
[51] See, for example, Sharp, *Letters from Italy*, 77–99.

He was also taken aback by the ubiquitous presence of ragged and half naked *lazzaroni*, who crowded the staircases and entrances to the theatre. A circumstance 'the less agreeable', he observed, 'as the Company sit with their Box Doors Open to Receive their Visitors and to Admit their Servants with Ice'. The company in the pit were 'low and dirty' with very few women present and soldiers prevented people from standing in the passages between the seats. In this description of the theatre Abbot adumbrated several themes which ran through his experience of the city, and that of many other travellers: Naples was a place where glittering splendour masked dirt and poverty; where the *lazzaroni* were a perpetual presence; and where personal freedom was at the mercy of an autocratic, feudal monarch, who could impose order in his theatre, or anywhere else, through military force.

Abbot was rehearsing a number of well-worn clichés about Naples, in particular the emphasis on the finery and display with which the Neapolitan elite were so much enamoured and the contrast with the poverty and squalor which it hid. This was a common theme to comments throughout Italy, but in Naples, where much of the focus was on the people and the social life, rather than the antiquities or paintings, the observations were made with all the more force. As John Mitford observed, 'The people of the lower class are the most dirtily miserable, & those of the higher class the most shabbily magnificent of any place in Italy, where misery & dirt, magnificence & shabbiness are the general characteristics.'[52] So, visitors set the scene of the evening promenade along the Chiaja, where carriages accompanied by a retinue of footmen were packed so tightly that they could only move at a walking pace.[53] But the footmen were really *lazzaroni* simply hired for the occasion, and dressed up in livery, rather than being real retainers. And in order to maintain such state, it was said, the nobility lived 'all the year round on a little macaroni and greens'.[54]

The density of population was another recurring, even dominant motif. After the beauty of the situation, the populousness of the city was probably its most frequently noted characteristic. Density of population indicated activity, commerce and vitality – attributes which were often absent from other cities which were in noticeable decline. Charles Burney found Naples amazingly populous, 'it has an air of bustle and business beyond even London or Paris'. The streets, he noted, were in

[52] Mitford journal GA D2002/3/4/1, vol. 5, 4.
[53] Flaxman journal BL Add. MS 39787, fol. 61r.
[54] Lady Holland to Duchess of Leinster, 21 Dec. 1766, Fitzgerald (ed.), *Correspondence*, I, 488.

general straight and wide with open spaces – not enclosed like squares in London, but nevertheless well paved and well built and full of people, 'which to me have a better look than ponds, trees or gardens'.[55] The Strada di Toledo, according to Francis Drake, was so full of people at all times of day and night that it was as troublesome to walk along as Cheapside.[56] Whilst the comparison with Cheapside may not seem initially flattering, given the frequency with which other Italian cities were described as deserted or moribund, the inference to be drawn was certainly a positive one.

Amidst the noise of human voices, continually employed in activities in the streets, observed John Moore, 'the noise of carriages is completely drowned in the aggregated clack of human voices'.[57] The noise of Naples was one of its defining characteristics – but not always appreciated, particularly at night, according to Philip Francis, whose early enthusiasm for the city was tempered after a few days of constant noise and interrupted sleep.[58] The persistent racket clearly unsettled other travellers as well as Francis. Arguably, these visitors might have been less disturbed by the incessant clamour from the streets were it not that the noise was also a constant reminder of unknown threats, represented by the *lazzaroni* who were the main offenders in generating the din. For much of the eighteenth century, up until around 1770, British visitors seem to have found the number, ubiquity and idleness of the *lazzaroni* threatening.[59] In effect, they were the physical embodiment of the idleness and danger associated with Naples, and accordingly featured prominently in travellers' accounts. In any other Italian city, by contrast, the labouring population was generally conspicuous by its absence in travellers' accounts.

Edward Thomas, travelling in 1750, clearly found the unfamiliar environment of Naples threatening and shocking. How far his fears

---

[55] Scholes (ed.), *Eighteenth-Century Musical Tour*, 243.

[56] Drake journal MCO MS MC F16 vol. 2, 36.

[57] Moore, *View of Society and Manners*, II, 128; Hall journal NLS MS 6327, fol. 2v: one of the few comments that Sir James Hall made about the city itself was a reference to the 'unimaginable noise'. See also Piozzi's complaints about the *lazzaroni* shouting and bawling all day in the streets: Piozzi, *Observations and Reflections*, 236.

[58] Francis journal BL Add. MS 40759, fol. 14.

[59] This fear of the Neapolitan labouring classes was not confined to British travellers: it was widely rehearsed by French authors as well, whose publications were also read by many English-speaking travellers. Laziness and greed, explained Jerome Richard in his *Description historique et critique de l'Italie*, 6 vols. (Dijon, 1766), were deeply entrenched and had turned the *lazzaroni* into devils. See Melissa Calaresu, 'Looking for Virgil's Tomb: the end of the Grand Tour and the cosmopolitan ideal in Europe', in Jás Elsner and Joan-Pau Rubiés, *Voyages and Visions: Towards a Cultural History of Travel* (1999), 138–61, 302–11.

had been provoked by the topographical literature he had been reading in preparation and how far his anxiety was a reaction to an unfamiliar environment cannot be ascertained. However, whilst he was at Naples, as he informed his correspondent Jeremiah Milles with a certain macabre triumph, five people had been murdered in the streets. The *lazzaroni* were, he wrote, 'the most diabolical race' and he never went out after nightfall during his stay. He was, he confessed, frightened of his own *valet de place*.[60] Francis Drake was equally damning: the Neapolitans were 'without controversy the greatest rogues and cheats' in Italy.[61] The familiar stereotype was rehearsed by another traveller in 1766, whose account is now in the Bodleian Library: 'The People are as lazy, idle, roguish, debauched as any upon the Earth, which gave rise to the saying Naples is a Paradise inhabited by Devils.'[62] The Neapolitans themselves seem to have played up to this image, providing the tourists with what was presumably a desirable frisson of danger: several travellers recorded in their diaries that their guide or their antiquary had freely admitted to having committed a murder. Winchilsea's antiquary boasted that he had killed three men and wounded several others. The 'calash man', however, dismissed this rodomontade and told Winchilsea that only one man had lost his life to the antiquary.[63] Charles Abbot also noted with some anxiety that the guide employed on his behalf by the antiquary Charles Clarke to take him to Pozzuoli had been charged with five murders; he proved, however, to be a model guide.[64] Robert Gray who also used Mr Clarke's services to procure a guide – possibly the same one – was likewise alarmed by the guide's boastful claim to a murderous reputation, but similarly came to no harm.[65] Naples was, after all, the birthplace of Salvator Rosa, and there was therefore an expectation that the landscape should contain some danger, some element of sublime horror. Tales of murderous guides were clearly circulated with relish amongst the British community and played to the expectations of travellers who imagined a landscape that was populated by *banditti* and ruffians.

Protestants felt particularly imperilled by the volatility of the Neapolitans. The presence of so many people on the streets, milling around with no apparent employment or purpose, seems to have intensified the sense

---

[60] Thomas to Jeremiah Milles, 30 Nov. 1750, BL Add. MS 19941, fol 25v.
[61] Drake journal MCO MS MC F16 vol. 2, 30.
[62] Tracy and Dentand journal Bodl. MS Add. A 366, fol. 63.
[63] Winchilsea to his mother, 18 May 1773, ROLLR Finch MSS DG 7/4/12 box 4953 bundle 32.
[64] Abbot journal TNA PRO 30/9/41, 282.
[65] Gray, *Letters during the Course of a Tour*, 402.

Figure 11 Interior view of the cathedral of San Gennaro depicting the moment of the liquefaction of the blood of San Gennaro, from Jean Claude Richard de Saint-Non, *Voyage pittoresque ou description des royaumes de Naples et de Sicilie*, 5 vols. (Paris, 1782–5).

of unease provoked by Catholic ritual and superstition. Superstition was not, of course, confined to Naples, but given that it was chiefly associated with the unthinking credulity of the labouring classes it was particularly prominent in Naples where the *lazzaroni* had such a visible presence. It became a defining characteristic of the city in a way that was not the case, even in Rome, where religion arguably assumed an even greater role in daily life. In Rome, the set pieces on religion revolved around observing the pope, the services of Holy Week and other ceremonies such as the blessing of animals on the feast of St Anthony, rather than the religion of the 'people'. For all its pageantry and display, it was not generally regarded by the British as threatening or sinister. In Rome, noted the Norwich merchant Robert Harvey, there was far less superstition than in other cities: 'a man passed by a church without pulling of his hat' and not even the *valet de place* genuflected on entering a church.[66] In Naples, however, superstition bred fanaticism and extremes of behaviour. And with such a large, mobile, anonymous population concentrated within the city, fanaticism could be manipulated to dangerous ends. One of the set pieces of the tourist experience was to describe the ceremony of the liquefaction of the blood of San Gennaro: it offered not only a prime example of priestcraft and superstition but also an opportunity to dwell on the danger heretics ran in being present (see Figure 11). Were the ceremony to fail to work and their presence be detected, the British feared they would be in danger of being lynched by an over-excited mob, whipped into a frenzy of fanaticism by priests looking for scapegoats to blame for the non-performance of the miracle.[67] One traveller, Peter Cowling, described how he had 'wish'd much' to have seen the ceremony, but was 'Advis'd by Many Englishmen & Natives, to resist the Temptation'. The common people, he was told, feared earthquakes and volcanic eruptions would ensue if the miracle did not succeed, and in such cases were always liable to attribute the failure of the miracle to the presence of heretics; in which cases, 'the mob have more than once rose upon them and ill treated them'.[68] Cowling evidently felt discretion was the better part of valour. Others were bolder, but not even the most anxious visitor, such as Miss Derbishire of

---

[66] Harvey journal NRO MS 20677, 202.

[67] Lalande had recorded this story in *Voyage en Italie*; British visitors who echoed it included: Francis Drake (MCO MS MC 16 vol. 2, 41) and Ann Flaxman (Flaxman Journal BL Add. MS 39787, fol. 62v); in a letter dated 3 June 1773, Lord Winchilsea explained to his mother that he had declined to attend the ceremony for fear of the danger, ROLLR Finch MSS DG 7/4/12 box 4953 bundle 30; see also Derbishire journal NRO DCN 118/6, 69.

[68] Cowling journal CUL Palmer MS c. 5, 36.

Figure 12 Masaniello haranguing the people of Naples in the Piazza del Mercato during the rebellion of 1647, From Jean Claude Richard de Saint-Non, *Voyage pittoresque ou description des royaumes de Naples et de Sicilie*, 5 vols. (Paris, 1782–5).

Norwich, was ever able to claim that the threatened danger had materialised. Yet, such fears did shape other more concrete experiences: Matthew Todd, a gentleman's gentleman travelling with his master shortly after 1815, found himself accosted by a Sister of Charity who was begging on behalf of the poor. As he recorded it, he tried to shake her off, but she stuck to him 'like a leech' and then started to scream, rousing the *lazzaroni* – 'who were laying by in scores like pigs and half naked'. Fearing that they would think he had struck her, he ran off, and only just in time, he claimed, to save himself. He raced back to his master's lodgings, told the landlord that the *lazzaroni* were after him; the latter instructed him to run upstairs and promised to put the pursuers on the wrong scent. He was as good as his word, and when the mob arrived he told them that the Englishman had gone around the corner, whereupon, wrote Todd, 'they set off like a pack of bloodhounds ... Fortunately', he concluded, 'we are to leave this Dangerous Place tomorrow.'[69]

Pickpocketing, theft and interpersonal violence were all a focus for anxiety, but the 'mob' or the *lazzaroni* taken en masse also presented the danger of insurrection, a threat that was as unpredictable as the earthquakes or volcanic eruptions with which popular discontent was often associated. One of the few events of Neapolitan history with which the British were familiar was the revolt of Masaniello (see Figure 12). Hester Piozzi, for example, set her heart upon purchasing an account of the revolt whilst in Naples, only to find that the pamphlet had been banned.[70] Masaniello, the fisherman from Amalfi, led a rebellion against the fiscal extortion of the Spanish viceroy, the Duke of Arcos, in 1647, calling for equality of noble and popular representation. He controlled Naples for a week, raised a militia and dispensed justice, before his hold on power began to crumble away. The memory of his rebellion and the shortlived republic that he headed proved much more enduring, and several editions of the account of the uprising were published in Britain during the eighteenth century.[71] And the fear that the people might rise up again lived on too: Joseph Addison was puzzled at how the Spanish

[69] Trease (ed.), *Matthew Todd's Journal*, 110.

[70] Piozzi, *Observations and Reflections*, 234, 'I wished exceedingly to purchase here the genuine account of Massaniello's far-famed sedition and revolt, more dreadful in a certain way than any of the earthquakes which have at different times shaken this hollow-founded country. But my friends here tell me it was suppressed, and burned by the hands of the common excecutioner.'

[71] An account of the uprising was first translated into English and published by James Howell in the seventeenth century: J[ames] H[owell], *An Exact History of the Late Revolutions in Naples and their Monstrous Successes* (1650). The eighteenth century saw the following publications: Francis Midon, *The History of the Rise and Fall of Masaniello, the Fisherman of Naples* (1729); Francis Midon, *The History of the Rise and Fall of*

kept the people from revolting and the heavily armed garrison that oversaw the city, it was assumed, were as much to keep the people in subjection as to defend the kingdom from hostile invaders.[72] Rather later in the century, Henry Swinburne acknowledged that in recent years plentiful food and the presence of a garrison had done much to keep the mob quiet, but was nevertheless convinced that given the right circumstances it might still prove a formidable challenge to government. During a recent eruption of Vesuvius, he noted, the people had taken offence at the new theatre being more frequented than the churches and assembled in great numbers to drive the nobility from the opera (a natural danger giving rise to another man-made one).[73] With memories of the seventeenth-century insurrection at the back of their minds, visitors' anxiety over the dangers of massed assemblies and the possibility of insurrection or riot were evidently heightened.

Although the depopulation of cities such as Rome was invariably represented as a symptom of poor government and economic decline, Naples' populousness was equally problematic. London, with which Naples was often compared, also had its critics who regarded its over-blown bulk as a danger to the public good. London's size was feared to be disproportionate, distorting the economy and draining resources from the rest of the country. The density of population undermined the maintenance of social order, facilitating crime and immorality. Migrants flocked to London, hoping for work, or at least a more remunerative life of begging, and on arrival were drawn into a cycle of theft, prostitution or worse.[74] Similar criticisms were raised against Naples, but all the more sharply as Naples was the only city of any size in the Neapolitan kingdom and its economy was clearly not prospering as was that of London. Nor could it be argued that the burgeoning population was economically productive. Instead of merchants and manufacturers, the Neapolitan middle classes were dominated by lawyers engaged in an

Masaniello, the Fisherman of Naples (2nd edn, 1747; repr. 1768 and ?1770); anon., *The History of the Surprizing Rise and Sudden Fall of Masaniello, the Fisherman of Naples* (1747); anon., *The History of the Surprizing Rise and Sudden Fall of Masaniello, the Fisherman of Naples* (Oxford, ?1748). On the revolt itself, see Peter Burke, 'The Virgin of the Carmine and the revolt of Masaniello', *P&P*, 99:1 (1983), 3–21.

[72] Addison, *Remarks on Several Parts of Italy*, 205.

[73] Swinburne, *Travels in the Two Sicilies*, II, 72. Swinburne's account, recording his travels in 1775–6, made no reference to the famine of 1763/4 or its consequences; Robert Harvey referred briefly to it in 1773, blaming it upon poor management, Harvey journal NRO 20677, 161.

[74] M. Byrd, *London Transformed: Images of the City in the Eighteenth Century* (New Haven and London, 1978); A. J. Weitzman, 'Eighteenth-century London: urban paradise or fallen city?', *Journal of the History of Ideas*, 36 (1975), 469–80.

endless round of futile litigation.[75] But it was the idleness of the swarms of *lazzaroni* that drew most comment. In London, as Samuel Sharp pointed out in 1766, such people would not have been on the streets but would have been shut up within doors in a workshop or manufactory. But in the balmy climate of Naples *lazzaroni* could afford to lie in the sun – like so many swine – reliant on the charity of the monasteries for their survival. In fact, he suggested provocatively, the galley slaves were better off than their free brethren: they received food and clothing and, with little hard labour to perform, they could even earn some extra income on the side.[76] Sharp certainly underestimated the realities of unemployment in London's economy, but the openly 'idle' behaviour of the *lazzaroni* was a recurrent motif in visitors' commentary on Naples. It was also a subject of major concern for the Neapolitan political economists who, like the British, saw it as yet another symptom of the pernicious consequences of the feudal system under which Naples still suffered.[77]

Sharp's observations related specifically to Naples and drew on long-standing stereotypes of the Italian character. But in the later eighteenth century, as Andrew Canepa has argued, these stereotypes became less critical and more sympathetic.[78] Many of the old prejudices, however, continued to exist, and given the suspicions that any kind of assembly of the labouring sort aroused in Britain in the 1790s and the horror stories emanating from Paris with regard to the activities of the sans culottes, it might be expected that the suspicion with which the *lazzaroni* were habitually regarded would have been sharpened and amplified: particularly given that the radical press in Britain was busy reinventing Masaniello as a hero of popular resistance to despotism – he featured in

---

[75] The dominance of the legal profession in Naples (where it has been calculated there was one lawyer for every 200 people) was one of Giannone's principal targets in his critique of Neapolitan society. See Rao, 'Feudal question, judicial systems and the Enlightenment'. The ubiquity of lawyers was another of the clichés surrounding Naples that featured in almost all guidebooks and travel literature. A visit to the *vicaria* or courts of justice was a common activity for tourists: see, for example, Lord Herbert's description of his visit, Herbert (ed.), *Henry, Elizabeth and George*, 235–6, or Mary Berry's account in Lewis (ed.), *Extracts of the Journals and Correspondence*, I, 78.

[76] Sharp, *Letters from Italy*, 100. Sharp's criticisms of the *lazzaroni* should be taken in the context of a publication that was consistently critical of Italy and indeed the value of the Grand Tour as an educational experience. But his views were more widely shared: for similar views from French writers, see Calaresu, 'Looking for Virgil's Tomb'. Sharp's comments also reflect topical concerns in Britain: moralists such as Henry Fielding and Jonas Hanway similarly railed against the ever increasing luxury of the London poor who were either drunk on gin or expected to be able to drink tea and ape the luxuries of their betters.

[77] Rao, 'The feudal question, judicial systems and the Enlightenment'.

[78] Canepa, 'From degenerate scoundrel to noble savage', esp. 133–46.

Thomas Spence's *Pig's Meat*, for example.[79] Regardless of this subversive potential, however, the *lazzaroni* were increasingly being represented in much more benign terms as essentially harmless, charming and childlike. If they were indolent, that was the fault of the climate rather than innate failings of moral fibre; if they were dependent upon alms rather than industry and agriculture, that was the fault of the twin evils of Catholicism and feudalism.

Naples re-imagined

This change in register that characterises so many accounts of the later eighteenth century demands explanation. Whilst it is possible to look to domestic factors (the topicality of the revolt of Masaniello in relation to contemporary events, the burgeoning interest in 'manners and customs'), it is important also to acknowledge the influence of Neapolitan reformers such as Giannone from the earlier eighteenth century and more latterly Genovesi, Filangieri and Galanti upon British visitors. By this time, many visitors were familiar, either directly or indirectly, with Giannone's *Civil History of the Kingdom of Naples* which had been translated into English in 1729.[80] They absorbed his critique of the Catholic church, even if they appear to have profited less from his history of the city itself. Giannone's criticisms found a natural sympathy with Protestant suspicions of the papacy and of the means by which the Catholic church enriched itself at the expense of both the state and the people and maintained its authority through cultivating superstition and through a monopoly on education. William Robertson had notably drawn on Giannone in his introductory essay on the history of Europe which prefaced his *History of the Reign of the Emperor Charles V* (1769) and this informed widely used accounts such as John Moore's *View of Society and Manners in Italy* (1781). Moore, for example, refused to blame the character of the people, but rather the system of government

---

[79] [Thomas Spence], *Pig's Meat: Or Lessons for the Swinish Multitude*, 3 vols. (1794–5), III, 22–55, 67–97, 123–36, 152–4, 185–7, 197–213. The popularity of Masaniello's story continued to grow in the nineteenth century and it became the subject of articles, short stories, two plays, an opera and a ballet: Brand, *Italy and the English Romantics*, 192–3.

[80] On the British reception of Pietro Giannone, see Hugh Trevor Roper, 'Pietro Giannone and Great Britain', *HJ*, 39:3 (1996), 657–75. Thomas Pelham was reading Giannone's history of Naples in Italian during his tour in 1777 and referred to him as a familiar text amongst the educated elite: 'The histories of Italian affairs, particularly those of Muratori and Gianone [sic], are so generally known and esteemed, and comprehend so minute an account of the origin and progress of the Pope's aggrandizement, that it would be superfluous to enter into any investigation of it here.' Pelham to his mother, 30 July 1777, BL Add. MS 33127, fol. 285v. See also Denham, *Temporal Government*, 6.

which oppressed them and made it futile for them to attempt to improve their situation by labour.[81] From the mid-eighteenth century, a second generation of reformers, including Ferdinando Galiani, Gaetano Filangieri and Giuseppe Maria Genovesi, further developed the study of political economy in Naples and drew attention to the pressing need for agricultural and economic reform. They saw the persistence of feudalism as the key to Naples' problems and developed a penetrating critique of the Neapolitan state and its economy.[82] Galanti's two-volume survey of Naples was not widely read amongst the British travelling public, and nor, apparently, was his much shorter guide to the city of Naples itself published in 1792. But Henry Swinburne, whose volumes on Naples were widely consulted by British travellers, was well acquainted with him and his circle, and it was largely through Swinburne's publications that the views of the Neapolitan reformers were filtered into the consciousness of British travellers.[83] Hence, an increasingly important element of travel writing about Naples in the latter part of the century entailed commentary on how the church and the feudal system had combined to inhibit the development of Naples' natural fertility and potential for commerce. It is for this reason that we find rather more attention given to the evils of the fiscal system, the role of the nobility and the need for reform in this period, which also informed a less condemnatory attitude towards the problem presented by the *lazzaroni*.[84]

By 1776, Anne Miller declared that the *lazzaroni* were honourable and harmless.[85] A few years later, Hester Piozzi compared them to 'tattowed Indians': they were primitive and semi-barbarous, but not, of themselves, threatening.[86] Marianna Starke whose *Letters from Italy* was published in 1800, carried this process of infantilising the *lazzaroni* even further. She too played down the danger they posed and dismissed their reputation as a homeless ungovernable rabble. Their character, she

---

[81] Moore, *View of Society and Manners*, II, 160.

[82] John Robertson, *The Case for Enlightenment: Scotland and Naples, 1680–1760* (Cambridge, 2005), ch. 7; Franco Venturi, 'The Enlightenment in southern Italy', in Franco Venturi, *Italy and the Enlightenment*, ed. S. Woolf and trans. S. Corsi (1972), 198–224.

[83] Davis, *Naples and Napoleon*, 46–8.

[84] Calaresu, 'Looking for Virgil's Tomb', 152; Canepa, 'From degenerate scoundrel to noble savage'; see also Martin Sherlock, *Letters from an English Traveller* (1780),102–4, who argued that the Neapolitans were 'naturally good' and 'absolutely' in the state of nature; they were guilty of crimes and rudeness, but only because they were unaware that they were doing wrong.

[85] Miller, *Letters from Italy*, II, 383–8.

[86] Piozzi, *Observations and Reflections*, 231. But it should be noted that Piozzi's pro-Italian agenda muted her expression of overt criticism of the Italians: see Turner, *British Travel Writers*, 172–8.

claimed, had been much mistaken by the traveller. On the contrary, they could be 'charmed by a joke' and 'governed by kind words'. Those who had not been tainted by commerce with the foreign visitors were of a 'noble disposition'.[87] Sympathy for the *lazzaroni* was not confined to female travellers: John Chetwode Eustace discussed them at some length, arguing that they were unfairly treated both by Neapolitan writers and travellers. He emphasised their good humour and defended them from the charge of idleness and ignorance. Eustace subscribed to the view that they were shaped by their circumstances, rather than that they were innately indolent. The influence of Neapolitans such as Giuseppe Maria Galanti, who depicted his fellow Italians as gentle, music-loving and predisposed to enjoy life, can also be detected here.[88] But this rehabilitation also owed a considerable amount to contemporary events in Europe. The loyalty that the *lazzaroni* had shown to the Bourbon monarchy during the upheavals of 1798–9, their 'warm attachment to liberty' and their 'abhorrence of oppression' (suitably allied with support for the monarchy) helped to transform their reputation from being a latent force for sedition to one of constancy and public spirit.[89] In the wake of the French Revolution, atheism and its sacrilegious destruction of the established order could be seen as a more potent threat than the misguided superstition of Roman Catholics. By the end of the Napoleonic Wars, the *lazzaroni* had been re-imagined as charming and picturesque: for the poet Samuel Rogers they were 'a noisy, gay & harmless race ... offering their little services on every occasion'.[90] British travellers' growing self-confidence in their membership of an enlightened and civilised society allowed them to view the *lazzaroni* less as dangerous devils than as the primitive and childlike members of a society, whose development had been halted by the pernicious effects of feudalism.

It should be noted, however, that the majority of comments on the innocence and charm of the *lazzaroni* come from published sources, where the authors were evidently articulating (and repeating) a fashionable rhetoric. Personal diaries and correspondence, in which there was

---

[87] Starke, *Letters from Italy* (1800 edn), II, 93–4.
[88] Galanti, *Breve descrizione della città di Napoli*, 268; see also his *Nuova descrizione storica e geografica dell'Italia*, 2 vols. (Naples, 1782).
[89] Eustace, *Classical Tour*, II, 39–42. It should be noted, however, that Eustace took care to distinguish these faithful and honest *lazzaroni* from the 'idle' and 'unprincipled' beggars who filled the churches of Naples and other public spaces (154).
[90] Hale (ed.), *Italian Journal*, 268. Henry Coxe, *Picture of Italy*, claimed that the *lazzaroni* had disappeared from Naples and were now all gainfully employed as porters, soldiers and scavengers (325).

less emphasis upon writing for a particular readership or creating a work that conformed to certain literary expectations, tended to be more critical of the *lazzaroni*, suggesting that visitors continued to find the confrontation with their outright poverty distasteful and discomforting. Their dirt, idleness and in particular their habit of picking vermin from each other's heads, rather than their beguiling innocence and picturesque charm, were the characteristics that attracted most comment in this more private format.[91]

But this is not to deny the fact that the street life of Naples had, by the early nineteenth century, become one of its positive attractions.[92] The evocation of a town through a description of its people and their way of life was not a development exclusive to Naples or a form of writing that was limited to the British. Such passages reflected the shift of focus in travel writing across Europe towards the description of 'manners and customs' and the pursuit of the picturesque. 'Manners and customs' provided a barometer by which to evaluate many other questions, such as the position of women or agricultural progress or the extent of superstition with which enlightened travellers liked to concern themselves in their study of society. Similarly, picturesque street scenes including labourers or beggars as staffage were becoming more common in topographical art, being appreciated as part of the urban aesthetic (evident, for example, in accounts of London such as J. T. Smith's *Vagabondia*).[93] Travellers were searching out and describing the picturesque qualities of street life in *any* town, not just Naples. But the emphasis upon the streets and their inhabitants, and the dynamic quality of these spaces, is much more marked in descriptions of Naples than elsewhere in Italy.[94] It was in Naples that tourists really began to make an effort to describe the appearance, pastimes and character of the people. To a certain extent, this seems to have happened because the buildings

---

[91] See, for example, Boswell's description written to Johnston, 19 Mar. 1765, 'The People are the most shocking race eaters of garlic and catchers of vermin an exercise which they scruple not to perform on the public Streets.' Walker (ed.), *Correspondence of James Boswell*, 159–60; see also Lady Holland's comments to her sister, Dec. 1766, 'their great occupation [is] to louse one another in the Street all day long in the sun', in Fitzgerald (ed.), *Correspondence*, I, 488; see also Bentham journal TNA PRO 30/9/43, 164; Derbyshire journal NRO DCN 118/6, 17.

[92] Melissa Calaresu, 'From the street to stereotype: urban space, travel and the picturesque in late eighteenth-century Naples', *Italian Studies*, 62:2 (2007), 189–203.

[93] Lucy Peltz, 'Aestheticizing the ancestral city: antiquarianism, topography and the representation of London in the long eighteenth century', *Art History*, 22:4 (1999), 472–94.

[94] Nelson Moe, *The View from Vesuvius: Italian Culture and the Southern Question* (Berkeley, 2002), 2–3, suggests that the picturesque became the main 'prism' through which Naples was viewed by northern European visitors in the later eighteenth century.

themselves – churches, palazzi, the fortresses – were not, as we have seen, so central to the visitor's experience of Naples as they were elsewhere, but it was also because the sheer density of population was so much higher – and so much more obvious. Thus it was that travellers first began trying to conjure up a sense of the atmosphere and to describe the day to day activities of its people: 'I am impatient to catch and convey the manners, dress, air, and folly of this gay and glittering city' wrote John Owen in 1796.[95] Every other shop was selling food according to Hester Piozzi, with people piling in from all directions and no specific purpose in mind. Even the Strada di Toledo, the impressive main street running for a mile and a half through the centre of Naples, was filled with stalls, mountebanks, puppet shows, shrines and wineshops. A set piece describing the manners and customs of the people became a customary element in descriptions of Naples. Joseph Forsyth, the author of *Remarks on Antiquities,* who generally confined himself to observations of a more architectural and antiquarian bent, found himself strangely fascinated by the swelling mass of humanity on the streets of Naples and its endless activity. But he was also disturbed by its lack of order, rationality and discipline. In London, the crowd represented a society that was governed by the principles of order, reason and application to industry; in Naples, it embodied the unreasoned attachment to superstition; the undisciplined indulgence in sensual pleasure; and the dangerously free play given to passion and excitement:

The crowd of London is uniform and intelligible: it is a double line in quick motion; it is the crowd of business. The crowd of Naples consists in a general tide rolling up and down, and in the middle of this tide a hundred eddies of men. Here you are swept on by the current, there you are wheeled round by the vortex. A diversity of trades dispute with you the streets. You are stopped by a carpenter's bench, you are lost among shoe-makers' stools, you dash among the pots of a *macaroni*-stall, and you escape behind a *lazarone's* night-basket. In this region of caricature every bargain sounds like a battle: the popular exhibitions are full of the grotesque; some of their church-processions would frighten a war-horse.[96]

With his vocabulary of the battle field, Forsyth still seems to have been feeling an undercurrent of danger at the extremes of Neapolitan street life. For the most part, however, visitors were simply captivated by the amount of activity going on in the streets, a reaction best

[95] Owen, *Travels into Different Parts of Europe,* II, 95.
[96] Forsyth, *Remarks on Antiquities,* 266. The passage was also reproduced in Coxe, *Picture of Italy,* 307. See also Anon., *The London Guide and Stranger's Safeguard* (1818), 15, 'Walking the streets has been reduced to a system in London; every one taking the right hand of another, whereby confusion is avoided.'

summed up in the novelist Lady Sydney Morgan's description of
Naples as she saw it in 1816:

Crowds, the most grotesque and characteristic, group round the stages of the
mountebanks; the pavement is strewed with mounds of oranges, and the air
resounds with that acute Babel like noise which belongs exclusively to Naples,
where the spirits of the people are all abroad, increased, but not overpowered, by
the clang of trumpets, the winding of horns, and the tinkling of guitars, which
summon the votarists of amusement to its several temples.[97]

But it was not, of course, just the *lazzaroni* who represented a threat in
Naples. The city was also associated with the dangers of sensuality and
licentiousness, modes of behaviour which were permitted indulgence
unconstrained by the regulatory norms of society with which the British
were familiar. In the 1790s, there was a shift in emphasis amongst
travellers as to where they located the perils of Neapolitan society: whilst
the danger associated with the *lazzaroni* appear to have been mitigated,
in its place there was a more pervasive anxiety about a permissive sexual
immorality. The association of Naples with sexuality was longstanding,
but although visitors frequently compared the luxury and indolence of
modern Naples with its sybaritic reputation in antiquity, the element of
sexual impropriety and licentiousness was not so explicitly articulated.
Swinburne, for example, never identified licentiousness or loose sexual
mores as a key element of the continuity with antiquity which he identified
elsewhere. Indeed, overt sexuality was not one of the principal dangers
associated with the city for most of the eighteenth century.[98] Around mid-
century, visitors often observed that prostitutes were less visible in Naples
and that there were fewer signs of jealousy from Italian men than in other
cities. Contrast this to Venice, where the dangers of the courtesans were
one of the set pieces of Grand Tour writing.[99] Lalande, whose tour was
widely used by British travellers, similarly commented upon the absence
of prostitutes in the streets.[100] Charles Abbot was one of those who

[97] Morgan, *Italy*, II, 333. Morgan's description bears some similarity to that of Goethe,
whose detailed and sympathetic account of the *lazzaroni* and Neapolitan street life
in *Italienische Reisen* (1816) was based upon observations made 1787–8. Goethe's
Reisen were not translated into English until 1849, however, when they were included
in A. J. W. Morrison's translation of *Autobiography of my Life* (London, 1849).
[98] Swinburne, *Travels in the Two Sicilies*, II, 79. Seventeenth-century travellers, however,
frequently commented upon the presence of prostitutes upon the streets. John Evelyn,
for example, claimed that there were 3,000 courtesans in Naples and that 'this towne is
so pester'd with these Cattel, that there needes no small mortification to preserve from
their inchantements, whilst they display all their naturall & artificiall beauty, play, sing,
feigne, compliment, & by a thousand studied devices seeke to inveigle foolish your
persons'. E. S. de Beer (ed.), *The Diary of John Evelyn*, 6 vols. (Oxford, 1955), II, 322.
[99] See Chapter 4.   [100] Lalande, *Voyage en Italie*, VI, 336.

travelled with the English translation in his luggage: in Naples, he noted in his journal that the prostitutes 'never Walk about the Streets of an Evening'; rather, their pimps came and approached men directly in their carriages.[101] It is impossible to establish whether or not this observation was informed by his reading of Lalande, but what should be noted is that his perception of the city was of a place where prostitution was more discretely arranged than in other Italian centres. The practice of soliciting through pimps was therefore an aspect of Neapolitan life that he thought worthy of record. William Forbes, another reader of Lalande, was similarly struck in 1792 by the fact that one could walk through the streets of Naples at night and never see a street walker, although he had supposed they would have been widespread. He concluded rather lamely that such transactions must all be concluded indoors.[102]

However, at around the same time that Forbes was recording his surprise (or possibly disappointment) at the absence of street walkers, an English clergyman, John Owen, complained that he had

seen no place in which nature is less restrained by the laws of morals, or even of decorum. That thin and flimsy veil, which, disguising the grossness of vice, renders it – if not less criminal – less offensive, seems here to be either unknown, or unregarded. The passions speak a language of the most licentious depravity.[103]

Forsyth, likewise a clergyman, as we have already seen, was similarly unsettled by the sensuality of Naples when he referred to its combination of danger and allure. He added that it 'continues to subvert the two great sexual virtues, guardians of every other virtue, – the courage of men and the modesty of women'.[104] In the easeful warmth of Naples, the barriers of sexual propriety melted into blurred indistinction. And yet another clergyman, Robert Gray, found the very air of Naples seductive and dangerous to virtue, unlike England where the values of virtue and fidelity were, he claimed, still felt.[105] Even more overt in his identification of Naples with sensuality – to the point of titillation – was the British merchant Nicholas Brooke, whose Observations on the Manners and Customs, purportedly written as a series of letters to 'a friend' during his travels in 1794–5, dwelled at length on the licentiousness he encountered throughout Italy, and in Naples in particular.[106]

[101] Abbot journal TNA PRO 30/9/41, 332.
[102] Forbes journal NLS MS 1542, fol. 214.
[103] Owen, Travels into Different Parts of Europe, II, 95.
[104] Forsyth, Remarks on Antiquities, 273.
[105] Gray, Letters during the Course of a Tour, 399.
[106] Nicholas Brooke, Observations on the Manners and Customs of Italy, with Remarks on the Vast Importance of British Commerce on that Continent (1798). James Boswell, inevitably perhaps, claimed to have been 'truly libertine' in Naples blaming the climate: 'my

In part, we have to see such comments as a product of the scope for reflection on social mores which was offered by the convention of describing manners and customs in the travel literature of the period. Naples' climate and historical reputation might be supposed to invite such remarks, if not the timing and the venom with which they were expressed. Certainly by the nineteenth century, the 'Italian south' was increasingly constructed as a place of sensuality, indolence and loose morality to be contrasted with the disciplined restraint of northern Europe and of the British in particular.[107] A significant role in the creation of this image is conventionally attributed to Mme de Staël's novel *Corinne* (1807), which became one of the most influential accounts of Italy of the early nineteenth century. It is easy to trace her influence, both implicit and explicit, in subsequent travellers' accounts which stress the emotional warmth and spontaneity of the south, breathing new life into Montesquieu's climatic explanation of national character.[108] But this anxiety about sensuality, amongst British travellers at least, clearly predated the publication of *Corinne*, although it does, perhaps, help explain why de Staël's representation of Italy had such resonance.

There are other contributory factors that need to be considered here, however. First, since mid-century the connection between the sexual licentiousness of the south in both antiquity and the present had been strengthened by the excavations at Pompeii and Herculaneum. These had produced particularly rich evidence of what one tourist described as the lack of modesty and decorum amongst the Romans, although many others declined even to comment upon the more explicit items uncovered by excavations.[109] In Rome, the vision of antiquity offered by the antiquaries and connoisseurs was frequently asexual.[110] At Pompeii,

---

blood was inflamed by the burning climate and my passions were violent'. Brady and Pottle (eds.), *Boswell on the Grand Tour*, 6.

[107] Moe, *View from Vesuvius*. Lemaistre commented on the easy morals of Neapolitan ladies in 1802, *Travels after the Peace of Amiens*, II, 72.

[108] See, for example, Blunt, *Vestiges of the Ancient Manners and Customs*, 282, who contrasted Italian volatility and expressiveness with the 'frigidity of an Englishman's constitution, and his almost utter exemption from every thing like corporeal expression of his feelings'. Joseph Luzzi, 'Italy without Italians: literary origins of a romantic myth', *Modern Language Notes*, 117 (2002), 48–83, argues that one of the key characteristics of foreigners' construction of Italy and the Italians was the absence of public moral code (51). They were also constructed as primitive, violent and effeminate.

[109] Armitage journal TCC Add. MS a 266 37 (2), fol. 23v; Lemaistre, *Travels after the Peace of Amiens*, II, 36: 'The subjects of some of these paintings are not very decorous, according to modern ideas of delicacy; and the symbol of the god of gardening appears rather too frequently in the decoration of houses.'

[110] Chard, 'Nakedness and tourism'. See also Smith, *Sketch of a Tour*, II, 120, on the brothel in Pompeii: 'Modern manners are shocked at such flagrant public obscenity.'

by contrast, the eighteenth-century traveller was brought face to face with the unexpurgated version of antique sexuality. But the discovery of phallic street signs and erotic wall paintings predated the upsurge of prudery which found a voice from the 1790s and cannot of itself account for the heightened disapproval shown from the 1790s onwards.[111]

More important, perhaps, was the changing profile of visitors in terms of gender balance and social class. The presence of increasing numbers of women, especially younger women, in family groups such as that of Sir William Forbes' wife and daughter, heightened the sensibilities of both men and women as to possible impropriety. Boys would be boys and the phallocentricity of antiquity may have delighted the members of the Society of Dilettanti, but it was not a pleasure that could be shared in mixed company.[112] The increasingly numerous and heterosocial middling presence contributed to the deepening tinge of disapproval and a stronger sense of prudishness. Thus, while the aristocratic Earl of Pembroke might have encouraged his son to seek out the sexually explicit statue of the satyr copulating with a goat, for Sir William Forbes a devout Episcopalian, it was a 'most beastly group', despite the highly finished workmanship.[113] A rising current of criticism against aristocratic licentiousness and immorality back in Britain would not have predisposed travellers to look leniently upon libertinism, ancient or modern.[114]

---

[111] Richard Payne Knight's *Discourse on the Worship of Priapus* (1786), which drew on the research of d'Hancarville and the supposed paganism of the cult of Isernia identified by Sir William Hamilton, argued for the phallocentric character of ancient mythology. It was, however, only privately printed and circulated amongst members of the Society of Dilettanti and cannot be attributed with influencing broader perceptions of the Neapolitan region from which many of his examples came. The volume was republished in 1818 as *In Inquiry into the Symbolic Language of Ancient Art and Mythology*, but shorn of much of the more explicit sexual content. Kelly, *Society of Dilettanti*, 241–66; Bruce Redford, 'Richard Payne Knight's *Discourse on the Worship of Priapus*', in Bruce Redford, *Dilettanti: The Antic and the Antique in Eighteenth-Century England* (Los Angeles, 2008), 113–28.

[112] On libertine masculinity, and in particular its relationship to classical antiquity, see Kelly, *Society of Dilettantti*, especially 61–89; Turner, *British Travel Writers*, similarly discusses the disruption of the traditional aristocratic discursive practice of classical nostalgia by increasing numbers of middle-class, professional and female travel writers (passim).

[113] Herbert (ed.), *Henry, Elizabeth and George*, 197; see also the disgust of Sir William Forbes: NLS MS 1541, fol. 108. Forbes was even more outraged, however, by the extortionate fee demanded by the guide for showing it.

[114] Boyd Hilton, *A Mad, Bad, and Dangerous People? England 1783–1846* (Oxford, 2006), 178, notes the sudden shift in attitude towards sexuality around 1800 in British culture. See also Anna Clark, *Scandal: The Sexual Politics of the British Constitution* (Princeton, 2004), 113–23; Vic Gatrell, *City of Laughter: Sex and Satire in Eighteenth-Century London* (2006), 418–82, and on late eighteenth-century concerns surrounding the corruption of contemporary morals, Innes, 'Politics and morals'.

Furthermore, in the more masculine militaristic climate of the 1790s tolerance levels for anything that smacked of effeminacy rapidly dissipated; effeminacy was equally the consequence of over-indulgence in sexual license as it was the manifestation of feminine habits of submission and servility.[115] In short, domestic morality was transported into Italy and asserted itself forcefully on the representation of Naples and its environs; so much so, that Robert Gray, whose horror at Neapolitan sensuality has already been quoted, was taken to task in the pages of the *Gentleman's Magazine* for offering a luridly distorted account of sexual and social mores in Italy.[116] The issue of the veracity of his comments is less important than the implication that he chose to project onto Italy, and Naples in particular, those very faults that he saw as threatening the social order at home and which he wished to believe were utterly foreign to the British character.

In 1766, Caroline Holland informed her sister that 'It is extremely entertaining to drive about the streets to see how very unlike everything is to what we see at home.'[117] But she did not expand upon her somewhat prosaic observation of alterity. Anything approximating to an emotional response to the city was left unspecified and unexplored. But by the early nineteenth century, an image was being constructed of Naples that depended less on its physical appearance than on a distinctive *atmosphere*, which drew upon a subjective and personal experience of the city. The enumeration of antiquities and monuments had never been such a dominant feature of descriptions of Naples as it had in Rome; nor did the city's history offer a salutary model with which the British visitor could identify. Rather, its associations were with the intangible qualities of leisure, pleasure and sensuality – an entirely different kind of urban experience to that offered by Florence, Rome or even Venice, let alone British cities. Naples was what British cities were not: unproductive, idle and disordered. But it also appeared carefree, joyous and unrestrained. For some, the city represented a dangerous lack of restraint; for others, the same lack of restraint represented freedom from the conventions and restrictions of their own society and was a quality to be relished. The early nineteenth century seems to have been a key moment in this reconceptualisation of Naples as a city with a distinctive appeal (or frisson, depending on one's view point) as opposed to being the point of departure for other activities.

---

[115] Wahrman, *The Making of the Modern Self*, 58–69.
[116] Arthur Greville, 'Remarks on Mr Gray's tour', *Gentleman's Magazine*, 65 (July 1795), 547–51.
[117] Lady Holland to Duchess of Leinster, 21 Dec. 1766, Fitzgerald (ed.) *Correspondence*, I, 488.

The evolving response to Naples illustrates more clearly than any other Italian city the influence of romantic travel writing upon perceptions of Italy. The 'romantic' traveller, it has been argued, developed a very different mode of tourism to the formalised and ostensibly objective mode of viewing which characterised so much of eighteenth-century travel literature. Romantic travellers saw transgression less as a danger than as a means of personal discovery. For male travellers in particular, the experience of travel offered the opportunity for temporary irresponsibility and abandonment of duty, rather than a continual performance of the norms of masculinity and taste. The dangers of southern indolence or effeminacy that Naples offered within the licensed context of travel could be apprehended as part of this temporary 'unmooring' of the self and become a source of pleasure as well.[118] Naples' dangerous allure was nothing new, but by the nineteenth century it had become integral to the image and reputation of the city, shaping both the visitor's perceptions and subsequent representations.

[118] Chard, *Pleasure and Guilt*, 11, 17–19, 36–8, 213–48; O'Connor, *Romance of Italy*, 53.

5   Venice: a place of singularity and spectacle

'In short every thing here is singular.' Thus Robert Wharton summarised his experience of Venice for his friends at home in Durham.[1] Generations of British tourists echoed his sentiment. Venice was unique and extraordinary. It was fascinating, but also discomfiting and alienating. It was unlike any other city they visited, whether in terms of topography and architecture, politics and government, or social and sexual mores. After Rome, it was also the city which had the strongest imaginative associations and which aroused the most heightened expectations of all the destinations of the Italian tour. But the British sense of familiarity with Venice was very different from that which was felt in Rome. The buildings and monuments were not invested with the same deep layers of meaning as Rome's antiquities, celebrated through generations of humanist scholarship. There was no equivalent to Basil Kennett's *Romae antiquae notitia* to imprint scenes of Venetian history on the schoolboy's imagination; the names of the doges never ran off the tongue with the same familiarity as the roll call of Roman emperors; nor could the battle of Lepanto command the instant recognition of the Carthaginians' defeat at Actium. Venice's fame was not so much a consequence of people or events, but of its reputation for having an exceptionally stable system of government and as an exemplar of timeless continuity.[2] But the city's unique culture and constitution were inextricably bound up with its extraordinary physical qualities. Venice's aquatic topography certainly endowed it with much of its renown and singularity, but it had also been a crucial factor in perpetuating the longevity of the Republic and its independence. It was the combination of the city's location with the distinctive social and political culture to which it had given rise that determined the city's place in the British imagination in the eighteenth century. Whilst Florence was

---

[1] Robert Wharton to Miss Lloyd, 10 May 1776, DUASC WHA 168 letterbook number 3, fol. 15v.
[2] Edward Muir, *Civic Ritual in Renaissance Venice* (Princeton, 1981), 13–61, on the 'myth of Venice'.

favoured because it offered a haven of home-like comforts and sociability, in Venice, British travellers found much that was unusual and curious, but much that was strange and unsettling too. This shaped the tenor of all their observations: visitors stressed what was different, rather than looking for similarities. Most visitors were fascinated, but many felt ill at ease and were glad to leave after a stay of only a week or two. Venice was, as Richard Pococke told his mother, 'an odd place that does not please me'.[3]

Expectations and preconceptions

British visitors to Venice in the eighteenth century were the heirs of both a longstanding interest in Venetian history within English political culture and the Venetians' own powerfully expressed sense of pride in their historic traditions of political liberty and stability and the city's commercial prosperity.[4] Unlike the majority of the other Italian city states, Venice had retained its independence and had never fallen under the sway of another territorial power since its foundation. This proud tradition of autonomy and civic identity affected the way in which Venice presented itself to visitors (not least in the guidebooks that were purchased by the British) and shaped the way that visitors responded to the city in turn.[5]

Venice's claim to a unique degree of freedom rested on the fact that it had never been conquered. It was supposed to have been founded in the fifth century by Romans fleeing Ostrogothic invasion. The Venetians, therefore, prided themselves on being the true heirs of the ancient Roman traditions of political liberty. Thanks to the city's impregnable defensive situation in the lagoon, it had never subsequently been invaded or conquered by other territorial powers. These founding myths and its subsequent history had been familiar to many English-speaking visitors from the sixteenth century: Contarini's *De magistratibus et republica Venetorum* (1543) was translated into English by Samuel Lewkenor as *The Commonwealth and Government of Venice* (1599) and Francesco Guiccardini's *Storia d'Italia* which offered an equally idealised view of

---

[3] Richard Pococke to his mother, 2 June 1734, BL Add. MS 22978, fol. 80r.

[4] J. G. A. Pocock, *The Machiavellian Moment. Florentine Political Thought and the Atlantic Republican Tradition* (Princeton, 1975), especially 272–330; David Wootton, 'Ulysses bound? Venice and the idea of liberty from Howell to Hume', in David Wootton (ed.), *Republicanism, Liberty and Commercial Society* (Stanford, 1994), 341–67; Hale, *England and the Italian Renaissance*, 21–5; John Eglin, *Venice Transfigured: The Myth of Venice in British Culture, 1660–1797* (Basingstoke, 2001),11–68.

[5] Venice's relationship to its own past, and particularly its early (and mythical) history is explored by Patricia Fortini Brown, *Venice and Antiquity* (New Haven and London, 1999).

the Venetian constitution, was similarly translated into English in 1579. Contarini celebrated the perfection of the Republic's mixed constitution, its stability, independence, its pacific record and its tolerance. The Venetians kept their spiritual overlord, the pope, at arm's length too and English Protestants, therefore, also admired the Venetians for resisting the encroachments of the counter-reformation papacy, even enduring a papal interdict. (James I had gone so far as to write a pamphlet in defence of the Republic.) Paolo Sarpi's defence of Venice's immunity from papal intervention was greatly admired in Britain, where it found many readers and contributed to the valorisation of Venice as a state that had avoided religious as well as secular tyranny. The influence of this idealised vision of Venice on the commonwealthmen of mid-century, such as James Howell and James Harrington, has been well documented.[6] Between 1668 and 1672, it has been calculated that there were at least ten publications that described the constitution of Venice for an English readership.[7] The ideal of Venice that was represented in these sources was based upon no very precise understanding of how the Venetian constitution actually worked, but as Edward Muir notes, it was peculiarly attractive to moderate reformers who opposed tyranny whilst being equally nervous about the implications of genuine popular democracy.[8] At the Glorious Revolution, whig politicians saw it as a model of constitutional government and the doge offered the ultimate example of limited monarchy.

At roughly the same time, however, this almost wholly positive evaluation was being challenged by a far more critical and sceptical analysis of the Venetian state, which drew upon works by French observers, such as Amelot de la Houssaye and St Didier, rather than the celebratory Venetian sources. These authors saw the falling off in the Republic's trade and its loss of political power and naval strength as the consequence of a fatally flawed system of government.[9] 'The constitution so beloved of English commonwealthmen', writes John Eglin, 'was depicted as the corrupted charter of the ineffectual government of an irreversibly declining state no more to be admired than any other earthly government.'[10] In the seventeenth century, the city had been held up as a paragon of stable republican government; by the eighteenth century, that image was reversed to one of oligarchic corruption, oppressive secrecy and

[6] James Howell, *SPQV a Survey of the Signorie of Venice, of her Admired Policy, and Method of Government* (1651); James Harrington, *Oceana* (1656).
[7] Hale, *England and the Italian Renaissance*, 34.
[8] Muir, *Civic Ritual in Renaissance Venice*, 54–5.
[9] Amelot de la Houssaye, *Histoire du gouvernement de Venise* (Paris, 1695).
[10] Eglin, *Venice Transfigured*, 18

commercial decline.[11] Venice ceased to be a model to which Britain might aspire, and became instead a warning of what Britain might become.

Yet, the British accepted the Venetian claims to be the true heirs of ancient Rome and, even when critical of other aspects of Venetian society, they still retained an admiration for the city which they believed provided a direct link to the spirit of ancient Rome.[12] Given that the majority of British travellers were Protestant, they also continued to admire the Venetians' determination to retain their spiritual freedom and to resist the temporal authority of the pope. Superstition was rarely a theme of visitors' comments in Venice as it was in Rome or Naples; indeed, its comparative absence often featured in visitors' observations: 'To say the truth', wrote one traveller, 'I have seen less of the Roman Catholic religion, less of its mummery, and less of its scenery in Venice, than in any other part of either France or Italy.'[13]

The analysis of Amelot de la Houssaye exercised a clear influence on several of the most widely used tours of the late seventeenth and early eighteenth centuries: Misson, Addison, Wright, Blainville and even the overtly whiggish Gilbert Burnet. In fact, all the standard published guides to Italy drew on these arguments, which rapidly assumed the status of truisms and irrevocably shaped the terms of reference through which Venice was viewed during the eighteenth century. It also fed into another set of associations that surrounded Venice – that of the 'città galante' – a city of luxury, carnival and pleasure. Since the renaissance period, Venice had been famous for its music, its theatres (it had seven, more than any other city in Italy), its masquerades, its gambling, its courtesans and its pursuit of pleasure. Whereas the traditions of freedom and a stable oligarchy provided the foundations of indigenous Venetian civic identity, this was a view of the city that was projected onto it by outsiders. Following the analysis of Amelot de la Houssaye and others, critics of Venice argued that its citizens were denied political participation and submitted to the oppressive regime of the Council of Ten because they were distracted by entertainment and pomp; the nobility, who were ciphers in government, were similarly bought off and were reduced to selling their votes in the Senate on the *broglio*. Liberty, as Bruce Redford notes, was a protean term that could have multiple

---

[11] Ibid., 11–43; Redford, *Venice and the Grand Tour*, 51–5; Iain Gordon Brown, 'Water, windows, and women: the significance of Venice for Scots in the age of the Grand Tour', *Eighteenth-Century Life*, 30:3 (2006), 1–50.

[12] See, for example, Eustace, *Classical Tour*, I, 64–5.

[13] George Ayscough, *Letters from an Officer in the Guards*, 205; Hester Piozzi claimed that there was no city in Italy 'more eminent for the decency with which divine service is administered', *Observations and Reflections*, 101.

meanings, and not all of the liberties exercised by the Venetians held equally positive connotations.[14] It was this myth of the 'città galante', the libertine city, that came to dominate in the eighteenth century. A narrative of a corrupt core, concealed by a deceptive exterior show of finery and display, provided the conceptual framework with which many visitors approached the city.

It was as a consequence of this evolution in Venice's reputation that Venetian analogies appeared with diminishing frequency in eighteenth-century political debate.[15] The idea of the city still retained a powerful presence in British political culture, however, if only as an illustration of the dangers posed by unbridled luxury to political and moral virtue. But Venice was not only familiar to those who made models of government their study: it was as widely known through the theatre and literature as through political debate. When visitors to Venice recalled events or sought out landmarks, it was *Venice Preserved* or the *Merchant of Venice*, not the works of Contarini or Sarpi, to which they referred.[16] The Rialto Bridge was admired as a piece of architecture (although most were disappointed to find its form obscured by the shops which lined it) but its principal significance for British tourists was as the location for the conspiracy between Pierre and Jaffeir in *Venice Preserved* or as the hub of Shylock's commercial activities in the *Merchant of Venice*. William Forbes, like many other tourists, engaged in an imaginative reverie upon the Rialto, conjuring up images of Pierre and Jaffeir, and embarked upon a futile inquiry to establish whether any of the family names used in the play still existed amongst modern Venetians.[17] But given that neither Shakespeare nor Otway had ever visited Venice, the evocation of the physical spaces of the city in their plays was sketchy. James Edward Smith, whose view of Venice was jaded to say the least, pointed out Otway's unfortunate solecism in locating a scene of secret deliberation in one of the most crowded spaces in the entire city.[18]

Venice was also a city which commanded a stronger visual presence in the British imagination than any other city apart from Rome. Canaletto's

---

[14] Redford, *Venice and the Grand Tour*, 55–8; on the cultural meaning of masquerade in the eighteenth century, with which Venice was particularly associated, see Terry Castle, *Masquerade and Civilization: The Carnivalesque in Eighteenth-Century English Culture and Fiction* (1986). On the significance of carnival for the city's eighteenth-century identity, see Jonathan White, ' "When the kissing had to stop": eighteenth-century Venice – apotheosis or decline?', in idem, *Italy the Enduring Culture* (Leicester, 2000), 171–201.

[15] Eglin, *Venice Transfigured*, 29.

[16] An exception was Sta Maria dei Servi, which was visited by some who sought to honour the memory of Paolo Sarpi who was buried there. See, for example, Jeremiah Milles' journal, BL Add. MS 15763, fol. 114.

[17] Forbes journal NLS MS 1540, fol. 167.   [18] Smith, *Sketch of a Tour*, II, 422.

vedute defined popular perceptions of Venice during his lifetime and long after. His views of Venice first started to attract attention in the 1720s but they have to be seen as part of a much longer tradition of topographical art. Maps of Venice, prints of its buildings and the costumes of the inhabitants had filtered into Europe since the sixteenth century creating a widespread visual familiarity with the city amongst the educated elite of Europe.[19] From the late seventeenth century, Luca Carlevaris had responded to the rising volume of visitor demand to produce a series of over one hundred etchings of buildings and townscapes in Venice, published as *Fabriche e vedute di Venetia* in 1703–4.[20] These were widely purchased by foreign visitors, such as Joseph Addison, who noted the 'very curious stamps' of the buildings 'that are most famous for their Beauty or Magnificence' that had recently been published in Venice.[21] Sets of measured drawings of north Italian and Venetian architecture were also produced in their hundreds, if not thousands, by Antonio Visentini and his studio assistants from the 1730s, which as John Harris notes 'catered to the *milordi* who saw them as the picture postcards of their day'.[22] Visentini is best known for having engraved a series of fourteen of Canaletto's *vedute* owned by Consul Joseph Smith, which were first published in 1735; these were so successful that they were re-issued in 1742 with an additional twenty-four engravings, and a further edition appeared in 1751.[23] Despite their apparent ubiquity, Canaletto and Visentini did not have a monopoly on representations of Venice in this period: visitors could also purchase views by Michele Marieschi such as *Magnificentiores selectioresque urbis Venetiarum prospectus* (1741).[24] Thanks to the widespread availability of prints, as well as the popularity of Canaletto's views, most of those who were in a position to travel already had some preconception of Venice's appearance, just as they were

[19] Bronwen Wilson, 'Venice, print and the early modern icon', *Urban History*, 35:1 (2006), 39–64.
[20] William Barchan, 'Townscapes and landscapes', in Jane Martineau and Andrew Robison (eds.), *The Glory of Venice: Art in the Eighteenth Century* (New Haven and London, 1995), 92–113. Some of Carlevaris' prints would later be used by Canaletto as the starting point for his own *vedute*: David Bomford and Gabriele Finaldi, *Venice through Canaletto's Eyes* (1998), 12.
[21] Addison, *Remarks on Several Parts of Italy*, 83.
[22] John Harris, 'The neo-palladians and mid-century landscape', in Jane Martineau and Andrew Robison (eds.), *The Glory of Venice: Art in the Eighteenth Century* (New Haven and London, 1995) 247–66.
[23] J. G. Links, *Views of Venice by Canaletto Engraved by Antonio Visenti* (1971). After Smith's death, the plates are thought to have been purchased from his widow by the publisher Furlinetto, who had them re-engraved. A new edition was published in 1833 and reprinted 1836.
[24] Harris, 'The neo-palladians and mid-century landscape', 247–66.

familiar with the appearance of Roman monuments. Thus, the countess of Pomfret assumed that there was no need to describe the Rialto to her correspondent, the Countess of Hertford, as 'you will have seen so many pictures of this in painted views which people have brought back to England'.[25] Philip Yorke's enthusiasm for describing the sights of Venice may have been waning when he omitted a description of the Doge's Palace in a letter to the Earl of Hardwick, on the grounds that 'your lordship will have seen [it] so often painted and engraved that it is scarcely worth describing it', but his assumption of familiarity on the part of his uncle is indicative of the place occupied by Venice in the cultural imagination of the British elite at this time.[26] Nor was this visual acquaintance with Venice limited to members of the aristocracy: prints of Venice like prints of Rome were widely available for those with pretensions to taste. Thus in *Emma*, Jane Austen had Mr Woodhouse and Mrs Weston entertain themselves at Donwell Abbey, whilst everybody else was out strawberry picking, by looking at prints of the Piazza San Marco (see Figure 13).[27]

Some travellers made their way to Venice before heading south to Florence and Rome; others visited the city on the return leg of their journey to Italy. Having been to Naples, they travelled back to Rome, across to Ancona to admire Trajan's Arch, and along the coast (crossing the Rubicon) to Venice, stopping off at northern Italian cities such as Bologna en route if these had not already been visited. Travellers aimed to be in Venice either during the extended season of carnival (which commenced on Twelfth Night), or the festivities surrounding Ascension Day when the famous *sposalizio* and the regattas took place, or during the season of masquerading which lasted from roughly 5 October to 16 December.[28] At these periods, the city was in full party mode, putting on a show for the thousands of visitors who would descend upon Venice from the neighbouring hinterland.[29] During carnival, there was a continual round of masquerades in fancy dress, concerts, regattas, gambling parties and other activities, and all seven theatres were open.[30] This was the principal attraction and outside such periods the city was, inevitably,

[25] Phillips (ed.), *Correspondence*, III, 242.
[26] Yorke to his uncle, 22 May 1778, BL Add. MS 35378, fol. 192v.
[27] Jane Austen, *Emma* (Oxford, 1982), 363.
[28] Aileen Ribiero, *Dress in Eighteenth-Century Europe* (New Haven and London, 2002), 247; visitors' accounts of the *sposalizio* are discussed by Redford, *Venice and the Grand Tour*, 58–65.
[29] Thomas Twisden in 1693 referred to the vast numbers of visitors coming to Venice during carnival, Bodl. MS Eng. misc. c 206, fol. 15v. Archenholz claimed that 42,480 visitors came to Venice for the festivities on Ascension Day in 1775, held in honour of the visit of Emperor Joseph II: *A Picture of Italy*, I, 37.
[30] See Joseph Spence's letter to his mother describing the variety of fancy dresses worn by the Venetians, and the role playing involved in Klima (ed.), *Letters from the Grand Tour*, 94–6.

Figure 13 The Piazza San Marco.

found to be 'stupid' or 'dull'.[31] When Philip Francis arrived at Venice in August 1772, out of season, he found it deeply disappointing: the only entertainment was provided by an Englishman, Mr Potts, who was performing feats of horsemanship.[32] Potts failed to impress.

Nor did the Republic offer the attractions of a royal court, where young men might polish their social skills, establish political connections and improve their horsemanship. The Venetian nobility, instead, were notoriously unwilling to entertain foreigners (the consequence, it was said, of a paranoid government which feared the betrayal of state secrets) and, as many visitors complained, aside from the theatres and masquerades during carnival, there was very little opportunity for mixing with local society. Venice was not attractive to the British as a city for longer-term residence. Unlike Rome, the British government was represented in Venice, but Venetian suspicion of foreigners, and the lack of a court culture, made it difficult for John Strange, British Resident in Venice 1774–86, for example, to offer the same kind of sociability and services as Sir Horace Mann and Sir William Hamilton provided to visitors in Florence and Naples. As Philip Yorke explained to his uncle, the Earl of Hardwick, even if Strange had not been ill during their residence in Venice he would not have been of any use 'with regard to presenting us to the Society of the place, for the being a foreign Minister is here a total exclusion'.[33] Edward Thomas found that the only entertainments to which he and his countrymen were invited were the receptions held by the French and imperial ambassadors. The Venetians who attended were 'very civil as far as bows go' but would not be engaged in conversation.[34] This, coupled with the fact that few visitors stayed in Venice more than a couple of weeks, meant that the pattern of dinners, conversazioni and sociability that grew up amongst the communities of British visitors in Florence, Rome and Naples was never replicated on the same scale.

Venice's place on the Grand Tour was, therefore, slightly equivocal: as an education in taste, it arguably offered little that could not be acquired elsewhere. It represented an object lesson in republican government and the power of commerce, certainly, but this had to be set against its associations with luxury, libertinism and licence. Parents, worried about the temptations of the city's notoriously brazen prostitutes and the culture of gambling, might advise against its inclusion in their offspring's

[31] Lord Kildare to the Duchess of Leinster, 12 Oct. 1768: 'it is a very stupid place except in Carnival', Fitzgerald (ed.), Correspondence, III, 539; see also Smith, Sketch of a Tour on the Continent, II, 364; Lemaistre, Travels after the Peace of Amiens, II, 211.
[32] Francis journal BL Add. MS 40579, fol. 7.
[33] Yorke to his uncle, 3 June 1778, BL Add. MS 35378, fol. 204.
[34] Thomas to Jeremiah Milles, 31 Mar. 1751, BL Add. MS 19941, fol. 37r.

itinerary.[35] The Countess of Chichester clearly did not think that her son, Thomas Pelham, would have much to gain from a visit to Venice; it might be interesting to visit, she allowed, but if he could not fit it in, it 'may be well conceived from a good Canaletti'.[36]

The spectacle of Venice

Like Rome, Venice was a city to be apprehended from a distance, with excitement and anticipation. Even the approach was different: visitors generally left their carriages at Fusina, where a large coach house had been specially constructed for the accommodation of visitors. The final leg of the journey was made in a barge along the river Brenta, allowing for views of the nobility's Palladian villas along the riverside.[37] Venice rose up from the sea as one approached, like a city floating upon water, with towers and spires instead of ships' masts and sails. 'At first sight', wrote Edward Thomas, 'it seemed to be set down into the sea like Swift's Flying Island in Guliver.'[38] Robert Gray approached Venice in the glow of evening sunlight, when the city appeared 'to have just risen, as the mother of Love is described, in elegant and classic imagery, from the waves of the sea' (making a rather heavy-handed play on the suggestive assonance of eighteenth-century pronunciations of 'Venice' and 'Venus').[39] It was a city that could be encompassed in one glance – there was no sprawl, no hills or woodland to obscure it: 'the many turrets, steeples, domes, palaces that lye all on a level, ... strike the eye all at once', remarked another traveller.[40]

All travellers knew that Venice stood in the midst of water, but this first sight of the city still had the capacity to surprise, even at the end of the eighteenth century. As Adam Ferguson remarked, when reporting on his arrival in Venice to his wife in 1793, 'knowing and seeing I find is different'.[41] One of its most striking features was the complete absence of city walls, which were rendered unnecessary by its aquatic location. Although mural defences had been allowed to fall into decay or had even been dismantled in most British cities by the eighteenth century, in

---

[35] Roger Robertson wrote to his father, 14 June 1752, acknowledged the latter's warning against the dangers of Venice: NLS Acc 12244.
[36] Countess of Chichester to Pelham, 13 June 1777, BL Add. MS 33127, fol. 261.
[37] Bentham journal TNA PRO 30/9/43, 106.
[38] Thomas to Jeremiah Milles, 3 Mar. 1751, BL Add. MS 19941, fol. 36r.
[39] Robert Gray, *Letters during the Course of a Tour*, 434. For other examples of this verbal punning, see Redford, *Venice and the Grand Tour*, 6.
[40] Drake journal MCO MS MC F16 vol. 2, 132.
[41] Brown, 'Water, windows and women', 2.

mainland Italy, where warfare continued intermittently throughout the century, no town or city of any size went unfortified. Walls defined a town and in Italy continued to serve a crucial defensive function.[42] For Venice, however, no protection other than the shallows of the lagoon was necessary and its limits were defined by seawater rather than bricks and mortar. Venice's 'fluid Bulwark', wrote Edward Wright, was far more effective than walls or ramparts, for 'let the Venetians but pluck up their Poles out of the Lagune, and they may defy any foreign Vessels coming near them by Water; and by Land there's no coming at them'.[43] Not everyone found the city's situation so pleasing, however. For John Moore, Venice's location in the midst of the sea was neither romantic nor delightful, but rather precisely what enabled the Council of Ten to exercise such oppressive rule. He looked across the sea to the terra firma and 'real freedom': a city surrounded by land was, in his opinion, a far more attractive sight than Venice's watery and inconvenient isolation.[44]

Venice was almost universally defined by the absence of streets and pavements (although, as most travellers eventually acknowledged, there was a complex network of narrow bridges and footpaths). Even Amsterdam, another city of canals, had systems of streets and pavements beside the waterways upon which pedestrians could walk, and quays outside the houses where goods could be unloaded. But Venice did not have this convenience and the water came right up to the thresholds of the houses: it was, as visitors observed, as if the city had been flooded.[45] It was only latterly that this came to be seen as a picturesque feature.[46] As a consequence, Venice could not be judged, as other cities were, by the quality of the pavements: even the expensive repaving of the Piazza San Marco in 1723 – beautifully represented in Canaletto's views of the square – went unremarked.[47] But if visitors could not pass comment on the cleanliness or otherwise of the streets, they could, and frequently did, make highly critical remarks on the stench rising up from the canals: a

---

[42] Observations on the strength and defensive capacity of the walls of cities were more frequent in the first half of the eighteenth century when the political balance of power within Italy was considerably less stable: see, for example, the accounts of Andrew Mitchell (BL Add. MSS 38315–19), Walter Bowman (St Andrews University Library MS 38271) and Francis Drake (MCO MS MC 16).

[43] Wright, *Observations*, I, 45.   [44] Moore, *View of Society and Manners*, I, 40.

[45] Northall, *Travels through Italy*, 427: 'Many noble buildings are on each side of it [the grand canal]: but wanting a beauty which the towns in Holland have, a quay or space between the houses and the canals, this makes it look like a town overflowed, the water coming close to the sides of the foundations of the buildings.' See also Sir James Hall's description NLS MS 6325, fol. 48v.

[46] Abbot journal TNA PRO 30/9/41, 413.

[47] Giovanni Albrizzi, *Forestiere illuminato intorno le cose più rare, e curiose, antiche e moderne della città di Venezia* (Venice, 1740), 47.

smell that was overpowering in summer and was not the least of the reasons why visitors were frequently so glad to leave the city.[48] 'I had rather not return a second time to row through stinking canals in those coffin-like Gondolas' confessed the bearleader Thomas Brand to his sister.[49] The sense of inundation was reinforced by the almost complete absence of any open public space apart from the Piazza San Marco. Sir Martin Folkes complained that there were no other squares of any size, nor even any gardens or yards.[50] Whilst his observation was certainly an exaggeration, what is important is the perception that he and others had formed that Venice occupied a uniquely densely inhabited space. The maps and plans produced for tourists would only have served to reinforce this impression of crowded in-filling. Venice appears in these prints as a mass of blocks of tightly packed buildings, intersected by narrow canals – unlike the plans of cities such as Rome or Turin which celebrated the grand open spaces and rectilinear streets so highly prized at the time.

Folkes also found Venice confusing and difficult to navigate: it was disorientating due to the absence of a regular street plan and the visitor was confronted with a labyrinthine network of canals and *calle*. There were no perspective views, no straight lines, no open vistas, except on the Grand Canal. It was only after he had purchased a plan of Venice that he was able to make any sense of the city spatially.[51] He was not alone in this: Jeremiah Milles similarly complained at the intricacy of the street plan and the 'prodigious number of turnings' that one had to make in order to arrive at any given destination.[52] It is hardly surprising, then, that as Heathcote Tatham noted, the reaction of most British visitors was simply to jump into a gondola rather than to attempt to find their way around the city themselves.[53] Unlike most cities, Venice was entirely flat, which made it all the harder to make sense of its layout, as there were no natural vantage points from which it might be surveyed.[54] In order better to understand the city, travellers were advised to ascend a tower – such as the clock tower in the Piazza San Marco – for the prospect view over the city, with the layout of the canals, the lagoon and the surrounding islands.[55] Only then

---

[48] Christopher Hervey, *Letters from Portugal, Spain, Italy and Germany, in the Years 1759, 1760 and 1761*, 3 vols. (1785), III, 463; Lindsey journal Bodl. MS Eng. c. 7052, fol. 38.
[49] Thomas Brand to his sister, 13 Apr. 1787, CUL Add. MS 8670 (c) 21.
[50] Folkes journal Bodl. MS Eng. misc. c. 444, fol. 27r.   [51] Ibid.
[52] Milles journal BL Add. MS 15763, fol. 104.
[53] Pearce and Salmon (eds.), *Charles Heathcote Tatham in Italy*, 67.
[54] Smith, *Sketch of a Tour*, III, 362.
[55] Folkes journal Bodl. MS Eng. misc. c. 444, fol. 13r; Abbot journal TNA PRO 30/9/41, 393.

could the form of the city and its dramatic location be fully appreciated. It was, as Robert Wharton told his family, an astonishing view:

directly under you is this <u>vast</u> city surrounded with water on all sides. Then come the Islands innumerable and each having its Town Village Convent Church or Building on it and lessening to the View in proportion to its distance and the View terminated on one side by the Expanse of Sea and on the other by the environs of Padua and the mountains of Verona.[56]

It is not surprising that the bird's eye view maps of Venice were such popular souvenirs amongst visitors.

In the absence of roads and streets, there was accordingly no conventional traffic. Without the deafening clatter of iron-rimmed wheels on cobbles or the constant passage of footsteps in the streets, Venice was eerily quiet. 'A dead melancholy stillness reigns', John Patteson informed his mother, 'and you hear nothing but the cry of the gondoliers on turning the corners, and quarrelling with each other.'[57] The splash of the gondoliers' oars and the sound of their singing offered a dramatic contrast to the hubbub of traffic and voices encountered in a city such as Naples or the commercial port of Leghorn. The silence was identified as a characteristic feature of Venice long before nineteenth-century romantics used it to evoke an atmosphere of decay and desolation, but it was indicative even then of the city's commercial decline. The Venetian air was also uncommonly clear: Canaletto's views of Venice may represent an idealised version of the city, but the bright atmospheric clarity which characterises his *vedute* of the 1750s was also noted by visitors. London, dependent on soft and grimy Newcastle coal, was a city of soot and smut. In Venice, where the principal fuel was wood and where there was little in the way of manufacturing industry, atmospheric pollution was not a problem.[58]

Venice may have been a labyrinth of canals, but few visitors appear to have explored much beyond the Grand Canal – with or without a gondolier.[59] The city was a spectacle to be viewed, rather than a place to be discovered. The only 'capital objects' to be seen in Venice, noted Charles Abbot, were the 'Palace [sic] of St Marks' and the Arsenale. San Marco itself 'was not worth visiting', apparently, despite its antiquity.

[56] Robert Wharton to Miss Lloyd, 10 May 1776, DUASC WHA 168 letterbook number 3, fol. 15v.

[57] Cubitt, Mackley and Wilson (eds.), *Great Tour of John Patteson*, 295.

[58] Sharp, *Letters from Italy*, 7.

[59] William Beckford, who found 'every day some new amusement in rambling about its innumerable canals and alleys' defied, yet again, the norms of eighteenth-century travel writing (William Beckford, *Dreams, Waking Thoughts and Incidents* (1783), 108).

His own journal, however, records that he also visited the Rialto, San Giorgio Maggiore and several of the palaces lining the Grand Canal. But by and large, the aspects of Venice that he chose to describe were confined to what could be seen on or around the Grand Canal and the Arsenale.[60] In this, he was entirely typical of British visitors.[61] Most went to il Redentore and San Giorgio; some visited Murano and other islands in the lagoon; those with a particular interest in art or architecture explored some of the other churches such as SS Giovanni e Paolo (which housed both Titian's masterpiece of the martyrdom of St Peter and the monuments to the doges) or the Scuola San Rocca. Unlike the palazzi of Roman nobility, however, where the public rooms were routinely open to foreign visitors, the Venetian nobility were less willing to put their homes and their collections on public display, thus Philip Francis, for example, was frustrated to find that he could only gain access to those of the Pisani and Barbarigo families. This perceived lack of openness was another factor in creating that sense of alienation and exclusion of which the British so often complained.[62] For the majority of British visitors, therefore, their experience of Venice was constructed around the Piazza San Marco and the churches and palaces along the serpentine curve of the Grand Canal.

For all their interest in the history of Venice – and in many of the published guides the political and constitutional history of Venice merited an extended discussion – the manner in which the city was viewed did not represent the physical monuments and spaces of the city as the embodiment of its history. Venice's history was not tied to particular places or specific monuments as was Rome's: it was Shakespeare and Otway who gave meaning to the Rialto, not the course of Venetian history. The Doge's Palace might elicit a disquisition on the nature of Venetian oligarchy, but the connection between the events of the past and their relationship to the physical structure that tourists saw before them was not made. As in Rome, visitors viewed a disconnected series of churches and buildings; they counted the piazzas (too few) and the bridges (too many, and too slippery) and noted the curiosity of the saracenic arches on the façades that lined the Grand Canal. But they rarely related the buildings to what they knew of the city's history – and even more seldom put a date to them. Instead, Venice was a city to be

[60] TNA PRO 30/9/41, 387–441.

[61] The contemporary Venetian guidebooks were all structured around descriptions of the *sestiere*.

[62] Francis journal BL Add. MS 40759, fol. 9. These were also the only palazzi mentioned by Philip Yorke in a letter to his uncle, 2 May 1778, BL Add. MS 35378, fol. 194.

viewed and described in the present tense: a spectacle to behold rather than a testimony to the past, for the past still lived on in the creaking traditions of the Republic.

But the spectacles were many and the Venetian love of colour and display that they occasioned fascinated the British. First and foremost was the daily performance of Venetian life in the Piazza San Marco. Just as Naples was defined by the British through its street scenes, the Piazza San Marco, or St Mark's Place as it was invariably known, was a lively crowded, space that epitomised the special character of the city. Maximilien Misson proclaimed it the 'Soul and Glory of the City'[63] and as such it elicited near universal approval. It was the social hub where everyone paraded and where all the news was to be heard. It was the stage upon which every activity in Venice converged. Visitors were delighted with the broad expanse of space that it offered and the variety of life to be seen. On certain days, it was the location of a busy market, but only a visitor such as the ever-practical Sarah Bentham – whose journal was largely innocent of the usual tropes and conventions of travel writing – described the entirely ordinary display of everyday cloth, second-hand pewter, fruit and vegetables that took place on market-day.[64] It was in St Mark's Place that visitors encountered the festivities of carnival and the masqueraders that defined so much of the popular image of Venice. Joseph Spence, who always sought to entertain his mother in his letters home, gave a lively account of the fancy dress and playacting in which the Venetians engaged at carnival: he had seen, he told her, not only the harlequins and ladies dressed as milkmaids, but a 'great fat fellow drest up like a Nurse' and 'one of the tallest gentlemen in Venice' trussed up like an infant in swaddling clothes, bawling and roaring for pap, which the 'nurse' duly fed to him. 'T'would be', he concluded 'a modest thing to say they are only half mad.'[65] Anne Miller's description in Letters from Italy reads much like a verbal description of one of Canaletto's scenes: 'here are the senators, nobles, merchants, fine ladies, and the meanest of the people: Jews, Turks, puppets, Greeks, mountebanks, all sorts of jugglers and sights'. Not even the most bizarre costume or language would attract notice in such an environment.[66] Hester Piozzi, a partial and effusive observer it must be allowed, declared that it rendered the spectator 'breathless with delight', but even the more cautious Francis Drake admitted that, despite its 'irregularities and deformities', it was one of the few sights in Italy that actually

[63] Maximilien Misson, A New Voyage to Italy, 2 vols. (1695), I, 154.
[64] Bentham journal TNA PRO 30/9/43, 110–11.
[65] Klima (ed.), Letters from the Grand Tour, 93.   [66] Miller, Letters from Italy, III, 247.

exceeded the expectations of one's imagination.[67] Drake felt himself to
be 'dropt on enchanted ground' when he found the Piazza full of
animals, rope dancers, acrobatic displays, astrologers and 'shows and
sights of all kinds and contrivancy'. Even the mechanicks and ordinary
people dressed up in the most extraordinary costumes.[68]

Irrespective of carnival, the piazza was a place of constant activity where
Venetian society was on display. Venice's singularity was manifested in
the dress of its inhabitants and St Mark's Place was the ideal location in
which to observe the different fashions and costumes: the nobility in their
silk robes and 'prodigious' wigs; the women in their dominos (a long,
black, all-encompassing silk cloak) and silk veils; and the masks worn by
both men and women during carnival and the masquerading season.[69]
Supposedly, women were not permitted to frequent the coffee houses and
casinos which occupied the arches of the portico around the square
without a mask, but, as many travellers observed, this convention was
frequently breached in another instance of Venetian licence.[70] But the
ubiquity of the masks and the domino which concealed the wearer's
identity also contributed to the sense of Venice as an alien, unknowable
city. Thomas Pelham wrote to his mother in 1777 trying to convey a sense
of the city's extraordinary qualities. He singled out not just its location
and the waterborne transport, but the twenty-four-hour culture of a city
where the theatres did not open until 10.00 in the evening, where the
company went to the casinos around the piazza for conversation and
gambling once the theatres had closed, and would then spend the small
hours of the morning perambulating around the square. As the market
sellers set up their stalls in the morning the late-night partygoers purchased food for their supper before returning home. The nobles who were
strolling around as dawn broke kept their eyes open, he claimed, 'by the
assistance of strong Coffee' – another facet of Venetian life that drew
frequent and critical comment from British observers. There were 'so
many objects of Attention and Curiosity that I really know no better sight
than Venice', he concluded.[71] Philip Yorke, whose letters to his uncle were

[67] Piozzi, *Observations and Reflections*, 80; Drake journal MCO MS MC F16, vol. 2, 157.
[68] Drake journal MCO MS MC F16, vol. 3, 11–12.
[69] Ribiero, *Dress in Eighteenth-Century Europe*, 246–7.
[70] Abbot journal TNA PRO 30/9/41, 395, 'Under the Arcades are Shops, Coffee Houses &
small Casino's. In the Rooms upon the first Floor are the Grand Casino's. The Small
Casino's are in the Mezzonine over the Coffee Houses, & are within the Arcade. They all
Open into a Passage behind the Building – The Great Casino's belong to Subscription
Clubs; one of them the Philharmonic consists of Four Card Rooms & a Ball Room
indifferently furnished.'
[71] Pelham to his mother, 23 Oct. 1777, BL Add. MS 33127, fols. 333–4. On the
consumption of coffee and its dangers, see also Piozzi, *Observations and Reflections*, 103.

a sanctimonious exercise in affirming his unwavering adherence to a path of virtue in the midst of temptation, primly observed that Venetian hours were 'much too late' for those accustomed to colder climes.[72]

Descriptions of St Mark's Place also provided the opportunity to depict the city's cosmopolitanism and to comment upon the manners and customs of the inhabitants, lounging in the coffee houses and the shops: 'Jews, Turks, Arabs, in short all sorts of dresses that one sees in books of travel', observed Adam Walker.[73] William Beckford was delighted by the Babel like mix of languages he encountered: Turkish, Arabic, Sclavonian, Greek, and he wandered about the square talking to Armenian priests and jewellers and Greek and Dalmatian merchants. Beckford's approach to Venice was highly unusual, however, sidestepping the conventional observations of travel writing and offering an entirely subjective and solipsistic perspective instead.[74] But for most visitors, the cosmopolitanism of the Piazza was simply an exotic spectacle to be admired from a distance, not something to be pursued any further. It certainly did not encourage them to visit the Greek quarter or to seek out the Jewish traders in their ghetto. For all the popularity of the *Merchant of Venice* there was no literary tourism to see where Shylock might have lived.[75] The Rialto sufficed (see Figure 14).

Despite their superficial familiarity with the appearance of Venice derived from paintings, prints and engravings, the city's architecture, and that of San Marco in particular, invariably came as a surprise, even a shock. San Marco represented in an extreme form the profusion of ornament and confusion of style which British visitors encountered in Venetian architecture throughout the city. It was like nothing they had seen before. The combination of pointed gothic arches and rounded Byzantine domes, enhanced by brightly coloured mosaics, is not to everyone's taste, even today when architectural eclecticism is more widely tolerated.[76] In the eighteenth century, it was a mixture of styles which went beyond comprehension. It is tempting to say that San Marco defied description. But that is not strictly true. Most made at least some effort to delineate what they saw as the bizarre quality of the church's

[72] Yorke to his uncle, 3 June 1778, BL Add. MS 35378, fol. 205.
[73] Walker, *Ideas Suggested on the Spot*, 146; Craven, *Journey through the Crimea*, 98.
[74] Redford, *Venice and the Grand Tour*, 105–15.
[75] Edward Wright evidently explored the ghetto because he described a circumcision that he had witnessed, but it was the ceremony rather than the place in which he was interested: Wright., *Observations*, I, 68. Brief references can also be found in some of the more compendious guides such as John Northall's *Travels through Italy*, but there is no indication of the author having actually visited the area.
[76] Jonathan Buckley and Hilary Robinson, *Venice: The Rough Guide* (1993), 42, describe the façade as 'bewildering' and the 'worst aesthetic mismatch in all Italy'.

Figure 14 The Rialto Bridge from the east.

fabric. But, given the limited terminology available in the eighteenth century with which to describe architecture that failed to conform to classical norms, they struggled to record its appearance in any detail. The bewilderment which was felt when confronted with the architecture of medieval Italy was more acute here than anywhere else.[77] Francis Drake was baffled. Even gothic architecture, he complained, followed some kind of system in its ornamentation but San Marco flouted even these rules: it was a jumble, a confused heap of different styles and ornaments; a mixture of Moorish, gothic, Greek and Saracenic.[78] 'It is neither Gothic nor regular', complained Thomas Broderick, 'in short, it is, with all its splendour and magnificence, neither one thing nor another.'[79] Others simply found it 'clumsy' and 'dismal'.[80] The uncertainty over its style persisted into the nineteenth century, despite the emergence of a more discerning appreciation of gothic architecture amongst most travellers. In 1803, Joseph Forsyth found it 'a very singular pile.' He was able to distinguish Greek and gothic elements but this was no ordered progression; rather it was 'a fortuitous jumble of all'.[81] But just as there was increasing recognition that churches such as San Pudentius or San Clemente represented a valuable document of primitive Christianity in early nineteenth-century Rome, so too some of the later visitors to Venice could recognise the basilica as an exemplar of early Christian architecture, even if they could not commend its beauty.[82]

Nor were the local guidebooks of much help in explaining the structure: the story of its foundation was recounted and all the stages of its successive construction, destruction and reconstruction but the building itself was not actually described. The spoils from Constantinople, the richness of the mosaics and the trophies in the treasury were enumerated in loving detail, but these were catalogues, not descriptions. The liturgical significance of the different elements of the basilica were described (the narthex, nave, baptistery and various chapels) but not their physical appearance. There was no question here of identifying an architectural style or influence.[83] It was enough simply to record the building's antiquity; the wealth it displayed in the richness of its façade; and the proof which its very size and opulence, as well as the haul of spoils from

[77] The reactions of British visitors to the Italian gothic are discussed more fully in Chapter 6.
[78] Drake journal MCO MS MC F16 vol. 2, 159.
[79] Thomas Broderick, *The Travels of Thomas Broderick Esq in a Late Tour through Several Parts of Europe*, 2 vols. (1754), I, 316.
[80] Derbyshire journal NRO DCN 118/6, 84.   [81] Forsyth, *Remarks on Antiquities*, 333.
[82] See, for example, the description in Lemaistre, *Travels after the Peace of Amiens*, II, 179.
[83] Albrizzi *Forestiere illuminato*, 10–18.

Constantinople, offered of the protection of its tutelary saint and the city's concomitant commercial success. Venetians did not have to justify the basilica's existence by locating it within a taxonomic model of architecture or explain its appearance by identifying different cultural influences.

Unlike the churches of Florence and Rome, or even some of the other churches in Venice, San Marco could not boast a succession of artistic masterpieces for the visiting connoisseurs to admire. The mosaics covering the walls of the narthex and the interior were a curiosity but little appreciated. In the seventeenth century, when the practice of decorating churches with mosaic was largely unknown in Britain, several writers, such as Maximilien Misson, went to some length to describe how mosaics had been made.[84] But the images depicted thereby scarcely interested him. Those inside the basilica were obscured by poor lighting and years of accumulated dirt and even when visible their style was deemed to be primitive and unattractive to the eighteenth-century eye. The iconography was seldom remarked upon, reflecting both the poor visibility of the interior and a distinct lack of interest on the part of the British. 'Awkwardly drawn and worse coloured', pronounced the Countess of Pomfret.[85] Guidebooks and *ciceroni* would have been able to enlighten them on such matters – the iconographical programme of the mosaics was an important element of any Venetian guidebook – but the subject matter was not the point: the mosaics were simply another manifestation of the singularity of Venice and an illustration of the barbarous times in which the basilica had originally been built. Towards the end of the century, attitudes were less dismissive, as interest in the middle ages and the period's cultural production increased, but the comments that were made were hardly more informative as to the iconography of the scenes represented: 'legends without end' was Adam Walker's banal but enthusiastic endorsement.[86]

St Mark's Place also comprised the physical embodiment of Venice's unique constitution: the Doge's Palace and the courts of justice. Like the basilica, the Doge's Palace featured in every traveller's account of the city. Observers appreciated the quality of the rose coloured marble, the impressive dimensions and the fact that it housed the Venetian Senate: 'Notwithstanding all the Gothicism about it, it may pass for a Palazzo

[84] Misson, *New Voyage to Italy* (1695 edn), I, 159.
[85] Phillips (ed.), *Correspondence*, III, 225.
[86] Walker, *Ideas Suggested on the Spot*, 148. For the shift in attitude towards the art and architecture of the medieval period, see Chapter 6.

superbissimo.'[87] But visitors were unable to render a verbal description of the building's appearance. 'It would perhaps be rash in a Man to undertake to give a perfect Description of it', as one writer excused himself.[88] Brief comments on the 'saracenic' arches (uncouth and out of all proportion, complained one guide) or the 'disproportioned' pillars sufficed.[89] The architecture of the palace could be read as a symbol of the government within: its intricacy, wrote Adam Walker in 1790, reflected 'the dark intriguing policy of this artful republic'.[90] Walker's view of Italy was heavily influenced by the aura of mystery and danger evoked by Ann Radcliffe's gothic novels, a tradition in which gothic architecture was invariably redolent of oppression and tyranny. But the interest of the building lay less in its exterior appearance, which was unequivocally grand and imposing whatever one thought about the style in which it had been built, than in the activities that took place around and within it. Hence, many visitors devoted far more attention to describing the chambers inside the palace, the different councils and tribunals which met there and the paintings by the Venetian masters which adorned the walls. Even for those who did not share Walker's literary gothic preoccupations, there was plenty within the palace to remind them of both the checks and the balances of Venice's mixed constitution and the less attractive aspects of its government.

Visitors liked to wind themselves up into a state of indignation against the oppression of the Venetian government. Joseph Spence, somewhat dramatically, told his mother that he had not dared to write anything in his letters about the Venetian people until he had reached the safety of Rome four hundred miles away.[91] (Possibly this was simply an excuse to exonerate himself from a lapse in letter-writing.) Coffee houses, Edward Wright had informed his readers in 1730, had no seats, 'nor dare the masters of them keep any; that Company may not with Ease to themselves stay long together in such occasional Places of Meeting'.[92] A visit to the Doge's Palace presented the opportunity for visitors to offer an analysis of the government and frequently to engage in a reflective passage critical of Venetian tyranny. The *bocca di leone*, the lions' mouths that gaped open to receive the anonymous evidence of secret informers against their neighbours, were symbols of the dark arts of the Council of Ten and the State Inquisition. The *piombi* under the roof and the *pozzi*

[87] Blainville, *Travels through Holland, Germany, Switzerland*, I, 521. [88] Ibid.
[89] Coxe, *Picture of Italy*, 427; Milles journal BL Add. MS 15763, fol. 126; Smith, *Sketch of a Tour*, II, 402.
[90] Walker, *Ideas Suggested on the Spot*, 150.
[91] Klima (ed.), *Letters from the Grand Tour*, 94. [92] Wright, *Observations*, I, 97.

below in the foundations, where prisoners had been housed before the construction of the imposing seventeenth-century prison facing the palace, were potent reminders of how limited the vaunted freedoms of the Republic were for those who fell foul of the state.

The Bridge of Sighs (the Ponte dei Sospiri) that connected the palace to the prison was present on the visitors' itinerary by virtue of its curious enclosed design long before Byron gave it literary immortality in *Childe Harold's Pilgrimage*. The unfailingly comprehensive Edward Wright and Georg Keysler had both mentioned it, for example, but simply as a part of their cataloguing of information rather than as a trigger for sensibility.[93] From mid-century, the rise of sentiment, however, wrought a palpable change in travellers' descriptions, as they sought to demonstrate their empathy with the prisoner condemned – possibly unjustly – to perish in the dungeons of the Venetian state. In 1750, Francis Drake spoke of the 'melting pity' he felt for the prisoners as he looked upon Contino's prison and the Ponte dei Sospiri. Robert Harvey was similarly moved by the fate of the 'poor devils' who passed over it to languish in the prison when he visited Venice in 1773.[94] The shudders of William Beckford, who was haunted by 'horrors and dismal prospects' after viewing the bridge, are better known today, yet Beckford's influence in his own time was limited: *Dreams, Waking Thoughts and Incidents* was published in 1783, but was suppressed and had only limited circulation.[95] The images of gothic horror that Beckford summoned up, therefore, when describing the prisons and bridge, could not have had a bearing upon the views of most travellers until it was republished in edited form in 1834. With the publication of *Childe Harold*, however, the bridge rapidly acquired another set of associations and visitors were moved not just by the imagined plight of the prisoners, but by their own response to Byron's verse.[96]

The physical environment of the Palace itself also attracted comment in observations which are indicative not so much of changing levels of tolerance towards dirt amongst British travellers, but of an evolution in their attitudes towards the political traditions that the Palace represented. It was commonplace in the first half of the century to comment upon the filth and human excrement that lay around the staircases and the entrances. Gilbert Burnet had complained of the propensity of the nobility to use it as a 'common house of office'.[97] Such observations

---

[93]   Ibid., I, 55 and Keysler, *Travels*, III, 280.
[94]   Drake journal MCO MS MC F16 vol. 2, 156, and Harvey journal NRO MS 20677, 214.
[95]   Beckford, *Dreams, Waking Thoughts and Incidents*, 106–7.
[96]   Waldie, *Sketches Descriptive of Italy*, IV, 106.   [97]   Burnet, *Some Letters*, 129.

were soon replicated in other published tours and acquired additional
ironic weight as a comment on Venetian liberty, which had been lacking
in Burnet's whiggishly sympathetic account of the constitution.
According to Edward Wright, there were 'such filthy heaps and nasty
lakes even at the entrance into the hall of the great council that one
scarce knows where to tread'. It was, he remarked, 'a top Instance of the
Venetian Liberty'.[98] Blainville continued this critique of the superficiality
of Venetian freedoms: 'This nasty Sight is so far from being disagreeable
to the Inhabitants, that they account it Part of their boasted Liberty, to
evacuate those Superfluities of Nature, when, where, and before whom
they please.'[99] The theme continued to crop up in a number of other
tours until the 1760s and the stench of waste in and around the Doge's
Palace operated as a potent metaphor for the corruption of the regime
as a whole.[100] In the latter part of the century, however, it is noticeable
that such observations became much rarer. Visitors continued to complain vociferously about the stench of Venice: as we have already seen,
there had always been complaints about the odours emanating from
the canals. But nastiness in the late eighteenth century was instead
a problem to be found throughout the city: in St Mark's Place itself,
upon the Rialto and, according to Sir William Forbes, in every street
and alley. It was, he suggested, a consequence of the enclosed situation
and poor management; the system of boats for removing rubbish
and nuisances from the canals was 'troublesome and expensive' and
ultimately inefficient.[101] Hester Piozzi likewise attributed the noxiousness of the canals to the want of police or proper regulation.[102] Neither
of them adduced the problem as proof of the corruption of political
virtue, however. This represents a significant shift in the focus of observations: the practicalities of civil police and sanitary regulation rather
than principles of political liberty were now the yardstick by which
urban governance was to be judged: British travellers had higher expectations of the urban environment in the wake of decades of domestic
urban improvement.

The city's reputation for 'licentiousness and pleasure' was another
recurrent theme in travellers' observations: particularly those who visited
the city in carnival season when such characteristics were at their most

---

[98] Wright, *Observations*, I, 56.

[99] Blainville, *Travels through Holland, Germany, Switzerland*, I, 505.

[100] See, for example, Northall, *Travels through Italy*, 437, and Sharp, *Letters from Italy*, 35.
On the connection between offensive smells and political corruption in eighteenth-
century discourse, see Clare Brant, 'Fume and perfume: some eighteenth-century uses
of smell', *Journal of British Studies*, 43:4 (2006), 443–63.

[101] Forbes journal MS 1540, fols. 181–2.   [102] Piozzi, *Observations and Reflections*, 88.

visible.[103] Discussion of the social and sexual mores was a common feature of accounts of any Italian city: *cicisbeism*, the behaviour of nuns, the prevalence of loose women were all customs that the British singled out as defining the character of Italians across the Italian states. But there was a general agreement in the literature that such traits were particularly marked in Venice. In the simple summary of Edward Thomas, the 'wickedness of the place is beyond all description'.[104] Comments on the outrageously lax lifestyle of the nuns or the cynicism of Venetian mothers in 'selling' their daughters to be the mistresses of younger sons[105] were simply a part of a broader interpretative framework: that is the narrative of political oppression accompanied by a dominating commercial ethos, under which luxury and the pursuit of wealth had triumphed over moral and political virtue. 'Gallantry' was encouraged in order to keep the nobility quiescent and to preserve the stability of the government; prostitution was sanctioned because younger sons were not allowed to marry in order to preserve the family inheritance; there was an excess of nuns because daughters were placed in convents, rather than being provided with a dowry in order to preserve the integrity of family estates.[106] But in compensation for this enforced seclusion, they were allowed freedoms that would never be permitted elsewhere, which, as the Countess of Pomfret noted with great disapproval, extended to their being allowed to go out masking during carnival.[107] Descriptions of young girls taking the veil in Venice, therefore, assumed an additional edge, as observers took the opportunity to expatiate on what they saw as the grotesque hypocrisy enacted before them.[108]

There are similarities here with other cities, of course, and particularly Naples, where fears of sexual licence and immorality were always present. In Naples, however, the anxiety focussed upon an excess of sensuality, engendered by the warmth and lassitude of the climate. No such climatic explanations were adduced in Venice, where sexual licence was seen purely as the consequence of luxury, greed and moral cynicism. In Naples, the prostitutes were said to be discreetly hidden; in Venice, they

---

[103] Thompson, *Travels of the Late Charles Thompson Esq*, I, 248.
[104] Thomas to Jeremiah Milles, 31 Mar. 1751, BL Add. MS 19941, fol. 37v.
[105] Misson, *New Voyage to Italy* (1695 edn), I, 188; Nugent, *Grand Tour*, II, 87; Broderick, *Travels of Thomas Broderick*, I, 331.
[106] Addison, *Remarks on Several Parts of Italy*, 95.
[107] Phillips (ed.), *Correspondence*, III, 238.
[108] Andrew Mitchell attended one such ceremony at San Zacharia in 1734 and recorded that 'I was much moved wt the sight, however great convenience it may be to the familie is to dispose of ye Children in yt manner, it is certainly very hard to betray them into a sort of perpetual emprisonment, and to cheat them of this life under the spurious pretence of providing for Eternity', BL Add. MS 58319, fol. 39v.

were brazen and bold. It was a businesslike commercial operation, coord-
inated through the pimping gondoliers. Misson famously described
'whole Streets of Ladies of Pleasure' with their 'Breasts open' and painted
faces[109] and the reputation of the Venetians for the bare-faced 'toleration
of strumpets' and of sodomy became a hackneyed commonplace.[110]
More than a century later, the clergyman John Owen echoed the description, but with powerful overtones of disapproval, as he described the sight
of 'windows of certain apartments thrown up, and females of a particular
class fantastically bedizened, dealing out their invitations'. (In Naples, his
comments were much less specific, focussing on the atmosphere of
licentiousness rather than the visible presence of prostitution.)[111] Owen's
explanation for such *laissez-faire* attitudes in Venice was the same as that
of Misson – 'nothing can render the mind so fit for the yoke of subjection,
as a free indulgence of the passions'.[112] Such reports certainly titillated
the fancy of James Boswell, and doubtless many others.[113] Given the
frequency with which descriptions of Venice repeated the stories of sexual
licence, it is hard to know when travellers were reporting their own
experience or simply rehearsing the clichés that were a part of the
common cultural currency back in Britain. Edward Thomas's account
of how he witnessed a gentleman's narrow escape from the clutches of a
prostitute and her pimp reads like a traveller's cliché, shaped by the
expectations (or anxieties) generated by Misson's account.[114] But some
travellers do appear to have been genuinely taken aback by what they
encountered. Richard Rawlinson was clearly discomfited by an overtly
sexual encounter with a man in the Piazza San Marco, who 'pretending
to piss held his yard in his hand and moved it about, as I passed to and fro
in a very lewd manner', while the same Edward Thomas was evidently
disconcerted to have been approached by a child of only eight, offering
her services, on the island of Murano.[115]

The dangers of the luxury and dissipation on offer in Venice could in
theory be mitigated by a serious application to art and culture but this

---

[109] Misson, *New Voyage to Italy* (1695 edn), I, 189.
[110] See, for example, Bernard Mandeville, *The Fable of the Bees* (1714), 69.
[111] See p. 195 above.   [112] Owen, *Travels into Different Parts of Europe*, II, 238–9.
[113] James Boswell told his friend John Johnston that 'When I got to Venice I had still some
small remains of disease, but strange gay ideas which I had formed of the Venetian
Courtesans turned my head, and away I went to an Opera-Dancer, and took Lord
Mounstuart with me. We both had her; and we both found ourselves taken in for the
punishment which I had met with at Rome.' Boswell to Johnston, 19 July 1765 in
Walker (ed.), *Correspondence of James Boswell*, 174.
[114] Thomas to Jeremiah Milles, 31 Mar. 1751, BL Add. MS 19941, fol. 37v.
[115] Rawlinson journal Bodl. MS Rawl. d. 1180, 774–5; Thomas to Jeremiah Milles,
31 Mar. 1751, BL Add. MS 19941, fol. 37v.

rarely featured as the dominant objective in the traveller's itinerary. For the seeker after virtù, the city had much to offer: notably paintings by Titian, Veronese and Tintoretto and the series of renaissance churches and palazzi by Palladio, Scamozzi and Sansovino. Following the publication of Isaac Ware's translation of Palladio's *I Quattro Libri dell' Architettura* (1738), the latter's work in Venice became much better known amongst English-speaking travellers and the more studious gave careful study to the buildings.[116] All the same, not even the finest Palladian church could rival the antique beauty of the Pantheon and antiquity could not be juxtaposed with the renaissance with the same edifying effect. Too many buildings presented nothing but a confused stylistic jumble.[117] Similarly, although Venetian art was admired, it was not as highly regarded as the collections in Bologna, Rome or Florence. Following Vasari's judgement, Venetian artists were praised for their colouring and their drapery, but criticised for the weakness of their design and composition. True greatness, as Jonathan Richardson reminded his readers, did not reside in 'Flutter or Gawdy Colours'.[118] Bassano and Veronese were frequently taken to task for including anachronistic dress and lowering the conception of their designs with domestic details. The judgement still held in the early nineteenth century: for Joseph Forsyth, despite the skill in colouring and fidelity to nature displayed in Venetian art, such paintings were 'deplorably vacant of interest, mind, drama, and historical truth'.[119] Unlike Florence, where latterly at least considerable interest was shown in the art of Giotto and Cimabue on the grounds that they were the instigators of the rebirth of painting, the precursors to Bassano and Giorgione were routinely ignored.[120]

---

[116] See, for example, the journal of Andrew Mitchell, BL Add. MS 38315, fols. 37–8; his interest in Palladianism predated the publication of Ware's translation of Palladio.

[117] Eustace offers an interesting exception in that he represented Venice as offering a case study of the progression of architecture: 'Hence, the attentive observer may discover the history of architecture in the streets of Venice, and may trace its gradation from the solid masses and the round arches, the only remains of the ancient grand style in the sixth, seventh, eighth and ninth centuries, through the fanciful forms and grotesque embellishments of the middle ages, to its revival and re-establishment in these latter times.' *Classical Tour*, I, 68.

[118] Jonathan Richardson, *An Essay on the Theory of Painting by Mr Richardson* (2nd edn, 1725), 93.

[119] Forsyth, *Remarks on Antiquities*, 339. See also Reynolds' criticisms of Venetian art in his fourth discourse, discussed by Barrell, *The Political Theory of Painting*, 103–4.

[120] On Florence see Chapter 2 above. The predecessors of the sixteenth-century school in Venice were routinely ignored even when early Florentine masters were gaining greater recognition. Edward Wright provided one of the fullest accounts of Venetian art and, for example, described the Carpaccio cycle in the Scuola of St Ursula as done in the 'very dry manner' typical of the time (*Observations*, I, 72). James Edward Smith simply referred to some 'curious old paintings' of her (St Ursula's) history in the Scuola: *Sketch of a Tour*, II, 373.

The revival of the arts was not a Venetian narrative in the eighteenth century. Viewing art, therefore, did not assume the same importance as it did in some of the other cities of the Italian tour. In fact, as in Naples, by the time that visitors arrived, they were frequently suffering from *ennui*. More than one excused him or herself for failing to take note of paintings in any detail by quoting Burnet's opinion that, after Rome, one was spoilt for seeing anything else.[121] The Richardsons, whose *Account of Some of the Statues, Bas-Reliefs, Drawings and Pictures in Italy* (1722) guided the observations of so many British travellers round the collections of Florence, Bologna and Rome, had not covered Venice, which meant that travellers would have had to rely on local guides.[122] The ever-compendious Misson failed to provide his readers with more than a minimal amount of information; although he noted that there were said to be as many fine pictures in Venice as at Rome, it was a subject 'I pretend not to enter upon.' Instead, he simply listed the three most celebrated paintings to be seen: Veronese's *Marriage at Cana*, Titian's *Presentation of the Virgin* and his *Martyrdom of St Peter Martyr*, and it was these three paintings that featured most consistently in all travellers' accounts across the century.[123] Even Anne Miller, whose commentary on paintings was otherwise so comprehensive, provided only very cursory lists of the Venetian paintings to be seen, on the grounds that she had already subjected her mother/putative reader to enough observations on art from other parts of Italy.[124]

No account of Venice was complete without a description of gondolas and gondoliers. Like the *lazzaroni* of Naples, the *gondolieri* had acquired an emblematic status in descriptions of the city. Their distinctive culture, manners, appearance, skill and musical prowess, as well as their extraordinary vessels, invariably invited comment and operated metonymically for Venice's many unique qualities. Visitors in the earlier eighteenth century, following authors such as Misson, often associated them with the system of prostitution and pimping and more than one visitor noted how well adapted the gondolas were to lovemaking. According to the late seventeenth-century critiques of Venetian governance, the gondoliers were also complicit in the network of spies and informants upon which the State Inquisition relied; a claim that was repeated by some authors into the 1790s.[125] But

[121] Robertson to his father, 14 Apr. 1752, NLS Acc 12244.
[122] Andrew Mitchell referred himself to the *Ritratto di Venezie* on the matter of paintings: BL Add. MS 58319, fol. 39.
[123] Misson, *New Voyage to Italy* (1695 edn), I, 171.
[124] Miller, *Letters from Italy*, III, 256.
[125] See, for example, the claims made by the German traveller Archenholz, *A Picture of Italy*, I, 62; Smith, *Sketch of a Tour*, II, 363.

just as the *lazzaroni* of Naples were rendered childlike and unthreatening in many accounts by the late eighteenth century, so too the *gondolieri* began to assume a less dangerous aspect. Joseph Baretti went to considerable lengths to defend the reputation of Venice from what he claimed to be the ill-founded and ill-informed prejudices of British travellers such as Tobias Smollett and Samuel Sharp, but even before his intervention was published, the tide of opinion had begun to change.[126] Even the critical Sharp had allowed that they were always clean and never without a spare shirt to change into. Their supplies of clean linen were noted by other visitors, who also observed their skill in handling the gondolas around tight corners and through congested canals with admiration: 'they whip round a sharp corner of these watery streets with more agility, than the best coachman in London can take a short turn there', enthused Anne Miller.[127] Their well-developed physique was the frequent object of admiration on the part of travellers, male and female alike. They were, to quote John Owen, a race of men 'distinguished by muscular force and manly form'.[128] Their reputation for singing was similarly well established by the second half of the century: Joseph Addison had noted the popularity of Tasso amongst the 'common people' of Venice in his *Remarks on Italy*, but this characteristic gradually became associated exclusively with the *gondolieri*.[129] Visitors arrived in Venice expecting to hear the canals echoing with the sound of gondoliers singing *Gerusalemme Liberata* and for Thomas Broderick their music making had a charm which exceeded anything he had heard in the opera houses. Some twenty years later in 1776, Robert Wharton was equally taken by their renditions of Tasso.[130] Rather than functioning as the 'pimps and spies' of the Republic's government, they were increasingly represented as musical, song-loving boatmen more akin to W. S. Gilbert's creation. In short, like the *lazzaroni* of Naples, they became charming and picturesque. This development undoubtedly reflected the increasing popularity of Tasso and Ariosto amongst the English reading public but it was also part of the diminishing sense of danger that the system of Venetian espionage represented, as we will explore more fully below.

---

126 Barretti, *Account of the Manners and Customs of Italy*.
127 Hall journal NLS MS 6325, fol. 63v; Miller, *Letters from Italy*, III, 246.
128 Owen, *Travels into Different Parts of Europe*, II, 236. See also Forbes' praise for their elegant musculature and dexterity, Forbes journal NLS MS 1540, fol. 178, and Coxe, *Picture of Italy*, 452.
129 Addison, *Remarks on Several Parts of Italy*, 104.
130 Broderick, *Travels of Thomas Broderick*, I, 315, 334; Robert Wharton to Miss Lloyd, 10 May 1776, DUASC WHA 168 letterbook number 3, fol. 15v.; Piozzi, *Observations and Reflections*, 89–90.

The gondolas themselves attracted a rather more equivocal response. These strangely shaped black boats epitomised the city's unique and alien qualities, so much so that even the most inept draughtsmen included sketches of their shape and the distinctive prow in their journals or correspondence. The standard observation was to compare them to hearses on account of their unremittingly black appearance: en masse, the flotillas of gondolas took on a depressing, even sinister appearance. Adjectives such as 'melancholy', 'funereal' and 'lugubrious' were frequently called into play. Whilst many visitors were entertained by the novelty of this form of transport, it soon wore off. Gondolas were inconvenient for sightseeing, being too low down for a proper view of the buildings lining the canal; they were claustrophobic; and they rendered one entirely dependent upon the gondolier. So, whilst Thomas Phillip Robinson appreciated the charm of stepping into one directly from the front door, he found it 'excessively inconvenient to be entirely at the disposal of your boatman' whose services were essential if he wished to escape from 'disagreeable company' or from the tedium of a 'stupid Play'.[131] Travellers used to the exercise of walking and to being in control of their own itineraries found this dependence on another individual particularly trying, but also suffered from the sheer physical frustration of being unable to stretch their legs. Lack of exercise had other dangerous consequences too, as Francis Drake noted: the young men of Venice were indolent, inactive and effeminate for want of manly exercise 'and [as they] are always carry'd in the soft conveyance of a Gondola, they appear in that state of nonage, where nature has left it undetermin'd whether to pronounce them a man or a boy'.[132] The dependence on the gondolier, which Robinson found so galling, similarly ran counter to British constructions of manly independence. The 'lolling Luxury' of a gondola was not suited to the 'freedom of British Limbs' as another visitor complained.[133] Gondolas, then, were complicit in the effeminisation of the Italian male. It was small wonder that the British looked upon them with such suspicion.

The cracks in the façade

Venice's importance as a European power in the eighteenth century had been dimmed, but was certainly not extinguished. For the first

[131] Thomas Philip Robinson, *The Grand Tour 1801–1803: Being Letters from Lord Grantham to his Mother, from Prussia, Saxony, Russia, Austria, Switzerland, Italy and France* (Penzance, 1979), 84.
[132] Drake journal MCO MS MC F16 vol. 2, 151.
[133] Walter Bowman to Arthur Balfour, 11 June 1734, St Andrews University Library Special Collections MS 38271/19/13.

two-thirds of the century at least, travellers still regarded Venice as a powerful state, economically and politically. According to Anderson's *Historical and Chronological Deduction of Commerce* (1764), Venice 'retains a considerable share of foreign commerce'.[134] The bustle of the Piazza San Marco, the cosmopolitan air and well-stocked shops, full of luxury and imported goods, seemed to betoken vigorous trade – particularly in comparison with towns such as Ferrara and Padua through which travellers had passed on their way to Venice. These were described as depopulated wastes, where grass grew in the streets, where trade had fled and where grandiose buildings had lost their raison d'etre. Addison noted the decay in commerce, but did not assume it was an inevitable downward spiral, observing that the Senate were looking to measures to improve the situation.[135] Nearly fifty years later, Francis Drake emphasised that Venice was still the most considerable power in Italy and an essential bulwark for Christendom against the Turks.[136] John Northall's 1766 guide to Italy claimed that the revenue from trade and manufactures amounted to 3 million ducats a year.[137] Given that Northall lifted lengthy passages wholesale from other volumes (including Addison's *Remarks on Several Parts of Italy*), the reliability of his information may legitimately be questioned, but John Moore, whose *View of Society and Manners in Italy* (1781) was at least based on first-hand experience, drew a similar conclusion. The Republic's trade, he noted, had declined, but its commerce was still considerable and the industrious poor were all employed in manufactures: he saw no traces of 'squalid beggary'.[138] Many visitors went to the Arsenale and noted down the information they had read or were provided with on the number of galleys in the fleet or the city's alleged defensive strength, without apparently questioning whether the Republic really was in a position to defend itself any longer.[139] For Robert Wharton in 1774, Venice was still the 'glorious seat of freedom and commerce'.[140]

Pace Wharton, there was nevertheless widespread recognition that the eighteenth-century Republic was not the commercial power house that formerly it was, that its government had become ossified and that its

[134] Anderson, *An Historical and Chronological Deduction*, I, vi.
[135] Addison, *Remarks on Several Parts of Italy*, 84.
[136] Drake journal MCO MS MC F16 vol. 3, 17.
[137] Northall, *Travels through Italy*, 425.   [138] Moore, *View of Society and Manners*, I, 238.
[139] Guidebooks to Venice included a lengthy description of the Arsenale and the Bucentoro; there were also separate publications devoted to descriptions of the Bucentoro and the various rituals and ceremonies, or 'pubbliche diverti'.
[140] Robert Wharton to Miss Lloyd, 10 May 1776, DUASC WHA 168 letterbook number 3, fol. 15v.

defensive capacities were largely illusory.[141] Admiration for what Venice had been coexisted with awareness of its decline in an uneasy tension which was not definitively ended until the Republic's fall in 1797. Whilst some visitors happily parroted the information they were given about the thousands employed in the shipyard and the quantity of weapons held in the armoury, the more observant began to look past the performance that was being staged for their benefit, to see a different reality behind the façade. They noted the absence of any sign of recent shipbuilding and saw that the arms and guns on display were rusty and old fashioned and of little use for modern warfare.[142] Even in 1694, the run-down state of the Arsenale was being excused, unconvincingly, to visitors on the grounds that all the arms and equipment were being used in the war in the Morea,[143] and less than ten years later, Addison found much of the weaponry in the armoury to be 'useless' and a hundred years out of date.[144] Robert Gray was shown twenty-four vessels on the stocks when he visited the Arsenale in 1792 – initially an impressive sight – but he soon recollected the accounts he had read by travellers many years earlier, who referred to seeing precisely the same number of galleys. This made him 'suspect that they are never finished, and kept merely for ostentation'.[145] For the perceptive visitor, it is evident that the Arsenale had become nothing more than a curiosity. With its rusty collection of obsolete armour and weaponry, it was more akin to a display of antiquities than a demonstration of defensive strength and seafaring power. Inevitably, the Arsenale drew comparisons with Britain's dockyards, an exercise which served only to highlight Venice's displacement by Great Britain as the world's leading maritime power. 'There was nothing to see', wrote one Miss Derbishire for hundreds of other patriotic Britons, secure in the confidence of Britain's naval strength, 'but was not superior at Plymouth or Portsmouth.'[146]

In the latter part of the eighteenth century, then, it appears that visitors were beginning to look beyond some of the myths surrounding

---

[141] Sharp, *Letters from Italy*, 26.

[142] In 1783, Sir James Hall dismissed the scene at the Arsenale as 'all for show': the workmen were evidently not working on the ships as there were no signs of woodchips or sawdust (NLS MS 6325, fol. 66). See also Thompson, *Travels of the Late Charles Thompson Esq*, I, 248–9: the Arsenale was only to be admired for what it had been rather than for 'what it is now' and Francis Drake's similarly sceptical observations made in 1752: MCO MS MC F16, vol. 2, 162.

[143] Twisden journal Bodl. MS Eng. misc. c 206, fol. 14v.

[144] Addison, *Remarks on Several Parts of Italy*, 88.

[145] Gray, *Letters during the Course of a Tour*, 440.

[146] Derbishire journal NRO DCN 118/6, 85; see also Adam Walker on the technological backwardness of the shipyards: *Ideas Suggested on the Spot*, 165–6.

Venice, its government and its social and political mores. The comments on the 'liberty' to defecate, noted above, the *bocca di leone*, and the Bridge of Sighs had all been elements of the broader denunciation of the Venetian regime. Some continued in this strain: Elizabeth Craven, evidently writing for sensationalist effect, claimed that the spies were just as intrusive in 1789.[147] In the 1780s, Arthur Young and Thomas Watkins both took the opportunity of making a speech against Venetian tyranny and John Moore voiced his incomprehension at the way Venetians tolerated such a regime.[148] But such rhetorical outpourings did not reflect the actual experience of most visitors, as many acknowledged. John Patteson, ever sceptical of the hype perpetrated by so many of his travelling compatriots, told his mother that he thought the stories greatly exaggerated.[149] Other travellers, who were likewise writing for their own personal record or for family members, rather than for publication, similarly avoided the extravagant claims of Craven and her ilk. Charles Abbot, for example, merely noted that the lions' mouths were much disused of late. For him, and many others, the Doge's Palace was simply a 'handsome' building and the piles of excrement which had apparently offended so many earlier visitors failed to make any impression on him at all.[150] In general, in the later eighteenth-century travellers began to display a more realistic evaluation of Venetian government: the practical reality of the constitution, they realised, was quite different from either the theoretical model or the tyranny of earlier critiques. As Eglin has argued, by this point there seems to have been a consensus that the myth of Venice had been overstated, and instead there was even some admiration for the oligarchy's relatively benign administration.[151] Peter Beckford found that the Council of Ten proceeded with 'lenity and circumspection' and marvelled at the fact that they were able to control such a large city without the support of a single soldier.[152] Viscount Palmerston came to a similar conclusion when he visited the city in 1764, arguing that the oligarchy's full powers were seldom abused and were in any case a valuable defence for the common people against the

---

[147] Craven, *Journey through the Crimea*, 94.
[148] Eglin, *Venice Transfigured*, 98–9, notes the protests of Arthur Young, John Moore and Thomas Watkins.
[149] Cubitt, Mackley and Wilson (eds.), *Great Tour of John Patteson*, 296.
[150] Abbot journal TNA PRO 30/9/41, 401. Abbot's observation may have been influenced by Barretti who had argued that the receptacles had long since fallen into disuse, *Account of the Manners and Customs of Italy*, II, 306. In Naples, he was alert to such unpleasantness (see p. 179 above).
[151] Eglin, *Venice Transfigured*, 101.
[152] Peter Beckford, *Familiar Letters from Italy to a Friend in England*, 2 vols. (Salisbury, 1805), II, 431–2.

tyranny of the nobility. Their government, he noted, was fair, the people happy, the taxes slight and the pursuit of pleasure positively encouraged in all ranks of people.[153] Moreover, for all the rumoured paranoia of the Council of Ten, no visitor ever claimed to have been the victim of oppression, or even the direct object of the government's suspicion, although many invoked the suspicion and secrecy of the government as an explanation for a perceived want of courtesy from the Venetian nobility – perhaps as a sop to offended national pride.

This tendency to challenge the conventional wisdom also extended to the iconographic tradition and is evident in a greater propensity to admit to disappointment upon seeing Venice: the reality of the city did not match the heightened expectations shaped by Canaletto's *vedute*.[154] Up until mid-century, travellers generally claimed that the beauty of Venice surpassed its depiction in art; that Canaletto's drawings and canvases could not capture its peculiar charm and splendour.[155] Even Samuel Sharp, who was far from being an uncritical observer of Italy, claimed that Venice's beauty exceeded Canaletto's views in his tour published in 1766.[156] But only four years later, Charles Burney was complaining that the views of Venice did not live up to the idea of the city that he had formed in his imagination 'particularly after seeing Canalettis ... There was neither the symmetry nor the richness of materials I expected.'[157] Arthur Young, who visited the city in 1789, was similarly disappointed: the city had some beautiful features, he allowed, 'but does not equal the idea I had formed of it from the pictures of Canaletti ... You have a palace of three magnificent stories, and near it a hovel of one. Hence, there is not that species of magnificence which results from uniformity; or from an uninterrupted succession of considerable edifices.'[158] Canaletto's views, echoed Lady Webster in a letter to Lady Sheffield in 1792, 'raise the Imagination to a Pitch which the Original does not fulfil'.[159] Visitors were now able to see through the sleight of Canaletto's

[153] Black, *Italy and the Grand Tour*, 148.

[154] These expressions of disappointment and anti-climax can be paralleled with the disillusionment felt by visitors in Rome upon discovery that the antiquities failed to match either the idealised image of Desgodetz's engravings or the sublime grandeur and monumentality of Piranesi's vision. See Chapter 2.

[155] Drake wrote: 'It is perhaps the only town in the world, where the several views really appear to the eye more beautiful than in prints, and even Canaletti's prospects of this place lose half their elegance on paper.' MCO MS MC F 16 vol. 2, 139.

[156] Sharp, *Letters from Italy*, 7.

[157] Scholes (ed.), *Eighteenth-Century Musical Tour*, 109.

[158] Young, *Travels in France and Italy*, 256. See also Ayscough, *Letters from an Officer in the Guards*, 199.

[159] Adeane (ed.), *Girlhood of Maria Josepha Holroyd*, 188–9.

hand that had made all the buildings appear fresh and new, banishing any unattractive features to oblivion.[160]

These more critical reactions were right, of course. Canaletto, like any topographical artist of the time, was wont to play fast and loose with scale and proportions – widening canals, increasing the height of buildings and even removing the miserable hovels of which Arthur Young complained if it suited his purpose.[161] The question arises, therefore, as to why it was only in the later eighteenth century that visitors ceased to see Venice as a *veduta* by Canaletto and began to observe it more critically, emphasising the distance between the idealised image and the reality of the city itself. Most immediately, Canaletto's œuvre was no longer cutting edge and fashionable. Although he did not die until the age of ninety-four in 1782, by the time that Arthur Young was voicing his disappointment, the paintings to which Young referred were well over a generation old. It was therefore easier to bring a critical eye to bear on them. But as in Rome, where travellers were also expressing similar sentiments of disappointment at the failure of the city to live up to the visual imagery, part of the explanation lies in the evolution of the genre of travel literature and the greater emphasis that was now placed upon the subjective experience, allowing more scope for emotional transports of delight but also for the expression of disappointment or even dissent from conventional wisdom.[162] The value that was now attached to the traveller's exploration of his or her individual response to a city opened up the possibility of more varied and less formulaic representations of place. But the sensation of disappointment and the impulse to chip away at the traditional image of Venice demands a broader explanation. Attitudes to Venice were also changing because of domestic developments which meant that the British travelled with a different framework of expectations: as the stability of Britain's mixed constitution appeared increasingly secure and as imperial and commercial expansion looked set to far exceed that of Venice, the story of the Venetian constitution lost much of its exemplary value. The stark polarities in which it was represented in an earlier period could be revised in more measured terms, which acknowledged the limitations of the oligarchy's control and even the benefits of their rule. And as visitors began to question the validity of the myths with which they were so familiar, equally they were prepared to look beyond the idealised version of Venice which prints and paintings had led them to expect, with the consequence that what they saw was a

---

[160] Ayscough, *Letters from an Officer in the Guards*, 199; Hervey, *Letters from Portugal, Spain, Italy and Germany*, III, 463.
[161] Bomford and Finaldi, *Venice through Canaletto's Eyes*, 12.   [162] See Chapter 3.

city that was beautiful in parts, but neither so perfect as that depicted by Canaletto, nor constitutionally so flawed as the one represented by Amelot de la Houssaye.

Conclusion

Venice's fall to Napoleon in 1797, it has been observed, was of little consequence in the European balance of power, but it marked an irrevocable turning point for Venice. It became a city in the past tense. Unlike Florence, Rome or Naples, where the upheavals of the Napoleonic era did not fundamentally change the way in which these cities were perceived, in Venice, the loss of autonomy signalled a sea change. The city's glory and its independence that had sustained its civic traditions were gone. Napoleon had stripped it of its works of art and sacked the Arsenale. Austria-Hungary had set up a puppet democracy and was now milking it for tax revenues. Venetian dominance of the eastern Mediterranean was unequivocally a thing of the past, as the Austrians made their naval base at Trieste, not Venice. The framework through which Venice was viewed had radically altered: it no longer offered even the ossified remains of the stable oligarchy that had once been so widely admired. For moralists, Venice's submission to Austria was the inevitable consequence of the city's earlier capitulation to luxury: the 'gallant' city had been living on borrowed time. It had become the 'foul abode of effeminacy, wantonness and debauchery' and the bold and manly sentiments that had sustained its glory had long since disappeared, leaving a degenerate body politic. 'Jacet ingens littore truncus' (Aeneid 2 1. 557–8) intoned John Chetwode Eustace, with an undertone of disapproval, on his arrival.[163]

Venice did not, of a sudden, become less noisome or more picturesque, but in the short term, the city lost much of its charm. For Lemaistre, the loss of its constitution and its commercial functions rendered the city less attractive and less interesting: it was, he complained, 'dull', 'tawdry', 'disappointing' and 'dirty'.[164] Even the gondoliers were found wanting. By the early nineteenth century, visitors had ceased praising their performance and were instead complaining of disappointment and Lemaistre could not find any gondoliers to sing for him at all in 1802.[165] Charlotte Lindsey was more fortunate, but deeply dissatisfied by the performance with which she was entertained in 1815 and Jane Waldie, whose patriotic chauvinism coloured almost every observation in her travels, flatly

---

[163] Eustace, *Classical Tour*, I, 75–6.
[164] Lemaistre, *Travels after the Peace of Amiens*, II, 174–6.   [165] Ibid., II, 175.

preferred the singing of the English gentlemen of her party to that of the gondoliers.[166] Byron's 'songless gondolier' was, perhaps, more than simply a poetic creation.[167] Subjugation to Austrian rule was a traumatic experience for the Venetians, but it had a profound effect on the way that visitors saw the city. The disappearance of the music loving *gondolieri* was symptomatic of a perception that Venice had lost the spirit that once had animated it.

Venice was now an empty shell which had to be populated in melancholy reveries, accompanied by memories of vanished grandeur and former glories.[168] This was a romantic mode of representation that relied much more heavily on an imaginative and affective response, which in turn was inspired by the poetry of *Childe Harold*, rather than the relentlessly factual content of guidebooks. It signalled a clear break with earlier perceptions of the city: for the eighteenth-century traveller, the appeal and interest of Venice had resided in its *singularity* – its peculiar government, its unique topography, the extraordinary architecture, the flamboyant costumes and the ceaseless round of pleasure and entertainment, rather than nostalgic regret or a sense of romance or mystery. Thus, Addison had dismissed it as a city of singularity and entertainment, with little to offer that was either edifying or improving.[169] A century later, Joseph Forsyth was similarly unimpressed by Venice: singularity could easily be delineated (and equally easily apprehended), he objected, unlike the sublime beauty of Naples or the Apollo Belvedere that demanded the discrimination of taste. Nor did Venice have any of the obscurity of antiquity that rendered a ruined temple or a gothic castle fascinating.[170] But even by 1815, Venice was beginning to acquire some of these more mysterious, evocative overtones, precisely because it was, metaphorically at least, a city in ruins where the imagination could have free play. The opportunity was created for visitors to engage in the same kind of melancholy reflection that they indulged in at Rome. Whilst the Republic remained constant and unchanging its past was still a part of the present. But after 1797, the Republic was gone and could be retrieved only through the exercise of the imagination. Lemaistre was disappointed in 1802, but other visitors started to recommend viewing it

---

[166] Lindsey journal Bodl. MS Eng. c. 7052, fol. 38; Waldie, *Sketches Descriptive of Italy*, IV, 166.

[167] Marianne Colston claimed to have found the last two remaining gondoliers who could sing Tasso's *Jerusalem* but was not impressed by their performance, *Journal of a Tour in France*, I, 79–80.

[168] John Pemble, *Venice Discovered* (Oxford, 1994), 87.

[169] Addison, *Remarks on Several Parts of Italy*, 85.

[170] Forsyth, *Remarks on Antiquities*, 332; see also Chard, *Pleasure and Guilt*, 132–3.

by moonlight; like the Coliseum – the other set piece of moonlit tourism – its charms were enhanced by the shadows cast and the concomitant air of melancholy obscurity.[171] In 1817, Henry Matthews walked through the Doge's Palace and mourned the loss of Venice's ancient power and splendour as he recalled the spirit of Dandalo, the twelfth-century doge. His account is redolent with nostalgia for its former grandeur.[172] For Marianne Colston, it became a place for pensive recollection and imaginary associations: visiting the city in 1820, she described how she fell into a state of 'visionary reverie', blending past, present and future, where 'dull realities are dimly felt'. Every step she took, she enthused, conjured up a different image from *Childe Harold*.[173] Venice's narrative arc had been changed for good.

---

[171] Waldie, *Sketches Descriptive of Italy*, IV, 145.

[172] Matthews, *Diary of an Invalid*, 227. See also Samuel Rogers, who found himself transported to the lands of 'antient fable' in St Mark's Place, Hale (ed.), *Italian Journal*, 172.

[173] Colston, *Journal of a Tour in France*, 273.

6   Medievalism on the Grand Tour

Introduction

In 1781, having made the conventional observation that travellers acquired an 'early partiality' for Rome by reading the classics and the history of the ancient republic in their youth, John Moore proceeded to note how little regard in comparison was paid to the 'transactions' of the last fourteen or fifteen centuries.[1] Moore's comment is significant in that he saw the need to acknowledge that this collective ignorance concerning the more recent events of Italian history existed, or was even regrettable. Prior to this date, observations on Italy's medieval past were conspicuous by their absence. As such, it is indicative of the fact that by the 1780s a more informed interest in the history of the middle ages and the 'gothic' era was already beginning to make itself felt amongst the literate travelling public, even in that most classical of environments, the Grand Tour. The Grand Tour as a cultural institution underwent a fundamental change in character during the nineteenth century, as we saw in the introduction, both in terms of itinerary and the composition of the travelling classes.[2] But it also underwent more qualitative changes: the traditional attractions of art and antiquities retained much of their appeal, but – particularly in cities beyond Rome – a different Italy was now being sought out: that of medieval towers and palazzi, of gothic churches and of the primitive simplicity of painting in an age in which the arts were first beginning to recover.

This is a theme that has already been anticipated in preceding chapters, but the purpose of this chapter is to consider more closely how the development of interest in the 'middle ages' in the eighteenth century

---

[1] Moore, *View of Society and Manners*, I, 69.
[2] On the changing nature of travel in the era after the Grand Tour, see Brand, *Italy and the English Romantics*; Buzard, *The Beaten Track*; O'Connor, *Romance of Italy*; John Pemble, *The Mediterranean Passion* (Oxford, 1987); Powell, *Italy in the Age of Turner*; Jonah Siegel, *Haunted Museum. Longing, Travel and the Art-Romance Tradition* (Princeton, 2005).

contributed to the emergence of this picturesque, medieval Italy in the
nineteenth century. A survey of the topographical literature, correspondence and journals of late eighteenth- and early nineteenth-century travellers reveals considerably more attention being given to the art and
architecture of the middle ages and the early renaissance than is often
given credit for. Travellers with antiquarian and architectural interests
struggled to incorporate the churches, cathedral and palazzi of medieval
Italy into a narrative of architectural development according to which
the emergence of the 'pointed arch' had to be understood as a distinctively English development. Those whose interest was fuelled rather by
the literary fashion for the gothic and the picturesque had different
priorities when it came to the description of medieval architecture, but
their interest was nevertheless directed away from a uniformly classical
view of Italy. As the medieval period and its achievements came into
sharper focus, itineraries within and between the towns and cities of Italy
changed. New associative meanings and different aesthetic ideals began
steadily to modify the dominant classical paradigm of the eighteenth-
century tour, well before the end of the Napoleonic Wars.

There are two aspects to the growth of interest in the middle ages from
the second half of the eighteenth century which need to be considered
here. One is the more scholarly and antiquarian approach, best represented for the purposes of this chapter by attempts to establish a 'system'
of gothic architecture.[3] Eighteenth-century antiquaries were engaged
upon a project to provide 'order' to the gothic style, in the same way
that classical architecture was analysed and understood in terms of
orders, each with its own rules of proportion and ornament and showing
chronological progression.[4] Such a model would moreover have the

---

[3] On eighteenth-century attitudes towards the gothic, see Kenneth Clark, *The Gothic Revival: An Essay in the History of Taste* (1928); Michael McCarthy, *Origins of the Gothic Revival* (New Haven and London, 1987); Chris Brooks, *The Gothic Revival* (1999; repr. 2001); Simon Bradley, 'The gothic revival and the Church of England 1790–1840', University of London, Courtauld Institute of Art, Ph.D. thesis (1996). The attempt to establish 'orders' for gothic architecture was, of course, ultimately futile, but was a reflection of how eighteenth-century perceptions of the gothic were shaped by assumptions derived from classical models.

[4] James Essex, 'Remarks on the antiquity and different modes of brick and stone buildings in England', *Archaeologia*, 4 (1777), 81–119 (esp. 108–9): 'for the Gothic, like the Grecian architecture, has its different orders or modes, and every order its peculiar members by which it may be distinguished from the rest; and as these are regulated by just proportions founded upon geometrical principles, as capable of demonstration as those of the Greek or Roman; we may judge of the whole from a part, with as much certainty as we may know the extent of a Roman temple from the length of a triglyph'. See also Richard Gough, *Anecdotes of British Topography* (1768), xx; James Dallaway, *Anecdotes of the Arts in England; or, Comparative Remarks on Architecture, Sculpture, and*

additional value of helping to identify the date of construction of buildings where no textual sources had survived, or where they appeared to conflict.[5] To this end, a basic chronology of the development of gothic architecture from the 'Saxon' (as the Romanesque was then termed by British antiquaries) through to what would eventually be termed the perpendicular was articulated long before Thomas Rickman's *Attempt to Discriminate the Styles of English Architecture* (1817) codified the styles in an accessible format for a wider reading public. Publications such as Thomas Warton's *Observations on Spenser's Faerie Queen* (1754) and James Bentham's *History and Antiquities of the Conventual Church of Ely* (1771), which provided the basis for more popular publications such as Francis Grose's *Antiquities of England and Wales* (1773–6) and articles in the *Gentleman's Magazine* ensured that the reading public was presented with a vocabulary with which to describe the different elements and styles of medieval architecture, and was being taught the means by which to discriminate between them.[6] Enthusiasts for gothic architecture in England drew strength from the increased interest in national history and the importance attached to the middle ages as a formative period in the nation's constitutional development.[7] As such, the gothic style was identified by many as the 'English' style and as the embodiment of national identity. The study of gothic antiquities received an additional fillip from patriotic sentiment during the French Revolutionary and Napoleonic Wars, particularly through the journalism of John Carter in the *Gentleman's Magazine*.[8] One consequence of these developments was that travellers, whether in Britain or abroad, were increasingly looking at buildings in order to establish *when* they were built, irrespective of whether they were gothic or classical in design.

The other approach to the medieval past was less rigorously antiquarian and more fanciful. It found expression in the fashionable 'gothick' architecture; in the vogue for the picturesque; and the sublime and in the gothic novel. The interest of eighteenth-century historians in the history of feudal relations and private property focussed their attention on the middle ages as a pivotal era of change,[9] but it was also being viewed more sympathetically

Painting Chiefly Illustrated by Specimens at Oxford (1800), 4, and John Milner, *A Treatise on the Ecclesiastical Architecture of England during the Middle Ages* (1811), vi–vii.

[5] These attempts to develop a typological model or historical account of gothic architecture were typical of eighteenth-century antiquarianism and were paralleled in other areas, most notably in Winckelmann's stylistic analysis of classical sculpture.

[6] Sweet, *Antiquaries*, 318–30.

[7] Newman, *Rise of English Nationalism*, 109–20; Sweet, *Antiquaries*, 243–67.

[8] J. Mordaunt Crook, *John Carter and the Mind of the Gothic Revival* (1995).

[9] Robertson, *History of the Reign*.

as a period of chivalry and courtly conduct, and one which was particularly important for the development of the arts as well as the constitution.[10] The idealisation of chivalric culture fed upon and contributed to a greater awareness of the art, poetry, architecture and sculpture of the middle ages, particularly from the late thirteenth century to the turn of the sixteenth, and gave the middle ages an imaginative appeal which analyses of feudal relations, however important in terms of the development of property relations and political liberty, could never match. Thus, Adam Walker could write that the walled village of Stagia 'puts one in mind of the days of Knight-Errantry, when Damosells were imprisoned in lofty towers, in wilds, and deserts; among rocks and precipices'.[11] But the 'gothic' was also a staple element of the picturesque: images of crumbling arches, festoons of ivy and the air of gentle decay popularised in publications such as William Gilpin's picturesque tours ensured a wider appreciation of the aesthetic, if not the archaeological, value of medieval buildings.[12] Equally, the gothic could appeal to the aesthetic of the sublime: conjuring up images of feudal oppression in the massy walls of castles and their cavernous dungeons, or a sense of religious awe through the vertiginous height and 'dim religious light' of a gothic cathedral. In the 1790s, the gothic novel reached the peak of its popularity and a generation of readers were educated to see a ruined abbey or deserted castle as inherently gloomy, sinister and threatening.[13] Given how many gothic novels, and those of Ann Radcliffe in particular, were set in Italy, the imaginative associations connected with the literary gothic gave an unmistakable flavour to many visitors' comments.[14] Increasingly, visitors travelled to Italy with two versions of the Italian past in mind. One was the rational and ordered world of classical antiquity; the other was the violent and dangerous era of the gothic past, characterised by 'blood, horror, violence and excess'.[15]

Seeing the gothic

Even in Italy, of course, it had never been possible entirely to ignore the imposing presence of the cathedrals, churches and palazzi which

[10] Richard Hurd, *Letters on Chivalry and Romance* (1762). On the growth of the cult of chivalry, see Mark Girouard, *The Return to Camelot: Chivalry and the English Gentleman* (New Haven and London, 1981).

[11] Walker, *Ideas Suggested on the Spot*, 341.

[12] The tension between the two is explored in Sweet, *Antiquaries*, 298–9.

[13] Brooks, *The Gothic Revival*, 105–26.

[14] Kenneth Churchill, *Italy and English Literature 1764–1930* (London and Basingstoke, 1980), 16–21. Churchill quotes Eustace's jibe at the over-reliance upon Italian settings for gothic novels in Eustace, *Classical Tour*, IV, 293–4.

[15] Chard, *Pleasure and Guild*, 234–5.

dominated the townscape of all but the most recently improved cities – although classically minded travellers might object to their obtrusion. No visitor to Milan could possibly overlook the dazzling white marble bulk of the duomo. For all the Palladian splendour of its churches, Venice was still dominated by two buildings which flouted every convention of the classical architectural rule book: San Marco and the Doge's Palace. Florence had the best collection of modern statuary in Italy, but much of it stood in the shadow of the fourteenth-century Palazzo Vecchio, whilst Brunelleschi's famous dome sat atop a thirteenth-century structure. But for Joseph Addison, and the majority of eighteenth-century travellers, the 'dark ages' which had given rise to these highly visible buildings were of so little interest that they were barely even conceptualised as having a distinctive style. The middle ages were seen as a period of rude barbarity, primitive and coarse, when none of the arts had flourished; when learning and taste fell into abeyance; and the architecture, distinguished only by its abnegation of all that was most admired in classical architecture, deserved little further notice. The profusion of ornament and decoration of buildings such as the duomos in Siena or Milan or the basilica of San Marco in Venice was simply unpalatable: for generations of travellers, influenced by accounts such as that of the fiercely Protestant Gilbert Burnet, such extravagance of ornament and profusion of decoration was simply a symbol of the fiscal extortion exercised by the Catholic church over its superstitious congregation.[16]

Thus, for the first half of the eighteenth century at least, few buildings preceding the revival of classical architecture in the fifteenth century were ever described in any detail. Even in a highly detailed tour, such as that of Johann Georg Keysler, upon which numerous British tourists relied, individual churches in Florence or Siena, for example, were named and the paintings and monumental epitaphs of note enumerated, but next to nothing was said about the physical fabric, except occasionally to note the date of construction or the name of the architect.[17] In general, this was more information than many tourists cared to transcribe into their journals or their correspondence. In most cases, the name of a church was sufficient, and was mentioned only to locate the paintings which were to be found inside. For those who did acknowledge the physical appearance of the exterior, the choice of adjective was telling – words such as ridiculous,

---

[16] Burnet, *Some Letters*, 107, 115, 170, 178, 193–4.
[17] Keysler, *Travels*, I, 451–80.

foolish, crude, whimsical and incorrect, or simply odd, were typically
used – signifying the failure of such buildings to conform to what were
believed to be the correct rules of architecture. For the most part,
travellers expressed distaste mixed with wonder at the sheer size and
cost of such structures, rather than admiration. George Parker
observed dryly to his father that the architect of the cathedral at Milan
'seems to have had nothing else in his head than the contrivance how
to lay out a prodigious sum of mony'.[18] But even in the midst of
incomprehension and disgust, the financial investment and craftsmanship which these buildings embodied still had the capacity to impress.
Joseph Addison described the cathedral at Siena as a 'masterpiece' of
gothic architecture: he wondered at the degree of ornament with
which even the water spouts were laden. He then went on to describe
the windows in terms which made up in vividness what they lacked in
technical accuracy: they were like 'so many scenes of perspective with
a multitude of little pillars retiring one behind another'. But, as if
ashamed of allowing himself to be seduced by such superficial attractions, in the final sentence he turned around and re-affirmed his
classical allegiances, declaring that 'nothing in the world can make a
prettier shew to those who prefer false beauties and affected ornaments to a noble and majestic simplicity'.[19] But many other travellers
were equally impressed: John Frederick, who travelled in Italy with his
brother Charles in 1737, was powerfully struck by the duomo at
Siena, observing that the marble façade covered with reliefs and
sculptures gave it a 'noble air' and that it 'pleases the eye wonderfully
even tho' the building is not in the taste which is now relished'.[20]
Similarly, the sheer height and scale of the thirteenth-century aqueduct at Spoleto often provoked admiring comment – and some
debate. So impressed were visitors by the feat of engineering that it
represented that they assumed that it must have been constructed by
the Romans, despite evidence to the contrary: 'There are few remains
of the kind equal in magnificence to the aqueduct here', observed
Thomas Broderick, 'it consists indeed of only one row of arches, but
there is all the Roman simplicity and grandeur in these.' However, he
continued, in amazement, 'here are not wanting travel writers who
mention it as Gothic: you will believe me, when I assure you, these

---

[18] Parker to his father, 7/18 Mar. 1721/2, BL Stowe MS 750, fol. 400.
[19] Addison, *Remarks on Several Parts of Italy*, 390–1.
[20] Frederick journal Surrey History Centre MS 4647/1, unfoliated MS. For details of the
Frederick brothers' itinerary, see Ingamells (ed.), *Dictionary of British and Irish Travellers*,
381–2.

bearleaders ... can have seen very little, or indeed can have read very little of the difference between the Roman and the Gothic taste, when they confounded them in this noble ruin'.[21]

By the 1780s, however, it is possible to detect a change in the tone of comments. Amidst the usual run of negative comments on the parti-coloured marble of Tuscan cathedrals, or the excessive ornamentation of Milan's duomo, travellers began to praise, for example, the lightness and delicacy of the gothic style. This was a trend which reflected the fashion-able, picturesque version of the 'gothick' epitomised by Horace Wal-pole's villa at Strawberry Hill. Elizabeth Craven wondered at the light and simple arches of the cloister at the Campo Santo at Pisa – they seemed to be held together by some magical power: 'if anything could reconcile me to the Gothic', she wrote, 'these arches would'.[22] Mary Berry, Walpole's friend and correspondent, similarly admired the light-ness and beauty of the gothic pillars in the duomo at Milan, although the apparent mixture of grecian and gothic styles offended her sense of architectural propriety.[23] The normally laconic Lord Herbert found the baptistery at Pisa to be 'Gothic and very beautiful in my opinion'.[24] The burgeoning interest in the literature of the middle ages also directed attention towards contemporaneous buildings: thus Hester Piozzi approved the church at Bergamo, with its mixture 'of Gothic and Grecian' because it reminded her of the verses she admired by her 'mezzo secoli' men.[25] Greater familiarity with the *Divine Comedy*, as we saw in Chapter 2, also manifested itself in travellers' accounts of the later eighteenth century: at Pisa they would identify the tower where Count Ugolino was supposed to have devoured his children; they visited Dante's tomb at Ravenna; and they recognised the Asinelli and Gari-senda towers in Bologna from the *Inferno*.[26] In the 1790s, the rising popularity of the gothic novel introduced a new set of literary associ-ations and its influence began to make itself felt in number of travellers' descriptions: buildings which had hitherto gone largely unnoticed began

---

[21] Broderick, *Travels of Thomas Broderick*, I, 393. See also Martin Folkes' comments: 'Between this and a much higher mountain is a deep valley over which water is still brought to the city by an Aqueduct built in the time of the latter empire', Bodl. MS Eng. misc. c. 444, fols. 78r–79r. Even in 1793, William Forbes continued to make a similar assumption, NLS MS 1545 fol. 20.

[22] Craven, *Journey through the Crimea*, 72.

[23] Lewis (ed.), *Extracts of the Journals and Correspondence*, I, 126.

[24] Herbert (ed.), *Henry, Elizabeth and George*, 328.

[25] Piozzi to the Revd Leonard Chappelow, 1 Sept. 1786, Bloom and Bloom (eds.), *The Piozzi Letters*, I, 209.

[26] Herbert (ed.), *Henry, Elizabeth and George*, 328; Finch journal Bodl. MS Finch e. 14, fol. 213r; Hale (ed.), *Italian Journal*, 184.

to feature as symbols of the gloom and horror of the middle ages. Adam Walker, for example, in 1790 observed that 'The gloomy Palace of Vicchio [sic] looks like the stone-den of some tyrant. It is Gothic, rustic, and black with age and smoke ... This palace contains a number of memorials of the barbarity, feudal fury, and ill-directed struggles for liberty, of the 12th, 13th, 14th and 15th centuries.'[27]

Describing the gothic

As travellers began to show more interest in the built environment of the middle ages, they often struggled to describe the buildings they saw. Even when they disliked what they saw, they described it rather more vividly: the stripes of black and white marble, characteristic of ecclesiastical architecture across Tuscany, for example, were variously compared to a harlequin's jacket or a zebra's coat.[28] In general, as we have seen, most travellers' observations on art, architecture and antiquities were highly derivative, drawing on a tradition of topographical and antiquarian literature that went back to the renaissance. Given the absence of any other works of reference, when they encountered medieval buildings they often adopted the descriptors used in Italian publications, of which the most significant was Giorgio Vasari's *Lives of the Artists*.[29] Vasari had never been much enamoured of the gothic style, which for him was unequivocally linked with the foreign invaders who had brought down the glory of Rome.[30] The narrative of the recovery of the arts which he offered in his *Lives of the Artists* held that the revival was due to the influence of artists and architects from Greece, where the skill and craftsmanship of antiquity had persisted longest and whose architects were the closest heirs to Rome. Any building, then, which approximated to what would now be called the Romanesque was denominated Grecian. Pisa, for example, was known to have had trading connections with Greece, and the eleventh-century Greek architect Buschetto, the

[27] Walker, *Ideas Suggested on the Spot*, 358.
[28] Watkins, *Travels through Switzerland, Italy, Sicily*, I, 295; Walker, *Ideas Suggested on the Spot*, 335.
[29] There was no translation of Vasari's *Lives of the Artists* into English during the eighteenth century, although William Aglionby's *Painting Illustrated in Three Dialogues* (1685) was essentially a translation of Vasari. His observations were also freely utilised in other works of art criticism, notably by Jonathan Richardson senior and junior, whose *An Account of Some of the Statues, Bas-Reliefs, Drawings and Pictures in Italy, with Remarks* (1722) was one of the most widely consulted works of reference on Italian art during the eighteenth century.
[30] E. S. de Beer, 'Gothic: origin and diffusion of the term; the idea of style in architecture', *JWCI*, 11 (1948), 145–8.

builder of the duomo, was commonly credited with having taken the first step towards bringing Italy out of the dark ages of gothic barbarism. The revival of the arts, according to this account, had spread eastwards into Italy from Pisa. (Vasari's Tuscan-centricity meant that he attributed little significance to the rather closer trading and cultural links of Venice with Byzantium.) But Pisa's baptistery displayed a combination of rounded and pointed arches – as did many other *trecento* and *quattrocento* structures in Italy – giving rise to the hybrid term greco-gothic (or greco-gotico), which was accordingly widely adopted by the British. The purely 'pointed' style, such as was found in the duomo at Milan, was identified with Germanic influence and was referred to as the *maniera tedesca*, whilst the more delicate and ornate style associated with the ogee arch, which was supposed to be particularly characteristic of Venice and southern Italy, was associated with eastern influences and was described as *arabesco* or *moresco*, or, in English, saracenic. This style, it was believed, had been disseminated through invasion: that is, the Moorish conquest of Spain and the Saracens' conquest of Sicily and parts of southern Italy;[31] through trading connections with Byzantium in the case of Venice; and through the cultural encounters of the Crusades.[32]

The limitations of this vocabulary betrayed the longstanding want of adequate terminology with which to describe the architecture of the middle ages and the confusion which still existed in the late eighteenth century as to how the different styles related both to each other and to the various ethnic groups which had invaded and conquered Italy and other parts of Europe. Thus, Adam Walker found that the duomo at Siena was 'a happy mixture of Gothic, with the first ideas of Grecian architecture that possessed the people of this country, after its long eclipse of Goth and Vandal darkness'. He was less impressed by the duomo at Florence, however, which was simply 'an unhappy jumble of Greek and Gothic architecture'.[33] But in general, rather than being conscious of the inadequacy of their terminology observers generally projected their confusion back onto the architecture, as did Jane Waldie when she referred to 'the strange medley of architectural orders

---

[31] Swinburne, *Travels in the Two Sicilies*, II, 116, 119, 149, 198, 222; Henry Swinburne *Travels through Spain in the Years 1775 and 1776*, 2 vols. (1787), I, 140, 298, II, 61, 260.

[32] The thesis that the pointed arch was brought back by returning crusaders, and was subsequently spread through Europe by itinerant freemasons, was adumbrated by Christopher Wren in 1713 in his reports on Westminster Abbey, but not published until 1750 in Christopher Wren, *Parentalia: Or, Memoirs of the Family of Wren* (1750), 295–303. It subsequently became one of the most widely held theories to explain its introduction into European architecture; it would be elaborated in much greater detail by John Ruskin in *The Stones of Venice* in 1851.

[33] Walker, *Ideas Suggested on the Spot*, 335, 342.

exhibited in buildings of lower ages'.[34] The apparent disorder of style was simply another instance of the barbarism of the period.

Nevertheless, regardless of the problems with the descriptive lexicon, the significant point to note is that by the end of the eighteenth century efforts were being made by many travellers to describe non-classical architecture, as opposed to passing over it in dismissive silence. The want of an appropriate descriptive vocabulary, however, was something which was beginning to provoke discussion amongst travellers, particularly those with antiquarian interests.

The rounded arches of the Romanesque churches of Tuscany and Lombardy, described by the Italians as greco-gothic, posed a problem for British observers. They clearly shared much in common with the rounded arches which were conventionally attributed to the Saxons or the Normans in Britain.[35] But the Saxons had never penetrated these areas of mainland Italy to bring with them their style of architecture. Similarly, the Lombards, who were evidently responsible for much of this architecture in northern Italy, had never reached the British Isles. English architects and antiquaries had appreciated early in the eighteenth century that the Saxon style of architecture was derived from Roman models – whether those left behind by the departing Romans, or introduced by Roman missionaries in the seventh century – but had been largely unaware of and uninterested in drawing comparisons with the comparable state of architecture in other parts of Europe.[36] But, as G. D. Whittington and many others pointed out, this style of building was simply a degeneration from Roman forms, and as such did not have to be associated with any particular ethnic group.[37] In fact, to make such a connection was positively misleading: hence the antiquary William Gunn first coined the term 'romanesque' in his *Inquiry into the Origins of Gothic Architecture* (1819), referring to the deviation from the Roman

---

[34] Waldie, *Sketches Descriptive of Italy*, I, 290–1.

[35] The eighteenth-century convention was to refer to rounded arches as 'saxon', following James Bentham's usage in *The History and Antiquities of the Conventual and Cathedral Church of Ely*, 2 vols. (Cambridge, 1771), despite the fact that it was widely accepted that the majority of the surviving buildings erected in this style were the work of the Normans and that the term was inherently misleading.

[36] See Thomas Cocke's discussion of early eighteenth-century attempts to identify and describe the Romanesque in 'Pre-nineteenth-century attitudes in England to Romanesque architecture', *Journal of the British Archaeological Association*, 36 (1973), 72–97. Smart Lethieullier, who travelled to Italy in 1737–9, noted that the font in Winchester cathedral was similar to those he had seen in Lombardy: Lethieullier to Charles Lyttelton, 15 July 1752, BL Stowe MS 752, fol. 68.

[37] G. D. Whittington, *An Historical Survey of the Ecclesiastical Antiquities of France; with a View to Illustrate the Rise and Progress of Gothic Architecture in Europe* (1810), 44–5.

norm, although this was not a term which caught on more widely until considerably later in the nineteenth century.[38]

Thus, this problem of nomenclature for the Romanesque style helped to crystallise awareness that architectural styles could not be pinned onto a single race of people such as the Goths or Saxons, and that architectural change could not be explained simply in terms of invasion and conquest. The Normans, with whom the rounded arch was generally associated in England, had conquered Sicily, but they had not been a territorial power in the areas where the architecture seemed to bear closest resemblance to the English Saxon style. Rather, Robert Smirke was intrigued to discover in Sicily what he believed to be some of the earliest specimens of the pointed arch, as well as numerous examples of the more florid architecture which was conventionally associated with eastern saracenic influences.[39] English antiquaries had long since appreciated that using the adjective 'gothic' to describe the pointed architecture which arose from the end of the twelfth century was misleading and inaccurate, but in the context of Italy it was positively erroneous: such buildings as could be dated to gothic rulers, such as San Vitale in Ravenna, built by Theodoric, did not bear the pointed arch. The gothic style to be found in the cathedrals of Pisa, Milan, Florence or Siena, moreover, displayed features which were rarely or never found in England, such as the twisted spiral shafts of columns, and other forms of ornamentation which were not introduced in English architecture until a much later date.[40] The evidence of Italian architecture showed up in even sharper relief the inadequacy of the existing terminology: for the antiquarian traveller, as opposed to the casual observer, the curious mixture that was Italian gothic presented numerous challenges.

---

[38] William Gunn, *An Inquiry into the Origin and Influence of Gothic Architecture* (1819); Thomas Cocke, 'The rediscovery of the Romanesque', in Tristram Holland, Janet Holt and George Zarnecki (eds.), *English Romanesque Art 1066–1200* (1984), 360–6; J. B. Bullen, 'The Romanesque revival in Britain, 1800–1840: William Gunn, William Whewell, and Edmund Sharpe', *Architectural History*, 47 (2004), 139–58; the term was used by Francis Palgrave in the *Handbook to Northern Italy* (1842); see also the use of the term 'debased Roman' by earlier antiquaries: Charles Lyttelton to Smart Lethieullier, 5 July 1757, BL Stowe MS 752, fol. 94. Cocke, 'Pre-nineteenth-century attitudes' (73), notes that James Essex used the term 'ancient Gothic' for Romanesque and coined the term 'Romano-Gothic' in his own notes, although did not use it in any of his published works.

[39] Robert Smirke, 'An account of some remains of gothic architecture in Italy and Sicily', *Archaeologia*, 15 (1806), 363–79.

[40] Thomas Kerrich noted that the only examples of 'twistifications' of which he was aware in England were on the tombs of Edward the Confessor and Henry III at Westminster Abbey, Kerrich to Francis Douce, 25 July 1818, Bodl. MS Douce d. 36, fol. 157 v.

One of the first to address this question in any detail in print, with reference to Italian examples, was James Dallaway, who had travelled to Italy in 1796 on his way back from Constantinople, where he had been chaplain to Sir Robert Liston's embassy.[41] Details of his travels do not exist beyond a few letters home to his family and the records of the Archivio di Stato Vaticano. We know for certain that he visited Livorno, Rome and Verona; how many other places he visited en route can only be surmised. In *Anecdotes of the Arts in England* (1800), Dallaway argued that a close examination of the varieties of gothic architecture would reveal differences 'as strongly marked as those of the Grecian orders'; differences which were analogous to the 'genius of the people' building them, 'so that the Gothic in Lombardy, in Spain, in Germany, in France, but especially in England, may be generically distinguished as decidedly as the Doric, the Ionic or the Corinthian'. He had an organic conception of the origins of gothic architecture and its local variations: rather than the Goths introducing their own style of architecture, the 'deterioration' from classical norms came about through a want of skill. In Italy, however, the availability of building materials such as columns and the remains of older structures which could act as frameworks or even models for later buildings, led to the development of a distinctive style. This was reminiscent of, but distinct from, what he termed the 'Grecian' style and equally distinct from the Saxon and gothic as practised in other parts of Europe: the use of circular arcades and porticos, for example, continued to be much more important features in Italian churches than they were in the rest of Europe.[42]

Dallaway was not isolated in his interests. The theme was taken up by G. D. Whittington who travelled through France and Italy in 1802–3 with a view to addressing precisely this question. His interpretation, *An Historical Survey of the Ecclesiastical Antiquities of France; with a View to Illustrate the Rise and Progress of Gothic Architecture in Europe* was published posthumously in 1810. Whittington argued that the Saxon and the Lombard styles simply represented different degrees of degeneration from Roman architecture; the pointed gothic style, contrary to those who argued that it had evolved out of the intersection of rounded arches,[43] for example, bore no relation to these at all, and could only be explained as an import – and following Wren, he argued that it was a

---

[41] Ingamells (ed.), *Dictionary of British and Irish Travellers*, 266.

[42] Dallaway, *Anecdotes of the Arts*, 1–7.

[43] This was a common interpretation amongst English antiquaries, particularly from the latter part of the eighteenth century, see, for example, John Milner in particular, *History of Winchester*, 2 vols. (Winchester, 1798), I, 151–2; Milner, *Treatise on the Ecclesiastical Architecture*, i–ii, 77–88. This was also the theory favoured by John Carter in his various

style brought back to Europe from the east by crusaders. The English, therefore, could lay no special claim to the gothic style and indeed the French had anticipated and exceeded the English in its design.[44] The architect Robert Smirke addressed himself to the same subject in a paper read before the Society of Antiquaries in May 1805.[45] He admitted that the study of gothic architecture during his continental tour had formed only a 'subordinate' part of his system of study, but 'as an Englishman' he could not help feeling a considerable attachment to it and an appreciation of its 'intrinsic merit'; he was, therefore, curious to see how it had been treated by foreigners. In Germany, he found numerous and splendid examples; in Italy, he found them more 'mixed' and 'unformed'. He noted the continued use of the rounded roman arch on structures such as the baptistery at Pisa, combined with pinnacles, crockets and other ornamentation normally associated with the pointed style (see Figure 15). This, he argued, showed that the gothic was introduced to Italy far earlier than in England and had assumed a degree of richness which did not appear in England until many years later.[46]

This exchange provoked a response from Thomas Kerrich, another antiquary, who had travelled to Italy during 1772–4. During his travels, he had made extensive notes on and sketches of the medieval tomb sculpture and architecture which he encountered in France, Germany and Italy.[47] His observations remained unpublished for many years until 1812, when he took up the challenge of identifying the different varieties of gothic architecture and explaining how and when the pointed arch emerged in the different countries of Europe. His comments are particularly arresting in that he rejected the conventional eighteenth-century model for explaining cultural change by invasions. The usual assumption was that any new cultural form, be it language, customs, legal system or architectural style, would have been introduced by invaders

publications: see, for example, *Ancient Architecture of England* (1805). Other antiquaries who adopted the theory in their publications included Dallaway, *Anecdotes of the Arts*; Edward King, *Munimenta Antiqua or Observations on Ancient Castles*, 4 vols. (1799–1805); Daniel and Samuel Lysons, *Magna Britannia; Being a Concise and Topographical Account of the Several Counties of Great Britain*, 6 vols. (1806–22).

[44] Whittington, *Historical Survey*, vi; see also George Haggitt, *Two Letters to a Fellow of the Society of Antiquaries on the Subject of Gothic Architecture* (Cambridge, 1813), 70–122, and Henry Hallam, *View of the State of Europe during the Middle Ages* (1818).

[45] Smirke, 'Account of some remains of gothic architecture in Italy and Sicily'.

[46] Henry Englefield had argued to the contrary that the cloisters had been built in different stages and that the tracery within the rounded arches had been added subsequently at a later date. Henry Englefield, 'Observations on the preceding paper respecting the remains of gothic architecture in Italy', *Archaeologia*, 15 (1806), 367–72.

[47] Kerrich's notes and sketches from his continental tour are to be found at BL Add. MSS 6728, 6729, 6736–40, 6743–5, 6749.

Specimen of the Architecture of the Baptistery at Pisa.

Figure 15 'Specimen of the Architecture of the Baptistery at Pisa', from Robert Smirke 'An account of some remains of gothic architecture in Italy and Sicily', *Archaeologia*, 15 (1806).

or immigrants, rather than arising as the product of internal cultural change. Instead, Kerrich found such arguments implausible and founded on 'improbable conjectures', according to which the Goths, Indians and Arabs were variously made responsible for the introduction of the pointed arch, simply because of certain similarities in architectural style. He was not interested in the hackneyed question of who had 'invented' the gothic or pointed arch – indeed, he did not believe that it was a question which could ever be resolved. Pointed or gothic arches, he explained, appeared to have been constructed in countries across Europe at the beginning of the twelfth century and by the end of it had become very common. Rather than identifying how and when the pointed arch came about, he was more concerned to trace its evolution and its regional variations.

He therefore set out an agenda for future research in order to try to resolve such questions, drawing attention to how few of the buildings constructed in either the 'German' (i.e. pointed gothic) or 'Lombard' style had been described by travellers in Italy, and proceeded to lay before the Society of Antiquaries his own descriptions and sketches, categorising the different cathedrals as to their dominant style of architecture. These included structures which had rarely been noted in any detail before by British visitors such as the cathedrals at Placentia, Parma, Modena, Cremona and Pavia (although he presumably had the church of San Michele rather than the cathedral in mind here), all of which he described as Norman. San Francesco at Placentia he identified as Norman gothic, whilst the churches of Sta Maria Novella and Sta Croce in Florence, the cathedrals at Arezzo, Orvieto, Siena and Perugia, San Antonio at Pistoia, San Frediano at Lucca and the de la Spina church in Pisa were all cited as examples of the 'light gothic'.[48] Elsewhere, in correspondence with the antiquary Francis Douce, he expounded his own typology for Italian architecture: it comprised, he suggested, the Norman or Saxon style; the 'light gothic' or *gotico tedesco*; and the more ornate *gotico arabesco*. He struggled to find vocabulary to describe the spiralling shafts characteristic of certain thirteenth- and fourteenth-century churches – resorting to the inelegant but apt 'twistifications' – and the prevalent use of cosmatesque, or what he

---

[48] Thomas Kerrich, 'Some observations on the gothic buildings abroad, particularly those in Italy; and on gothic architecture in general', *Archaeologia*, 16 (1812), 292–304; for further evidence of his interest in the development of the arts in the fourteenth century, see 'Observations upon some sepulchral monuments in Italy and France', *Archaeologia*, 18 (1817), 186–97.

called mosaic ornamentation. Kerrich believed that the style had been introduced by the Saracens via Sicily and southern Italy and was a variation of 'Moorish' architecture, which he characterised by a horseshoe arch, and which was found predominantly in Spain.[49] But in general, Kerrich was suspicious of language which attempted to identify a particular style of architecture with any race or country, being very much aware of the ease by which styles crossed geographical or national boundaries. Instead, he favoured a system, like that used by Vasari to categorise paintings, which identified a style simply by the century in which the artist or architect worked.[50] This would, he argued, make for far greater precision. Kerrich's observations are interesting not only because he was attempting to draw up a general European model of architectural development through the middle ages, but because he singled out for attention so many buildings which had hitherto been largely unnoticed by British travellers to Italy but whose importance would be recognised in the nineteenth century. Similarly, he also highlighted the architectural importance of destinations such as Assisi, which would attract increasing numbers of visitors in the nineteenth century by virtue of their gothic architecture.[51]

The first Englishman to employ the term 'Romanesque', as already noted, was another clergyman and fellow of the Society of Antiquaries, well known to Kerrich, William Gunn, who travelled to Italy in 1785 and again with his wife in 1792–3. Gunn's other claim to fame was to have conducted the marriage between Prince Augustus and Lady Augusta

---

[49] Kerrich wrote to Francis Douce, 29 Mar. 1814: 'What the Saracenic Architecture is when quite free from any mixture of Gothic I am not able to tell you: I have not seen enough but I think the re-entering or Horse-shoe Arch clearly is not essential to it, as it undoubtedly, I suppose, is to the Moorish. The grandest Characteristic of it seems to be the twisted pillar; the Norman and Gothic both sometimes have channels twisting round them in spirals, or astragals twisting round their staffs in the same manner – but in the Arabesc the shaft itself is twisted at such a rate sometimes, that I believe a thin rod might be thrust down from the top to the bottom, through the middle of it, almost without touching it. It has the same profusion of mosaics with the Moorish architecture ... I may add that the Cathedral of Florence, which is otherwise a Gothic Church, has a mixture of Saracenic Twistifications and I thought I traced some small mixture of Saracenic, even with what we should call Norman, or Saxon, in the body of the great church at Siena.' Bodl. MS Douce d. 36, fol. 117r.

[50] Kerrich habitually referred to sculpture and architecture as 1 cento, 2 cento, 3 cento, 4 cento in his notes (equivalent to twelfth, thirteenth, fourteenth and fifteenth centuries). See Bodl. MS Douce d. 36, fol. 22.

[51] Kerrich, 'Observations on the gothic buildings abroad', 292–304. See also William Gunn's list of churches in Italy, which he suggested should be studied scientifically to elucidate the development of Romanesque and Gothic architecture in Italy: Gunn, *Inquiry into the Origins and Influence of Gothic Architecture*, 73.

Murray in Rome.[52] He never published a tour of Italy, but in his *Inquiry into the Origin and Influence of Gothic Architecture* (1819), he drew on his familiarity with Italian buildings, particularly those of Pisa, to argue that the origins of the gothic style, the 'pointed arch' lay in the 'declension of Roman architecture', and that it had evolved alongside the rounded arch: hence their appearance together in buildings such as the duomo at Pisa.[53] The pointed arch, was not, he insisted, introduced from the east; rather, its use could be traced back through Roman architecture: the two had coexisted.[54] Moreover, because it was known at what date construction in Pisa had begun, antiquaries such as Gunn were able to establish a chronological framework around which they could build up their account of the revival of the art of architecture.

Popularising the gothic

It must be acknowledged, however, that architects and antiquaries such as Whittington, Gunn, Smirke, Kerrich and Dallaway were not necessarily representative of the broader travelling public in their efforts to establish a chronology for the emergence of the gothic style of architecture and its national or regional variations. The broader question remains, therefore, of the extent to which their investigations were reflected at all in the itineraries and observations of travellers, beyond the circle of the Society of Antiquaries, during this same period or found their way into the publications which were most popular amongst the travelling public. Published guides and unpublished journals and correspondence do indicate that these interests were filtering through and influencing the itinerary of the tour in Italy and the agenda of sightseeing.

---

[52] On Gunn's tour to Italy see Michael Riviere, 'The Rev. William Gunn, B.D: a Norfolk parson on the Grand Tour', *Norfolk Archaeology*, 33 (1962–5), 351–98. Gunn's journals of his travels in 1792–4 are at NRO WGN2/1–4.

[53] Gunn was particularly concerned to refute the suggestion put forward by Italian antiquaries, such as da Morrona, that the different styles evident in the duomo were the consequence of two different phases of building.

[54] Gunn, *Inquiry into the Origin and Influence of Gothic Architecture*, 6. Gunn was not the first to make this observation: James Barry had made a similar point in 1768 with regard to the cathedral at Viterbo arguing that gothic had arisen in Italy as a barbaric corruption of Roman forms, rather than coming from the east, or arising autonomously. See *The Works of James Barry Esq*, 2 vols. (1809), I, 125, 130–1, 179. See also William Gunn and Arthur Taylor, 'Remarks on the gothic architecture of the duomo, battistero and Campo Santo of Pisa', *Archaeologia*, 20 (1824), 537–52; Edward Ledwich, 'Observations on ancient churches', *Archaeologia*, 8 (1787), 165–94; and John Whitaker, *The Ancient Cathedral of Cornwall Historically Surveyed*, 2 vols. (1804), I, 82–95.

Descriptions of Pisa, published and unpublished, were always particularly rich and offer evidence of the broader diffusion of interest in Italian gothic architecture. No other medieval complex attracted such attention from British visitors during this period and it had done so long before William Gunn made it the focal point of his analysis of the origins of gothic architecture. The architectural ensemble of the leaning tower, the duomo, the baptistery and the Campo Santo had always been an important stopping point in the tourist itinerary through Tuscany: the image of the leaning tower, even in the eighteenth century, was one familiar to British eyes, and widely reproduced in prints.[55] Lord Herbert recorded how he and his companions made straight for it, 'as we had all four heard of the leaning Tower of Pisa in our Cradles'.[56] But beyond the curiosity of the leaning tower, Pisa merited attention because it seemed to offer a showcase illustrative of the rise of the arts of civilisation from their 'rebirth' in the thirteenth century to the *seicento*.[57] This became an increasingly important factor in Pisa's attraction to travellers. In the cloisters of the Campo Santo, visitors could view the progress of painting through the frescos which spanned the period from its first revival (the earliest were then believed to have been executed by Giotto) to the sixteenth century; whilst the sculptures of the Pisano dynasty, juxtaposed with the specimens of classical monumental sculpture and statuary collected in the cloisters, showed how the revival of the art of sculpture had been directly inspired by the ancient models. The duomo and the baptistery, as already noted, similarly illustrated the evolution of architectural form, from the rounded 'grecian' arches through to the pointed arch. Pisa was, as Mariana Starke informed her readers, 'the cradle of the arts'.[58]

Starke's account of 1800, which owed much to the notes of the English artist, William Artaud, was the fullest then available in English, and given the popularity of her guide, and its subsequent incarnations, it would have informed the view of many early nineteenth-century visitors.[59] Even

---

[55] George Lewis Langton visited the duomo, tower and Campo Santo of Pisa in December 1737, noting that he 'spent the morning in seeing what ev'ry book of Italy describes'. Colyer, 'A Breconshire gentleman in Europe', 283–4.

[56] Herbert (ed.), *Henry, Elizabeth and George*, 328. Edward Wright had similarly commented on the familiarity of the image of the leaning tower from prints fifty years earlier in *Observations*, II, 388.

[57] On the re-evaluation of the frescos as aesthetic objects in the early nineteenth century, see J. B. Bullen, 'The English romantics and early Italian art', in Bullen, *Continental Crosscurrents*, 9–34.

[58] Starke, *Letters from Italy* (1800 edn), I, 198.

[59] Ibid., 198–216; Starke's interest was primarily in the frescos of the Campo Santo, however, rather than the architecture of the complex. By 1828, the content of *Letters from Italy* had been revised and repackaged as *Instructions for Travellers*. This volume provided considerably more detail on the architecture, describing the duomo

writers with a more classical bias were unable to ignore the complex's significance. Joseph Forsyth, whose *Remarks on Antiquities, Arts and Letters, during an Excursion in Italy* (1813) was highly regarded in the early nineteenth century, visited Pisa in 1802. Given that his architectural ideal was the stark simplicity of ancient Greece, it is unsurprising that he was not attracted to the buildings. But despite his distaste for the gothic style, he was able to appreciate that the Italian version displayed significant differences from that which was to be found in Britain. The architecture at Pisa was 'not surely the Gothic of the north; for here are no pointed arches, no clustered pillars, no ribs nor tracery in the vaults'.[60] Forsyth's dislike of unnecessary columns, 'mean' arches, stunted proportions and other 'irregularities' was a more articulate version of the earlier eighteenth-century revulsion at what appeared to be architectural deformity. But he was also much more observant in his critique and, despite himself, appreciative of the rich detail of the ornamentation, noting elements which earlier visitors had never even observed such as the intricately carved figures of domestic and wild beasts.

Pisa in the second half of the eighteenth century was also unusual in the extent to which local antiquaries were engaged in research upon its medieval, republican past, describing and recording the art, architecture and sculpture in unprecedented detail, building upon the case first made by Vasari for Pisa's importance in the revival of the arts. British antiquaries, such as William Gunn and Robert Finch, drew heavily on this body of research and descriptive analyses by local antiquaries including da Morrona, Rosini and Lanzio.[61] But the availability of published accounts of the architecture and frescos is in itself an important reason why visitors' accounts were so much fuller in this respect for Pisa than

---

as 'greco-arabo-pisano' in style, and the baptistery as 'German gothic', 193. On William Artaud, see A. C. Sewart, 'The life, work and letters of William Artaud, 1763–1823', University of Manchester MA thesis (1951).

[60] Forsyth, *Remarks on Antiquities*, 8–9.

[61] Giuseppe Martini, *Theatrum basilicae Pisanae* (Pisa, 1705–23); there were several brief tourist guides including Anon., *Descrizione della città di Pisa per servire da guida* (Pisa, 1792), Anon., *Pregi di Pisa* (Pisa, 1816) and Anon., *Pisa antica e moderna* (Pisa, 1821); Giovanni Rosini, *Lettere pittoriche sul Campo Santo di Pisa* (Pisa, 1810), and Giovanni Rosini, *Pregi di Pisa compendiati da Alessandro da Morrona* (Pisa, 1816); Alessandro da Morrona, *Pisa illustrata nelle arti del disegno da Alessandro da Morrona*, 3 vols. (2nd edn, Livorno, 1812); Ranieri Prosperi, *Descrizione della città di Pisa* (Pisa, 1792), were based on da Morrona and were more informative on the subject of architecture than the other brief guides. On the frescos, see Carlo Lasinio, *Pitture a fresco del Campo Santo* (Pisa, 1812); Roscoe, *History of Painting*, I, 4–10. Robert Finch's detailed description of the buildings in Pisa offers a clear instance of a visitor drawing upon the locally available expertise: Bodl. MS Finch e. 17, fols. 72–83.

for other Tuscan cities which flourished in a similar era.[62] The Pisans'
interest in this period, however, as Robyn Cooper has shown, was driven
primarily by the patriotic impulse to recover and celebrate former glory.
They did not share the interest of the English antiquaries in accommo-
dating Pisa, let alone Italian gothic more broadly defined, into a chronological model of the development of gothic architecture, or in
pinpointing the origins of the pointed arch in either time or space.

The complex of duomo, baptistery and tower at Pisa may have been
particularly well known, but the more antiquarian minded travellers
were increasingly taking note of the variations and design of 'gothic'
buildings elsewhere, even if they did not share Gunn's fascination with
the emergence of the pointed arch. Robert Finch, another clergyman
with antiquarian leanings and an amateur interest in architecture, wrote
extensive notes on the ornamentation of the Romanesque churches of
Lombardy, which he described as a 'rude heavy gothic somewhat like the
Saxon'. But he was intrigued by the richness of the carvings, paying
particular attention to the lizards on the backs of lions which supported
the portico of the principal entrance to the duomo at Parma. At
Piacenza, Finch similarly took detailed notes on the bas reliefs illustrat-
ing the history of Charlemagne on the façade of the duomo (the fact that
Finch bothered to identify and record the subject matter of the reliefs is
in itself indicative of a significant shift in interest) and the slender
columns in the nave, ornamented with distinctive flowered capitals in
the east end. He was more impressed, however, by the delicacy of the
'greco-gothic' taste and the lancet windows, such as those which he
found at the duomo in Florence.[63] Such observations soon began to be
echoed by those with less explicit interest in gothic antiquities: Charlotte
Eaton similarly noted the widespread 'barbarism' of 'crouching lions'
supporting columns in northern Italy, supposing them to be of Lombard
origin.[64] Even John Chetwode Eustace, the author of the *Classical Tour*,
could not ignore the 'gothic' structures of northern Italy and, writing in
1813, his qualified admiration was expressed in terms which were
already considerably more observant than those of his predecessors
and showed some understanding of the different styles of gothic architecture, rather than a single generic 'gothick' type, evident in his

[62] Robyn Cooper, '"The crowning glory of Pisa": nineteenth-century reactions to the
Campo Santo', *Italian Studies*, 37 (1982), 72–100; see also Hilary Gatti, 'Il Campo
Santo di Pisa nella letteratura Inglese', *Annali della Scuola Normale Superiore di Pisa:
classe di lettere e filosofica*, 16, no. 1 (1986), 239–70.
[63] Finch journal Bodl. MS Finch e. 14, fol. 238. The rest of the building he found squat,
inelegant and awkward.
[64] Eaton, *Rome in the Nineteenth Century*, I, 47.

description of the cathedral at Lucca, for example. This was, he noted, a mixture of the heavy Saxon style, and with its light arabesque he allowed that it had 'no small claim' to beauty. The interior arcades were thick and clumsy but supported a second range which comprised light and airy pointed arches ornamented with fretwork of 'admirable grace and delicacy'.[65]

Finch and Eustace were unusually assiduous in their architectural observations. But the more general tourist itinerary was also beginning to expand to take in other centres, notable chiefly for their medieval or early renaissance architecture, even before the end of the eighteenth century. For much of the eighteenth century, Orvieto was known chiefly for its wine, rather than its cathedral. Few guides even mentioned the city, except as a possible staging post in the journey to Rome.[66] The poor quality of the rocky road from Bolsena made it relatively inaccessible to visitors travelling by coach. By the 1790s, the duomo's reputation was beginning to grow: John Flaxman spent several weeks at Orvieto in 1792 studying the reliefs on the cathedral façade and the frescos within by Signorelli, with another British artist, William Young Ottley.[67] But it was not just artists who were making the detour from Bolsena: Thomas Martyn's 1787 guide to Italy contained a lengthy footnote praising the beauties of the gothic façade.[68] Thomas Kerrich, James Dallaway and William Gunn had each visited it on their tours through Italy, for they all described its architecture in their subsequent publications,[69] and Robert Finch visited it on his journey from Florence to Rome in April 1815.[70] But by the end of the Napoleonic Wars, Orvieto was also entering the

---

[65] Eustace, *Classical Tour*, II, 250–1.

[66] Nugent, *Grand Tour*, III, 363, offered a brief account of the city, but tellingly described the cathedral as a handsome building, 'though of Gothic architecture'.

[67] David Irwin, *John Flaxman 1755–1826: Sculptor, Illustrator, Designer* (1979), 40–2. See also essays by Brigstocke on Flaxman and Ottley in Brigstocke, Marchand and Wright, *John Flaxman and William Young Ottley*, 3–24, 342–59. Ottley's response to the frescos featured in William Young Ottley, *The Italian School of Design Being a Series of Fac-similes of Original Drawings by the Most Eminent Painters and Sculptors of Italy* (1808–23) and *A Series of Plates, Engraved after the Paintings and Sculpture of the Most Eminent Masters of the Early Florentine School* (1826). John Flaxman's observations on gothic churches were also unusually detailed for the time, see, for example, his admiring description of the duomo at Milan, BL Add. MS 39786, fols. 21–2, written in 1787.

[68] Martyn, *Gentleman's Guide*, 302: 'The Cathedral is a very fine gothic building; the front at least as beautiful as that of Siena, and very rich in sculpture and mosaic. Nicola Pisano had some hand in it as sculptor, but was not an architect. It contains a great deal both of sculpture and painting within. Of the latter, a chapel painted by Signorelli, with the last judgement, is most remarkable, particularly because Michelangelo used to study it.'

[69] Kerrich, 'Some observations on the gothic buildings abroad', 301; Dallaway, *Anecdotes of the Arts*, 4; Gunn, *Inquiry into the Origin and Influence of Gothic Architecture*, 61.

[70] Finch journal Bodl. MS Finch e. 15, fol. 57v.

standard tourist itinerary in publications such as Henry Coxe's 1815 guide.[71] Assisi similarly began to attract more visitors, particularly as the route via Perugia between Rome and Florence became more popular. When Henry Swinburne visited Assisi in 1779, the only church he described was that of Sta Maria Minerva, which had been converted from the Roman Temple of Minerva.[72] Gradually, however, the conventual church attracted more attention, both on account of the frescos within, particularly those that were believed to be by Giotto, and its unmistakably pointed gothic architecture.[73] Sir Richard Colt Hoare, visiting Assisi in 1789, noted that the church of the Franciscan convent was particularly interesting, being constructed as three churches, one on top of the other: 'The middle one', he observed, 'is dark and vaulted and at present the usual one of devotion: the upper one is of an elegant gothic form, of a fine proportion and painted in various patterns of ancient mosaic: the architecture is of a good proportion and elegant and light in its form.'[74] In 1792, the conventual church was singled out in John Smith's *Select Views in Italy*, for the 'singularity of its construction'; the accompanying plate, however, failed to depict its gothic qualities in any detail (see Figure 16).[75] But by 1842, Henry Gally Knight had identified it as the best and most complete example of the pointed style of architecture in Italy.[76]

This new mode of perception even began to influence the descriptions of Rome, a city which, as we have seen, had hitherto been defined almost exclusively in terms of its classical architecture.[77] Joseph Forsyth's account of Rome included a subsection entitled 'Works of the middle ages' which described the basilicas of early

[71] Coxe, *Picture of Italy*, 369, described it as a 'very fine' gothic building, whose front was as magnificent as that of Siena's, and noteworthy for the sculpture of Niccolò Pisano.
[72] Henry Swinburne, *The Courts of Europe at the Close of the Last Century*, 2 vols. (1895), I, 245.
[73] See, for example, Eustace, *Classical Tour*, II, 162–3; Starke, *Letters from Italy* (1800 edn), II, 175; Hale (ed.), *Italian Journal*, 204; Kerrich and Gunn similarly referred to it as one of the finest examples of gothic architecture in Italy.
[74] Sir Richard Colt Hoare, 'Journey from Florence to Rome 1789', CUL Add. MS 3546, fol. 12.
[75] John Smith, *Select Views in Italy with Topographical Descriptions in England and France*, 2 vols. (1792–6), I, plate 12.
[76] Henry Gally Knight, *The Ecclesiastical Architecture of Italy: From the Time of Constantine to the Fifteenth Century*, 2 vols. (1842), II, plate XIX. See also William Hazlitt's description in *Notes of a Journey*, 334–5.
[77] This discussion concentrates on English accounts of Rome, but it is worth noting that Italian descriptions of the city also began to take note of gothic features, for example, Guattani, *Roma descritte ed illustrata*, singled out 'il bei chiostri Gothici' in San Paolo (II, 63) and described Sta Maria sopra Minverva as 'Una delle più antiche Chiese in cui si vedono gl'archi sesto-acuti, detti Gotici' (II, 120).

Figure 16 View of Assisi, from John Smith, *Select Views in Italy with Topographical Descriptions in England and France*, 2 vols. (1792–6).

medieval Rome. Forsyth, as we have seen, was no enthusiast for the gothic, and noted with some relief that Rome had been largely 'preserved from the Gothic taste'.[78] But by 1821, the English clergyman Edward Burton was warning his readers that 'the total absence of the Gothic or pointed style of architecture in the Roman churches, can hardly fail to be noticed by an English eye.' He proceeded to itemise the few remnants of what was 'properly or improperly' called gothic, identifying features which had rarely, if ever, before been drawn to the attention of British visitors. Further, he exploited the evidence of engravings to establish the presence of gothic structures which had been subsequently destroyed or improved, such as the transept of the old church of St John Lateran, and windows in the old church of St Peter's. He also engaged with the question *why* so few buildings of gothic architecture were to be found in Rome, given that there were so many specimens further south in Naples and Sicily – it could not have been simply that the style had not penetrated as far south as Rome. This was not a question which had ever suggested itself to earlier observers.[79] But he was unable to come up with a satisfactory answer.[80] Burton's attention to the gothic – which he effectively equated with the architecture of the Christian church – was indicative of a greater interest in Rome as the centre of early Christianity: a re-orientation in perspective which drew upon the increasingly evangelical religious sensibilities of nineteenth-century travellers.

Rome's brief period as a republic in the fourteenth century also began to attract more interest amongst British visitors, even if it was an episode that was more rarely celebrated within Rome itself. One aspect of the reception of Gibbon's *Decline and Fall* which is less frequently commented upon was its value in providing visitors to Rome with an account of the city's history after 476: a narrative which had otherwise largely been lacking.[81] The contours of the middle ages and the early renaissance gradually assumed a more defined appearance. For example, prior to Gibbon, such references as there were to Cola di Rienzo, who led a short-lived attempt to revive the Roman Republic in 1347, had been for the most part derogatory and brief: Keysler, upon whom many travellers

---

[78] Forsyth, *Remarks on Antiquities*, 156–64.

[79] Gunn, *Inquiry into the Origins and Influence of Gothic Architecture*, pointed out that the reasons for the absence of gothic architecture in Rome needed to be identified, but did not enter into an explanation (164). He claimed to have located only two examples of the gothic in Rome: two pointed arches in the convent of the Annunziata, and the ciboria of the altars in 'several of the basilica churches' (ibid.).

[80] Burton, *Description of the Antiquities*, 368–70.

[81] See, for example, Hobhouse, *Historical Illustrations*.

relied, had dismissed him in a footnote as 'this petty tyrant'.[82] But in chapter 70 of *Decline and Fall*, Gibbon's readers would have found an elegant and accessible summary of the careers of both Petrarch and Cola di Rienzo and an account of the doomed attempt to revive the Roman Republic.[83] Gibbon took a coolly measured view of Rienzo's career, but in the changed political landscape of the early nineteenth century, when a Roman Republic had temporarily existed in 1798, the self-styled tribune's story gained a new contemporary cogency and evinced a less equivocal response. Approbatory references to Rienzo became more frequent, particularly from visitors who identified with his attempts to revive political liberty and oppose the secular power of the papacy.[84] Cola di Rienzo's house, or what was believed to have been his house, attracted more attention on the tourist itinerary, both because of what it represented politically and because its architecture seemed to 'exhibit the first dawnings of architecture, in the fourteenth century'.[85] The building, with its 'massive walls irregularly spotted with little gothic casements' was, noted Lady Morgan, 'curious as a specimen of the domestic architecture of Rome in the fourteenth century'.[86] For those who hoped that the pope's authority might be tempered by another latter day Rienzo, the Capitol now inspired reflection, not simply because it was the location of the formative events of Roman history, but in recognition of its associations with Rienzo's career.[87] This was a process of imaginative reinterpretation which culminated in Bulwyer Lytton's eponymous novel, *Rienzi* (1835).

Further south, the presence of gothic architecture in Naples and Sicily was, however, much less remarked upon.[88] This is partly to be explained

---

[82] Keysler, *Travels*, II, 222. Before Gibbon made use of it in his own account, there appears to have been little interest in or notice of the account by Jean Antoine de Cerceau and Pierre Brumoy, *Memoirs of Nicholas Gabrini de Rienzi* (1740).

[83] Edward Gibbon, *The History of the Decline and Fall of the Roman Empire*, 7 vols. (Oxford, 1925), VII, 300–15.

[84] William Forbes, for example, wrote out a lengthy passage based upon the *Memoirs of the Life of Petrarch* concerning Rienzo's career into his own journal: NLS MS 1543, fols. 235–49.

[85] Weston, *Viaggiana*, 150. See also Finch journal Bodl. MS Finch e. 16, fol. 172v; Eaton, *Rome in the Nineteenth Century*, II, 293–5. For an overview of Cola di Rienzo's reputation in the eighteenth and nineteenth centuries and the fortune of his (presumed) house, see Carrie E. Beneš, 'Mapping a Roman legend: the house of Cola di Rienzo from Piranesi to Baedecker', *Italian Culture*, 26 (2008), 57–83.

[86] Morgan, *Italy*, II, 257n.

[87] Hobhouse, *Historical Illustrations*, 257.

[88] Mme de Staël, for example, claimed in *Corinne* that there were scarcely any gothic buildings or feudal castles to be found in the south of Italy: *Corinne*, trans. Raphael, 188. Saint-Non's *Voyage pittoresque*, another text which was well known amongst English readers, illustrated a number of gothic buildings from Magna Graecia and Sicily in volumes III and IV, such as the cathedral at Palermo; the letterpress was largely silent

by the relative infrequency with which the British, even in the early nineteenth century, penetrated into the *mezzogiorno* and beyond. It also reflects the tropes around which accounts of these areas were written: Naples, for example, had never been a city which was widely admired by the British either for its architecture or its art. As Chapter 4 showed, although visitors were impressed by the sumptuous extravagance of the marble and the silver plate in the churches, they did not generally find the florid baroque style of the city's architecture to their taste and barely even noticed the buildings of an earlier date. Thanks to the frequency with which earthquakes had damaged the city, few remains of classical antiquity remained intact or visible within the city itself. The consequence was that Naples, as we have seen, was generally described in terms of the beauty of its natural setting, the crowded streets, the richness and ritual of Catholic superstition, but not in terms of its physical fabric or its medieval past. Comments on such buildings tended to be laconic or dismissive, such as Mary Berry's observation in her journal that the cathedral was 'a very bad sort of gothic without any beauty'[89] or Mariana Starke's disgust at the excessive ornamentation in Sta Chiara, which made it look, she said, more like a ballroom than a Christian church.[90] Increased familiarity with Dante meant that the fate of Conradin, imprisoned in the Castel dell'Ovo by Charles of Anjou,[91] was sometimes alluded to, but the broader history of the Angevin dominance of Naples did not offer a model of stable oligarchy (as in Venice) or a combination of commerce and the arts (as in Florence) or even a vision of republican idealism to match the dreams of Petrarch and Rienzo in Rome.[92] Only the assiduous John Breval made mention of the importance of the Angevin building programmes in Naples' growth, but his interest was in the historical exercise of power that such edifices

---

upon the subject of gothic architecture. With regard to the cathedral, Saint-Non simply commented that 'l'extérieur de celle-ci est un des beaux Monumens qui nous restent du douzième siècle, pour le style, ainsi que pour les détails prodigieux de cette Architecture gothique qui sont à l'infini, & qui donnent à ce vaste Edifice, ainsi qu'à la Place sur laquelle il est construit, un air & un caractère Asiatique qui nous plut assez' (*Voyage Pittoresque*, IV, 140–1).

[89] Lewis (ed.), *Extracts of the Journals and Correspondence*, I, 79.
[90] Starke, *Letters from Italy* (1800 edn), II, 69.
[91] The story of Conradin's fate was recounted by earlier authorities such as Misson, *New Voyage to Italy* (1695 edn), I, 304, but little commented upon until the latter part of the century: see, for example, Flaxman journal BL Add. MS 39787, fol. 63, and Forbes journal NLS MS 1541, fols. 174–5.
[92] Although Neapolitan guidebooks and more compendious French and English language tours provided an overview of Neapolitan history, few if any visitors showed any interest at all in either the early origins of Naples or its subsequent history under the Romans, Normans, Angevins and Aragonese.

represented, not the style in which they were constructed.[93] The built environment, therefore, did not illustrate any historical narrative to which the British attached much meaning and there was no impulse to read the city's history through its architecture in the way that was beginning to happen in Florence, Rome or Venice.[94]

The history of the Venetian Republic had been closely studied by English authors for lessons in political virtue since the seventeenth century and the Doge's Palace celebrated as the centre from which la Serenissima had been governed, but the other Italian republics had never commanded the same attention, having failed to display political stability comparable to that which was so admired in Venice.[95] Their public buildings, therefore, similarly went unnoticed. In the later eighteenth century, this attitude began to change as appreciation of the early development of art and literature in the fourteenth and fifteenth centuries began to develop.[96] We have already seen how attitudes to Florence's history as a republic changed from it being regarded as an unedifying period of political factionalism overshadowed by the magnificence of the Medici dukes, to it being celebrated as the centre of political liberty and the cultivation of the arts, with much greater notice accordingly being given to the art and architecture, the 'monuments of republican dignity'. The republican era of other Italian city states acquired new significance for having given rise to the 'first flowering' of the arts in the *trecento*, not just in Florence, but in Pisa and Siena also.[97] One of the consequences of the French Revolutionary and Napoleonic Wars was further to stimulate such interest in Italian history. Jean Charles Léonard de Sismondi's *Histoire des républiques Italiannes du moyenne âge*, 16 vols, (1809–18)

[93] Breval, *Remarks on Several Parts of Europe* (1738 edn), I, 59–60.
[94] It should also be noted that few Italians had shown any interest in describing the development of Neapolitan art and architecture. Vasari and his successors, such as Lanzio, concentrated on Florence, Rome and the northern Italian schools, rather than looking further south. Swinburne's account of Naples in *Travels in the Two Sicilies* offers a partial exception in that his comments on the history and architecture of Naples were far fuller than those of most British visitors, but he was deeply unsympathetic to gothic architecture as a style. Lady Sydney Morgan's comments on Naples, published in 1821, begin to show some appreciation of how the city's historical evolution could be traced through its built form without entering into any detail on the appearance of style of the architecture: 'The antiquities of Naples, and its environs, are its sites, its buried cities, and classic ports; its historical recollections are the perpetuated horrors of a foreign despotism, registered in its Moorish, Spanish, and Arabic architecture.' *Italy*, II, 335.
[95] Eglin, *Venice Transfigured*, 11–67.
[96] Hale, *England and the Italian Renaissance*, 82–107; Bullen, *Myth of the Renaissance*, 19–50; Toynbee, *Dante in English Literature*, I, passim.
[97] Gunn, *Inquiry into the Origin and Influence of Gothic Architecture*, 58–9, drew a direct connection between the commercial, mercantile economy of Pisa and other Tuscan cities and the flourishing state of the arts.

was not widely read until translated into English in 1832, but exercised considerable indirect influence before that date through Henry Hallam's *View of the State of Europe during the Middle Ages* (1818).[98] Hallam was heavily reliant upon both Gibbon and Sismondi for his account of Italy and took from Sismondi in particular an ideal of autonomous urban communes which seemed to anticipate the political freedom that was being sought in the nineteenth century. There were other translations too, such as Pierre-Antoine-Noel-Bruno Daru's *Histoire de le République de Venise* (1822) and Lorenzo Pignotti's *History of Tuscany* (1822).[99] Equally, there was a series of publications in French and Italian which were devoted to charting the development of Italian art and literature in this period and celebrated the early renaissance as the period of the rebirth of civilisation.[100] This interest in the republican era of the city states had a clear impact on what was seen and recorded: the range of buildings which attracted travellers' attention was expanded, and structures which had hitherto been routinely ignored now came into sharper focus. As in Florence, the history of the town or city was increasingly being read through its buildings – the towers of Siena were no longer spoken of as architectural infelicities but as memorials of the men who had rendered essential services to the Sienese Republic;[101] those at Pisa were described by Forsyth as 'patrician towers' of grave magnificence;[102] for Sydney Morgan, the architecture of Milan bore the stamp of its importance in the middle ages;[103] and James Hakewill singled out the duomo as 'affording, perhaps, the completest specimen in Europe of what the art of the middle ages is capable of producing'.[104] Verona had always been a favoured destination for travellers on account of its

---

[98] Mary Shelley notably relied heavily on her reading of Sismondi's 'delightful' publication (as well as Machiavelli and Villani) to inform her novel, *Valperga, or the Life and Adventures of Castruccio Prince of Lucca* (1823), set amidst the fourteenth-century conflict between the Guelfs and the Ghibellines. Stuart Curran, 'Valperga', in Esther Schor (ed.), *The Cambridge Companion to Mary Shelley* (Cambridge, 2003), 103–15.

[99] Brand, *Italy and the English Romantics*, 175–93.

[100] Girolamo Tiraboschi, *Storia della litteratura Italiana*, 18 vols. (Florence, 1774–82); Lanzi, *Storia pittorica dell'Italia*; Séroux d'Agincourt, *Histoire de l'art d'après les monuments depuis sa decadence au IVe siècle jusqu'à son renouvellement au XVIe siècle* (Paris, 1823).

[101] Milford, *Observations, Moral, Literary and Antiquarian*, I, 240.

[102] Forsyth, *Remarks on Antiquities*, 8–9.

[103] Morgan, *Italy*, I, 72. See also comments on republican architecture in Florence in Chapter 2. By the 1840s, architectural writers such as Lord Lindsay could argue that these civic buildings offered the best specimens of gothic architecture in Italy; the cathedrals and churches, by comparison, were found wanting: Alexander William Crawford, Lord Lindsay, *Sketches of the History of Christian Art*, 3 vols. (1847), II, 17, 36–7.

[104] James Hakewill, *A Picturesque Tour of Italy from Drawings Made in 1816, 1817* (1820), plate 60.

amphitheatre, which had survived in a better state of restoration than had the Coliseum,[105] but by the early nineteenth century, the fourteenth-century Scaligieri tomb was also beginning to attract attention, both because of its historical associations and its exquisite workmanship. It was described by Joseph Forsyth as 'the most elegant Gothic, light open, spiry, full of statues caged in their fretted niches'.[106] Tourists even began to express concern at the damage that was being inflicted upon medieval, as well as classical, antiquities.[107]

The fact that greater attention was being paid to gothic architecture in Italy, however, did not necessarily signify unqualified admiration. On the contrary, the Italian version of gothic was frequently found wanting, particularly in comparison with what the British traveller was familiar with in his or her own country. On one level, this was presented purely as an aesthetic preference: thus, for Henry Matthews there was nothing in Italy 'so *beautiful*, as the light, elegant and graceful ruins of a Gothic Abbey', although the associations of a classical ruin were indubitably more inspiring.[108] But the critique of Italian gothic architecture, ruined or not, also drew strength from the widely rehearsed, if erroneous, argument, that the gothic was the national English style; the Italians could not, therefore, be allowed any superiority in this domain. Even in the first half of the eighteenth century, the more discerning antiquarian traveller, such as Martin Folkes, had noted that the 'gothic' architecture of Italy had not evolved into such a distinctive style as in England, displaying a greater debt to the classical traditions and forms, however debased: 'ours is a sort of taste by itself'.[109] This was a theme which was articulated with increasing emphasis as appreciation of English, or northern European, gothic developed over the course of the eighteenth and nineteenth centuries. Thus, the tabernacle work of the choir at Siena was very elegant, according to Adam Walker, but not equal to that of York Minster.[110] Visitors noted how Italian gothic never attained the

---

[105] Alexander Gordon's translation of Scipione Maffei's treatise on amphitheatres, *A Compleat History of the Ancient Amphitheatres* (1730), had helped its fame to spread amongst English-speaking travellers.

[106] Forsyth, *Remarks on Antiquities*, 348. See also Smith, *Sketch of a Tour*, III, 17, and William Stewart Rose, *Letters from the North of Italy Addressed to Henry Hallam*, 2 vols. (1819), I, 44–5.

[107] Armitage journal TCC MS a 226 37 (1), unfoliated MS, 2 Oct. 1790, Whaley Armitage noted the damage being caused to the cathedral at Milan by visitors.

[108] Matthews, *Diary of an Invalid*, 223.

[109] Folkes journal Bodl. MS Eng. misc. c. 444, fol. 56r.

[110] Walker, *Ideas Suggested on the Spot*, 137. Similarly, Mary Berry compared the baptistery at Parma to the chapter house at York: Lewis (ed.), *Extracts of the Journals and Correspondence*, I, 48. Sharp, *Letters from Italy*, 232. York Minster was regarded by many as the finest gothic building in the country.

soaring verticality or delicacy of ornamentation of early English or decorated gothic. Thus, Jane Waldie complained that the horizontal stripes, as found on the duomo at Siena, cut across the pointed arches and thereby diminished the imposing sense of height which such buildings normally commanded. Unlike Matthews, Waldie's objections were as much associative as aesthetic – the stripes, she complained 'effectually destroy all that similarity to the groves and forests appropriated to the worship of the Deity by the Druids and early priests of the northern nations where this peculiar architecture originally arose'. But it was the inferiority of Italian to English gothic that was the real sticking point.[111] As Edward Burton warned his readers, 'any specimen of that light and majestic architecture which prevails in our English cathedrals ... will in vain be sought for in Italy'. Even Milan's duomo was, in his opinion, a clear instance of the decline of gothic architecture.[112]

The view that the pointed arch was an English creation had never been universally held, and would become increasingly untenable after 1815 as knowledge of continental gothic architecture increased. But travellers could always argue that the pointed arch had reached its perfection in England, or that its use in England for religious structures was more appropriate than the Italian habit of remodelling the pagan temples of antiquity as Christian churches. Thus, J. B. S. Morritt was prepared to allow that St Peter's was the most magnificent building in the world, but, he noted, it failed to impress the mind with the 'religious, gloomy awe' that one experienced so naturally when walking through the lengthy aisles of a gothic building such as York Minster.[113] Travellers could find fault with Rome on new grounds: Robert Finch had approached the 'mistress of the world' with eager anticipation, only to be disappointed by the flatness and uneven elevation of the prospect view, which he found far less imposing than the prospect of an English townscape, punctuated with towers and steeples.[114] As such, the claims being made for the pre-eminence of English gothic complemented the rhetoric which increasingly asserted the superiority of the Christian British Empire over that of ancient, pagan Rome that we saw in Chapter 3.

---

[111] Waldie, *Sketches Descriptive of Italy*, I, 291; Robert Willis was rather more analytical in his objections: the gothic never really flourished in Italy, he explained, because of the pervasive presence of 'grecian' models of architecture, which were based upon horizontal principles of 'lateral extension' as opposed to the verticality which defined the gothic style: Robert Willis, *Remarks on the Architecture of the Middle Ages, Especially of Italy* (Cambridge, 1835), 2–3.

[112] Burton, *Description of the Antiquities*, 373.

[113] Morritt, *A Grand Tour*, 297.

[114] Finch journal Bodl. MS Finch e. 15, fol. 59r.

The experience of travel in Italy is frequently split between the era of the eighteenth-century Grand Tour and the period of romantic travel in the early nineteenth century, separated by the hiatus created by the French Revolutionary and Napoleonic Wars. Given the interruption to travel which was consequent upon war, it is easy to start the narrative of Anglo-Italian relationships afresh in 1815 and to identify new trends, new interests and new preoccupations, paying less regard to the continuities with the earlier period. But it would be unwise to assume that the French Revolutionary and Napoleonic Wars marked such an abrupt transition in the development of Britain's relationship with Italy, its culture and its history. The perceptions of medieval and early renaissance Italy in the post-Napoleonic era, as this chapter has shown, are a case in point. Whilst the nineteenth-century interest in 'Christian architecture' and the 'primitives' of the thirteenth and fourteenth centuries was clearly radically opposed to the classical priorities of eighteenth-century travellers, it is important to understand the stages by which this transition in values and taste came about, and to see how the eighteenth-century Grand Tour gradually evolved into a different kind of itinerary which incorporated the picturesque gothic, but nevertheless retained much of the original structure of the classical tour. As it did so, the range of cities to which visitors were attracted expanded and the meanings and values associated with them transformed. Although this chapter has focussed on the awareness and appreciation of the gothic style of architecture in Italy in order to explore these changes, it is a story which was shaped by the wider re-evaluation of the middle ages as the formative period of European history; by an approach to art and antiquities which was increasingly sensitive to the historical value of tracing stylistic changes over time and which was prying itself free from the hegemony of classicism; by a change in religious sensibilities which was less hostile to the architecture of the Catholic church and more appreciative of its significance as a testament to the history of early Christianity; and, as we have already seen in Chapter 3, by the reconfiguration of Britain's relationship with that of ancient Rome, from one of emulous admiration to confident equality and superiority.

Conclusion

By 1820, the relationship between Britain and Italy had changed fundamentally from that at the start of our period. In 1700, Italy, to the aspiring British traveller, seemed to represent the best of Europe's cultural achievements: the legacy of classical antiquity; the renaissance recovery of the arts; the splendours of baroque town planning and architecture. Although the political power of the papacy had been seriously curtailed since its early sixteenth-century apogée under Julius II, the pope was still a major figure in international diplomacy and the dangers of Catholicism were keenly felt by a generation who had lived through the policies of the later Stuarts and who were currently negotiating a political world where Jacobites looked to Catholic France and the pope for support. The Italian city states may have become shadows of their former glory, suborned by despotic princely power or stultified by oligarchic complacency, but their size and physical appearance and the memory of what they once had been could still command the respect of travellers from a country where few towns outside London could boast of anything approaching comparable elegance or size. Britain itself was still a long way from 'Great Power' status: its military, naval and financial strength were sorely tested in the War of the Spanish Succession, and dynastic stability at home was far from assured. It was, however, entering upon a phase of commercial, agricultural and manufacturing growth, stimulated by a rapid rise in population, which, in addition to the acquisition (and loss) of overseas empire, would contribute to unprecedented urbanization and create an increasingly prosperous and dynamic middle class. By 1820, London was the largest city in Europe, if not the world, by some distance; but even the second-tier towns such as Manchester, Liverpool or Birmingham were proud symbols of the country's commercial and manufacturing might and boasted imposing public buildings, pavements and street lighting. British towns and cities displayed increasing self-confidence in their own wealth, modernity and improvement and saw themselves as exemplars of culture and progress. Similarly, Britain's place in Europe was now one of political leadership and increasing imperial dominance. Over a century's worth of recurrent warfare had welded the British state into a more cohesive and powerful organism and turned 'Britishness' into a meaningful expression of identity.[1] Italy, meanwhile, had only receded in importance. The weakness of the papacy on the international stage had been exposed long before Napoleon's assault on Italy. Under Napoleonic rule, however, the Italian states were effectively reduced to the status of French colonies; the period marked a nadir in their fortunes, following a long period of gradual decline. Politics aside, the commercial and manufacturing expansion and demographic growth that characterised so many British cities in this period were largely absent from Italy and urban improvement lagged similarly behind.

This recalibration in the political, religious and cultural relationships between Britain and Europe, and Italy in particular, was manifest in the ways in which the cities of the Italian tour were described and represented. The pope's declining authority drew some of the venom with which papal influence and the catholic church were criticised, evident in accounts of Rome and of Naples, but also lesser cities, such as Ferrara, which were part of the Papal States, or Loreto. The shift also had other consequences: as British visitors became increasingly conscious of the vitality of urban and commercial society in their own country, their appreciation of Florence, which seemed to offer an early exemplar of the successful combination of commercial prosperity and cultural patronage to which the British aspired, was clearly heightened. More generally, we find a greater propensity to criticism: whilst travellers in the earlier part of the eighteenth century frequently found much to admire in Italian cities – whether the provision of water supplies in Pisa; the elegance of the street plan in Turin; or patrician charity in Genoa – in the latter part of our period, the tendency was to temper praise with criticism or to draw unfavourable comparisons with British cities.[2] Rome was no longer unassailable in its superiority, and Venice became a relic of former glory, not a living city with a future. Even Turin's celebrated street plan – compared by John Flaxman to the window panes drawn on a child's slice of bread and butter – fell out of favour for being too regular to the point of oppression, whilst its buildings were dismissed for looking shabby and unfinished.[3]

---

[1] Linda Colley, *Britons: Forging the Nation 1707–1837* (New Haven and London, 1992).

[2] See, for example, Duncombe (ed.), *Letters from Italy*, 103 (Pisa); Mitchell journal BL Add. MS 58319, fol. 54 (Genoa); Mitchell journal BL Add. MS 58315, fol. 8v, and Klima (ed.), *Letters from the Grand Tour*, 74 (Turin).

[3] John Flaxman to William Hayley, 17 July 1787, BL Add. MS 39780, fol. 43v; Armitage journal TCC Add. MS a 226 37 (1), 27 Sept. 1790.

Over the course of the eighteenth century, the British increasingly identified themselves as modern, whilst Italy and its cities lay in the past.[4] The attributes of modern urbanity – street lighting, street paving, street cleansing – with which the British identified themselves became criteria through which modern Italian cities all too often displayed their deficiencies. We have seen this already in Rome and in Venice, but the examples could be multiplied across Italy as comments on dark streets (illuminated only by wayside shrines) and malodorous nuisances demonstrated the absence of good civic police. Back home, complaints about the state of London's streets abounded, but once across the English Channel, the cleanliness of the urban environment was increasingly used by travellers to define themselves against the Italians (and other foreign nations), whether delighting in the pristine pavements of Florence or taking offence at the noisesomeness of Venetian canals and Roman piazzas. Cleanliness was the outward and visible sign of other less tangible qualities with which the British identified: it was indicative of a well-ordered society, where individuals enjoyed liberty and took responsibility for their actions; where by-laws regulated irresponsible behaviour and were observed; where a practical concern for function and order took precedence over a tawdry desire for magnificent display. As Lady Lyttelton lamented in Naples in 1819, 'Oh England! England! Dear, clean, delicate, virtuous England, catch me out of you when once I get to you!'[5] The only city that consistently proved the exception to the rule was Livorno, or Leghorn, where the bustling trade, the shops and the people – as well as the presence of English merchants – elicited frequent praise and prompted successive travellers to compare it to England.[6] 'Most cities in Italy', observed Robert Harvey, 'are devoted to the dead ... but Leghorn is built in the land of the living and everything is in perpetual movement.'[7]

The growth of towns and cities in Britain was not, of course, universally well received amongst contemporaries; indeed, there was a powerful tradition of criticism that found expression in fulminations against the corruption of moral values, the fracturing of social relations and the deleterious consequences of urban living upon physical health.[8] But this

---

[4] Luzzi, 'Italy without Italians'.   [5] Wyndham (ed.), *Correspondence*, 220.
[6] Lewis (ed.), *Extracts of the Journals and Correspondence*, I, 122; Piozzi, *Observations and Reflections*, 178; Gray, *Letters during the Course of a Tour*, 341; Watkins, *Travels through Switzerland, Italy, Sicily*, I, 320.
[7] Harvey journal NRO MS 20677, 130.
[8] The classic analysis of the literary reaction to nineteenth-century urbanisation is Raymond Williams, *The Country and the City* (1973).

was also a period *before* the most intense phase of urbanisation and the full horror of urban squalor and degradation that would be laid bare in the reports of Victorian reformers or the novels of Dickens still lay in the future. Thus, there was no sense in which Italy, or Italian cities, were being represented as the anti-type to the negative consequences of British urbanisation.[9] Although one can find a rhetoric of nostalgia in depictions of medieval institutions and monastic almsgiving in domestic urban antiquarian and topographical literature, there is little evidence that this was transposed to Italy.[10] At most, the lack of improvement and progress represented picturesque charm and simply reaffirmed the image of Italy as a country which inhabited the past, rather than being an active participant in the progress of modernity. Italian commerce and manufactures were routinely decried and found wanting. Modern Italy, as we have seen, was constantly compared to its historical antecedents: the shops of Naples were compared to those of Pompeii; the labouring classes played the same games and wore the same dress as those of ancient Rome; the women around Bologna looked like figures from a painting by Raphael or Titian.[11] The transformation of *lazzaroni* and *gondolieri* from a dangerous, violent and threatening presence to a primitive and charming addition to the townscape was another facet of this trope that denied Italy's pretensions to modernity. This backwardness, this sense of unchanging continuity with the past would soon become an important element in Italy's attraction for British visitors, but in 1820, it was not as yet fully articulated. Thus, Ferrara in 1826, long described by the British as dull, decayed and desolate, represented 'enchantment' for William Hazlitt. 'It is the *ideal* of an Italian city, once great, now a shadow of itself. Whichever way you turn, you are struck with picturesque beauty and faded splendours, but with nothing squalid, mean, or vulgar.'[12]

British travellers by the end of our period, then, were increasingly confident of their place in the world as 'moderns' and this was a quality that grew out of conscious pride in the country's cities and the commercial and manufacturing wealth that they represented, as well as the expansion of empire. In part, this can be attributed to the fact that by

---

[9] Hilary Fraser suggests that by the Victorian era 'English visitors to Italy compared an Italy still in touch with its historical roots with an England forever dislocated from its past by industrialization and modernization.' *The Victorians and Renaissance Italy* (Oxford, 1992), 3.

[10] Sweet, *Antiquaries*, 38.

[11] The perpetuation of ancient practices in modern Italy was elaborated in book length form by Blunt, *Vestiges of the Ancient Manners and Customs*.

[12] Hazlitt, *Notes of a Journey*, 343.

the nineteenth century increasing numbers of travellers came not from the landed elite, but from the commercial and professional classes, or from the urban gentry, that is from those who were themselves products of urban society. But that is not to say that the landed classes set themselves up in opposition to all things urban or that they would not have shared an appreciation of how much of Britain's wealth and influence was dependent upon the growth of towns, and of London in particular. The increasing importance of Parliament in the business of government and the rise of the London Season had helped to generate a uniquely metropolitan identity for the political and social elite, many of whom owned property in London, had investments in London's stock market and put their names to the commissions and subscriptions that improved the city's amenities and appearance. For the rest of the year, when not on their estates, they might visit Bath, Brighton or other of the spas and resort towns that had grown up to cater for leisured tastes. Thus, travellers were, for the most part, experienced and discerning judges of the urban environment.

Britain's own experience as an urbanising nation provides a crucial context through which to evaluate and understand changes in the patterns of viewing, describing and representing the cities of the Italian Grand Tour. It is not of itself, however, a sufficient explanation of how or why the changes took place: we need to consider not only the implications of an increasingly heterogeneous travelling class, but also the influence of much broader phenomena which affected not just British culture but that of Europe as a whole: changes in travel writing, developments in antiquarian and historical thought and a general rejection of the classically informed cosmopolitanism of the earlier period in favour of a clearer expression of national sentiment.

One of the underlying themes of the preceding chapters has been the evolving conceptualisation of the city from something akin to a cabinet of curiosities to an organic entity. Descriptions of cities in any language in the early part of our period – published or unpublished – were typically rendered as a catalogue of items, sometimes annotated to include brief descriptions: the principal churches; the most magnificent palaces; the number of squares, gates and bridges; and the important events with which the city was connected. These lists were a shorthand that informed the reader about the nature of the city's administrative structure (parishes, wards, *sestiere*); the influence of the church (the number of religious foundations); the wealth of the city and its nobility (the public buildings and the palazzi); the provision of public services and charitable foundations; the economy (the market, the gates); its defensive strength (the walls, the gates, the barracks) and the taste and munificence of its elite (in the lists of paintings, statues and other items which comprised the accounts of the palazzi).

This pattern was changing in the last third of the eighteenth century under the rising influence of sentiment, as travellers increasingly used the medium of travel writing as a record of their refined sensibility and their personal impressions of what they had seen. The late eighteenth century has been identified by some as a critical era in the emergence of modern subjectivity – the 'modern self', characterised by a sense of interior sensibility and individuality. The *ancien régime* self, by contrast, was constructed through surface effect rather than emotional depth: one's social identity was defined through the observance of externally imposed patterns of behaviour. By the end of the century, this had come to seem artificial and inauthentic to those who sought to be true to their inner feelings.[13] In terms of what travellers recorded, this shift can help us conceptualise some of the changes taking place in itineraries and ways of seeing. Visiting a city such as Rome, one had had to 'perform' the role of the polite traveller: visiting the antiquities, expressing the correct sentiment, making the appropriate allusions that demonstrated one's taste. Even in the early nineteenth century, an element of summary listing was often retained when it came to describing a particular town or city, as visitor and guide both attempted to impose some order on what was to be seen; but the exercise of describing a city also offered an opportunity for travellers to explore their own sense of self through their emotional response to the urban environment and to express their individuality through the originality of their observations. This encouraged a different kind of writing – one which demanded rather more literary artifice and descriptive imagery. Descriptions became more attentive to detail, more evocative of mood and atmosphere and frequently far more contrived. The aspiring literary traveller could no longer rely on a simple enumeration of what had been seen, but had to convey it in a lively and imaginative way that expressed his or her taste and sensibility. Tuscan architecture, such as the duomo of Florence, which had earlier been baldly characterised by its stripes of black and white marble, was, by the late eighteenth century, being compared variously to a zebra's coat, an Indian tea chest or a harlequin's jacket.[14]

The ostensibly dry and empirical mode of description dominated the published works of the first half of the eighteenth century, and even

---

[13] Charles Taylor, *Sources of the Self: The Making of the Modern Identity* (Cambridge, 1989), 185–98, 285–302; Wahrman, *The Making of the Modern Self*.

[14] Watkins, *Travels through Switzerland, Italy, Sicily*, I, 295; Walker, *Ideas Suggested on the Spot*, 335; Sadleir (ed.), *An Irish Peer on the Continent*, 126.

unpublished diaries and correspondence showed a similar tendency to collect and itemise information, rather than discuss it in a more discursive fashion. Observations on the peculiar social mores and forms of behaviour in foreign parts had always been part of the discourse of travel but at the start of our period these tended to be treated as curiosities – singularities, possibly dangerous, to be wondered at rather than understood. Thus, earlier writers such as Gilbert Burnet might comment at some length on the domestic arrangements of the Venetians, remarking on the strange design of their houses, the lack of domestic convenience and the peculiar polished red plaster floors.[15] Fifty years or so later, John Moore noted very similar features, but for him it was an opportunity to explore how Venetian domestic architecture was shaped by the need to facilitate commerce and trade and by the demands of the aquatic location. The red plaster floors were practical, being fire-resistant; the architecture was adapted to Venice's climate – the habit of living on the second floor was a response to the inevitable dampness emanating from the canals and also ensured better light.[16] The 'everyday' aspects of life in Venice – or indeed any other city – acquired greater validity as the object of description, being indicative of the manners and customs of that society, its degree of civility and of the principles that governed its order. For Moore, the distinctive and unusual properties of the buildings of Venice were the product of its topography, climate and local custom. The influence of Scottish Enlightenment sociology was evident.[17]

More generally, as we have seen, the Enlightenment interest in manners and customs, and the importance of recording one's own impressions, meant that the inhabitants of any given city and the personal encounters that took place became a much more substantive component of urban descriptions. For the earlier travellers, comments on social behaviour almost always pertained to the social elite, with whom the travellers mixed, rather than the 'popular customs' of the labouring classes. But by the later eighteenth, these had become interesting of themselves as manifestations of local culture, of the 'manners and customs' that gave a place its distinctive qualities.[18] This was not a topic that lent itself to lists: people could not be accommodated in

[15] Burnet, *Some Letters*, 150–1. [16] Moore, *View of Society and Manners*, I, 251–3.
[17] The *ODNB* describes Moore as 'very much a product of the Scottish Enlightenment'. H. L. Fulton, 'Moore, John (1729–1802)', *ODNB*, (www.oxforddnb.com/view/article/19130, accessed 31 July 2011).
[18] John Brand, *Observations on Popular Antiquities* (Newcastle, 1777); Marilyn Butler, 'Popular antiquarianism', in Iain McCalman (ed.), *An Oxford Companion to the Romantic Age: British Culture, 1776–1832* (Oxford, 1999), 328–38; Sweet, *Antiquaries*, 334–40.

summary descriptions of bridges, gates and fountains. They occupied the streets and the market places with bustle and activity; they hung their washing out to dry between the palazzi; they ate and drank; they sang and played music; and they loved, quarrelled and murdered. They contributed, as we saw in Naples, to the evocation of place and atmosphere, whereby the travellers sought 'to catch and convey the manners, dress, air, and folly', as John Owen put it.[19] By describing people, the observer was led into commentary on where they lived, where they bought and sold, where they partook of their pleasure: thus streets, rather than just the individual buildings, came into focus. Monuments such as the Coliseum were viewed from a different perspective as visitors noted the taverns and workshops occupying the vaults; and areas of the town associated with the lower orders – such as Trastevere in Rome – attracted new interest. In sum, the cities of early nineteenth-century accounts were far more obviously populated than those of a century before.

The descriptions of the early eighteenth century categorised and itemised everything; they gave the impression of orderly omniscience. All that was worth knowing about the city was encompassed within the totalising description. What could not be identified and accommodated was not included: hence the confusion and complaints of visitors at the anonymous ruins and fragments that they could not comprehend. By the end of our period, there is a sense of greater complexity in many accounts: an acknowledgement of partial knowledge and a willingness to see the potential of the unknown. It was sufficient to wonder and admire. Thus Adam Walker was surprised to see huge perpendicular 'flutings' along the city wall in Rome, extending 'for a mile in length'. He refused to believe his *cicerone*'s claim that they were the Baths of Domitian: 'what can downward chasms in a high wall have to do with baths?' he asked. Instead, he preferred simply to reflect on their sublime grandeur.[20] Walker's *Ideas Suggested on the Spot* is highly suggestive of a different way of perceiving and experiencing the physical spaces of the cities he visited. In the Baths of Titus, he was taken underground and described his sense of wonder at walking through the subterranean passages 'almost two miles, and to suppose that half of those passages remained yet unexplored'.[21] We have here the recognition of a city that existed beyond the limits of the tourist's knowledge or itinerary. Elsewhere, we start to find references to both the opportunity to explore and the possibility of getting lost. A visitor to Florence in 1816 was intrigued

[19] Owen, *Travels into Different Parts of Europe*, II, 95.
[20] Walker, *Ideas Suggested on the Spot*, 229.   [21] Ibid., 281.

by the myriad of alleys or 'obliquities', as he put it, which branched off the main streets 'in so strange a manner that a person walking by himself and not understanding the Florentine dialect may easily be embarrassed.'[22] William Forbes was a man who liked to take 'solitary perambulations' rather than relying always on a guide; this could, however, lead him into difficulties: on another occasion he and a companion tried to find their own way to the catacombs, but they 'very soon found ourselves in a part of the City to which we were both total Strangers, & neither his skill in Italian nor mine very well sufficed to procure a direction.'[23] Lewis Engelbach suffered a similarly disorientating experience as a consequence of dismissing his guide before finding his own way down from St Elmo into Naples. 'I totally lost my way, and became bewildered in a maze of small narrow lanes, the poor inhabitants of which answered my repeated enquiries with a good-natured, but to me unintelligible patois.'[24] For both Forbes and Engelbach, Naples was not just a city of fashionable society and grandiose architecture, but a place where the conventions of elite cosmopolitan society that sustained the Grand Tour could break down when they strayed away from the established conventions of 'grand tourist' behaviour: their inability to communicate with the locals to procure directions was symptomatic of their finding themselves in an environment in which their education gave them no advantages, offered them no means to interpret or understand where they were. They had entered upon the unfamiliar and the unknown.

This is all a long way from Eleanor Lavish throwing away the Baedecker and dragging Lucy Honeychurch off to 'drift' through the backstreets of Florence in pursuit of 'local colour', but it is still a significant departure from earlier modes of seeing, where the traveller was dependent upon the guide who showed him or her a prescribed set of antiquities or art that *ought* to be seen.[25] Yet, even in 1820, Jane Waldie was advising her readers that the best way to become familiar with Rome was simply to wander, unguided, and to delight in the unexpected discovery of 'some lonely column or ruined portico'.[26] From an exercise in recognition and certainties, the idiom was changing to one of exploration and discovery. The distinction between traveller and tourist, the latter being tied to hackneyed itineraries, the former engaged in the pursuit of authenticity, had yet to be fully articulated in the discourse of travel,[27] but in some of the travellers – like Forbes or

---

[22] Coxe, *Picture of Italy*, 379.
[23] Forbes journal NLS MS 1541, fol. 174; MS 1542, fol. 133.
[24] Engelbach, *Naples and the Campagna Felice*, 17.
[25] E. M. Forster, *A Room with a View* (Harmondsworth, 1986), 36–9.
[26] Waldie, *Sketches Descriptive of Italy*, I, 339.
[27] Buzard, *The Beaten Track*, esp. 1–6.

Engelbach – we can detect an incipient willingness to look beyond the prescriptive advice of the travel literature. Wandering or rambling through the streets was, of course, a well-established practice amongst inhabitants of London, and had spawned a specific genre of literature.[28] But it implies on the part of the pedestrian, walking through the streets rather than riding in a coach or following a *cicerone*, a level of engagement with the quotidian as well as the magnificent in the cities which they visited; a perspective which would encourage a different mode of observation and representation. We should also, perhaps, consider whether this move away from prescriptive itineraries was connected to practices of tourism in Britain: many of those travelling to Italy (including Forbes) had already engaged upon travel within the British Isles where self-guided exploration was far easier (no language problems, unless in Wales or the Scottish Highlands) and less threatening. There is certainly evidence from the journals of travellers such as John Byng of resistance to the advice of guidebooks and a determination to go beyond the artificial creation of the tourist itinerary to find the undocumented and the 'authentic'.[29] This willingness to go 'off the beaten track', as a later generation would term it, also reflected the emergent sense that towns and cities had characters – a combination of people, climate, topography and history – that could only be discovered through personal investigation.

It should be remembered, however, that these were also developments that had been stimulated by practical changes in the way that people moved about cities. As we have already seen, the later eighteenth century saw an increase in the number of travellers who were willing to forgo a guide, whether for reasons of economy or simply personal preference. At the same time, there was an ever-increasing availability of guides containing directions and street plans, thus enabling the visitor to find their own way through the town with much greater ease and independence. Maps and plans had become a pervasive feature of daily life by the end of the century, being used much more widely as a means of representing information, whether estate maps for absentee landlords and surveyors, enclosure maps for Parliament or town plans for urban improvement and development. The travellers of the later eighteenth century were therefore more map-literate than their predecessors. There were also

---

[28] Alison O'Byrne, 'The art of walking: representing urban pedestrianism in early nineteenth-century London', *Romanticism*, 14:2 (2008), 94–107; Paul Tankard, 'Johnson and the walkable city', *Eighteenth-Century Life*, 32:1 (2007), 1–22.

[29] William Rupp, 'A new perspective on British identity: the travel journals of John Byng, 1781–94', University of Warwick Ph.D. thesis (2011).

other technologies of urban navigation becoming available: street names were increasingly standardised and were marked at both street level and on maps; house numbering was also being introduced across the major European cities (not necessarily to help the visitor, but in order to facilitate fiscal extraction).[30] In London, John Trusler advised newcomers that 'you may always find your way, if, before you set out, you will consult a map of London, and attend to the names of the streets and courts, which are always painted on a board against the houses, at the corner of each street or court.'[31] And so too Charles Abbot found that the streets of Florence were similarly inscribed in 1784, noting that 'The Houses are Lofty, and the Name of Each Street is Painted at the House Corner, and the Number upon the Wall.'[32] As a consequence of these changes, we find travellers making more frequent reference to street names, describing their passage from one part of a town to another, locating buildings on streets, showing a greater awareness of the town, not as a composite collection of buildings, but as a network of connected spaces.

This book has also sought to emphasise the importance of recognising the presence of a very significant number of women amongst those who made the tour of Italy. By ignoring their presence, or simply conflating them with men, we achieve a distorted impression of what the experience of travel was like – it was far less homosocial than is often assumed – and also misunderstand the nature of Anglo-Italian cultural ties. Women, as well as men, were great admirers of Italy in the eighteenth century, and through travel, correspondence and publication were important mediators of Italian culture (Anne Miller brought the practice of the *conversazione* back to Batheaston, as well as publishing her *Letters from Italy*). Secondly, the increasing heterogeneity of the travelling class – of which women were an important but not the only element – was a crucial factor in the evolving diversification of the tour away from the original classical paradigm derived from the masculine traditions of civic humanism. This is not to say, however, that gender did not have an impact on what was seen or how it was experienced, or that gender

---

[30] David Garrioch, 'House names, shop signs and social organization in western European cities, 1500–1900', *Urban History*, 21:1 (1994), 37, 42; Reuben Rose-Redwood, 'Indexing the great ledger of the community: urban house numbering, city directories, and the production of spatial legibility', *Journal of Historical Geography*, 34:2 (2008), 286–310.

[31] John Trusler, *The London Adviser and Guide* (1786), 135. See also Alison O'Byrne, 'Walking, rambling and promenading in eighteenth-century London: a literary and cultural history', University of York, Ph.D. thesis (2003), 9.

[32] Abbot journal TNA PRO 30/9/41, 166–7.

norms were not reinforced through travel. As preceding chapters have demonstrated, there were some very practical constraints on what both men and women could or could not see: certain spaces were out of bounds for both sexes. There were also clear differences in emphasis in terms of what men and women were expected to be interested in, the most obvious being the assumption that women would have a lower tolerance threshold for the study of antiquities but a better appreciation of art. This was borne out by many of the female travellers, such as the Duchess of Leinster or Sarah Bentham, but there were equally women – Anne Miller, Sydney Morgan or Charlotte Eaton, for example – who displayed genuine interest in what antiquities revealed about the places they visited, even as they took care to distance themselves rhetorically from the discourse of 'spoony antiquarians'.[33] Guides were clearly accustomed to showing women as well as men around the sights, and adjusted their itineraries accordingly (to avoid over-exertion or improprieties) and tailored their information to suit the anticipated interest of a female audience.

Sociability was always a critical element of the Grand Tour: in terms of the tour's educational value, it was essential in preparing the young man for an adult life of negotiating fashionable society. But it was also key to the enjoyment of the tour itself: it is overwhelmingly evident that the reaction of travellers to particular places was deeply influenced by the extent to which they found themselves a part of congenial company, and congeniality for most men was improved by the presence of women. We know less about the sociability of the Grand Tour for the first half of the eighteenth century. This is partly because the more detailed comments have come down to us from female correspondents and diarists, and in the earlier period there were fewer female travellers to record such matters. Young men and their tutors tended not to dwell on social engagements, largely because their letters were intended to demonstrate time well spent in acquiring taste and virtue. As George Parker well knew, what his father wanted to hear was that he was fully occupied in Rome in 'learning Architecture' and 'going about the curiosities of the place', rather than details of the dalliances he had entered into.[34] So there is some degree of optical illusion when we look at the journals of Derbishire, Gibbes or Bentham with their daily accounts of tea drinking, walks, *conversazione* and balls, but nonetheless the presence of women was unquestionably a stimulus to such activities. These journals, and also those of male travellers such as Sir William Forbes, demonstrate

---

[33] Morgan, *Italy*, II, 186.
[34] Parker to Earl of Macclesfield, 26 Apr. 1721, BL Stowe MS 750, fol. 368.

that by the 1780s and 1790s the British formed a sizeable and sociable community in the major cities. They entertained each other and, to a lesser extent, were entertained by local Italian society, with a succession of group outings, receptions, balls and even cricket matches in the Borghese gardens or on the beach at Pozzuoli.[35] Henry Matthews complained that the English ladies had turned Rome into a watering place; his implied reproach was directed at their assumed inability to appreciate the significance of their surroundings, but it is also a reminder of the extent to which the major Italian cities had become part of a wider network of communities of fashionable expatriate society throughout mainland Europe.[36]

Female travellers, as we have seen, tended to record the rituals of sociability in greater detail. They have also been particularly associated with comments concerning the 'everyday' encountered by walking through the streets, the practicalities of domestic life, the social conventions and manners of society; indeed, many of the more perceptive and detailed observations discussed in this book were made by women. This is not altogether surprising, given that the prevailing expectation at the time was that women would find such matters – the domestic, the particular, the personal – of greater interest than would men, as it was their 'natural' sphere of activity. Their upbringing and the dictates of social convention meant that by and large they conformed to these cultural norms, as we saw in Chapter 1. Certainly, the comments of individuals such as Sarah Bentham or the Dean of Norwich's travelling companion, Miss Derbishire, offer rather different perspectives on Rome or Naples from those of their male counterparts. But whilst it is important to be aware of the extent to which the experience of any given city was gendered, it would be crudely reductionist to attribute greater interest in day to day living arrangements or the practice of cleanliness solely to women. Such matters were never an exclusively feminine prerogative: it was Sir James Hall, for example, who noted the arrangements for taking a shower in the private houses near the barracks in Pompeii.[37] The 'everyday' had become validated as an object of study in its own right because it was the very stuff of 'manners and customs'; it could illuminate, as John Moore recognised, the study of past and present societies.

---

[35] For references to cricket matches, see Forbes journal NLS MS 1541, fol. 212; Gibbes journal TNA PRO 30/9/7/10, 28 Mar. 1790; Oppé (ed.), *Memoirs of Thomas Jones of Penkerrig*, 93; Taylor (ed.), *Taylor Papers*, 9.
[36] Matthews, *Diary of an Invalid*, 163. On expatriates in Paris, see Robin Eagles, *Francophilia in English Society, 1748–1815* (Basingstoke, 1999), 94–119.
[37] Hall journal NLS MS 6327, fol. 40.

Gender was not consistently the most important factor in shaping a visitor's experience: birth, education, wealth and age all had a bearing for both sexes. Ann Flaxman's beer-swilling ascent and unceremonious descent on her bottom of Vesuvius would have been inconceivable for Lady Caroline Holland, for example, even assuming the latter to have had the stamina. But women's gender did make a difference: in some instances they were constrained by gendered beliefs and customary practices, but the very fact that they were women was also to their advantage: they were effectively freer to have a less prescriptive and more personal experience of Italy. And, for all that women authors only made up a fraction of the total of travel books published by the 1820s, their influence should not be underestimated; Benjamin Colbert has suggested that they were 'statistically more likely than men to capture the public mood and become popular (and controversial)'.[38] Certainly, as far as the historian is concerned, the female travellers of the late eighteenth and early nineteenth centuries broaden our understanding of the social experience of travel and remind us that they were not simply docile companions in a predominantly masculine institution; rather, they were active participants in an experience which allowed them to gain personal and cultural breadth, knowledge and useful connections.

The case for the gradual emergence of a more complex view of the city as an entity that evolved and changed over time, and whose history could be read through its physical fabric, has also been rehearsed throughout the preceding chapters. This development was not unconnected with the observation of the everyday noted above, but owed as much to the greater sense of historicism that became manifest during the eighteenth century. Throughout the early modern period, Europe's educated elite had devoted great efforts to devise chronologies of the past. They could divide history up into chronicles of reigns and empires in masterly fashion, but they had been less interested in or indeed able to differentiate – the periods of the past in terms of social or political development.[39] This approach to the study of the past was challenged from two directions: one being the influence of Enlightenment historical sociology, the other being the increasing sophistication of antiquarian research. The two were not, of course, unconnected and the respective practitioners drew upon many of the same intellectual currents, but the published œuvres were distinct.

---

[38] Colbert, 'Bibliography of British travel writing'.
[39] On the 'death' of the chronicle, see D. R. Woolf, *Reading History in Early Modern England* (Cambridge, 2000), 11–78.

As far as history writing was concerned, two significant changes took place that are of particular relevance here: first, was the rise of philosophical and conjectural history, which sought to explain the historical development of society and civilisation, not least through the study of manners and customs. Second, was the emergence of a new focus of study, that is the study of national history, as opposed to classical history or the narrative of recent political events. Prior to the eighteenth century, the history of medieval and renaissance Europe had not been the subject of considered historical analysis. But Voltaire's *Essai sur les moeurs et l'ésprit des nations* (1756) followed by the works of historians such as Robertson and Gibbon, filled that gap, telling the story of Europe's triumphal recovery from barbarism towards the civilised and enlightened – and apparently increasingly peaceful – world of the eighteenth century. The Europe of the eighteenth century enjoyed greater prosperity and greater liberty than had ever existed under Rome, and by extension, the achievements of its civilisation were more secure. This was a story in which the wealth and dynamism of Italian city states, not just Rome, had major roles to play.[40] Travellers became increasingly knowledgeable about the conflict between the Guelfs and the Ghibellines, the fate of Rienzo, the rise of the Medici or the fortunes of the Sforza. Changing literary tastes, such as the popularity of Dante's poetry and a fascination with chivalry, were also a factor in directing attention towards the thirteenth, fourteenth and fifteenth centuries which had hitherto been little regarded. The currency gained by Voltaire's *Essai sur les moeurs* and Robertson's *View of the Reign of the Emperor Charles V* clearly had an influence upon the way in which visitors approached former city states such as Florence and encouraged them to interpret the physical environment as testimony to its earlier commercial and artistic importance. Equally, as we saw in Chapter 3, Gibbon's powerful narrative provided the framework through which to conceptualise Rome's history after the city's fall.

Italians were also writing, and had written, their own histories too, of course, and their presentation of the past can also be seen to have contributed to shaping British attitudes to Italy. Many travellers were familiar with Machiavelli's history of Florence or Sarpi and Contarini on the Venetian Republic, and although he never achieved the recognition of Gibbon or Voltaire, Giannone's history of the Neapolitan kingdoms was certainly a contributory factor to the more sympathetic re-evaluation of the city and its kingdom in the last third of the eighteenth

---

[40] O'Brien, *Narratives of Enlightenment*.

century that we saw in Chapter 4. The influence of Italian historians upon British perceptions of Italy would become rather more evident in the period immediately after 1820. Italy's republican era – and therefore the cities themselves – attracted greater attention from the 1820s, both because of the topicality lent by movements such as the Carbonari and because of the influence of publications such as Sismondi's *Histoire des républiques Italiannes du moyenne age* (1809–18) which located an alternative to Napoleonic centralisation in the municipalities of medieval Italy as the basis for a united Italian state.[41] Although Sismondi's direct influence was apparent upon only a handful of travellers such as Sydney Morgan (visiting Italy in 1819), as Chapter 6 indicated, the longer-term effect was to direct the attention of British travellers towards the history of former Republics such as Lucca, Pisa and Pistoia, as well as the better-known examples of Florence and Genoa, and to valorise the study of the buildings erected in that period.

There was much more reference to Italian scholarship in the field of antiquarianism, however. Given the dependence of the British on Italian *ciceroni*, particularly in Rome and Naples, this is only to be expected. Moreover, the antiquities of ancient Rome were regarded as the common heritage of the educated elite of western Europe, not just of the Italians; indeed, the British not infrequently expressed the view that they would be better custodians of the antiquities than were the modern Romans. Antiquarian research was either assimilated directly through a *cicerone* such as Ficoroni, or by British antiquaries/dealers such as Gavin Hamilton, Thomas Jenkins or James Byres, who had made their career as antiquaries and were part of the antiquarian community of Rome.[42] There was, nevertheless, a reluctance to engage with Italian antiquarianism beyond the level of collecting and the pursuit of taste; Edward Gibbon was, of course, the outstanding exception to this rule. This was partly determined by a distaste for pedantry, but also from a desire to maintain some distance from the particular enthusiasm of the local patriot. Thus, Ficoroni's interest in the continuity between ancient and modern Rome and his fascination with the city that was still buried were

---

[41] Adrian Lyttelton, 'The national question in Italy', in R. Porter and M. Teich (eds.), *The National Question in Europe in Historical Context* (Cambridge, 1994), 74.

[42] The literature on these figures is extensive: see the series of articles by Brinsley Ford in *Apollo* (1974); Bignamini and Hornsby, *Digging and Dealing*; Brendan Cassidy, 'Gavin Hamilton, Thomas Pitt and statues for Stowe', *Burlington Magazine*, 1221 (2004), 806–14; Viccy Coltman, *Classical Sculpture and the Culture of Collecting in Britain since 1760* (Oxford, 2009), chs. 2–4; David R. Marshall, Susan Russell and Karin Wolfe (eds.), *Roma Britannica: Art Patronage and Cultural Exchange in Eighteenth-Century Rome* (2011); S. R. Pierce, 'Thomas Jenkins in Rome', *Antiquaries Journal*, 45 (1965), 200–29; Jonathan Scott, *The Pleasures of Antiquity* (New Haven and London, 2003).

disregarded by his clients; Piranesi's determination to establish the indigenous origins of Roman architecture amongst the Etruscans, rather than the Greeks, and his imaginative renderings of the ancient city were routinely dismissed; Catholic antiquaries' recognition of the importance of palaeochristian antiquities were not taken up for more than a century, until John Chetwode Eustace, a Catholic himself, recognised their import. Even the insights of Eschinardi and Venuti published in mid-century were not incorporated into British texts for over fifty years. Similarly, in Florence, Gibbon aside once more, few visitors displayed much interest in the Florentines' research on Etruscan antiquities and civilisation: their focus was rather on the treasures of the tribuna and the Pitti.[43] But, nonetheless, the level of antiquarian knowledge increased over the period, particularly in the context of architecture: descriptions of buildings became more detailed and more technical, as were the accompanying illustrations, and the inclusion of ground plans became more commonplace. The debt of Lumisden, Forsyth and Eustace to Roman antiquaries noted in Chapter 3, for example, was in marked contrast to most of their predecessors. Architectural literacy amongst the travelling public had also increased, facilitated by the increasing availability of architectural texts in the public domain, and by the fact that, in order to succeed as an architect at home, would-be British architects had to study in Italy. This meant that more detailed studies of Rome's architectural monuments were being made – a number of which were published in order to demonstrate their authors' credentials[44] – and that these same architects were also showing British visitors around the city in order to earn additional income and to attract potential future patrons.[45]

This sophistication was also part of a more analytical approach to antiquities that was increasingly receptive to the artefact and its appearance, rather than simply its relationship to a text, a person or an event. Whether it was the study of classical sculpture, monumental tombs or gothic architecture, antiquarian scholarship in eighteenth-century Europe was characterised by a greater analytical rigour of form and design, a clearer appreciation of the visual and aesthetic properties of

---

[43] James Byres also started collections towards a history of the Etruscans: NLS MS Dept 184/4.

[44] Frank Salmon, 'The impact of the archaeology of Rome on British architects and their work, 1750–1840', in Clare Hornsby (ed.), *The Impact of Italy: The Grand Tour and Beyond* (Rome, 2000), 219–43; Salmon, *Building on Ruins*, 26–52.

[45] Kerry Bristol, 'The social world of James "Athenian" Stuart', in Susan Weber Soros (ed.), *James 'Athenian' Stuart 1713–88: The Rediscovery of Antiquity* (New Haven and London, 2007), 147–94.

objects or buildings and an attempt to categorise antiquities (archaeo-logical, sculptural, artistic or textual) according to a chronological framework of typological development. Coupled with this was a growing corpus of aesthetic theoretical literature through which individuals could analyse their response to the beautiful and the sublime and also describe it. Winckelmann famously led the way in applying this approach to sculpture, but, as we saw in Chapter 3, there was also a much greater readiness to identify the different periods of architectural style, so that the visitor could trace the history of Rome through the solid simplicity of Etruscan masonry to the ornate excess and hubris of Empire, followed by the inevitable decline and corruption of both style and government. But other cities could be viewed in this way too: the attentive observer, as Joseph Forsyth pointed out, 'may discover the history of architecture in the streets of Venice'.[46] Accompanying this shift in emphasis was a greater recognition of the potential of any antiquarian artefact to yield up information about the past and it is here in particular that we find a confluence of antiquarian and historical thought. The 'manners and customs' of antiquity could be studied through the everyday objects, revealed so compellingly at Herculaneum and Pompeii, as well as the manners and customs of the modern Italians.

There was one area of antiquarian research where the British had less in common with the Italian antiquaries and that was the study of medi-eval and gothic antiquities. Italian antiquaries, such as Ludovico Muratori, were certainly interested in the middle ages, but Muratori's perspective was primarily a textual one and his focus was upon the religious rituals, customs and beliefs of the medieval period, not the architecture.[47] For all that Italians took pride in their medieval buildings – and the contemporary guidebooks to Venice, Naples or Florence demonstrably show that they did – there was little interest in the gothic as an architectural style and certainly no enthusiasm for debating the precise origin and location of the pointed arch or the relationship of Romanesque to gothic. These were questions that were investigated by British antiquaries in what was an essentially northern European debate. The enthusiasm with which the subject was pursued derived from the significance of the gothic as an expression of a national English style and of English national character. (Although discussion was generally framed in terms of 'English' history, the gothic was a style with which a broader British constituency could identify.) No such con-nections were made in Italy, however. Whilst the Campo Santo at Pisa

---

[46] Eustace, *Classical Tour*, I, 68.
[47] Ludovico Muratori, *Antiquitates italicae medii aevi*, 6 vols. (1738–42).

exemplified the city's liberty and wealth before it fell to Florence, the pointed arches which so intrigued the English antiquaries did not carry the same freight of meaning for the Italians. It is unsurprising, then, that, as noted in Chapter 6, there was a reluctance on the part of travellers to admit that any of the gothic buildings of Italy were a match for the glories of York Minster or Westminster Abbey; Rome in particular, the *non pareil* in so many other contexts, was found deficient in this regard.

This book has been primarily concerned with cities, with spaces and places, but the relationship between travel and national identity has been implicit throughout. Other historians, notably Gerald Newman, have argued that during the eighteenth century a stronger sense of English identity was forged against the elite 'cosmopolitanism' associated with cultural practices such as the Grand Tour.[48] The tour's raison d'être was undeniably cosmopolitan in its pursuit of a common cultural heritage of art, literature and antiquities. Although this study has focussed on the British, it is important to remember that they were fellow travellers with an international mix of French, Germans, Dutch, Russians, other Europeans and also Americans who read the same texts,[49] viewed the same antiquities, patronised the same artists and expressed very similar sentiments and reactions to many of the British.[50] This cosmopolitanism, and the ideals of Enlightenment universalism and the neo-classicism that sustained it, ran counter to longstanding traditions of xenophobia and local chauvinism, as well as the quickening sense of national particularism that Newman identifies. It was this aspect of the Grand Tour, as well as its suspect association with foreign fashions, effeminate manners and aristocratic immorality, that accounts for much of the suspicion with which it was regarded by those who stayed behind. But even though the classical Grand Tour was predicated upon values that transcended national boundaries, it was also about experiencing difference. Foreign travel was always widely praised for the opportunity it presented to remind the individual of the benefits and superiority of his or her own

---

[48] Newman, *Rise of English Nationalism*, esp. 1–47; on elite cosmopolitanism see also Eagles, *Francophilia*.

[49] Their education was based upon a common foundation of Latin texts, but there was also a high degree of commonality in the published guides: French texts such as those by Barthélemy, Cochin, Dupaty, Lalande, Misson, Richard and Saint-Non were widely read by British (and other) travellers; similarly, key texts in English, such as Addison's *Remarks on Several Parts of Italy* were translated into French.

[50] For a European perspective on the representation of Italy through the literature of the Grand Tour (and subsequently) see Marie-Madeleine Martinet, *Le voyage d'Italie dans les literatures européenes* (Paris, 1996). See also de Seta, *L'Italia del Grand Tour*, esp. 155–94 and Attilo Brilli, *Il viaggio in Italia: storia di una grande tradizione culturale* (Rome, 2006).

country.[51] Yet, the return home for many people was a relief: as Adam Walker remarked, 'God send us safe in Old England again, for (notwithstanding the fine sights) that is the country to really live in.'[52] Travellers did not leave their sense of English or British identity behind them at Dover; they hugged it around them like a protective cloak whenever they felt particularly threatened or discomfited by foreign surroundings, and they returned with a firm sense of their own national superiority intact.

Whether this sense of national superiority was English or British is a moot point: contemporaries were as inconsistent and ambiguous in their usage of English and British as most English are today, and it would be unwise to attempt to draw hard and fast distinctions.[53] However, it is noticeable that the more introspective comments about national characteristics tended to be framed in terms of Englishness and discussions of the nation's international and imperial role in terms of Britishness. Thus, the exercise of finding fault served to reinforce those characteristics that were generally assumed to be innately English. Whilst the British found much to admire in Italy from the past, their experience of difference in the present was frequently framed in negative terms. By defining what was wrong or what was odd, they asserted a sense of shared norms and values that provided a foundation upon which national identity might be built.[54] In this sense, Italy was no different from France, Germany or the other parts of Europe and beyond through which the British travelled. Indeed, the Italians could be interchanged with the French in many cases as the foil against which English qualities were defined: both nations were associated with servility and a loss of independence; with effeminacy and an excess of luxury; with Catholicism, superstition and hypocrisy; with the want of cleanliness; and with the execrable quality of the food. Some criticisms were more specific to Italy, however, notably the suspect sexual and marital mores and the custom of the *cicisbeo*; the alleged confinement of women; and the jealousy and violence of the men, all of which drew on cultural stereotypes that went back to the sixteenth century.[55]

---

[51] Lassels, *Voyage of Italy*, preface; Duncombe (ed.), *Letters from Italy*, 119–20.

[52] Walker, *Ideas Suggested on the Spot*, 183.

[53] Paul Langford, *Englishness Identified: Manners and Character, 1650–1850* (Oxford, 1999), 12–14.

[54] The literature on the construction of national identity in this period is extensive: see in particular Colley, *Britons*, Newman; *Rise of English Nationalism*; and Kathleen Wilson, *The Island Race: Englishness, Empire and Gender in the Eighteenth Century* (2003), esp. 1–28.

[55] See in particular Andrews, *Characteristical Views of the Past and Present State*; Canepa, 'From degenerate scoundrel to noble savage'.

Travellers arrived in Italy with these prejudices well entrenched. As John Patteson admitted to his mother, 'I am astonished when I consider with how despicable an opinion of the Italians I entered Italy. I don't know how I came by it, but most assuredly I expected to have found them a set of people universally addicted to every species of villany and vice.' He was surprised and gratified to find those whom he met were more congenial than both he and his ever-anxious mother expected.[56] To a certain extent, it is clear that the Italian *ciceroni*, innkeepers and *valets de place* also deliberately played up to the expectations of the British: they knew what the foreign visitors expected and obligingly provided it, as their livelihoods depended upon the flow of money from foreign pockets. Obviously, they showed the travellers what they wanted to see, be it antiquities, paintings or nuns behind a grate in a convent, but there was also an element of performing a part for the satisfaction of the visitors, who then had their national stereotypes comfortingly reinforced. Thus, in Naples, they claimed to be murderous *banditti*; in Venice, the gondoliers offered to procure sexual services for their male clients as well as supplying a vocal rendition of *Gerusalemme Liberata*; and at Imola, 'a good humoured friar' showed Elizabeth Gibbes' party the scourges with which the monks allegedly flagellated themselves.[57] The Italians were not passive agents in this process of cultural encounter and reflected back to the foreigners what they wanted to see or hear, the better to secure their custom.

The expression of Englishness that emerges from these travel narratives offers no real surprises and mirrored many of the characteristics that foreign observers detected in the English: in contrast to the Italians, they were modern, they were clean, they were Protestant, they were industrious, they were independent and enjoyed liberty (men and women alike) and they were honest.[58] (The less reputable behaviour of the wilder young men on the tour was rarely discussed in the context of national characteristics but rather deplored in moralising literature back home.) The explanations that were put forward to explain the differences between Italy and Britain were partly climatic, notably in Naples, where the warmth encouraged lassitude, indolence and sensuality and a greater propensity to hot-headed violence. But – particularly in the more temperate northern states – such arguments held less sway and explanations for the peculiarities of Italian behaviour drew on analyses of the

---

[56] Cubitt, Mackley and Wilson (eds.), *Great Tour of John Patteson*, 233.
[57] Gibbes journal TNA PRO 30/9/7/10, 4 Nov. 1789.
[58] See also the chapter headings in Langford, *Englishness Identified*: energy, candour, decency, taciturnity, reserve, eccentricity.

role of legal and political institutions in shaping national character, reflecting the view of William Robertson that 'the dispositions and manners of men are formed by their situation, and arise from the state of society in which they live'.[59] Further, for much of the eighteenth century, it was generally accepted, Anglo-Saxon anti-gallicanism notwithstanding, that all Europeans were descended from a common gothic origin. Thus, the variations between English liberty and foreign despotism were the product of historical circumstance and there was no more a racial basis to the critique of Italians than there was to that of the French.[60] Accordingly, it was argued that the Italians had been rendered servile by domestic disunion which had permitted foreign conquest and the loss of liberty.[61] Benighted Catholic nations suffered alike under arbitrary and absolute rule. In England, by contrast, liberty flourished hand in hand with Protestantism and engendered the kind of manly independence that could never submit to a lifetime of lounging around Venice in a gondola or dancing attendance on a woman as a *cicisbeo*. Hence, the value of seeing for oneself the different forms of government and society in Europe to appreciate the blessings of the English constitution.

Over time, the force of some of these criticisms was abated; in particular, the stridency of anti-Catholic sentiment, as we have seen, was moderated amongst many travellers by the later eighteenth century as the force went out of anti-Catholicism in political life. Protestantism was certainly still a crucial component of British identity, particularly amongst the majority of the population that never travelled in Europe, and with the establishment of Protestant chaplaincies in the nineteenth century, it became a more visible focus for expatriate society. However, it was accompanied by a greater openness to the merits as well as the offences of Roman Catholic Christianity.[62] Anglo-Saxon exceptionalism, which was closely tied to Protestantism in the nineteenth-century imagination, was also becoming stronger. The timeless universalism of the classical Grand Tour was giving way to an approach to Italy which was more historically aware, more diverse in its foci and more ready to

---

[59] William Robertson, *The History of America*, 2 vols. (1777), I, 417; see also David Hume, 'Of national characters', in David Hume, *Essays Moral, Literary and Political* (1742).

[60] Kidd, *British Identities before Nationalism*, 211–49.

[61] Andrews, *Characteristical Views of the Past and Present State*, 196.

[62] The formal presence of an Anglican ministry in Rome dates back to 1816, although Anglican chaplaincies had existed in port cities such as Livorno or Genoa from an earlier date to minister to the English factories. On the development of Anglican chaplaincies in Europe, see John E. Pinnington, 'Anglican chaplaincies in post-Napoleonic Europe: a strange variation on the Pax Britannica', *Church History*, 39:3 (1970), 327–44.

question the superiority that was once accorded to Rome. And just as the aristocratic cosmopolitanism of neo-classicism was being eroded, so too the sense of a common European 'gothic' heritage was gradually ceding to a more restrictive view, that confined the traditions of Anglo Saxon liberties and virtue to the German and Nordic nations. Southern Latin nations, such as Italy, Spain and even France, were categorised as ethnically distinct, and there were increasingly racial undertones to the characterisation of the Italians of the south as indolent and lazy.[63]

This study has been principally concerned with the construction of a sense of place in the major cities of the Grand Tour and its evolution from a ritualised performance of taste devised for a masculine social elite to a more subjective and personal experience that was accessible to a broader range of travellers of both sexes. The two are related because the articulation of the distinctiveness of a specific town or city in terms of its physical environment, its atmosphere and its history became clearer over the course of our period as travellers used the medium of travel writing to explore their own subjectivity and to express their personal response to the places through which they travelled. They sought to discover and describe not just the character of the people whom they encountered, but also the character of the towns and cities in which they stayed. The relationship of travellers to the built environment changed demonstrably both in terms of how they found their way around urban space, but also in terms of how they conceptualised their surroundings. This book has also offered a story of changing taste: on one level this can be explained simply through the shifting composition of the travelling public, itself the consequence of greater affluence in Britain. Although their participation could be seen as an act of cultural emulation, the priorities, tastes and agenda of the middling sort could not be smoothly subsumed within the rigid framework of the classical tour that sustained aristocratic hegemony. But not even the aristocracy with whom the Grand Tour originated could be untouched by the changes in British society or by Britain's increasingly dominant role in international geo-politics. It may be objected that those who travelled to Italy were only a small minority of the overall population; the significance of their experiences, therefore, should not be assumed to be representative of the population as a whole. The point is a valid one, but at the same time, it should also be remembered that there was a far larger penumbra of readers at home whose knowledge of Europe – and of Italy in particular – was mediated through

---

[63] Kidd, *British Identities before Nationalism*, 212; Moe, *View from Vesuvius*. There is an irony in the fact that even as the British supported the ideal of Italian unification, they became more aware of the regional variations within the geo-political unit of Italy itself.

these texts, and whose imagined identification with what it meant to be English or British was reinforced at the same time that their knowledge of foreign cities and civilisation was extended. The reactions of visitors to Italy and to Italian cities has also to be understood as part of the complex process through which a clearer sense of national identity and self-confidence came to be expressed.

Bibliography

MANUSCRIPT SOURCES

BODLEIAN LIBRARY OXFORD

MS Douce 67 anon., 'Remarks on several parts of Flanders, Brabant, France and Italy in the Year 1717'.

MS Don. c. 181, journal of Richard Chiswell, 1696.

MS Eng. misc. d. 213 journal of Edmund Dewes, 1773.

MS Douce d. 36 correspondence of Francis Douce and Thomas Kerrich.

MSS Finch e. 14–e17 journals of Robert Finch, 1814–15.

MS Eng. misc. c. 444 journal of Sir Martin Folkes, 1733–4.

MS Eng. c. 7052–3 journal of Charlotte Lindsey, 1815.

MS Eng. Lett. c. 368 correspondence of John Nichols.

MS Rawl. d. 1180–6 journals of Richard Rawlinson, 1720–6.

MS Add. A 366 'A journal kept by Mr Tracy and Mr Dentand during their travels through France and Italy', 1766.

MS. Eng. misc. c. 206 Thomas Twisden, tour upon the continent 1693–4.

BRITISH LIBRARY

Add. MS 75743 Althorp papers.

Add. MS 39780 correspondence of John and Ann Flaxman with relatives in England, 1787–94.

Add. MS 39786 journal of John Flaxman, 1787–8.

Add. MS 39787 journal of Mrs Ann Flaxman, 1787–8.

Add. MS 40759 journal of Sir Philip Francis, 1772.

Add. MS 36249 journal of William Freeman, 1726–8.

Add. MS 39790 correspondence of William Gunn and John Flaxman, 1793–1821.

Add. MS 3488 correspondence of John Baker Holroyd and his family, 1764–5.

Add. MSS 6728, 6729, 6736–40, 6743–5, 6749 notebooks of Thomas Kerrich.

Stowe MS 752 correspondence of Smart Lethieullier and Charles Lyttelton.

Add. MS 15763, fol. 114, journal of Jeremiah Milles, 1733–4.

Add. MSS 58315–9, journals of Andrew Mitchell, 1732–4.

Add. 48244 memoirs of the Earl of Morley, 1793–4.

Stowe MS 750 correspondence of George Parker and his father, first Earl of Macclesfield, 1719–22.

Add. MS 33127 correspondence of Thomas Pelham and his parents, the Earl and Countess of Chichester, 1777.

Add. MS 22978 correspondence of Richard Pococke with his mother, 1733–4.

Add. MS 38837 journal of James Robson 1787.

Add. MS 47031 correspondence of Edward Southwell and Lord Percival, 1725–6.

Add. MS 19941 correspondence of Edward Thomas with Jeremiah Milles, 1751.

Add. MS 35378 correspondence of Philip Yorke and his uncle, second Earl of Hardwick, 1779.

BUCKINGHAMSHIRE ARCHIVES

Centre for Buckinghamshire Studies D – DR/8/2 correspondence of William Drake.

CAMBRIDGE UNIVERSITY LIBRARY

Add. MS 8670 (c) /1–40 correspondence of Thomas Brand with his sister Susan Brand.

Add. MS 3545–55 diaries of Sir Richard Colt Hoare on the continent.

Add. MS 4155 Sir Richard Colt Hoare's notes on paintings.

Palmer MS c. 5 journal of Peter Cowling, 1786.

DURHAM UNIVERSITY ARCHIVES AND SPECIAL COLLECTIONS

WHA 167–9 correspondence of Robert Wharton, 1775–6.

GLOUCESTERSHIRE ARCHIVES

D 2002/3/4/1 journal of John Mitford, 1776.

MAGDALEN COLLEGE OXFORD

MS MC F15 and F16 journal of Francis Drake, 1751–2.

NATIONAL ARCHIVES

PRO 30/9/40–1 journal of Charles Abbot, Baron Colchester, 1788.
PRO 30/9/43–4 journal of Mrs Sarah Bentham, 1793–4.
PRO 30/9/7/10 and 11 journal of Miss Elizabeth Gibbes, 1789–90.

NATIONAL ARCHIVES OF SCOTLAND

GD 267/33/1 journal of Jane Graham (Mrs Patrick Home), 1772.
GD 267/33/4 account book of Patrick Home, 1772.
GD 267/33/2 journal of Patrick Home, 1772.
GD 267/22/5 letterbook and list of people met by Patrick Home in Italy in 1772.

NATIONAL LIBRARY OF SCOTLAND

Brand MSS Acc 10061 correspondence of Thomas Brand with his sister, Mrs Carr.
MS 10339 James Byres, 'Journal of my gant to Sicily in company with Mr Wilbraham', 1766.
Byres MS Dept 184/4 James Byres' notes on Etruscan antiquities.
MSS 1539–45 journal of Sir William Forbes, 1792–3.
MSS 6324, 6325, 6326, 6327 journal of Sir James Hall, 1783–4.
Acc 7952 diary of Joseph Mercer, 1778.
Acc 12604 John Murray Archive, including correspondence of Murray with Mariana Starke, Charlotte Eaton and Jane Waldie.
Acc 12244 letterbook of Roger Robertson of Ladykirk, 1750–3.

NATIONAL LIBRARY OF WALES

Wynnstay MSS Box 115/1 expenses and disbursements of Sir Watkin Williams Wynn, 1768–9.

NORFOLK RECORD OFFICE

DCN 118/6 journal of Miss Derbishire, 1788.
WGN2/1–4 journal of William Gunn, 1792–3.
MS 20677 journal of Robert Harvey, 1773.
LEST/NF 2 journal of Hamon le Strange, 1709–14.

PAUL MELLON CENTRE, BRINSLEY FORD ARCHIVE

Extracts of correspondence between Richard and John Newdigate, 1739–40, made by Brinsley Ford.
Transcript of Thomas Orde's journal at Florence and Siena, 1772.
Xerox of letters from Father John Thorpe to Lord Arundel, 1769–91.

RECORD OFFICE FOR LEICESTER, LEICESTERSHIRE AND RUTLAND

Finch MSS DG 7/4/12 box 4953 bundle 32 correspondence of George Finch, Earl of Winchilsea, with his mother, 1772–3.

ST ANDREWS UNIVERSITY LIBRARY

Special Collections MS 3671/6, journal of Walter Bowman, 1737.
MS 38271 correspondence of Walter Bowman, 1731–2.

SOCIETY OF ANTIQUARIES

MS 677 journal of Hudson Gurney, 1802–3.

SURREY HISTORY CENTRE

MS 1248/5 and 6 Brodrick family papers including correspondence between Thomas and Alan Brodrick from Italy, 1723–4.
MS 4647/1 journal of Sir John Frederick, 1737.

TRINITY COLLEGE CAMBRIDGE

Add. MS a 226 37 (1)–(3) journal of Whaley Armitage, 1790–1.

WADHAM COLLEGE OXFORD

Wadham MS A11.5 journal of John Swinton, 1730–1.

PRINTED PRIMARY SOURCES

Place of publication is London unless otherwise stated.

Anon., *Cronica Veneta sacra e profana o sia un compendio di tutte le cose più illustri ed antiche della città di Venezia* (Venice, 1736).

A Description of Ancient Rome, Containing a Short Account of the Principal Buildings, Places, etc, Noticed in the Annexed Plan of that City, Drawn from an Actual Survey by Leonardo Bufalino, in the Year 1551 (1761).

The History of the Surprizing Rise and Sudden Fall of Masaniello, the Fisherman of Naples (1747).

The History of the Surprizing Rise and Sudden Fall of Masaniello, The Fisherman of Naples (Oxford, ?1748).

L'Antiquario fiorentino o sia guida per osservar con metodo le cose notabili della città di Firenze (Florence, 1765).

The Polite Traveller: Being a Modern View of Italy, Spain, Portugal, and Africa, 4 vols. (1783).

Descrizione della città di Pisa per servire da guida (Pisa, 1792).

Pregi di Pisa (Pisa, 1816).

The London Guide and Stranger's Safeguard (1818).

Pisa antica e moderna (Pisa, 1821).

Addison, Joseph, *Remarks on Several Parts of Italy etc in the Years 1701, 1702, 1703* (1705).

Adeane, Jane H. (ed.), *The Girlhood of Maria Josepha Holroyd* (2nd edn, 1897).

Aglionby, William, *Painting Illustrated in Three Dialogues* (1685).

Albrizzi, Giovanni Battista, *Forestiere illuminato intorno le cose più rare, e curiose, antiche e moderne della città di Venezia e dell'isole circonvicine con la descrizione delle chiese, monisterj, ospedali, tesoro di San Marco, fabbriche pubbliche, pitture celebri, e di quanto v'e di più riguardevole* (Venice, 1740; revised edns 1765 and 1796).

Algarotti, Francesco, *An Essay on Painting Written in Italian by Count Algarotti* (1764).

Alison, Archibald, *Essays on the Nature and Principles of Taste* (Dublin, 1790).

Anderson, Adam, *An Historical and Chronological Deduction of the Origin of Commerce, from the Earliest Accounts to the Present Time*, 2 vols. (1764).

Andrews, John, *Characteristical Views of the Past and Present State of the People of Spain and Italy* (1808).

Archenholz, W., *A Picture of Italy: Translated from the Original German of W. De Archenholtz*, trans. Joseph Trapp, 2 vols. (1791).

Austen, Jane, *Emma* (Oxford, 1982).

Ayscough, George, *Letters from an Officer in the Guards to his Friend in England* (1778).

Baillie, Marianne, *First Impressions on a Tour upon the Continent in the Summer of 1818, through Parts of France, Italy, Switzerland, the Borders of Germany and a Part of French Flanders* (1819).

Barretti, Joseph, *An Account of the Manners and Customs of Italy; with Observations on the Mistakes of Some Travellers, with Regard to that Country*, 2 vols. (1768).

Barry, James, *A Letter to the Dilettanti Society, Respecting the Obtention of Certain Matters Essentially Necessary for the Improvement of Public Taste* (1798).

The Works of James Barry Esq, 2 vols. (1809).

Barthélemy, J. J., *Voyage en Italie de M l'Abbé Barthélemy* (Paris, 1801).

Batty, Elizabeth Frances, *Italian Scenery from Drawings Made in 1817* (1820).

Beckford, Peter, *Familiar Letters from Italy to a Friend in England*, 2 vols. (Salisbury, 1805).

Beckford, William, *Dreams, Waking Thoughts and Incidents* (1783).

Bellicard, Jerome Charles and Charles Nicolas Cochin, *Observations upon the Antiquities of the Town of Herculaneum, Discovered at the Foot of Mount Vesuvius* (1753).

Bentham, James, *The History and Antiquities of the Conventual and Cathedral Church of Ely*, 2 vols. (Cambridge, 1771).

Berchtold, Leopold, *An Essay to Direct and Extend the Inquiries of Patriotic Travellers*, 2 vols. (1789).

Bianchi, Giuseppe, *Raggualgio delle antichità e rarità che si conservano nella Galleria Mediceo-Imperiale di Firenze* (Florence, 1759).

Bianconi, Girolamo, *Nuova guida di Milano per gli amanti delle belle arti e delle sacre e profane antichità Milanesi* (2nd edn, Milan, 1795).

Blackburne, Francis (ed.), *Memoirs of Thomas Hollis Esq FR and ASS*, 2 vols. (1780).

Blainville, Henry de, *Travels through Holland, Germany, Switzerland and Other Parts of Europe; but Especially Italy*, 3 vols. (1767).

Bloom, Edward A. and Lilian D. Bloom, *The Piozzi Letters: Correspondence of Hester Lynch Piozzi, 1784–1821*, 6 vols. (London and Toronto, 1989).

Blunt, John James, *Vestiges of the Ancient Manners and Customs, Discoverable in Modern Italy and Sicily* (1823).

Bocchi, Francesco and Giovanni Cinelli, *Le bellezze della città di Firenze dove a pieno di pittura di scultura di sacri templi, di palazzi, i più notabili artifizj, e più preziosi si contengono* (Florence, 1677).

Bonnard, Georges A. (ed.), *Gibbon's Journey from Geneva to Rome* (1961).

Boschini, Marco, *Descrizione di tutte le pubbliche pitture della città di Venezia e isole circonvicine o sia rinnovazione delle ricche minere di Marco Boschini, colla aggiunta di tutte le opere, che uscirono dal 1675 fino al presente 1733* (Venice, 1733).

Boyd, Henry, *A Translation of the Inferno of Dante Alighieri, in English Verse* (1785).

Brady, Frank and Frederick A. Pottle (eds.), *Boswell on the Grand Tour: Italy, Corsica and France 1765–1766* (1955).

Brand, John, *Observations on Popular Antiquities* (Newcastle, 1777).

Breval, John, *Remarks on Several Parts of Europe Relating Chiefly to the History, Antiquities and Geography of those Countries*, 2 vols. (1726).
    Remarks on Several Parts of Europe Relating Chiefly to their History and Antiquities ... since 1723, 2 vols. (2nd edn, 1738).

Brigstocke, H., Eckart, M. and A. E. Wright, *John Flaxman and William Young Ottley in Italy*, Walpole Society, 72 (2010).

Broderick, Thomas, *The Travels of Thomas Broderick Esq in a Late Tour through Several Parts of Europe*, 2 vols. (1754).

Brooke, Nicholas, *Observations on the Manners and Customs of Italy, with Remarks on the Vast Importance of British Commerce on that Continent* (1798).

Brown, John, *An Estimate of the Manners and Principles of the Times* (1757).

Bruno, Raffaello del, *Ristretto delle cose più notablili della città di Firenze* (5th edn, Florence, 1745).

Brydone, Patrick, *A Tour through Sicily and Malta*, 2 vols. (2nd edn, 1776).

Burgess, Richard, *The Topography and Antiquities of Rome*, 2 vols. (1831).

Burnet, Gilbert, *Some Letters Containing an Account of what Seemed Most Remarkable in Switzerland, Italy, etc 1686* (repr. Menton, 1972).

Burton, Edward, *A Description of the Antiquities and Other Curiosities of Rome* (Oxford, 1821).

Callcott, Maria, *Description of the Chapel of the Annunziata dell'Arena or Giotto's Chapel in Padua* (1835).

Cameron, Charles, *The Baths of the Romans Explained and Illustrated* (1772).

Campbell, Harriet Charlotte Beaujolais, *A Journey to Florence in 1817*, ed. G. R. de Beer (1951).

Carter, John, *The Ancient Architecture of England (1795–1807)* (1805).

Chapone, Hester, *Letters on the Improvement of the Mind Addressed to a Young Lady*, 2 vols. (1773).

Cochin, Charles Nicholas, *Le Voyage d'Italie de Charles-Nicolas Cochin (1758)*, ed. Christian Michel (Rome, 1991).

Colles, John Mayne (ed.), *The Journal of John Mayne during a Tour on the Continent upon its Reopening after the Fall of Napoleon, 1874* (1909).

Colston, Marianne, *Journal of a Tour in France, Switzerland, and Italy, during the Years 1819, 20, 21*, 2 vols. (Paris, 1822).

Colt Hoare, Richard, *A Tour through the Island of Elba* (1814).
Hints to Travellers in Italy (1815).
Recollections Abroad, during the Year 1790: Sicily and Malta (Bath, 1817).
A Classical Tour through Italy and Sicily (1819).

Coronelli, Vincenzo, *Guida de' forestieri sacro-profana per osservare il più ragguardevole nella città di Venezia* (Venice, 1700).

Courtenay, John, *The Present State of the Manners, Arts, and Politics of France and Italy* (Dublin, 1794).

Coxe, Henry, *Picture of Italy; Being a Guide to the Antiquities and Curiosities of that Classical and Interesting Country* (1815).

Craven, Elizabeth, *A Journey through the Crimea to Constantinople* (1789).

Crawford, Alexander William, Lord Lindsay, *Sketches of the History of Christian Art*, 3 vols. (1847).

Creed, Richard, *The Journey to Rome with the 5th Earl of Exeter*, ed. and trans. Alice Thomas (Oundle, 2002).

Cresy, Edward and G. L. Taylor, *Architecture of the Middle Ages: Illustrated by a View, Plans, Sections, Elevations, and Details of the Cathedral, Baptistery, Leaning Tower or Campanile, and Campo Santo, at Pisa* (1818).
The Architectural Antiquities of Rome, 2 vols. (1821).

Cubitt, D., A. L. Mackley and R. G. Wilson (eds.), *The Great Tour of John Patteson, 1778–1779*, Norfolk Record Society, 67 (2003).

d'Agincourt, Séroux, *Histoire de l'art d'après les monuments depuis sa decadence au IVe siècle jusqu'à son renouvellement au XVIe siècle* (Paris, 1823).

Dallaway, James, *Anecdotes of the Arts in England; or, Comparative Remarks on Architecture, Sculpture, and Painting Chiefly Illustrated by Specimens at Oxford* (1800).

Dalmazzoni, Angelo, *The Antiquarian or the Guide for Foreigners to go the Rounds of the Antiquities of Rome* (Rome, 1803).

de Beer, E. S. (ed.), *The Diary of John Evelyn*, 6 vols. (Oxford, 1955).

de Cerceau, Antoine and Pierre Brumoy, *Memoirs of Nicholas Gabrini de Rienzi* (1740).

Denham, Thomas, *The Temporal Government of the Pope's State* (1788).

Desgodetz, Antoine Babuty, *Les edifices antiques de Rome* (1682).

Dickens, Charles, *Pictures from Italy*, ed. Kate Flint (1995).

Donati, Alessandro, *Roma vetus ac recens utriusque aedificiis ad eruditam cognitionem expositis* (1638).

Drummond, Alexander, *Travels through Different Cities of Germany, Italy, Greece, and Several Parts of Asia* (1754).

Du Fresnoy, *The Art of Painting* (1716).

Duncombe, J. (ed.), *Letters from Italy in the Years 1754 and 1755 by the Late Right Honourable John Earl of Corke and Orrery* (1773).

Dupaty, C. M. J. B. M., *Travels through Italy in a Series of Letters; Written in the Year 1785, by the Abbé Dupaty* (1788).

Duppa, Richard, *A Journal of the Most Remarkable Occurrences that Took Place in Rome, upon the Subversion of the Ecclesiastical Government, in 1798* (1799).

Eaton, Charlotte, *Rome in the Nineteenth Century*, 3 vols. (Edinburgh, 1820).

Edinburgh Review.

Elliott-Drake, Lady (ed.), *Lady Knight's Letters from France and Italy 1776–95* (1905).

Engelbach, Lewis, *Naples and the Campagna Felice in a Series of Letters Addressed to a Friend in England in 1802* (1815).

Englefield, Henry, 'Observations on the preceding paper respecting the remains of gothic architecture in Italy', *Archaeologia*, 15 (1806), 367–72.

Entick, John, *The Present State of the British Empire*, 4 vols. (1775).

Eschinardi, Francesco, *Descrizione di Roma e dell'Agro Romano, fatta gia' ad uso della carta topografica del cingolani dal padre Francesco Eschinardi della Compagnia di Gesù* (Rome, 1750).

Essex, James, 'Remarks on the antiquity and different modes of brick and stone buildings in England', *Archaeologia*, 4 (1777), 81–119.

Eustace, John Chetwode, *A Tour through Italy*, 2 vols. (1813).

A Classical Tour through Italy, 2 vols. (1814; revised edn, 4 vols., 1817).

Fabretti, Raffaello, *De aquis et aquaeductibus veteris Romae* (Rome, 1680).

Fenton, Richard, *A Historical Tour through Pembrokeshire* (1810).

Ficoroni, Francesco de', *Le memorie piu singolari di Roma, e sue vicinanze, notate in una lettera da Francesco Ficoroni diretta all'illustrissimo Signor Cav Bernard Ingelese, aggiuntavi nel fine le spiegazione d'una medaglia d'Omero* (Rome, 1730).

Le vestigie e rarità di Roma antica ricercate, e spiegate da Francesco de' Ficoroni (Rome, 1744).

Fitzgerald, Brian (ed.), *The Correspondence of Emily Duchess of Leinster*, 3 vols. (Dublin, 1957).

Folkes, Martin, 'On the Trajan and Antonine pillars at Rome', *Archaeologia*, 1 (1770), 117–11.

Ford, Brinsley (ed.), *Letters of Jonathan Skelton from Rome 1758*, Walpole Society, 31 (1956).

Forsyth, Joseph, *Remarks on Antiquities, Arts and Letters, during an Excursion in Italy, in the Years 1802 and 1803* (2nd edn, 1816).

Fremantle, Anne (ed.), *The Wynne Diaries*, 3 vols. (Oxford, 1937).

Galanti, Guiseppe Maria, *Nuova descrizione storica e geografica dell'Italia*, 2 vols. (Naples, 1782).

Breve descrizione della città di Napoli e del suo contorno (Naples, 1792).

Garden, Francis Lord Gardenstone, *Travelling Memorandums, Made in a Tour upon the Continent of Europe in the Years 1786, 87 and 88*, 3 vols. (Edinburgh, 1791).

Gargiolli, L. F. M., *Description de la ville de Florence et de ses environs précedée d'un abrége d'histoire Florentine*, 2 vols. (Florence, 1819).

Gell, William and John P. Gandy, *Pompeiana: The Topography, Edifices, and Ornaments of Pompeii* (1817–19).

Gentleman's Magazine

Gerard, Alexander, *An Essay on Taste* (1759).

Giannone, Pietro, *The Civil History of the Kingdom of Naples*, 2 vols. (1729).

Gibbon, Edward, *The History of the Decline and Fall of the Roman Empire*, 7 vols. (Oxford, 1925).

Goethe, J. Wolfgang, *Autobiography of my Life*, ed. and trans. A. J. W. Morrison (1849).

Goethe, J. Wolfgang, *Italian Journey*, ed. and trans. W. H. Auden and Elizabeth Mayer (Harmondsworth, 1982).

Goldsmith, Oliver, *Enquiry into the Present State of Polite Learning* (1759).

Gough, Richard, *Anecdotes of British Topography* (1768).

Gower, R. S., *Selections from the Letters of de Brosses* (1897).

Granville, Castalia Countess (ed.), *Lord Granville Leveson Gower (First Earl Granville). Private Correspondence 1781–1821*, 2 vols. (1916).

Gray, Robert, *Letters during the Course of a Tour through Germany, Switzerland and Italy, in the Years MDCCXCI and MDCCXCII* (1794).

Gray, Thomas, 'Criticism on architecture and painting during a tour in Italy', in John Mitford (ed.), *The Works of Thomas Gray*, 4 vols. (1836–43).

Grimani, A., *A Topographical and Historical Description of Antient and Modern Rome* (Bath, 1783).

Grosley, Pierre, *New Observations on Italy and its Inhabitants*, 2 vols. (1769).

Guattani, Giuseppe Antonio, *Roma descritta ed illustrata*, 2 vols. (Rome, 1805).

Gunn, William and Arthur Taylor, 'Remarks on the gothic architecture of the duomo, battistero and Campo Santo of Pisa', *Archaeologia*, 20 (1824), 537–52.

Gunn, William, *An Inquiry into the Origins and Influence of Gothic Architecture* (1819).

Gwynn, John, *London and Westminster Improved* (1766).

Haggitt, George, *Two Letters to a Fellow of the Society of Antiquaries on the Subject of Gothic Architecture* (Cambridge, 1813).

Hakewill, James, *A Picturesque Tour of Italy from Drawings Made in 1816, 1817* (1820).

Hale, J. R. (ed.), *The Italian Journal of Samuel Rogers Edited with an Account of Rogers's Life and of Travel in Italy in 1814–1821* (1956).

Hallam, Henry, *View of the State of Europe during the Middle Ages* (1818).

Hardwick, Nora (ed.), *The Grand Tour: William and John Blathwayt of Dyrham Park 1705–1708* (Bristol, 1985).

Harrington, James, *Oceana* (1656).

Hazlitt, William, *Notes of a Journey through France and Italy* (1826).

Herbert, Lord (ed.), *Henry, Elizabeth and George (1734–1780): Letters and Diaries of Henry, 10th Earl of Pembroke and his Circle* (1939).

Hervey, Christopher, *Letters from Portugal, Spain, Italy and Germany, in the Years 1759, 1760 and 1761*, 3 vols. (1785).

Heywood, Robert, *A Journey to Italy in 1826* (1918).

Hinde, C. A., *Journal of a Tour Made in Italy in the Winter of the Years 1819 and 1820*, ed. M. Merlini, Biblioteca del viaggio in Italia, 12 (Geneva, 1982).

Hobhouse, Benjamin, *Remarks on Several Parts of France, Italy, &c. in the Years 1783, 1784, and 1785* (1796).

Hobhouse, J. C., *Historical Illustrations of the Fourth Canto of Childe Harold: Containing Dissertations on the Ruins of Rome and an Essay on Italian Literature* (1818).

Houssaye, Amelot de la, *Histoire du gouvernement de Venise* (Paris, 1695).

Howell, James, *SPQV a Survey of the Signorie of Venice, of her Admired Policy, and Method of Government, &c with a Cohortation to All Christian Princes to Resent her Dangerous Condition at Present* (1651).

H[owell], J[ames], *An Exact History of the Late Revolutions in Naples and their Monstrous Successes* (1650).

Hume, David, 'Of national characters', in David Hume, *Essays Moral, Literary and Political* (1742).

Hurd, Richard, *Letters on Chivalry and Romance* (1762).
Dialogues on the Uses of Foreign Travel Considered as a Part of an English Gentleman's Education (1764).

Ingamells, John (ed.), *John Ramsay's Italian Diary 1782–4*, Walpole Society, 65 (2003).

James, Thomas, *The Italian Schools of Painting with Observations on the Present State of the Art* (1820).

Jameson, Anna, *Diary of an Ennuyée* (1826).

Jefferies, David, *A Journal from London to Rome, by Way of Paris, Lyons, Turin, Florence, etc and from Rome back to London, by Way of Loretto, Venice, Milan* (2nd edn, 1755).

Jerdan, William (ed.), *Letters from James Earl of Perth, Lord Chancellor of Scotland etc to his Sister, the Countess of Erroll, and Other Members of his Family*, Camden Society (1845).

Kennett, Basil, *Romae antiquae notitia: Or, the Antiquities of Rome in Two Parts* (10th edn, 1737).

Kerrich, Thomas, 'Some observations on the gothic buildings abroad, particularly those in Italy; and on gothic architecture in general', *Archaeologia*, 16 (1812), 292–304.
'Observations upon some sepulchral monuments in Italy and France', *Archaeologia*, 18 (1817), 186–97.

Keysler, Johann Georg, *Travels through Germany, Bohemia, Hungary, Switzerland, Italy, and Lorrain*, 4 vols. (1756).

King, Edward, *Munimenta Antiqua or Observations on Ancient Castles*, 4 vols. (1799–1805).

Klima, Slava (ed.), *Joseph Spence: Letters from the Grand Tour* (Montreal and London, 1975).

Knight, Cornelia, *Description of Latium; or, La Campagna di Roma* (1805).

Knight, Henry Gally, *The Ecclesiastical Architecture of Italy: From the Time of Constantine to the Fifteenth Century*, 2 vols. (1842).

Knight, Richard Payne, *Discourse on the Worship of Priapus* (1786).

Knox, Vicesimus, *Liberal Education: Or, a Practical Treatise on the Methods of Acquiring Useful and Polite Learning*, 2 vols. (9th edn, 1788).

Lalande, J. J., *Voyage d'un François en Italie, fait dans les années 1765 & 1766*, 8 vols. (Yverdon, 1769).

Lami, Giovanni, *Lezioni di antichità Toscane e spezialmente della città di Firenze recitate nell'accademia della crusca* (Florence, 1766).

Lanzi, Luigi, *Storia pittorica dell'Italia* (Florence, 1809).

Lassels, Richard, *The Voyage of Italy* (1670).

Lastri, Marco, *L'Osservatore fiorentino sugli edifizi della sua patria per servire alla storia della medesima*, 3 vols. (Florence, 1776).

Laugier, Marc Antoine, *An Essay on the Study and Practice of Architecture*. (1756).

Ledwich, Edward, 'Observations on ancient churches', *Archaeologia*, 8 (1787), 165–94.

Lemaistre, J. G., *Travels after the Peace of Amiens, through Parts of France, Switzerland and Italy*, 3 vols. (1806).

Lewis, M., *The Bravo of Venice* (1805).

Lewis, Lady Theresa (ed.), *Extracts of the Journals and Correspondence of Miss Berry from the Year 1783–1852*, 3 vols. (1865).

Lewis, W. S. (ed.), *Horace Walpole's Correspondence*, 48 vols. (New Haven, 1937–83).

Ligorio, Pirro, *Libro di M. Pyrrho Ligori Napolitano, delle antichità di Roma, nel quale si tratta de' circi, theatri, & anfiteatri* (Venice, 1553).

Lumisden, Andrew, *Remarks on the Antiquities of Rome and its Environs* (1797).

Lysons, Daniel and Samuel Lysons, *Magna Britannia; Being a Concise and Topographical Account of the Several Counties of Great Britain*, 6 vols. (1806–22).

Lyttleton, George, *Dialogues of the Dead* (Dublin, 1760).

Maffei, Scipione, *A Compleat History of the Ancient Amphitheatres*, trans. Alexander Gordon (1730).

Magnan, Dominique, *La ville de Rome ou description abrégée de cette superbe ville, avec deux plans généraux & ceaux de ses XIV quartiers, gravés en taille douce pour la commodité des étrangers*, 4 vols. (Rome, 1778).

La città di Roma ovvero breve descrizione di questa superba città, divisa in quattro tomi ed ornata di 385 stampe in Rame (Rome, 1779).

Malcolm, J. P., *Londinium redivivum; or, an Antient History and Modern Description of London*, 4 vols. (1802).

Manazzale André, *Rome et ses environs avec une description générale trés exacte de tous ses monuments anciens, & un abrégé de ses beautés les plus remarquables, en moderne, comme les meilleures Peintures, Sculptures & Architectures* (Rome, 1794).

Itinéraire instructif de Rome et de ses environs, 2 vols. (Rome, 1802).

Mandeville, Bernard, *The Fable of the Bees* (1714).

Martinelli, Fioravante, *Roma ricercata nel suo sito con tutte le curiosità* (Rome, 1769).

Martini, Giuseppe, *Theatrum basilicae Pisanae*, 2 parts (Pisa, 1705–23).

Martyn, Thomas, *A Gentleman's Guide in his Tour through Italy* (1787).

Martyn, Thomas and John Lettice, *The Antiquities of Herculaneum; Translated from the Italian* (1773).

Mason William (ed.), *The Works of Thomas Gray*, 4 vols. (3rd edn, 1807).

Matthews, Henry, *The Diary of an Invalid Being the Journal of a Tour in Pursuit of Health in Portugal, Italy, Switzerland and France in the Years 1817, 1818 and 1819* (2nd edn, 1820).

Middleton, Conyers, *A Letter from Rome: Shewing an Exact Conformity between Popery and Paganism, or the Religion of the Present Romans to be Derived Entirely from that of their Heathen Ancestors* (1729).

Middleton, W. E. Knowles (ed.), *Lorenzo Magalotti at the Court of Charles II: His relazione d'Inghilterra of 1688* (Waterloo, Ont., 1980).

Midon, Francis, *The History of the Rise and Fall of Masaniello, the Fisherman of Naples* (1729).

The History of the Rise and Fall of Masaniello, the Fisherman of Naples (2nd edn, 1747; repr. 1768 and ?1770).

Milford, John, *Observations, Moral, Literary and Antiquarian Made during a Tour through the Pyrenees, South of France, Switzerland, the Whole of Italy and the Netherlands, in the Years 1814 and 1815*, 2 vols. (1818).

Miller, Anne, *Letters from Italy, Describing the Manners, Customs, Antiquities, Paintings etc of that Country*, 3 vols. (1776).

Milner, John, *History of Winchester*, 2 vols. (Winchester, 1798).

A Treatise on the Ecclesiastical Architecture of England during the Middle Ages (1811).

Misson, Maximilien, *A New Voyage to Italy*, 2 vols. (1695).

A New Voyage to Italy, 4 vols. (1739).

Montesquieu, Charles de, *The Spirit of the Laws*, 2 vols. (1750).

Montfaucon, Bernard de, *The Antiquities of Italy: Being the Travels of the Learned and Reverend Bernard de Montfaucon, from Paris through Italy, in the Year 1698 and 1699* (1725).

Moore, John, *A View of Society and Manners in Italy; With Anecdotes Relating to Some Eminent Characters*, 2 vols. (1781).

More, Hannah, *Strictures on the Modern System of Female Education* (1799).

Morgan, Sydney, *Italy*, 2 vols. (1821).

Morritt, J. B. S., *A Grand Tour: Letters and Journeys 1794–96*, ed. G. S. Marindin (1985).

Morrona, Alessandro da, *Pisa illustrata nelle arti del disegno da Alessandro da Morrona*, 3 vols. (2nd edn, Livorno, 1812).

Moschini, Giannantonio, *Guida per la città di Venezia all'amico delle belle arti*, 4 vols. (Venice, 1803).

Muratori, Ludovico, *Antiquitates italicae medii aevi*, 6 vols. (Mediolani, 1738–42).

Nardini, Famiano, *Roma antica* (Rome, 1666).

Nelthorpe, Frances (ed.), *Mrs Mary Carter's Letters* (1860).

Nibby, Antonio, *Le mura di Roma disegnate da Sir William Gell* (Rome, 1820).

Nicolson, William, *The English Historical Library* (2nd edn, 1714).

Northall, John, *Travels through Italy* (1766).

Nugent, Thomas, *The Grand Tour, or, a Journey through the Netherlands, Germany, Italy and France*, 4 vols. (2nd edn, 1756).

Oppé, Paul (ed.), *Memoirs of Thomas Jones of Penkerrig, Radnorshire, 1803*, Walpole Society, 32 (1946–8).

Otter, William, *The Life and Remains of the Rev. Edward Daniel Clarke* (1824).

Ottley, William Young, *The Italian School of Design Being a Series of Fac-similes of Original Drawings by the Most Eminent Painters and Sculptors of Italy* (1808–23).

A Series of Plates, Engraved after the Paintings and Sculpture of the Most Eminent Masters of the Early Florentine School (1826).

Otway, Thomas, *Venice Preserved* (1682).

Overbeke, Bonaventura, *Degli avanazi dell'antica Roma* (Rome, 1739).

Owen, John, *Travels into Different Parts of Europe, in the Years 1791 and 1792: With Familiar Remarks on Places, Men and Manners*, 2 vols. (1796).

Palgrave, Francis, *Handbook to Northern Italy* (1842).

Palladio, Andrea, *L'antichità di Roma di M. Andrea Palladio, raccolta brevemente da gli auttori antichi, & moderni* (Rome, 1554).

Parrino, Dominico Antonio, *Nuova guida de' forastieri per osservare, e godere le curiosità più vaghe e più rare della fedelissima gran Napoli città antica, e nobilissima* (Naples, 1725).

Patch, Thomas, *The Life of Masaccio* (Florence, 1772).

Patoun, William, 'Advice on travel in Italy', in John Ingamells (ed.), *A Dictionary of British and Irish Travellers in Italy, 1701–1800* (New Haven and London, 1997), xxxix–lii.

Pearce, Susan and Frank Salmon (eds.), *Charles Heathcote Tatham in Italy*, Walpole Society, 67 (2005).

Penrose, Thomas, *A Sketch of the Lives and Writings of Dante and Petrarch* (1790).

Phillips, R., (ed.), *Correspondence between Frances, Countess of Hartford (afterwards Duchess of Somerset), and Henrietta Louisa, Countess of Pomfret, between the Years 1738–42*, 3 vols. (1805).

Philpot, Charles, *An Introduction to the Literary History of the Fourteenth and Fifteenth Centuries* (1798).

Piles, Roger de, *The Art of Painting and the Lives of the Painters* (1706).

Pinelli, Bartolomeo, *Raccolta di cinquanta costumi pittoreschi* (Rome, 1809).

Piozzi, Hester, *Observations and Reflections Made in the Course of a Journey through France, Italy and Germany*, ed. Herbert Barrows (Ann Arbor, 1967).

Piranesi, Giovanni Battista, *Vedute di Roma* (Rome, n.d.).

Della magnificenza ed architettura de' Romani (Rome, 1761).

Il Campo Marzio dell'antica Roma (Rome, 1762).

Pollnitz, Charles Lewis, *The Memoirs of Charles Lewis Baron de Pollnitz: Being the Observations He Made in his Late Travels from Prussia thro' Germany, Italy, France, Flanders, Holland, England etc in Letters to his Friend*, 2 vols. (1739).

Prosperi, Ranieri, *Descrizione della città di Pisa* (Pisa, 1792).

Richard, Jerome, *Description historique et critique de l'Italie*, 6 vols. (Dijon, 1766).

Richardson, Jonathan, *A Discourse on the Dignity Certainty, Pleasure and Advantage of the Science of a Connoisseur* (1715).

An Account of Some of the Statues, Bas-Reliefs, Drawings and Pictures in Italy, with Remarks (1722).

An Essay on the Theory of Painting by Mr Richardson (2nd edn, 1725).

Robertson, William, *The History of the Reign of the Emperor Charles V: With a View of the Progress of Society in Europe, from the Subversion of the Roman Empire to the Beginning of the Sixteenth Century*, 3 vols. (1769).

The History of America, 2 vols. (1777).

Robinson, Thomas Philip, *The Grand Tour 1801–1803: Being Letters from Lord Grantham to his Mother, from Prussia, Saxony, Russia, Austria, Switzerland, Italy and France* (Penzance, 1979).

Roscoe, William, *The Life of Lorenzo de' Medici, Called the Magnificent*, 2 vols. (Liverpool, 1795).

Roscoe, Thomas, *The History of Painting in Italy, from the Period of the Revival of the Fine Arts to the End of the Eighteenth Century: Translated from the Original Italian of the Abate Luigi Lanzi*, 6 vols. (1828).

Rose, William Stewart, *Letters from the North of Italy Addressed to Henry Hallam*, 2 vols. (1819).

Rosini, Giovanni, *Lettere pittoriche sul Campo Santo di Pisa* (Pisa, 1810).

Pregi di Pisa compendiati da Alessandro da Morrona (Pisa, 1816).

Rossini, Giovanni Pietro, *Il Mercurio Errante delle grandezze di Roma, tanto antiche, che moderne; cioè de' palazzi, ville, giardini, & altre rarità della medesima* (Rome, 1693).

Ruskin, John, *The Stones of Venice* (1851).

Russel, James, *Letters from a Young Painter Abroad to his Friends in England*, 2 vols. (2nd edn, 1750).

Sade, J. de, *The Life of Petrarch*, trans. Susannah Dobson, 2 vols. (1776).

Sadleir, Thomas U. (ed.), *An Irish Peer on the Continent (1801–1803): being a Narrative of the Tour of Stephen, 2nd Earl Mount Cashell, through France, Italy, etc as Related by Catherine Wilmot* (1920).

Saint-Non, Jean Claude Richard de, *Voyage pittoresque ou description des royaumes de Naples et de Sicilie*, 5 vols. (Paris, 1782–5).

Salmon, J., *An Historical Description of Ancient and Modern Rome*, 2 vols. (1800).

Samber, Robert, *Roma illustrata: Or a Description of the Most Beautiful Pieces of Painting, Sculpture, and Architecture, Antique and Modern, at and near Rome* (1722).

Sarnelli, Pompeo, *Nuova guida de' forestieri, e dell'istoria di Napoli* (Naples, 1772).

Scholes, Percy A. (ed.), *An Eighteenth-Century Musical Tour in France and Italy*, 2 vols. (Oxford, 1959).

Semple, Robert, *Observations on a Journey through Spain and Italy to Naples and thence to Smyrna and Constantinople*, 2 vols. (1807).

Sharp, Samuel, *Letters from Italy, Describing the Customs and Manners of that Country in the Years 1765 and 1766* (1766).

Shelley, Mary, *Valperga, or the Life and Adventures of Castruccio Prince of Lucca* (1823).

Sherlock, Martin, *Letters from an English Traveller* (1780).

Sigismondo, Giuseppe, *Descrizione della città di Napoli e suoi borghi*, 3 vols. (Naples, 1788).

Sismondi, Jean Charles Léonard de, *Histoire des républiques Italiennes du moyen âge*, 16 vols. (Paris, 1809–18).

Smirke, Robert, 'An account of some remains of gothic architecture in Italy and Sicily', *Archaeologia*, 15 (1806), 363–79.

Smith, James Edward, *Sketch of a Tour on the Continent in the Years 1786 and 1787*, 3 vols. (1793).

Smith, John, *Select Views in Italy with Topographical Descriptions in England and France*, 2 vols. (1792–6).

Smollett, Tobias, *Travels through France and Italy*, 2 vols. (1766).

The Expedition of Humphry Clinker (1771).

Spence, Joseph, *Polymetis: Or, an Enquiry Concerning the Agreement between the Works of the Roman Poets, and the Remains of the Antient Artists* (1747).

[Spence, Thomas], *Pig's Meat: Or Lessons for the Swinish Multitude*, 3 vols. (1794–5).

Staël, Mme de, *Corinne, or Italy*, trans. Sylvia Raphael (Oxford, 1998).

Stanhope, Philip, *Letters Written by the Late Right Honourable Philip Dormer Stanhope, Earl of Chesterfield, to his Son, Philip Stanhope*, 4 vols. (1774).

Starke, Mariana, *Letters from Italy between the Years 1792 and 1798*, 2 vols. (1800).

Letters from Italy between the Years 1792 and 1798, 2 vols. (2nd edn, 1815).

Travels on the Continent: Written for the Use and Particular Information of Travellers (1820).

Instructions for Travellers (1828).

Sterne, Laurence, *A Sentimental Journey through France and Italy* (1768).

Stevens, Sacheverell, *Miscellaneous Remarks Made on the Spot, in a Late Seven Years Tour through France, Italy, Germany and Holland* (1756).

[Stuart, James], *Critical Observations on the Buildings and Improvements of London* (2nd edn, 1771).

Swinburne, Henry, *Travels in the Two Sicilies in the Years 1777, 1778, 1779 and 1780*, 2 vols. (1783).

Travels through Spain in the Years 1775 and 1776, 2 vols. (1787).

The Courts of Europe at the Close of the Last Century, 2 vols. (1895).

Taylor, Ernest (ed.), *The Taylor Papers: Being a Record of Certain Reminiscences, Letters and Journals in the Life of Lieut-Gen Sir Herbert Taylor* (1913).

Thompson, Charles, *The Travels of the Late Charles Thompson Esq. Containing his Observations on France, Italy, Turkey in Europe, the Holy Land, Arabia and Egypt*, 3 vols. (1744).

Tiraboschi, Girolamo, *Storia della litteratura Italiana*, 18 vols. (Florence, 1774–82).

Titi, Filippo, *Nuovo studio di pitture* (Rome, 1674).

Totti, Pompilio, *Ritratto di Roma moderna* (Rome, 1638).

Trease, Geoffrey (ed.), *Matthew Todd's Journal: A Gentleman's Gentleman in Europe 1814–20* (1968).

Trusler, John, *The London Adviser and Guide* (1786).

Tucker, Josiah, *Instructions to Travellers* (1758).

Ulyssess, Charles, *Travels through Various Provinces of the Kingdom of Naples in 1789* (1795).

Vasari, Giorgio, *Lives of the Artists, Sculptors and Architects*, trans. Gaston du C. De Vere and ed. David Ekserdjian, 2 vols. (1996).

Vasi, Giuseppe, *Itinerario istruttivo diviso in otto stazioni o giornate per ritrovare con facilità tutte le antiche e moderne magnificenze di Roma* (Rome, 1763).
Itinerario istruttivo per ritrovare con facilità tutte le magnificenze antiche e moderne di Roma (Naples, 1770).
Vasi, Mariano, *Itinerario istruttivo di Roma antica e moderna* (Rome, 1804).
Venuti, Ridolfino, *Descrizione di Roma e dell'Agro Romano, fatta gia ad uso della carta topografica del cingolani dal padre Francesco Eschinardi della Compagnia di Gesù* (1750).
Accurata, e succinta descrizione topografica delle antichità di Roma dell'Abate Ridolfino Venuti Cortonese, 2 vols. (Rome, 1763).
Voltaire, *The General History and State of Europe*, 3 vols. (Edinburgh, 1758).
Waldie, Jane, *Sketches Descriptive of Italy in the Years 1816 and 1817*, 4 vols. (1820).
Walker, Adam, *Ideas Suggested on the Spot in a Late Excursion through Flanders, Germany, France and Italy* (1790).
Walker, Ralph (ed.), *Correspondence of James Boswell and John Johnston of Grange* (1966).
Warton, Thomas, *The History of English Poetry*, 4 vols. (1774–81).
Watkins, Thomas, *Travels through Switzerland, Italy, Sicily, the Greek Islands to Constantinople, Greece, Ragusa, and the Dalmatian Isles*, 2 vols. (2nd edn, 1794).
Webb, Daniel, *An Inquiry into the Beauties of Painting* (1761).
Weston, Stephen, *Viaggiana: Or, Detached Remarks on the Buildings, Pictures, Statues, Inscriptions etc of Ancient and Modern Rome* (1776).
Whitaker, John, *The Ancient Cathedral of Cornwall Historically Surveyed*, 2 vols. (1804).
White, T. H., *Fragments of Italy and the Rhineland* (1841).
Whitehouse, B. (ed.), 'Extract of a tour in Italy in 1792 and 1793 by four ladies', *The Antiquary*, 33 (1897), 273–8, 296–9.
Whittington, G. D., *An Historical Survey of the Ecclesiastical Antiquities of France; with a View to Illustrate the Rise and Progress of Gothic Architecture in Europe* (1810).
Wilcocks, Joseph, *Roman Conversations* (1792).
Willis, Robert, *Remarks on the Architecture of the Middle Ages, Especially of Italy* (Cambridge, 1835).
Winckelmann, J. J., *Reflections on the Painting and Sculpture of the Greeks*, trans. Henry Fuseli (1765).
Wren, Christopher, *Parentalia: Or, Memoirs of the Family of Wren* (1750).
Wright, Edward, *Some Observations Made in Travelling through France, Italy, &c in the Years 1720–21 and 1722*, 2 vols. (1730).
Wyndham, Mrs Hugh (ed.), *Correspondence of Sarah Spencer, Lady Lyttelton, 1787–1870* (1912).
Young, Arthur, *Travels during the Years 1787, 1788 and 1789* (Bury St Edmunds, 1792).

SECONDARY SOURCES

Place of publication is London unless otherwise stated.

Adler, Judith, 'Origins of sightseeing', *Annals of Tourism Research*, 16:1 (1989), 7–29.
'Travel as performed art', *American Journal of Sociology*, 94:6 (1989), 1366–91.

Byrd, M., *London Transformed: Images of the City in the Eighteenth Century* (New Haven and London, 1978).

Calaresu, Melissa, 'Looking for Virgil's Tomb: the end of the Grand Tour and the cosmopolitan ideal in Europe', in Jás Elsner and Joan-Pau Rubiés (eds.), *Voyages and Visions: Towards a Cultural History of Travel* (1999), 138–61, 302–11.

'From the street to stereotype: urban space, travel and the picturesque in late eighteenth-century Naples', *Italian Studies*, 62:2 (2007), 189–203.

Canepa, Andrew M., 'From degenerate scoundrel to noble savage: the Italian stereotype in eighteenth-century British travel literature', *English Miscellany*, 22 (1971), 107–46.

Capra, Carlo, 'Habsburg Italy in the age of reform', *Journal of Modern Italian Studies*, 10 (2005), 218–33.

Carter, Philip, 'James Boswell's manliness', in Tim Hitchcock and Michèle Cohen (eds.), *English Masculinities 1660–1800* (1999), 111–30.

Cassani, Silvia (ed.), *In the Shadow of Vesuvius: Views of Naples from Baroque to Romanticism, 1631–1830* (Naples, 1990).

Cassidy, Brendan, 'Gavin Hamilton, Thomas Pitt and statues for Stowe', *Burlington Magazine*, 1221 (2004), 806–14.

Castle, Terry, *Masquerade and Civilization: The Carnivalesque in Eighteenth-Century English Culture and Fiction* (1986).

Cavaliero, Roderick, *Italia Romantica: English Romantics and Italian Freedom* (London, 2005).

Certeau, Michel de, *The Practice of Everyday Life*, trans. Steven Randall (Berkeley, 1984).

Chadwick, Owen, *The Popes and European Revolution* (Oxford, 1981).

Chaney, Edward, *The Evolution of the Grand Tour: Anglo-Italian Cultural Relations since the Renaissance* (1998)

Chard, Chloe, 'Nakedness and tourism: classical sculpture and the imaginative geography of the Grand Tour', *Oxford Art Journal*, 18:1 (1995), 14–28.

Pleasure and Guilt on the Grand Tour: Travel Writing and Imaginative Geography 1600–1830 (Manchester, 1999).

Chard, Chloe and Helen Langdon (eds.), *Transports: Travel, Pleasure and Imaginative Geography 1600–1830* (New Haven and London, 1996), 179–205.

Churchill, Kenneth, *Italy and English Literature 1764–1930* (London and Basingstoke, 1980).

Claridge, Amanda, 'Archaeologies, antiquaries and the *memorie* of sixteenth- and seventeenth-century Rome', in Ilaria Bignamini (ed.), *Archives and Excavations*, Archaeological Monographs of the British School at Rome 14 (2004), 33–54.

Clark, Anna, *Scandal: The Sexual Politics of the British Constitution* (Princeton, 2004).

Clark, Kenneth, *The Gothic Revival: An Essay in the History of Taste* (1928). *The Nude* (1956; repr., 1980).

Clarke, M. and Penny, N., *The Arrogant Connoisseur: Richard Payne Knight, 1751–1824* (Manchester, 1982).

Clarke, M. L., *Classical Studies in Britain 1500–1900* (Cambridge, 1959).

Clay, Edith, *Sir William Gell in Italy* (1976).

Coates, Victoria C. Gardner and Jon L. Seydl (eds.), *Antiquity Recovered: The Legacy of Pompeii and Herculaneum* (Los Angeles, 2007).

Cochrane, Eric, *Florence in the Forgotten Centuries, 1527–1800* (1973).

Tradition and Enlightenment in the Tuscan Academies (Rome, 1961).

Cocke, Thomas, 'Pre-nineteenth-century attitudes in England to Romanesque architecture', *Journal of the British Archaeological Association*, 36 (1973), 72–97.

'The rediscovery of the Romanesque', in Tristram Holland, Janet Holt and George Zarnecki (eds.), *English Romanesque Art 1066–1200* (1984), 360–6.

Coffin, R. Pine, *Bibliography of British and American Travel in Italy to 1860* (Florence, 1974).

Cohen, Michèle, *Fashioning Masculinity: National Identity and Language in the Eighteenth Century* (1996).

'Manliness, effeminacy and the French: gender and the construction of national character in eighteenth-century England', in Tim Hitchcock and Michèle Cohen (eds.), *English Masculinities, 1660–1800* (1999), 44–62.

'"To think, to compare, to combine, to methodise": girls' education in Enlightenment Britain', in Sarah Knott and Barbara Taylor (eds.), *Women, Gender and Enlightenment* (Basingstoke, 2005), 224–42.

Colbert, Benjamin, 'Bibliography of British travel writing, 1780–1840: the European Tour, 1814–18 (excluding Britain and Ireland)', *Cardiff Corvey Articles*, XIII.1, www.cardiff.ac.uk/encap/journals/corvey/articles/cc13_n01. html, accessed 31 July 2009.

Colley, Linda, *Britons: Forging the Nation 1707–1837* (New Haven and London, 1992).

Collins, Jeffrey, *Papacy and Politics in Eighteenth Century Rome* (Cambridge, 2004).

Coltman, Viccy, *Fabricating the Antique: Neoclassicism in Britain, 1760–1830* (Chicago, 2006).

Classical Sculpture and the Culture of Collecting in Britain since 1760 (Oxford, 2009).

Colyer, R. J., 'A Breconshire gentleman in Europe, 1737–8', *National Library of Wales Journal*, 21 (1979–80), 265–97.

Connell, Brian, *Portrait of a Whig Peer: Compiled from the Papers of the Second Viscount Palmerston, 1739–1802* (1957).

Constantine, David, *Fields of Fire: A Life of Sir William Hamilton* (2001).

Cooper, Robyn, '"The crowning glory of Pisa": nineteenth-century reactions to the Campo Santo', *Italian Studies*, 37 (1982), 72–100.

Corbin, Alain, *The Foul and the Fragrant: Odor and the French Social Imagination* (Leamington Spa, 1986).

Corp, Edward, *The Stuarts in Exile 1719–66: A Royal Court in Permanent Exile* (Cambridge, 2011).

Cowan, Brian, 'An open elite: the peculiarities of connoisseurship in early modern England', *Modern Intellectual History*, 1:2 (2004), 151–83.

Cristefani, M., 'Sugli inizi dell' "Etruscheria": la pubblicazione del *De Etruria regali* di Thomas Dempster', *Mélanges de L'École Française de Rome: Antiquité*, 90 (1978), 577–625.

Crook, J. Mordaunt, *The Greek Revival: Neo-Classical Attitudes in British Architecture, 1760–1870* (1972).

John Carter and the Mind of the Gothic Revival (1995).

Crowley, John, 'The sensibility of comfort', *AHR*, 104 (1999), 749–82.

Curran, Stuart, 'Valperga', in Esther Schor (ed.), *The Cambridge Companion to Mary Shelley* (Cambridge, 2003), 103–15.

Darley, Gillian, *John Soane: An Accidental Romantic* (New Haven and London, 1999).

Davis, John A., *Naples and Napoleon: Southern Italy and the European Revolutions 1780–1860* (Oxford, 2006).

de Beer, E. S., 'Gothic: origin and diffusion of the term; the idea of style in architecture', *JWCI*, 11 (1948), 145–8.

Dee, E. E., *Views of Florence and Tuscany by Giuseppe Zocchi 1711–1767* (New York, 1968).

di Mauro, Leonardo, 'Naples and the South', in Ilaria Bignamini and Andrew Wilton (eds.), *Grand Tour: The Lure of Italy in the Eighteenth Century* (1997), 144–50.

Ditchfield, Simon, 'Reading Rome as a sacred landscape, c. 1586–1635', in Will Coster and Andrew Spicer (eds.), *Sacred Space in Early Modern Europe* (Cambridge, 2005), 167–92.

Dixon, Susan M., 'Piranesi and Francesco Bianchini: *capricci* in the service of pre-scientific archaeology', *Art History*, 22:2 (1999), 184–213.

'The sources and fortunes of Piranesi's archaeological illustrations', *Art History*, 24:4 (2002), 469–87.

Dolan, Brian, *Ladies of the Grand Tour* (2001).

Doran, Dr, *'Mann' and Manners at the Court of Florence, 1740–86*, 2 vols. (1876).

Du Prey, Pierre de la Raffinière, *John Soane: The Making of an Architect* (Chicago, 1982).

Eagles, Robin, *Francophilia in English Society, 1748–1815* (Basingstoke, 1999).

Edwards, Catharine, *Writing Rome: Textual Approaches to the City* (Cambridge, 1996).

(ed.), *Roman Presences: Receptions of Rome in European Culture, 1789–1945* (Cambridge, 1999).

Eglin, John, *Venice Transfigured: The Myth of Venice in British Culture, 1660–1797* (Basingstoke, 2001).

Elsner, Jás and Joan-Pau Rubiés (eds.), *Voyages and Visions: Towards a Cultural History of Travel* (1999).

Ely, John Wilton, *Piranesi as Architect and Designer* (New Haven and London, 1993).

'"Classic ground": Britain, Italy, and the Grand Tour', *Eighteenth-Century Life*, 28 (2004), 136–65.

Evans, Harry B., *Aqueduct Hunting in the Seventeenth Century: Raffaello Fabretti's De aquis et aquaeductibus veteris Romae* (Ann Arbor, 2002).

Figgis, Nicola F., *The Roman Property of Frederick Augustus Hervey, 4th Earl of Bristol and Bishop of Derry (1730–1803)*, Walpole Society 55 (1989–90).

Finn, Margot, 'Men's things: masculine possession in the consumer revolution', *Social History*, 25:2 (2000), 133–55.

Fischer, Bernerd, *Allan Ramsay and the Search for Horace's Villa* (Aldershot, 2001).

Fitzgerald, Elizabeth, *Lord Kildare's Grand Tour, 1766–1769* (Cork, 2000).

Fleming, John, 'The Hugfords of Florence (Part II): with a provisional catalogue of the collection of Ignazio Enrico Hugford', *Connoisseur*, 136 (1955), 197–206.

'Lord Brudenell and his bear-leader', *English Miscellany*, 9 (1958), 127–41.

Robert Adam and his Circle in Edinburgh and Rome (1962).

Ford, Brinsley, 'Sir Roger Newdigate and Piranesi', *Burlington Magazine* (July 1972), 466–72.

'The earl-bishop: an eccentric and capricious patron of the arts', *Apollo*, 99 (1974), 426–34.

'James Byres: principal antiquarian for the English visitors to Rome', *Apollo*, 99 (1974), 446–61.

'Sir John Coxe Hippesley: an unofficial English envoy to the Vatican', *Apollo*, 99 (1974), 440–5.

'Sir Watkin Williams-Wynn: a Welsh maecenas', *Apollo*, 99 (1974), 435–9.

'Thomas Jenkins: banker, dealer and unofficial English agent', *Apollo*, 99 (1974), 416–25.

Forster, E. M., *A Room with a View* (Harmondsworth, 1986).

Fothergill, Brian, *Sir William Hamilton, Envoy Extraordinary* (1969).

Fraser, Hilary, *The Victorians and Renaissance Italy* (Oxford, 1992).

French, Henry and Mark Rothery, '"Upon your entry into the world": masculine values and the threshold of adulthood among landed elites in England, 1680–1800', *Social History*, 33:4 (2008), 402–22.

Garrioch, David, 'House names, shop signs and social organization in western European cities, 1500–1900', *Urban History*, 21:1 (1994), 18–46.

Gaston, Robert, 'British travellers and scholars in the Roman catacombs 1450–1900', *JWCI*, 46 (1983), 144–65.

Gatrell, Vic, *City of Laughter: Sex and Satire in Eighteenth-Century London* (2006).

Gatti, Hilary, 'Il Campo Santo di Pisa nella letteratura Inglese', *Annali della Scuola Normale Superiore di Pisa: classe di lettere e filosofica*, 16:1 (1986), 239–70.

Girouard, Mark, *The Return to Camelot: Chivalry and the English Gentleman* (New Haven and London, 1981).

Golinski, Jan, *British Weather and the Climate of Enlightenment* (Chicago, 2007).

Gossman, Lionel, *Medievalism and the Ideologies of the Enlightenment: The World and Work of La Curne de Sainte-Palaye* (Baltimore, 1968).

Grell, Chantal, *Le dix-huitième siècle et l'antiquité en France 1680–1789*, 2 vols. (Oxford, 1995).

Gross, Hanns, *Rome in the Age of Enlightenment: The Post-Tridentine Syndrome and the Ancien Regime* (Cambridge, 2002).

Habel, Dorothy, *The Urban Development of Rome in the Age of Alexander VII* (Cambridge, 2002).

Hale, J. R., *England and the Italian Renaissance: The Growth of Interest in its History and Art* (1954; repr. 1996).

'Art and audience: the Medici Venus, c. 1750–1850', *Italian Studies*, 31 (1976), 37–58.

McCarthy, Michael, 'The education in architecture of the man of taste', *Studies in Eighteenth-Century Culture*, 5 (1985), 337–53.

Origins of the Gothic Revival (New Haven and London, 1987).

'Andrew Lumisden and Giovanni Battista Piranesi', in Clare Hornsby (ed.), *The Impact of Italy: The Grand Tour and Beyond* (2000), 65–81.

Mack, Robert L., *Thomas Gray: A Life* (New Haven and London, 2000).

Mckay, Peter, 'The Grand Tour of the Honourable Charles Compton', *Northamptonshire Past and Present*, 7 (1986–7).

'Northamptonshire travellers in Italy, 1690–1775', *Northamptonshire Past and Present*, 9 (1995–6), 121–32.

McKeon, Michael, *The Secret History of Domesticity: Public, Private, and the Division of Knowledge* (Baltimore, 2006).

McKitterick, Rosamund and Roland Quinault (eds.), *Edward Gibbon and Empire* (Cambridge, 1997).

Macnaughton, Donald A., *Roscoe of Liverpool: His Life, Writings and Treasures 1753–1831* (Birkenhead, 1996).

Manwaring, Elizabeth, *Italian Landscape in Eighteenth-Century England* (1965).

Marrano, Harold, 'Italy and the Italians of the eighteenth century seen by Americans', *Italian Quarterly*, 16 (1972), 41–72.

Marshall, David R., Susan Russell and Karin Wolfe (eds.), *Roma Britannica: Art Patronage and Cultural Exchange in Eighteenth-Century Rome* (2011).

Marshall, Roderick, *Italy in English Literature 1755–1818: Origins of the Romantic Interest in Italy* (1934).

Martinet, Marie-Madeleine, *Le voyage d'Italie dans les literatures européenes* (Paris, 1996).

Matheson, C. S., '"A shilling well laid out": the Royal Academy's early public', in David Solkin (ed.), *Art on the Line: Royal Academy Exhibitions at Somerset House, 1780–1836* (New Haven and London, 2002), 39–54.

Michaelis, Adolf, *Ancient Marbles in Great Britain* (Cambridge, 1882).

Miles, Robert, *Ann Radcliffe: The Great Enchantress* (Manchester, 1995).

Miller, Peter (ed.), *Momigliano and Antiquarianism: Foundations of the Modern Cultural Sciences* (Toronto, 2007).

Moe, Nelson, *The View from Vesuvius: Italian Culture and the Southern Question* (Berkeley, 2002).

Moloney, Brian, *Florence and England: Essays on Cultural Relations in the Second Half of the Eighteenth Century* (Florence, 1969).

Moore, Andrew, *Norfolk and the Grand Tour* (Fakenham, 1985).

Moore, James, Ian Macgregor Morris and Andrew J. Bayliss (eds.), *Reinventing History: The Enlightenment Origins of Ancient History* (2009).

Mount, Harry, 'The monkey with the magnifying glass: constructions of the connoisseur in eighteenth-century Britain', *Oxford Art Journal*, 29:2 (2006), 167–84.

Muir, Edward, *Civic Ritual in Renaissance Venice* (Princeton, 1981).

Murray, Peter (ed.), *Five Early Guides to Rome and Florence* (Florence, 1972).

Naddeo, Barbara Ann, 'Topographies of difference: cartography of the city of Naples, 1627–1775', *Imago Mundi*, 56:1 (2004), 23–47.

'Cultural capitals and cosmopolitanism in eighteenth-century Italy: the historiography of Italy and the Grand Tour', *Journal of Modern Italian Studies*, 10 (2005), 81–99.

Newman, Gerald, *The Rise of English Nationalism: A Cultural History, 1740–1830* (New York, 1997).

Nicassio, Susan Vandiver, *Imperial City: Rome under Napoleon* (Chicago, 2005).

Nitchie, Elizabeth, *The Reverend Colonel Finch* (New York, 1940).

Nola, Annalisa di, 'Percorsi reali e percorsi simbolici nelle guide di Roma tra XVI et XIX secolo', in Sofia Boesch Gajano and Lucretta Scaraffia (eds.), *Luoghi sacri e spazi della sanctità* (Turin, 1990), 483–506.

O'Brien, Karen, *Narratives of Enlightenment: Cosmopolitan History from Voltaire to Gibbon* (Cambridge, 1997).

Women and Enlightenment in Eighteenth-Century Britain (Cambridge, 2009).

O'Byrne, Alison, 'The art of walking: representing urban pedestrianism in early nineteenth-century London', *Romanticism*, 14:2 (2008), 94–107.

O'Connor, Maura, *The Romance of Italy and the English Imagination* (1998).

Oxford Dictionary of National Biography, Oxford University Press, 2004 (www. oup.com/oxforddnb).

Parslow, Christopher Charles, *Rediscovering Antiquity: Karl Weber and the Excavation of Herculaneum, Pompeii and Stabiae* (Cambridge, 1995).

Parsons, Nicholas, *Worth the Detour: A History of the Guidebook* (Stroud, 2007).

Peltz, Lucy, 'Aestheticizing the ancestral city: antiquarianism, topography and the representation of London in the long eighteenth century', *Art History*, 22:4 (1999), 472–94.

Pemble, John, *The Mediterranean Passion* (Oxford, 1987).

Venice Discovered (Oxford, 1994).

Phillips, Mark Salber, 'Adam Smith and the history of private life: social and sentimental narratives in eighteenth-century historiography', in Donald R. Kelley and David Harris Sacks (eds.), *The Historical Imagination in Early Modern Britain: History, Rhetoric and Fiction, 1500–1800* (Cambridge, 1997), 318–42.

'"If Mrs Mure be not sorry for poor King Charles": history, the novel, and the sentimental reader', *History Workshop Journal*, 43 (1997), 111–31.

Society and Sentiment: Genres of Historical Writing in Britain, 1740–1820 (Princeton, 2000).

Pierce, S. R., 'Thomas Jenkins in Rome', *Antiquaries Journal*, 45 (1965), 200–29.

Pinnington, John E., 'Anglican chaplaincies in post-Napoleonic Europe: a strange variation on the Pax Britannica', *Church History*, 39:3 (1970), 327–44.

Pocock, J. G. A., *The Machiavellian Moment: Florentine Political Thought and the Atlantic Republican Tradition* (Princeton, 1975).

Barbarism and Religion, vol. II: Narratives of Civil Government (Cambridge, 1999).

Pollack, Martha D., *Turin 1564–1680: Urban Design, Military Culture and the Creation of the Absolutist Capital* (Chicago and London, 1991).

Pomian, Krysztof, *Collectors and Curiosities in Paris and Venice, 1500–1800* (Cambridge, 1987).

Porter, Dennis, 'Uses of the Grand Tour: Boswell and his contemporaries', in
    Dennis Porter, *Haunted Journeys: Desire and Transgression in European Travel
    Writing* (Princeton, 1991), 25–68.
Porter, Roy, *Edward Gibbon: Making History* (1988).
Potts, Alex, *Flesh and the Ideal: Winckelmann and the Origins of Art History* (New
    Haven and London, 1994).
Powell, Cecilia, *Italy in the Age of Turner: 'The Garden of the World'* (1998).
Pratt, Mary Louise, *Imperial Eyes: Travel Writing and Transculturation* (2nd edn.
    2008).
Prown, David Jules, 'A course of antiquities at Rome', *Eighteenth-Century
    Studies*, 31:1 (1997), 90–100.
Purdue, A. W., 'John and Harriet Carr: a brother and sister from the north-east
    on the Grand Tour', *Northern History*, 30 (1994), 122–38.
Rao, Anna Maria, 'The feudal question, judicial systems and the
    Enlightenment', in Girolamo Imbruglia (ed.), *Naples in the Eighteenth
    Century: The Birth and Death of a Nation State* (Cambridge, 2000), 95–117.
    'Antiquaries and politicians in eighteenth-century Naples', *Journal of the
    History of Collections*, 19:11 (2007), 165–75.
Redford, Bruce, *Venice and the Grand Tour* (New Haven and London, 1996).
    'Richard Payne Knight's *Discourse on the Worship of Priapus*', in Bruce Redford,
    Dilettanti: The Antic and the Antique in Eighteenth-Century England (Los
    Angeles, 2008), 113–28.
Ribiero, Aileen, *Dress in Eighteenth-Century Europe* (New Haven and London,
    2002).
Ridley, Ronald T., *The Eagle and the Spade: Archaeology in Rome during the
    Napoleonic Era* (Cambridge, 1992).
Ritter, Richard de, '"This changeableness in character": exploring masculinity
    and nationhood on James Boswell's Grand Tour', *Scottish Literary Review*,
    2:1 (2010), 23–40.
Riviere, Michael, 'The Rev. William Gunn, B.D.: a Norfolk parson on the Grand
    Tour', *Norfolk Archaeology*, 33 (1962–5), 351–98.
Robertson, John, *The Case for Enlightenment: Scotland and Naples, 1680–1760*
    (Cambridge, 2005).
Roeck, Bernd, *Florence 1900: The Quest for Arcadia*, trans. Stewart Spencer (New
    Haven and London, 2009).
Roettgen, Steffi, *Anton Raphael Mengs 1728–1779 and his British Patrons* (1993).
Rose-Redwood, Reuben, 'Indexing the great ledger of the community: urban
    house numbering, city directories, and the production of spatial legibility',
    Journal of Historical Geography, 34:2 (2008), 286–310.
Salmon, Frank, 'Charles Cameron and Nero's Domus Aurea: "una piccola
    esplorazione"', *Journal of the Society of Architectural Historians*, 36 (1993),
    69–93.
    Building on Ruins: The Rediscovery of Rome and English Architecture (Aldershot,
    2000).
    'The impact of the archaeology of Rome on British architects and their work,
    1750–1840', in Clare Hornsby (ed.), *The Impact of Italy: The Grand Tour and
    Beyond* (Rome, 2000), 219–43.

'Stuart as antiquary and archaeologist in Italy and Greece', in Susan Weber Soros (ed.), *James 'Athenian' Stuart: The Rediscovery of Classical Antiquity* (New Haven, 2007), 103–45.

San Juan, Rose Marie, *Roma: A City out of Print* (Minneapolis and London, 2001).

Schnapp, Alain, *The Discovery of the Past: The Origins of Archaeology*, trans. Ian Kinnes and Gillian Varndell (New York, 1997).

Schudt, Ludwig, *Le guide di Roma: Materialen zu einer Geschichte der Römischen Topographie* (Vienna, 1930).

Scott, Jonathan, *The Pleasures of Antiquity* (New Haven and London, 2003).

Seta, Cesare de, *Napoli* (revised edn, Naples, 1999).

L'Italia del Grand Tour da Montaigne a Goethe (3rd edn, Naples, 2001).

Sicari, G., *Bibliografia delle Guide di Roma in Lingua Italiana dal 1480 al 1850* (Rome, 1991).

Siegel, Jonah, *Haunted Museum: Longing, Travel and the Art-Romance Tradition* (Princeton, 2005).

Simpson, Gareth, 'The rise and fall of the Roman historian: the eighteenth century in the Roman historical tradition', in James Moore, Ian Macgregor Morris and Andrew J. Bayliss (eds.), *Reinventing History: The Enlightenment Origins of Ancient History* (2009), 187–218.

Skinner, B. C., *Scots in Italy in the Eighteenth Century* (Edinburgh, 1966).

Sloan, Kim, 'Charles Francis Greville: shaping private and public collections', in C. Frank (ed.), *Rome and the Constitution of a European Cultural Heritage in the Early Modern Period: The Impact of Agents and Correspondents on Art and Architecture* (forthcoming, Rome).

Solkin, David, *Painting for Money: The Visual Arts and the Public Sphere in Eighteenth-Century Britain* (New Haven and London, 1992).

(ed.), *Art on the Line: Royal Academy Exhibitions at Somerset House, 1780–1836* (New Haven and London, 2002).

Spacks, Patricia Meyer, 'Splendid falsehoods: English accounts of Rome, 1760–1798', *Prose Studies*, 3:3 (1980), 203–16.

Stabler, Jane, 'Taking liberties: the Italian picturesque in women's travel writing', *European Romantic Review*, 13:1 (2002), 11–22.

'Subduing the senses? British romantic period travellers and Italian art', *Nineteenth-Century Contexts*, 26:4 (2004), 320–8.

Stainton, Lindsay, *'Hayward's List': British Visitors to Rome, 1753–1775*, Walpole Society, 39 (1983).

Stirling, A. M. W., *Coke of Norfolk and his Friends* (1912).

Stoye, John, *English Travellers Abroad, 1607–1667: Their Influence in English Society and Politics* (London, 1952).

Sweet, Rosemary, *The Writing of Urban Histories in Eighteenth-Century England* (Oxford, 1997).

'Topographies of politeness', *TRHS*, 6th ser., 12 (2002), 355–75.

Antiquaries: The Discovery of the Past in Eighteenth-Century Britain (2004).

Szechi, Daniel, 'The image of the court: idealism, politics and the evolution of the Stuart court, 1689–1730', in Edward Corp (ed.), *The Stuart Court in Rome: The Legacy of Exile* (Aldershot, 2003), 49–64.

Tankard, Paul, 'Johnson and the walkable city', *Eighteenth-Century Life*, 32:1 (2007), 1–22.

Taylor, Charles, *Sources of the Self: The Making of the Modern Identity* (Cambridge, 1989).

Tinkler-Villani, Valeria, 'Translation as a metaphor for salvation: eighteenth-century English versions of Dante's *Commedia*', *Journal of Anglo-Italian Studies*, 1 (1991), 92–101.

Towner, John, 'The Grand Tour: a key phase in the history of tourism', *Annals of Tourism Research*, 12 (1985), 308–12.

Toynbee, Paget, *Dante in English Literature from Chaucer to Cary c. 1380–1844*, 2 vols. (1909).

Trevor Roper, Hugh, 'Pietro Giannone and Great Britain', *HJ*, 39:3 (1996), 657–75.

Turner, Frank M, 'British politics and the demise of the Roman Republic: 1700–1939', *HJ*, 29:3 (1986), 577–99.

Turner, Katherine, *British Travel Writers in Europe 1750–1800: Authorship, Gender and National Identity* (Aldershot, 2001).

Vance, Norman, *The Victorians and Ancient Rome* (Oxford, 1997).

Venturi, Franco, 'The Enlightenment in southern Italy', in Franco Venturi, *Italy and the Enlightenment*, ed. S. Woolf and trans. S. Corsi (1972), 198–224.

Vickery, Amanda, *The Gentleman's Daughter: Women's Lives in Georgian England* (New Haven and London, 1998).

'His and hers: gender, consumption and household accounting in eighteenth-century England', *P & P*, supplement 1 (2006).

Behind Closed Doors: At Home in Georgian England (New Haven and London, 2009).

Viviès, J., *English Travel Narratives in the Eighteenth Century: Exploring Genres* (Aldershot, 2002).

Wahnbaeck, Thomas, *Luxury and Public Happiness: Political Economy in the Italian Enlightenment* (Oxford, 2004).

Wahrman, Dror, *The Making of the Modern Self: Identity and Culture in Eighteenth-Century England* (New Haven and London, 2004).

Walchester, Kathryn, *Our Own Fair Italy: Nineteenth-Century Women's Travel Writing and Italy 1800–1844* (Bern, 2007).

Wallbank, M. V., 'Eighteenth-century public schools and the education of the governing elite', *History of Education*, 8 (1979), 1–19.

Webb, Timothy, '"City of the soul": English romantic travellers in Rome', in Michael Liversidge and Catherine Edwards (eds.), *Imagining Rome: British Artists and Rome in the Nineteenth Century* (Bristol, 1996), 20–37.

Weinbrot, Howard, *Augustus Caesar in 'Augustan' England. The Decline of a Classical Norm* (Princeton, 1978).

Weitzman, A. J., 'Eighteenth-century London: urban paradise or fallen city?', *Journal of the History of Ideas*, 36 (1975), 469–80.

West, Shearer (ed.), *Italian Culture in Northern Europe in the Eighteenth Century* (Cambridge, 1999).

White, Jonathan, '"When the kissing had to stop": eighteenth-century Venice – apotheosis or decline?', in Jonathan Wright, *Italy the Enduring Culture* (Leicester, 2000), 171–201.

Whitehead, Jane, 'British visitors to the Uffizi, 1650–1789', in Paola Barocchi and Giovanna Ragionieri (eds.), *Gli Uffizi: quattro secoli di una galleria* (Florence, 1983), 287–307.

Whyman, Susan E., *The Pen and the People: English Letter Writers, 1660–1800* (Oxford, 2009).

Williams, Raymond, *The Country and the City* (1973).

Wilson, Arline, '"The Florence of the north"? The civic culture of Liverpool in the early nineteenth century', in Alan J. Kidd and David Nicholls (eds.), *Gender, Civic Culture and Consumerism: Middle-Class Identity in Britain, 1800–1940* (Manchester, 1999), 34–46.

William Roscoe: Commerce and Culture (Liverpool, 2008).

Wilson, Bronwen, 'Venice, print and the early modern icon', *Urban History*, 35:1 (2006), 39–64.

Wilson, Kathleen, *The Island Race: Englishness, Empire and Gender in the Eighteenth Century* (2003).

Withey, Lynne, *Grand Tours and Cook's Tours. A History of Leisure Travel, 1750–1915* (New York, 1997).

Wood, Carol Gibson, *Jonathan Richardson* (New Haven and London, 2000).

Woolf, D. R., 'A feminine past? Gender, genre, and historical knowledge in England, 1500–1800', *AHR*, 102 (1997), 645–79.

Reading History in Early Modern England (Cambridge, 2000).

The Social Circulation of the Past: Historical Culture in Early Modern England, 1500–1730 (Oxford, 2003).

Woolf, Stuart, *A History of Italy 1700–1860: The Social Constraints of Political Change* (1979).

Wootton, David, 'Ulysses bound? Venice and the idea of liberty from Howell to Hume', in David Wootton (ed.), *Republicanism, Liberty and Commercial Society* (Stanford, 1994), 341–67.

UNPUBLISHED THESES AND DISSERTATIONS

Bradley, Simon, 'The Gothic Revival and the Church of England 1790–1840', University of London, Courtauld Institute of Art, Ph.D. thesis (1996).

Brown, Iain Gordon, 'Sir John Clerk of Penicuik (1676–1755). Aspects of a virtuoso life', University of Cambridge Ph.D. thesis (1980).

Ceserani, Giovanna, 'The study of Magna Graecia: classical archaeology and nationalism since 1750', University of Cambridge Ph.D. thesis (2000).

Edgar, Katharine, 'Edward Daniel Clarke (1769–1822) and the collecting of classical antiquities', University of Cambridge Ph.D. thesis (2001).

Griggs, Tamara Ann, 'The changing face of erudition: antiquaries in the age of the Grand Tour', Yale University Ph.D. thesis (2003).

Henry, Maura Aileen, 'The fourth Duchess of Beaufort's Grand Tour (1769–1774) and the making of the aristocracy', Harvard University Ph.D. thesis (1996).

Meyer, Wendel William, 'The church of the catacombs: British responses to the evidence of the Roman catacombs, 1578–1900', University of Cambridge Ph.D. thesis (1985).

O'Byrne, Alison, 'Walking, rambling and promenading in eighteenth-century London: a literary and cultural history', University of York Ph.D. thesis (2003).

Rupp, William, 'A new perspective on British identity: the travel journals of John Byng, 1781–94', University of Warwick Ph.D. thesis (2011).

Sewart, A. C., 'The life, work and letters of William Artaud, 1763–1823', University of Manchester M.A. thesis (1951).

Vaughan, Gerard, 'The collecting of classical antiquities in England in the eighteenth century: a study of Charles Townley (1737–1805) and his circle', University of Oxford D.Phil. thesis (1988).

Index

Abbot, Charles
  on Bernini, 61
  on coffee houses in Venice, 214
  on Florence, 86, 277
  on the Medici as merchants, 89
  on museum at Portici, 50
  on Naples, 178, 181, 193
  on prints of Florence, 68
  on Venice, 58, 211, 230
Academy of Cortona, 85
Addison, Joseph, *Remarks on Several Parts of Italy*, 5, 6, 12, 16
  on Naples, 185
  on Rome, 109, 112, 154
  on Siena, 241
  on Venice, 204, 226, 228, 234
Alison, Archibald, 24
Amiens, Peace of, 10, 12
anglophilia, 80
antiquarianism
  developments in, 282–5
  and travel writing, 6
archaeology, development of in Rome, 113–22
Ariosto, Ludovico, 36
Armitage, Whaley, 18, 153, 264
Artaud, William, 253
Assisi, 257
Ayscough, George, *Letters from an Officer in the Guards*, 103

Baretti, Joseph (Giuseppe), 226
Barrell, John, 59
Barry, James, 91, 252
Batoni, Pompeo, 63
Beaufort, Elizabeth Berkeley, fourth Duchess of, 26, 31
Beckford, Peter, 230
Beckford, William, 211, 215, 220
Benedict XIV, Pope (Prospero Lorenzo Lambertini), 150, 154
Bentham, James, 245

Bentham, Sarah, 17, 102
  observations on the everyday, 44–5
  on Rome, 35
  on social life in Rome, 39–40, 140
  on Venice, 213
Bernini, Gian Lorenzo, 61
Berry, Mary, 34, 44, 52, 56, 136, 142, 187, 242, 264
Berwick, Anna Vernon, Baroness, 26
Bianchini, Giuseppe, 117
Blainville, Henry de, 99, 158, 221
Blathwayt, John, 158
Bologna, 44, 53
  Palazzo Bovi, 57
  Palazzo Zampieri, 53, 54
  Piazza Nettuno, 59
Boswell, James, 16, 18, 30, 36, 191, 194, 223
Bowman, Walter, 137, 209, 227
Boyd, Henry, 97
Brand, Thomas, 210
Breval, John, *Remarks on Several Parts of Europe* (1726), 6
Breval, John, *Remarks on Several Parts of Europe* (1738)
  on Florence, 58, 86
  on Florentine effeminacy, 87
  on Naples, 172, 261
Broderick, Thomas, *Travels of Thomas Broderick*, 217, 226, 241
Brooke, Nicholas, *Observations on the Manners and Customs of Italy*, 194
Bruni, Leonardo, 76
Burgess, Richard, *Topography and Antiquities of Rome*, 159
Burnet, Gilbert, *Some Letters Containing an Account*, 6
  anti-Catholicism, 147
  on the catacombs, 158
  on Catholic church in Naples, 176
  on depopulation of the *campagna*, 16
  on Rome, 110, 147

on Venice, 220, 273
Burney, Charles, 106, 179, 231
Burton, Edward, *Description of the*
    Antiquities and Curiosities of Rome,
    100–16, 123, 127, 128, 129,
    145, 157, 259
  on the duomo at Milan, 265
Buzard, James, 47, 129
Byres, James, 34, 85, 102, 158
Byron, George Gordon, Lord, 104
  Childe Harold's Pilgrimage, 9, 13,
    37–8, 220

Cameron, Charles, 113
Campbell, Lady Charlotte, 26, 58
Canaletto (Giovanni Antonio Canal), 203,
    231–2
Canova, Antonio, 61
Carlevaris, Luca, 204
Carpaccio, 224
Carr, John, 26
Catholicism
  attitudes towards, 147–50
  greater sympathy towards, 157–60
Cento, 53
Chard, Chloe, 41, 61
Charles III (Carlo Borbone), 177
Chichester, Annetta Pelham, Countess of,
    208
Chiswell, Richard, 8, 69
chivalry, cult of, 95, 239, 281
cicisbei, 9, 41
Cimabue, 83
Clarke, Charles, 181
Clarke, Edward Daniel, 134, 157
Clement XIII, Pope (Carlo Rezzonico), 43
Clement XIV, Pope (Giovanni Vincenzo
    Antonio Ganganelli), 150
Cocchi, Antonio, 81
Coke, Lady Mary, 78
Colbert, Benjamin, 280
Colston, Marianne, *Journal of a Tour in*
    France, Switzerland and Italy, 38,
    126, 234, 235
Colt Hoare, Sir Richard, 11, 58, 93,
    104, 111, 257
connoisseurship, 23, 24, 28, 29, 32, 46
Contarini, Gasparo, *De magistratibus et*
    republic Venetorum, 200
convents
  ceremony of taking the veil, 41–2, 222
  out of bounds to men, 56
Cork and Orrery, John Boyle, fifth Earl of,
    70, 86
Correggio, Antonio Allegri da, 53

Coutts, Susan, 28
Cowling, Peter, 108, 183
Coxe, Henry, *Picture of Italy*, 8, 15
  on crime in Rome, 135
  on Florence, 94
  on Rome, 134, 136, 149
Craven, Elizabeth, Lady Craven, 41, 73,
    230, 242
Cresy, Edward, *Architectural Antiquities of*
    Rome, 117
cricket, played by the British in Italy, 279

Dallaway, James, 247
Dante, *Divine Comedy*, 94–6, 242, 261
de Brosses, Charles, 77
Derbishire, Miss, 40, 42, 50, 51, 55,
    183, 229
Dewes, Edmund, 19
dirt, attitudes towards, 45–7, 269
  see also Florence, and cleanliness; Rome,
    and dirt
Drake, Francis, 17
  on actresses in Florence, 72
  on Florence, 55, 77, 80, 83, 86
  on Naples, 172, 180, 181
  on Rome, 154
  on Venice, 213, 217, 220, 227, 228
Drake, William, 45

Eaton, Charlotte, *Rome in the Nineteenth*
    Century, 89
  on antiquarianism, 29, 30
  on the Coliseum, 126
  on dirt, 47
  on dirt in Rome, 143
  on gothic antiquities, 255
  on prudery, 58
  on Rome, 120, 121, 142
  on the Trasteverini, 134
effeminacy, 25, 29, 64, 197, 198, 233, 286
Eglin, John, 201, 230
Elba, 11
Engelbach, Lewis, *Naples and the*
    Campagna Felice, 275
Englefield, Henry, 248
Entick, John, *Present State of the British*
    Empire, 124
Essex, James, 237
Etruscan antiquities, 85
Eustace, John Chetwode, *Classical Tour*, 12,
    16, 38, 52
  on catacombs, 159
  on early Christianity in Rome, 155–6
  on excavations in Roman forum, 122
  on gothic architecture, 255

Eustace, John Chetwode, *Classical Tour*
(cont.)
    on maps, 104
    on Naples, 171, 190
    on Rome, 113, 125
    on Venice, 224, 233
Evelyn, John, 193

Fea, Carlo, 122
Ferguson, Adam, 208
Ferrara, 37, 270
Ficoroni, Francesco de', 28, 111, 116, 282
Filangieri, Gaetano, 189
Finch, Robert, 11, 16
    on catacombs, 159
    on female visitors to Rome, 28
    on Florence, 93
    on Pisa and Lombardy, 255
    on prudery, 58
    on Rome, 141, 145, 155, 265
    on St Peter's, 153
    use of maps, 107
Flaxman, Ann
    climbs Vesuvius, 55–6
    on dirt in Rome, 142
    on Florence, 73, 76
    goes to Paestum, 55
    on museum at Portici, 32
    on Rome, 31, 99
    on Trastevere, 133
    on Trasteverini, 134
Flaxman, John, 71, 99, 256, 268
Florence, 26
    and absence of crime, 71–2
    absence of prostitutes, 72
    architecture of, 77–8
    attractions for women, 78–9
    and availability of English goods, 73–5
    and cleanliness, 75–6
    baptistery, 82
    Brancacci Chapel, 92
    campanile, 82
    ducal galleries, 30, 34, 56, 59, 81
    duomo, 59, 82
    Gabinetto de Antichi Quadri, 92
    medieval architecture of, 93–4
    Palazzo Pitti, 77
    Palazzo Vecchio, 94, 243
    Piazza della Signoria, 86
    Ponte Sta Trinità, 75
    Ponte Vecchio, 86
    as a Republic, 65, 66, 67, 89, 94, 296
    San Lorenzo, 82
    Sta Croce, 82, 94
    Sta Trinità, 82

Santissima Annunziata, 82
Santo Spirito, 82
    tribuna, 33, 68, 78
Folkes, Sir Martin, 210, 242, 264
Forbes, Sir William, 17, 41, 54, 275
    on climbing Vesuvius, 55
    on Florence, 86
    on gondoliers, 226
    on *Leda and the Swan*, 57
    on Naples, 174, 177, 194, 196
    on Rome, 102, 110, 125
    on social life in Rome, 140
    on Venice, 203, 221
Forsyth, Joseph, 10, 12
    Remarks on Antiquities
        on gothic architecture, 254, 257, 264
        on Grand Duke Leopold, 71
        on guidebooks, 104
        on Naples, 164, 171, 192, 194
        on Rome, 115, 123, 125, 128
        on Venetian art, 224
        on Venice, 217, 234
Fortescue, Lady Mary, 33
Francis Stephen, Grand Duke of
    Tuscany, 70
Francis, Philip, 102, 180, 207, 212
Frederick, John, 241

Galanti, Giuseppe Maria, 190
    Breve descrizione della città di Napoli, 175
Galiano, Ferdinando, 169, 189
Garden, Francis, Lord Gardenstone, 89
Genoa, 5, 75
    Albergo dei Poveri, 137
    Palazzo Spinola, 46
Genovesi, Giuseppe Maria, 189
Ghiberti, Lorenzo, 93
Giambologna, 59
Giannone, Pietro, *Civil History of the
    Kingdom of Naples*, 188
Gibbes, Elizabeth, 52–3, 55, 56, 61,
    135, 168
Gibbon, Edward, 81, 85, 86, 282
    Decline and Fall, 97, 113, 124, 259
Giordano, Luca, 174
Giotto, 82
Goethe, J. W., *Italienische Reisen*, 193
Gori, Antonio Francesco, 85
gothic architecture
    and civic republicanism, 262–3
    theories of, 237–8, 245–52
Gray, Robert, *Letters during the Course of
    a Tour*, 105, 181, 194, 197, 208, 229
Gray, Thomas, 137
Greek revival, 123

Guattani, Giuseppe Antonio, *Roma
    descritta ed illustrata*, 115, 257
Guercino, Giovanni Francesco Barbieri, 54
Gunn, William, 245, 252
Gurney, Hudson, 175
Gwynn, John, *London and Westminster
    Improved*, 124

Hadfield, Charles, 73
Hakewill, James, 263
Hale, John, 59
Hall, Sir James, 17, 77, 95, 180, 229, 279
Hallam, Henry, *View of the State
    of Europe*, 263
Hamilton, Sir William, 55, 177, 196
Harrington, James, 201
Harvey, Robert, 13–14, 63
    on *Leda and the Swan*, 57
    on Livorno, 269
    on Naples, 186
    on Pius VI, 150
    on Rome, 113, 136, 138, 139
    on San Stefano Rotundo, 155
    on Venice, 220
Haynes, Clare, 148
Hazlitt, William, 47, 270
Herbert, George Augustus, Lord, 103, 187,
    242, 253
Herculaneum, *see* Pompeii
Hobhouse, John Cam, *Historical
    Illustrations*, 122, 163
Holland, Caroline Fox, Baroness, 31, 33,
    49, 55, 197
Holroyd, John Baker, 41, 43
Home, Mrs Patrick, 55
Home, Patrick, 26, 40
Houssaye, Amelot de la, 201, 202
Howell, James, 201

Jacobites, *see* Rome, Jacobite court
Jameson, Anna, 106
Jefferies, David, *A Journey from London to
    Rome*, 132
Jenkins, Thomas, 139
Jones, Thomas, 27, 75, 102, 151

Kerrich, Thomas, 248–51
Keysler, Johan Georg, 240
Kildare, William Fitzgerald, Marquess of,
    19, 39, 43, 75, 150, 207
Knight, Cornelia, 121
Knight, Henry Gally, 257

Lalande, Abbé de, *Voyage en Italie*, 53, 170,
    174, 183, 193

Lami, Giovanni, 85
Langton, George Lewis, 6, 253
Lassels, Richard, *Voyage of Italy*, 6, 23
Lastri, Marco, 84
Leinster, Emily Fitzgerald, Duchess of,
    see Holland, Caroline Fox, Baroness;
    Kildare, William Fitzgerald,
    Marquess of
Lemaistre, J. G., *Travels after the Peace
    of Amiens*, 169, 177, 195,
    233, 234
Leopold, Grand Duke of Tuscany, 70–2,
    89, 92
Lethiullier, Smart, 245
Lindsay, Alexander William Crawford,
    Lord, 263
Lindsey, Lady Charlotte, 26, 49, 156, 233
Livorno, 69, 73, 269
    English burial ground, 149
Loreto, 157
Lucca, 256
Lumisden, Andrew, *Remarks on the
    Antiquities of Rome*, 116, 121
Lyttelton, Lady Sarah, 269

Magnan, Dominique, *La ville de Rome*, 105
Malcolm, J. P., *Londinium Redivivum*, 163
Mann, Sir Horace, 70, 79
manners and customs, study of, 8, 120,
    134, 191, 215, 272–4, 279, 284
maps, use of, 104–5, 106–7, 276
Martyn, Thomas, *A Gentleman's Guide*,
    83, 256
Masaccio, 92
masculinity, 23–5, 30, 51
Matthews, Henry, *Diary of an Invalid*
    on dirt in Rome, 141
    on gothic architecture, 264
    on gothic novels, 38
    on ladies in Rome, 279
    on prudery, 61
    on Venice, 235
Mayne, John, 106, 128
Medici, Cosimo de', third Grand Duke, 68
Medici, Lorenzo de', 84, 87, 90
Michelangelo, 58, 82, 92, 93, 130
Michele, Marieschi, 204
Middleton, Conyers, *Letter from Rome*,
    24, 148
Milan, 44, 263
    duomo, 242, 265
    Palazzo Brera, 58
Milford, John, *Observations, Moral, Literary
    and Antiquarian*, 11
Millard, John, *see* Coxe, Henry

Miller, Anne, *Letters from Italy*, 31, 277
  on catacombs, 158
  on the dangers of the sun, 35
  on Florence, 73
  on the museum at Portici, 32, 50
  on Naples, 168
  on Pompeii, 49
  on prudery, 58
  on Roman guidebooks, 103
  on Rome, 149
  on St Peter's, 151
  on souvenirs, 44
  on Venice, 213, 225, 226
  on the *Venus de Medici*, 79
  on viewing art, 52, 53–4
  on women in Venice, 40
Milles, Jeremiah, 203, 210
Misson, Maximilien, *New Voyage to Italy*,
  6, 24, 147, 158, 213, 218, 223,
  225, 261
Mitchell, Andrew, 76, 137, 209, 222,
  224, 225
Mitford, John, 46, 130, 150, 179
Moir, Patrick, 54, 102
Montesquieu, Charles Louis de Secondat,
  Baron de, *Espirt de Lois*, 167
Moore, John, *View of Society and Manners*
  on connoisseurship, 29
  on Giambologna, 59
  on middle ages, 236
  on Naples, 180, 188
  on Rome, 125
  and Scottish enlightenment, 273
  on Venice, 209, 228
  on *Venus de Medici*, 59
More, Hannah, 46
Morgan, Sydney, *Italy*
  on Cola di Rienzo, 260
  on the Coliseum, 126
  on Florence, 94
  on Naples, 175, 193, 262
  on Rome, 145
  on Trasteverini, 134
Morritt, J. B. S., 126, 265
Murray, John, 11

Naples, 44
  antiquarianism in, 172–3
  the Chiaja, 45, 170, 178, 179
  climate of, 167–8
  comments on architecture of, 170–1
  comments on art, 173–4
  and comments on Catholicism,
  171–2, 176
  comments on history of, 175–6

  comments on superstition, 185
  dangers of sensuality, 193–7
  influence of Neapolitan reformers, 188–9
  lazzaroni, 179
  reevaluation of, 189–91
  Masaniello, Revolt of, 185–6, 187–8
  and medieval architecture, 260–2
  and noise, 180
  observations on street life, 191–3
  population of, 169, 179–80, 186–7
  and prostitutes, 193
  San Gennaro, 182
  Sta Chiara, 261
  theatres, 178–9
Napoleonic Wars
  impact on Grand Tour, 10–12
Nardini, Famiano, 117
national identity, 285–9, 303
Northall, John, *Travels through Italy*, 15,
  173, 228
Nugent, Thomas, *Grand Tour*, 7, 15, 131,
  171, 256

Orde, Thomas, 71
Orvieto, 256
Ottley, William Young, 91, 256
Otway, Thomas, *Venice Preserved*, 36, 203
Owen, John, *Travels into Different Parts of
  Europe*, 9, 142, 192, 194, 223, 226

Paestum, 54, 123
Palladianism, 77
Palladio, Andrea
  Antichità di Roma, 112
  I Quattro Libri dell'Architettura, 224
Palmerston, Henry Temple, Viscount, 230
papacy, attitudes towards, 149–51
Parker, Hon. George, 28, 171, 241, 278
Patch, Thomas, 91, 92
Patoun, William, 103, 138, 149
Patteson, John, 30, 63, 145, 287
  on Venice, 211, 230
Patteson, Martha, 149
Payne Knight, Richard, 196
Pelham, Thomas, 43, 70, 102
  on Giannone, 188
  on Rome, 109, 139
  on Venice, 214
Pembroke, Henry Herbert, tenth
  Earl of, 57
Perugia, 32
Petrarch (Francesco Petrarca), 37, 94, 260
Philpot, Charles, *Introduction to the Literary
  History of the Fourteenth and Fifteenth
  Centuries*, 88

Piacenza, 255
Pinelli, Bartolomeo, 134
Piozzi, Hester Thrale, *Observations and
    Reflections*, 35, 56
  on catacombs, 158
  declines to visit Paestum, 54
  on Florence, 65, 73, 143
  on gothic architecture, 242
  on *lazzaroni*, 189
  on Masaniello, 185
  on Naples, 192
  on Roman antiquities, 34
  on Rome, 133
  on St Peter's, 151
  on Venice, 213, 221
Piranesi, Giovanni Battista, 111, 283
Pisa, 253–5
  Campo Santo, 242
Pius VI, Pope (Giovanni Angelo Braschi),
    132, 150
Pococke, Richard, 24, 200
Pomfret, Henrietta Louisa Fermor,
    Countess of
  on Florence, 76
  on Roman antiquities, 108
  on San Paolo, Rome, 32
  on social life, 38
  on Venice, 205, 222
Pompeii, 47–51, 195, 279
  influence on archaeology at
    Rome, 120
Portici, museum at, 32, 49–50, 57, 168

Radcliffe, Ann, 38
Raphael, 130
Rawlinson, Richard, 58, 59, 68, 223
Redford, Bruce, 202
Reynolds, Sir Joshua, 51, 92
Richard, Jerome, *Description historique et
    critique d'Italie*, 170, 180
Richardson, Jonathan, *Account of
    Some of the Statues*, 78, 82,
    173, 224
Rienzo, Cola di, 260
Robertson, Roger, 13, 18
  on the museum at Portici, 50
  on Naples, 167
  on Rome, 101, 138
Robertson, William
  History of America, 288
  *History of the Reign of the Emperor
    Charles V*, 90, 188
Robinson, Thomas Philip, 227
Rogers, Samuel, *Italian Journal*, 96,
    190, 235

Romanesque, 238, 245–6, 251
Romano, Giulio, 57
romanticism, 12
Rome, 24, 27–9, 30, 31–2, 35, 39, 44, 67
  anfiteatro castrense, 56
  and antiquarianism, 107–12
  Arch of Vespasian, 45
  Baths of Trajan, 114
  Campo di Fiore, 135
  catacombs, 157–60
  charitable foundations, 136
  and *ciceroni*, 101–3
  Circus Maximus, 125
  Cloaca Maxima, 127
  Coliseum, 34, 117, 125, 136, 154
  compared with Britain, 124–5, 147
  and dirt, 140–5
  and disappointed expectations, 129
  Domus Aurea, 114
  economy of, 135–6
  empire, criticisms of, 126
  forma urbis Romae, 120
  forum, 110, 113
    excavation of, 113–22
  and guidebooks, 103–7, 131
  interest in early Christianity, 155–7
  Jacobite court, 138
  maps of, 104–5, 106–7
  Napoleon's influence on, 146
  observations on gothic architecture, 155,
    257–9
  Palazzo Ruspigliosi, 51
  Pantheon, 47, 129
  Piazza del Popolo, 99, 145
  Piazza della Rotunda, 143, 145
  Piazza di Pietra, 101
  Piazza Navona, 133, 135
  and picturesque, 112–13
  Republic, admiration of, 127
  St Peter's, 130, 151–3, 265
    compared with St Paul's, 151–3
  San Clemente, 93, 155, 156
  San Paolo, 32
  San Pudentius, 159
  San Stefano Rotundo, 155
  Sta Costanza, 35
  Sta Maria Maggiore, 111
  smell of, 141–2
  sociability, 139–40
  Temple of Jupiter Stator (Castor and
    Pollux), 117
  theatres, 140
  Trajan's Column, 124, 128, 142
  Trasteverini, 133–5
  Villa Lantri, 40

Roscoe, William
  and Italian primitives, 91
  The Life of Lorenzo de'Medici, 90
Russel, James, 33, 42, 110, 127

Saint-Non, Jean Claude Richard de,
  Voyage pittoresque, 260
Sarpi, Paolo, 201
sexuality, attitudes towards in art, 56–61,
  196
Sharp, Samuel, *Letters from Italy*, 9, 55,
  149, 187, 226, 231
Shelley, Mary, *Valperga*, 263
Sherlock, Martin, *Letters from an English
  Traveller*, 189
shopping, 43–4
Sicily, 55, 244, 246, 259, 260
Siena, 263
  duomo, 241, 244, 265
Sigismondo, Giuseppe, *Descrizione della
  città di Napoli*, 176
Sismondi, Jean Charles Léonard de,
  Histoire des républiques, 262, 282
Sixtus V, Pope (Felice Paretti di Montalto),
  99, 131, 145
Smirke, Robert, 246, 248
Smith, James Edward, *Sketch of a Tour*
  on Anne Miller, 54
  on Florence, 89
  on guidebooks in Rome, 103
  on Rome, 154
  on Venice, 203
Smith, John, *Select Views in Italy*, 257
Smollett, Tobias, *Travels in France and Italy*,
  16, 104, 140
Soane, Sir John, 54
souvenirs, 44
Spence, Joseph, 26
  on Naples, 167
  Polymetis, 148
  on Rome, 109
  on Venice, 205, 213, 219
Spence, Thomas, 188
Spencer, (Margaret) Georgiana, Countess
  Spencer, 177
Spoleto, 241
Staël, Germaine de, *Corinne*, 9, 37–8, 91,
  195, 260
Starke, Mariana, *Instructions for
  Travellers*, 63
Starke, Mariana, *Letters from Italy*, 11, 106
  on Florence, 73
  on Naples, 171, 189
  on Pisa, 253
Sterne, Laurence, *Sentimental Journey*, 9

Stevens, Sacheverell, *Miscellaneous
  Remarks*, 149
Strange, John, 207
Stuart, Charles Edward, the Young
  Pretender, 138
Stuart, James, 113
Stuart, James Francis Edward, the Old
  Pretender, 138
Swinburne, Henry, 168, 186, 189, 193,
  257, 262
Swinton, John, 73, 149

Tasso, Torquato, 36
Tatham, Heathcote, 210
Taylor, G. L., *see* Cresy, Edward
Templetown, Elizabeth Boughton,
  Baroness, 26
Thomas, Edward
  on Naples, 180
  on Rome, 137
  on Venice, 207, 222, 223
Thompson, Charles, *Travels of the Late
  Charles Thompson*, 77, 229
Tintoretto (Jacopo Comin), 53
Titian (Tiziano Vecellio)
  Venus de Medici, 17
Todd, Matthew, 19, 75, 185
travel and education of youth, 23–5
Tucker, Josiah, 25
Turin, 268
Twisden, Thomas, 171

Vasari, Giorgio, *Lives of the Artists*, 83,
  86, 243
Vasi, Giuseppe, *Itinerario Istruttivo*, 104,
  105, 137
Venice, 39
  absence of street noise, 211
  absence of superstition, 202
  after 1797, 235
  Arsenale, 228–9
  carnival, 205–7, 213–14
  comments on paintings, 223–5
  commerce of, 227–8
  dirt, attitudes towards, 220–1
  Doge's Palace, 218–21
  and freedom for women, 40–1
  gondolas, 227
  gondoliers, 37, 225–7
  Palazzo Barberigo, 58
  Piazza San Marco, 213–15
  Ponte dei Sosperi, 220
  printed images of, 203–6
  reputation, 200–3
  Rialto Bridge, 203

San Giorgio (monastery of), 56
San Marco, 215–18; and gothic
    architecture, 215–17
Scuola San Rocco, 53
sexual mores of, 221–3
and shops, 44
Venus de Medici, 59–61, 79, 81
Venuti, Ridolfino, *Antichità di Roma*, 103
Verona, 33, 36, 263
Veronese, Paolo, 56
Vesuvius, ascent of, 55–6
Vienna, Treaty of, 12
Villani, Giovanni, 85
Visentini, Antonio, 204
Voltaire, 80
    Essai sur les moeurs, 281

Walchester, Kathryn, 37, 47
Waldie, Jane, *Sketches Descriptive of Italy*,
    26, 31, 37, 275
    on gothic architecture, 244, 265
    on the Palazzo Pietra, 101
    on Venice, 233
Walker, Adam, *Ideas Suggested on the Spot*,
    239, 286
    on Florence, 80, 243
    on gothic architecture, 244
    on Rome, 120, 133, 136, 163, 274
    on Venice, 215, 219
Walpole, Horace, 54, 137
Warton, Thomas, *History of English Poetry*, 95

Watkins, Thomas, 82, 150, 165
Watts, Susanna, 37
Webster, Elizabeth, Lady, 36, 231
Welch, Saunders, 28
Westmorland, Jane, Countess of, 28
Weston, Stephen, *Viaggiana*, 116
Wharton, Robert, 199, 211, 226, 228
Whittington, G. D., 247
Willis, Robert, 265
Wilmot, Catherine, 35, 42, 55
Winchilsea, George Finch, ninth Earl of,
    19, 43, 76, 120, 170, 172,
    181, 183
Wren, Christopher, 244
Wright, Edward, *Observations Made in
    Travelling*, 6
    description of circumcision in
        Venice, 215
    on Florence, 79, 83
    on Naples, 171
    on Pisa, 253
    on Rome, 28, 111, 120, 149, 154
    on Venice, 209, 219, 221, 224
Wynne, Elizabeth (Betsey), 33
Wynne, Sir Watkin Williams, 68

Yorke, Philip, 81, 95, 139, 205, 207, 214
Young, Arthur, 71, 88, 231

Zocchi, Giuseppe, 68
Zoffany, Johann, 68, 78

Made in the USA
Lexington, KY
27 September 2016